L

OF

MARYLAND CHURCH RECORDS

Compiled and edited by

Edna A. Kanely

As part of a on-going project of the Church Records
Committee of the Genealogical Council of Maryland

FAMILY LINE PUBLICATIONS
Silver Spring, Maryland

Published by

FAMILY LINE PUBLICATIONS
13405 Collingwood Terrace
Silver Spring, Maryland 20904

Genealogy/History/Early Maps
for
Maryland, Delaware and Washington, D.C.

Catalog on request

International Standard Book Number   0-940907-03-8

CONTENTS

iii

PREFACE

In 1695 shortly after the establishment of the Anglican Church as the state church in the Province of Maryland, the Anglican church vestries were charged with recording births, marriages and deaths for all persons within their respective parishes regardless of the person's religion. Before that time the county clerks were supposed to record such information, and some county records exist before 1695 for Kent, Talbot, Somerset and Charles counties.

Understandably, the surviving Anglican church records are spotty in their coverage. Doubtless many events went unrecorded due to lack of cooperation of the persons involved and due to the laxity of the church officials in performing their duty. The situation was then compounded by ravages of time in the disappearance of registers. The other religious sects also began to keep track of their adherents so that church records are existent for several different religious groups in the colonial period.

After the Revolutionary War county clerks were supposed to issue and record marriage licenses, but the various churches continued to record information on their members, and many still do.

Baltimore City commenced collecting vital statistics in 1875. In 1880 a state-wide requirement was established but resulted in no surviving records. The law was strengthened in 1898, but compliance was slow in coming. For example in 1909 it was estimated that 60% of the births and 100% of the deaths were recorded. In the last half century civil records provide the information and church records have decreased in importance.

Thus for a major part of Maryland's past, church records are indispensible to the genealogist. However there has been no comprehensive summary of the location and availability of Maryland church records. Recognizing the need, the Genealogical Council of Maryland embarked on a project to make such a comprehensive summary. Hopefully all past churches can be identified and a determination made as to the existence and scope of their records. To date some 2600 churches have been covered and this first volume summarizes the information on those churches.

The Council is grateful to the members of its sponsoring societies who have contributed information to this current volume and hopes that its publication will encourage further work on the project. A special thanks is due to Edna Kanely, Chairperson of the Church Records Committee of the Council. She has managed the project, soliciting cooperation of the member societies, and has personally located more than 50% of the information in the first volume.

S. E. Clements, Chairman
Genealogical Council of Maryland

INTRODUCTION

The Genealogical Council of Maryland was organized in September 1976 to serve as a clearinghouse for activities of the various genealogical societies in the state of Maryland. Membership of the Council consists of representatives from genealogical and historical organizations, libraries and archives. Any interested group may be eligible for associate membership.

For a long time, Maryland genealogists have felt a strong need for more information on church records prior to the twentieth century. Although a significant number of records have been lost or no longer exist, many are still available in books, hand written copy, microform and photocopy. Researchers of history and genealogy face the problem of determining where to look, whom to contact, and what library or archives to visit.

In the Fall of 1983 the Genealogical Council of Maryland decided to gather information on the location and availability of Maryland church records - and to publish a directory of these records. In pursuit of this goal we sought to determine the location of the original records of all churches in the state of Maryland, the location of copies of records and the periods of churches' existence. All churches built before 1910 were to be included.

Member societies of the Genealogical Council of Maryland were asked to gather information in their geographical area (usually a county). A procedure was established and a church record form prepared with an instruction sheet. Participants in this project visited (and revisited) churches, telephoned and wrote letters - in order to complete the church record forms. As church record forms were received photocopies were made and placed in binders at the Maryland Historical Society Library, arranged alphabetically by name of church and by county. These binders were made available to genealogists, researchers, historians and the general public. Today, they are used extensively by staff and patrons of the Library not only in locating church records but also in identifying and locating the churches themselves at various periods of Maryland history. Copies of the church record forms were also furnished to the Maryland State Archives and to the Upper Shore Genealogical Society.

This Directory is a condensed summary of the information appearing in the church record forms. The first part of this book contains a listing of churches alphabetically arranged by county with Baltimore City and County combined. The religion is shown followed by the name of the church and its address if the address is known. The date that the church was established is given in parentheses. The earliest and ending record dates are shown with an asterisk to indicate original records, whereas the number sign signifies the existence of copies of records. Abbreviations that follow each symbol indicate the location of the records. Additional information is given in parentheses.

The second part of this book contains a listing of names and addresses of churches arranged by religion, alphabetically by county. In gathering the information many sources were used but frequently complete addresses were not available. In some instances we received more than one address for the same church; sometimes church addresses and mailing addresses differed. In

INTRODUCTION

these instances both addresses are shown. A major effort was made to obtain
current addresses. There is one exception - addresses of Reformed churches
were taken from a 1911 list from which we have removed names of churches
which have merged with other churches or whose structures have been turned
over to another denomination altogether. We thought this information might
prove to be useful to researchers.

Information on the location of churches was gathered by personal contact and
through letters and visits to church archives and libraries. A listing of
the various sources used is included in an appendix at the end of this book.

Many churches have yet to respond to our request for information regarding
their records. We hope that member societies of the Genealogical Council of
Maryland and interested individuals will continue to contact churches in an
effort to complete as many church record forms as possible. As this new
information becomes available to the Genealogical Council of Maryland it
will be added to the binders at the Maryland Historical Society Library,
Maryland State Archives and Upper Shore Genealogical Society. These
additions will also become a part of future revisions to this Directory.

So many societies, archives, libraries and individuals participated in this
project it would be difficult to name and acknowledge each and everyone. My
sincere thanks to them all for their cooperation and support.

Edna Agatha Kanely, Chair
Maryland Church Records Committee

ABBREVIATIONS USED

*	original
#	copy, copies
&	and
abt	about
ACGS	Allegany County Genealogical Society, 611 Washington St, Cumberland 21502
ACPHS	Adams County Pennsylvania Historical Society, Lutheran Theological Seminary, Gettysburg PA 17325
Adv	Adventist
Afric	African
Al	Alley
Amer	America, American
Apos	Apostolic
Arc	Archives
Assem	Assembly
Assn	Association
Assoc	Associate
Ave	Avenue
Balto	Baltimore
Bap	Baptist
bet	between
Bldg	Bldg
Blvd	Boulevard
Breth	Brethren
Cath	Catholic
Cath Cen	Chancery, The Catholic Center, 320 Cathedral St, Balto 21201
CCHS	Carroll County Historical Society, 210 E Main St, Westminster 21157
CCPL	Carroll County Public Library, 50 E Main St, Westminster 21157
cert	certificates
ch	church
CHI	Concordia Historical Institute, Department of Archives, 801 DeMun Ave, St Louis MO 63105
Chris	Christian
Clev	Cleveland
Co	County, Counties
Com	Community
Cong	Congregational
Conserv	Conservative
Ct	Court
DAR	DAR Library, 1776 D St NW, Washington, DC 20006

Dept	Department
Disc	Disciples of Christ
Disc HS	Disciples of Christ Historical Society, 1101 19th St S, Nashville TN 37212
Div	Division
Dr	Drive
E	East
E&RA	Evangelical & Reformed Archives, Lancaster Central Archives & Library, 555 W James St, Lancaster PA 17603
Eng	Emgland, English
ep	Enoch Pratt Free Library, 400 Cathedral St, Balto 21201
Epis	Episcopal
estab	established
Evan	Evangelical
Ext	Extended
FHL	Friends Historical Library, Swarthmore College, Swarthmore PA 19081
fr	from
Fund	Fundamental
GUL	Georgetown University Library, Special Collections Division, 37th & O Sts NW, Washington DC 20057
Ger	German, Germany
Haverford	Haverford College, James P Magill Library, Haverford PA 19041
His	Historical
HPL	Hagerstown Public Library, 100 S Potomac St, Hagerstown 21740
Hts	Heights
Hwy	Highway
Ind	Indiana
Indep	Independent
Insti	Institutional
Inter	Inter Denominational
Isl	Island
Jeh Wit	Jehovah's Witnesses
Jud	Judaism
LCA	Lutheran Church in America, 7604 York Rd, Balto 21204
LDS	Genealogical Library, Church of Jesus Christ of Latter Day Saints, 35 North West

ABBREVIATIONS USED

	Temple St, Salt Lake City UT 84150
LL	Lovely Lane United Methodist Church, 2200 St Paul St, Balto 21218
Ln	Lane
LTS	Lutheran Theological Seminary, Abdel Ross Wentz Library, Gettysburg PA 17325
Luth	Lutheran
MBHS	Maryland Baptist Historical Society, 1313 York Rd, Lutherville 21093
MCHS	Montgomery County Historical Society, 103 W Montgomery Ave, Rockville 20840
Md	Maryland
MDA	Maryland Diocese Archives, Episcopal Diocese of Maryland, 201 W Monument St, Balto 21201
Meet	Meeting
Menn	Mennonite
Meth	Methodist
MGS	Maryland Genealogical Society, 201 W Monument St, Balto 21201
MGS Bull	Maryland Genealogical Society Bulletin
MHS	Maryland Historical Society Library, 201 W Monument St, Balto 21201
MHS Mss Div	Maryland Historical Society Library, Mss Division, 201 W Monument St, Balto 21201
mi	mile, miles
misc	miscellaneous
MMG	Maryland Magazine of Genealogy
Morav	Moravian
MSA	Maryland State Archives, P.O. Box 828, Annapolis 21401
Mt	Mount
N	North
Natl	National
Naz	Nazarene
nr	near
Orth	Orthodox
OT	Old Town, Balto

Peabody	George Peabody Library of the Johns Hopkins University, 17 E Mt Vernon Pl, Balto 21202
Pent	Pentecostal
PGCGS Bull	Prince George's County Genealogical Society Bulletin
Phila	Philadelphia
PHS	Presbyterian Historical Society, 425 Lombard St, Philadelphia PA 19147
Pk	Park
Pkwy	Parkway
Pl	Place
Presb	Presbyterian
Prim	Primitive
Prot	Protestant
Pt	Point
R	Roman
Rd	Road
Ref	Reformed
Rm	Room
Rt	Route
Rus	Russian
S	South, Southern
Salva	Salvation
Sch	School
Sci	Science, Scientist
7th Day Adv	Seventh Day Adventist
SL	Evangelical & Reformed Historical Society, Philip Schaff Library, Lancaster Theological Seminary, 555 W James St, Lancaster PA 17603
Soc	Society
Sq	Square
SSGL	Silver Spring Genealogy Library, 500 E Randolph Rd, P.O. Box 4119, Silver Spring 20904
St	Saint, Street
Sta	Station
Sulp	Sulpician Archives
Sun	Sunday
Swarthmore	Friends Historical Library of Swarthmore College, Swarthmore PA 19081
'Swed	Swedenborgian
Syn	Synagogue

ABBREVIATIONS USED

Tenn	Tennessee
Ter	Terrace
UCC	United Church of Christ
UMHS	United Methodist Historical Society, Lovely Lane Museum, 2200 St Paul St, Balto 21218
Ukra	Ukrainian
Unit	United
Unitar	Unitarian
Univ	Universalist
W	West
WCFL	Washington Co Free Library, 100 S Potomac St, Hagerstown 21740
Wes	Wesleyan
Wit	Witnesses
WMG	Western Maryland Genealogy (magazine)
YCHS	York County Historical Society Library, 250 E Market St, York PA 17403

Prot Epis	Allen, Rev Ethan 1777-1806 * MHS Mss Div (notes on Allegany parishes)
Presb	Barrelville Presb Ch, Rt 1 Box 160-C, Mt Savage 21545 (1918) 1918- * ch (in 1933 became a mission of First Presb Ch, Cumberland)
Evan	Calvary Evan Ch. SEE: Calvary Unit Meth Ch
Evan Unit Breth	Calvary Evan Unit Breth Ch. SEE Calvary Unit Meth Ch
Unit Meth	Calvary Unit Meth Ch, 30 E Mary St, Cumberland 21502 (1905) 1914- * ch (1905-1948 known as Calvary Evan Ch, 1948-1967 Calvary Evan Unit Breth Ch, 1967- Calvary Unit Meth Ch)
Unit Meth	Centre Street Unit Meth Ch, 217 N Centre St, Cumberland 21502 1863- * ch (began in early 1780's "Mother church of Methodism of Western Maryland," in 1799 the 'Methodist Meeting House' was built on Fayette at Smallwood St, 1816 a bigger ch built on N Centre St)
Prot Epis	Christ Ch Parish. SEE: St George's Ch
Luth	Christ Luth Ch, Vocke Rd at Martz Ln, LaVale 21502 1894- * ch
Epis	Ch of the Holy Cross, 612 Brookfield Ave, Cumberland 21502 (1891) 1910- * ch, prior to 1910 * Emmanuel Epis Ch, Cumberland, 1891-1894 * MDA, 1896-1964 # MSA
Afric Meth Epis	Dickerson Afric Meth Epis Ch, 146 Mechanic St, Frostburg 21532 (1845) 1845-1924 * ch (1845 known as Hall's Chapel located on Ormand St, 1881 name changed to Dickerson relocated on Mechanic & Pine Sts)
Epis	Emmanuel Ch, 16 Washington St, Cumberland 21502. * ch, 1803-1964 # MSA, 1804-1840's missing 1840-1984 # ACGS
Epis	Emmanuel Epis Ch. SEE: Ch of the Holy Cross
Epis S	Emmanuel Epis South. SEE: Emmanuel Unit Meth Ch
Meth	Emmanuel Meth Ch. SEE: Emmanuel Unit Meth Ch
Unit Meth	Emmanuel Unit Meth Ch, 24 Humbird St, Cumberland 21502 1901- * ch (previously Emmanuel Meth, Emmanuel Epis South)
R Cath	Father Slattery's Cathedral. SEE: St Peter's, 172 Church St, Westernport 21562
Cong	First Cong Ch, Bowery St, Frostburg 21532 (1872) 1872- * ch (originally known as Shiloh Welsh Cong Ch, many records in Welsh language)
Bap	First Eng Bap Ch, 136 E Main St, Frostburg 21532 (1871) 1871 * ch (formerly Mt Zion Welsh Ch)
Meth Epis	First Meth Epis Ch, Frostburg 1838-1939 # MSA
Presb	First Presb Ch, 11 Washington St, Cumberland 21502 (1810) 1837- * ch
Unit Meth	First Unit Meth Ch, 14 Church St, Lonaconing 21539 (1850) 1870's- * ch
Presb	First Unit Presb Ch, 31-33 Broadway, Frostburg 21532 (1858) * ch
Meth Epis	Frostburg Meth Epis Ch. SEE: Frostburg Unit Meth Ch
Meth Epis S	Frostburg Meth Epis Ch South. SEE: Frostburg Unit Meth Ch
Unit Meth	Frostburg Unit Meth Ch, 48 W Main St, Frostburg 21532 (1832) 1859- * ch (in 1861 became Frostburg Meth Epis, 1899 Meth Epis South)
Meth	Grace Chapel. SEE: Grace Unit Meth Ch
Meth Epis	Grace Meth Ch, South, Frostburg 1898-1922 # MSA

Unit Meth	Grace Unit Meth Ch, 130 Virginia Ave, Cumberland 21502 (1884) 1893- * ch (originally known as Grace Chapel)
Afric Meth Epis	Hall's Chapel. SEE: Dickerson Afric Meth Epis Ch
Unit Meth	Kingsley Unit Meth Ch, 248 Williams St, Cumberland 21502 1870- * ch, 1871-1964 # MSA
Bap	Mt Zion Welsh Ch. SEE: First Eng Bap Ch
R Cath	Our Lady of Mt Carmel Ch, Morgantown 1903-1926 * St Peter's, 172 Church St, Westernport 21562
Unit Meth	Rawlings Unit Meth Ch, P.O.Box 228, Rawlings 21557 (1881) 1940- * ch (records lost in fire in 1926)
R Cath	R Cath Chapel. SEE: St Patrick's Cumberland R Cath Congregation
R Cath	St Gabriel's, Eutaw St, Barton 21521, mailing address 172 Church St, Westernport 21562. 1871- * ch (mission ch of St Peter's)
Prot Epis	St George's Ch, Mt Savage 1855-1964 # MSA (called Christ Ch Parish 1841-1845)
Prot Epis	St John's Ch, Frostburg (1841) 1867-1920 * MSA, 1867-1964 # MSA
Cath	St Mary of the Annunciation, 8 St Mary's Terrace, Lanaconing 21539 (1865) 1858-1984 # MSA
R Cath	St Mary's Ch. SEE: St Patrick's Cumberland R Cath Congregation
R Cath	St Michael Parish, Frostburg 1852-1984 # MSA
R Cath	St Patrick's Cumberland R Cath Congregation, 201 N Centre St, Cumberland 21502 (1791) 1818- * ch, 1818-1983 # MSA (began in 1791 as R Cath Chapel, in 1819 known as St Mary's Ch, named St Patrick in 1848)
R Cath	St Patrick's R Cath Ch, Little Orleans 21766. 1840's- * St Peter's Cath Ch, Hancock
Evan Luth	St Paul's Evan Luth Ch, 34 W Main St (P.O.Box 227) Frostburg 21532 (1808) 1861- * ch (first meetings held in Neff Meet House at Wright's Crossing, separated from Cumberland Congregation in 1841, ch built on present site in 1865)
Luth	St Paul's Luth Ch, 15 N Smallwood St (Washington & Smallwood Sts) Cumberland 21502 (1794) 1790- * ch
R Cath	St Peter's, 172 Church St, Westernport 21562 (1857) 1857- * ch (known as Father Slattery's Cathedral)
Epis	St Peter's Epis Ch, 2 St Peter's Pl, Lonaconing 21539 (1839) * ch, 1895-1960 # MSA
Epis	St Philip's Chapel, 612 Brookfield Ave, Cumberland 21502 (1891) 1891-1910 * Emmanuel Epis Ch, 1910- * Holy Cross, 1910-1964 # MSA (a black ch)
R Cath	SS Peter & Paul Monastery, 125 Fayette St, Cumberland 21502. 1845- * ch
UCC	Salem UCC, 78 Broadway, Frostburg 21532 (1867) 1867- * ch
Cong	Shiloh Welsh Cong Ch. SEE: First Cong Ch
Presb	Southminster Presb Ch, 310 Race St, Cumberland 21502 (1907) 1919- * ch (began in Woodman Hall)
Meth	Trinity Indep Meth Ch. SEE: Trinity Unit Meth Ch
Meth Epis S	Trinity Meth Epis Ch South. SEE: Trinity Unit Meth Ch

Allegany County

Unit Meth	Trinity Unit Meth Ch, 120 Grand Ave, Cumberland 21502 (1872) 1897- * ch (first known as Trinity Indep Meth Ch on S Centre & Union Sts, Trinity Meth Epis Ch South in 1898)
Unit Meth	Unit Meth, Mt Savage 21545. 1890- * ch
UCC	Zion UCC, 160 E Main St, Frostburg 21532 (1853) * ch

Anne Arundel County

Meth	Adams Chapel. SEE: Mt Zion Unit Meth Ch
Prot Epis	All Hallows Ch (All Hallows Parish) nr Davidson (1692) 1669-1980 * and # MSA, 1685-1899 # MHS, 1691-1858 # LDS
Friends	Annapolis Monthly Meet 1970-1979 # MSA
Meth Epis	Annapolis Station Meth Epis Ch. SEE: Asbury Meth Ch
Meth Prot	Anne Arundel Circuit of the Meth Prot Ch 1844-1891 * MHS Mss Div, 1830-1894 # MHS, 1866-1894 # LDS
Unit Meth	Arnold-Asbury Unit Meth Ch, 78 Church Rd, Arnold 21012 (1859) 1898- * ch
Unit Meth	Asbury Broadneck Unit Meth Ch, 657 Broadneck Rd, Annapolis 21401 (1851) 1851- * ch
Meth	Asbury Meth Ch, Annapolis 1890-1924 # MSA (formed from Annapolis Station Meth Epis Ch abt 1836/7)
Unit Meth	Baldwin Memorial Unit Meth Ch, 981 General's Hwy, Millersville 21108 (1777) 1873- * ch
Meth	Calvary. SEE: Chesapeake Charge Meth Epis Ch South
Meth	Calvary Meth Ch, Annapolis (1921) 1822-1957 * and # MSA (formed by merger of First Meth Epis Ch (1833) and Maryland Avenue Meth Epis Ch (1895))
Unit Meth	Cape St Claire Unit Meth Ch, 855 Chestnut Tree Dr, Annapolis 21401 (1954) 1956- * ch
Meth	Cedar Grove. SEE: Chesapeake Charge Meth Epis Ch South
Meth	Centenary. SEE: West River Charge Meth Epis Ch
Prot Epis	Chapel of St James the Less in St James Parish. SEE: Christ Ch, Owensville
Meth Epis S	Chesapeake Charge Meth Epis Ch, South 1904-1916 # MSA (in 1904 re-united with West River Charge keeping name Chesapeake Charge; includes Calvary, Cedar Grove, Emmanuel, Oakland, Shiloh, Wesley)
Meth	Chew Chapel. SEE: Mt Zion Unit Meth Ch
Prot Epis	Christ Ch nr Guilford 1712-1939 * MDA # MSA, 1711-1857 # MHS LDS
Prot Epis	Christ Ch, Owensville 1860-1971 # MSA (originally Chapel of St James the Less in St James Parish)
Epis	Christ Epis Ch, 220 Owensville Rd, West River 20078. 1860- * ch
Evan Luth	Christ Evan Luth Ch, 8245 Jumpers Hole Rd, Millersville 21108 (1908) 1902 * ch (area known as Elvaton)
Epis	Ch of St Christopher, 116 Marydell Rd, Linthicum Hts 21090 (1951) 1952- * ch
R Cath	Ch of St Mary's. SEE: St Mary's Parish, Annapolis
S Bap	College Avenue Bap Ch 1899-1957 # MSA

3

Bap	College Parkway Bap Ch, P.O.Box 217, 301 College Pkwy, Arnold 21012 (1959) 1959- * ch
Unit Meth	Community Unit Meth Ch, 8680 Fort Smallwood Rd, Pasadena 21122 (1925) 1929- * ch
R Cath	Dodon Chapel. SEE: St Mary's Parish, Annapolis, Our Lady of Sorrows, Owensville
Unit Meth	Eastport Unit Meth Ch, 926 Bay Ridge Ave, Annapolis 21403 (1895) 1899- * ch
Epis	Ellicott's Chapel 1840-1918 * MDA. SEE ALSO: St Peter's Ch, Odenton
Bap	Elvaton Bap Ch, P.O.Box 1317, Glen Burnie 21061 (1972) 1972- * ch
Meth	Emmanuel. SEE: Chesapeake Charge Meth Epis Ch South
Luth	Emmanuel Luth Ch of Stoney Creek, 8615 Fort Smallwood Rd, Pasadena 21122 (1947) 1948- * ch
Epis	Epiphany Chapel 1918-1939 * MDA
Epis	Epiphany Church, Morgan Rd, Odenton 21113 (1918) 1918- * ch
Meth	Epworth League. SEE: West River Charge Meth Epis Ch
Unit Meth	Ferndale Unit Meth Ch, 117 Ferndale Rd, Glen Burnie 21061 (1924) 1924- * ch
Luth	First Evan Luth Ch, P.O.Box 3 (Rt 170 & Odenton Rd) Odenton 21113 (1940) 1940- * ch
Meth Epis	First Meth Epis Ch. SEE: Calvary Meth Ch, Annapolis
Presb	First Presb Ch, Annapolis 1845-1960 * MSA, 1845-1941 # MSA
Meth	Friendship. SEE: Mt Zion Unit Meth Ch, West River Charge Meth Epis Ch
Meth	Friendship Charge Meth Ch 1942-1969 # MSA
Meth Epis	Friendship Charge Meth Epis Ch 1920-1938 # MSA
Meth	Galesville. SEE: West River Charge Meth Epis Ch
7th Day Adv	Glen Burnie 7th Day Adv, 508 Aquahart Rd, Glen Burnie 21061 (1935) 1935 * ch
Unit Meth	Glen Burnie Unit Meth Ch, 7 Second Ave SE, Glen Burnie 21061 (1874) 1894- * ch
Luth	Glen Luth Ch, 106 Carroll Rd, Glen Burnie 21061 (1955) 1955- * ch
Luth	Gloria Dei Luth Ch, 461 College Pkwy, Arnold 21012 (1982) 1982- * ch
Presb	Harundale Presb Ch, 1020 Eastway, Glen Burnie 21061 (1948) 1948- * ch, 1948-1981 # MSA
Bap	Heritage Bap Ch. SEE: College Avenue Bap Ch
R Cath	Hillsmere Mission. SEE: St Mary's Parish, Annapolis
Meth	Hogans. SEE: Mt Zion Unit Meth Ch
R Cath	Holy Family, Davidsonville. SEE: St Mary's Parish, Annapolis, Our Lady of Sorrows, Owensville
R Cath	Immaculate Conception. SEE: St Mary's Parish, Annapolis
Friends	Indian Spring Preparative Meet, Orth 188-1841 # MSA
Bap	Jessup Bap Ch, P.O.Box 308, Jessup 20794 (1967) 1963- * ch
Unit Meth	John Wesley Unit Meth Ch, 2114 Bay Ridge & Forest Hill Ave, Annapolis 21403 * ch
Meth	Lancaster. SEE: Mt Zion Unit Meth Ch
Luth	Luth Ch of Our Redeemer, 7606 Quarterfield Rd, Glen Burnie 21061 (1957) 1957- * ch
Meth	Magothy Meth Ch, Hog Neck Peninsula 1881-1899 # MGS Bull
Meth Epis	Magothy Meth Epis Ch 1878-1929 * and # MSA

Unit Meth	Magothy Unit Meth Ch of the Deaf, 3703 Mountain Rd, Pasadena 21122 (1982) 1982- * ch
Meth Epis	Maryland Avenue Meth Epis Ch. SEE: Calvary Meth Ch, Annapolis
Unit Meth	Mayo Memorial Unit Meth Ch, 1012 Turkey Pt Rd, Edgewater 21037 (1878) 1913- * ch (many records lost in fire 1975)
Unit Meth	Mayo Memorial Unit Meth Ch, Rt 214, Mayo 21106 (1803) 1970- * ch
Meth	McKendree. SEE: Mt Zion Unit Meth Ch, West River Charge Meth Epis Ch
Unit Meth	Melville Chapel Unit Meth Ch. SEE: Elkridge Unit Meth Ch, 6166 Lawyers Hill Rd, Balto 21227
Unit Meth	Mt Tabor Unit Meth Ch, P.O.Box 93, Crownsville 21032 (1858) 1858- * ch
Meth	Mt Zion. SEE: West River Charge Meth Epis Ch
Unit Meth	Mt Zion Unit Meth Ch 1837-1897 # MSA (includes Adams Chapel, Chew Chapel, Friendship, Hogans, Lancaster, McKendree, Mt Zion, Owensville, Sylven Chapel, Union, Wesley Chapel, West River)
Meth	Oakland. SEE: Chesapeake Charge Meth Epis Ch South
R Cath	Our Lady of Perpetual Help, Woodland Beach, Edgewater. SEE: St Mary's Parish, Annapolis
R Cath	Our Lady of Sorrows, 101 Owensville Rd, West River 20778 (1866) 1865- * ch, 1865-1980 # MSA (includes Holy Family, Davidsonville; Dodon Chapel. SEE ALSO: St Mary's Parish, Annapolis
R Cath	Our Lady of the Cape Chapel, Cape St Clair. SEE: St Mary's Parish, Annapolis
R Cath	Our Lady of the Fields, Millersville. SEE: St Mary's Parish, Annapolis
Luth	Our Redeemer Luth Ch, 7606 Quarterfield Rd, Glen Burnie 21061 (1957) 1957- * ch
Luth	Our Shepherd Luth Ch, P.O.Box 626, 400 Benfield Rd, Severna Pk 21146 (1958) 1958- * ch
Meth	Owensville. SEE: Mt Zion Unit Meth Ch, West River Charge Meth Epis Ch
Luth	Peace Luth Ch, 416 Wellham Ave, Glen Burnie 21061 (1958) 1958- * ch
Presb	Prince of Peace Presb Ch, 1657 Crofton Pkwy, Crofton 21114 (1967) 1967- * ch
Friends	Quarterly Meet for Western Shore 1680-1951 # MSA
Epis	Queen Caroline Parish 1771, 1855-1865 * MDA, 1805 # MSA. SEE ALSO: St John's Ch, Kingsville, Balto & Harford Co
Epis	St Andrew the Fisherman Ch, P.O.Box 175, Mayo 21106. 1959- * ch
Prot Epis	St Anne's Ch, Annapolis 1705-1981 * and # MSA
Prot Epis	St Anne's Parish 1687-1857 # MHS
R Cath	St Augustine's, Annapolis. SEE: St Mary's Parish, Annapolis
Prot Epis	St Christopher's by the Sea Chapel, Gibson Isl 1925-1965 # MSA
R Cath	St Gerald's, Gerardton. SEE: St Mary's Parish, Annapolis
Prot Epis	St James Ch 1663-1856 * MSA, 1663-1952 # MSA, 1659-1896 # MHS, 1862-1869 # LDS

R Cath	St John the Evangelist, Severna Pk 1958-1980 # MSA (prior to 1959, SEE: St Mary's Parish, Annapolis)
R Cath	St John's, Severna Pk. SEE: St Mary's Parish, Annapolis
Prot Epis	St John's Ch, Ellicott City 1834-1957 # MSA
Luth	St John's Luth Ch, 300 W Maple Rd, Linthicum Hts 21090 (1919) 1919- * ch
R Cath	St Joseph's, Odenton. SEE: St Mary's Parish, Annapolis
R Cath	St Lawrence, Jessup 1921-1980 # MSA (prior to 1921 records at St Mary's, Laurel; St Augustine's, Elkridge; or St Mary's, Annapolis)
Prot Epis	St Margaret's Ch, St Margaret's 1680-1885 * and # MSA
Prot Epis	St Margaret's Prot Epis Ch, Westminster 1673-1885 # MHS, 1699-1885 # LDS
Evan Luth	St Martin's Evan Luth Ch, Spa Rd & Hilltop Ln, Annapolis 21403 (1874) 1874- * ch, 1874-1967 # MSA
Epis	St Martin's in-the-Field Epis Ch, 375 Benfield Rd, Severna Pk 21146 (1954) 1954- * ch
Prot Epis	St Mary's Ch, Hooversville (now Jessup) 1871-1907 * MDA # MSA
R Cath	St Mary's Immaculate Conception. SEE: St Mary's Parish, Annapolis
R Cath	St Mary's Parish, Annapolis 1851-1980 # MSA (includes Ch of St Mary's, Immaculate Conception; Chesterfield Mission; Dodon Chapel; Hillsmere Mission; Holy Family, Davidsonville; Our Lady of Perpetual Help, Edgewater; Our Lady of Perpetual Help, Woodland Beach; Our Lady of Sorrows, Owensville; Our Lady of the Cape Chapel, Cape St Clair; Our Lady of the Fields, Millersville; St Augustine's, Annapolis; St Gerard's, Gerardton; St John's, Severna Park; St Joseph's, Odenton; St Mary's Immaculate Conception; Santa Maria de Immaculate Conception
Prot Epis	St Peter's Ch, Odenton 1918-1939 * MDA, 1848-1918 # MSA (Ellicott's Chapel)
Prot Epis	St Philip's Chapel, Annapolis 1892-1962 # MSA
Prot Epis	St Stephen's Ch, Millersville 1869-1927 * MSA, 1857-1969 # MSA
Meth Epis	Severn & South River Circuit 1842-1868 * MHS Mss Div
Unit Meth	Severna Pk Unit Meth Ch, 731 Benfield Rd, Severna Pk 21146 (1965) 1965- * ch
Meth	Shiloh. SEE: Chesapeake Charge Meth Epis Ch South
Meth	Sylven Chapel. SEE: Mt Zion Unit Meth Ch
Prot Epis	Trinity Ch, two miles n of Waterloo 1866-1909 # MSA
Unit Meth	Trinity Unit Meth Ch, 1300 West St, Annapolis 21401. 1915- * ch
Meth	Union. SEE: Mt Zion Unit Meth Ch
Meth	Weems Meth Meet, Friendship 1833-1851 # MSA
Meth	Wesley. SEE: Chesapeake Charge Meth Epis Ch South, West River Charge Meth Epis Ch
Meth Epis	Wesley Chapel 1844-1851 # MSA (a chapel of Calvary Meth Epis in Annapolis) SEE ALSO: Mt Zion Unit Meth Ch
Meth	Wesley Grove Charge Unit Meth Ch 1890-1920, 1953-1969 # MSA
Meth	West River. SEE: Mt Zion Unit Meth Ch
R Cath	West River. SEE: Our Lady of Sorrows, Owensville
Friends	West River & Clifts Monthly Meet 1662-1814? # MHS

Anne Arundel County

Meth Epis   West River Charge Meth Epis Ch 1884-1915 # MSA (includes
                     Centenary, Epworth League, Galesville, Friendship,
                     McKendree, Mt Zion, Owensville, Wesley)
Meth Epis S   West River Charge Meth Epis Ch, South 1882-1905 # MSA
Meth Epis S   West River Circuit 1835-1894 # MSA
Friends   West River Meet 1655-1824 # MGS Bull

Baltimore City and Baltimore County

Ref Presb   Abbott Memorial Ref Presb Ch, 3426 Bank St (Bank St & Highland
                     Ave) Balto 21224 (1882) 1882-1983 * and # Presb Ch (USA)
                     Dept of History, 425 Lombard St, Phila, Pa 19147 1983- * ch
                     (Until 1983 ch was known as Abbott Memorial Unit Presb Ch)
Presb   Aisquith Presb Ch, 7515 Harford Rd, Balto 21234 1854- * ch
                     (Original name Aisquith Street Presb Ch located at Aisquith
                     & Edwards Sts)
Unit Meth   .Aldersgate Unit Meth Ch, 42nd St & Falls Rd, Balto 21210.
                     1918- * ch
Cath   All Saints, Liberty Heights & Eldorado Ave, Balto 21207
                     (1912) 1912- * ch
Epis   All Saints Ch, Balto 1867-1969 * MDA
Epis   All Souls Ch, Brooklyn, Balto 1972-1984 * MDA
Meth Epis S   Alpheus W Wilson Memorial Meth Epis Ch South 1915-1972 # MSA
Unit Meth   Alpheus W Wilson Memorial Unit Meth Ch, Charles St at
                     University Pkwy, Balto 21218 (estab 1915 as Calvary Meth
                     Epis Ch South) 1915- * ch
Meth Epis   Ames. SEE: Balto Circuit Meth Epis Ch
Meth   Ames Chapel SEE: Stone Chapel
Meth   Ames Memorial Meth Ch, 1429 Carey St, Balto 21217 1940- * ch
                     (estab in 1850 as Western Chapel located on Division St)
Unit Meth   Andrew Chapel Unit Meth Ch, 4100 Frankford Ave, Balto 21206
                     (1853) * ch
Meth Epis   Appold Meth Epis Ch 1877-1948 # MSA. SEE ALSO: Northwood
                     Appold Unit Meth Ch
Unit Meth   Arbutus Unit Meth Ch, 1227 Maple Ave, Balto 21227 (1906)
                     1917- * ch
Meth Epis S   Arlington Meth Epis Ch, South 1876-1935 * Arlington Unit Meth
                     Ch
Unit Meth   Arlington Unit Meth Ch, 5268 Reisterstown Rd, Balto 21215 *
                     ch
Unit Presb   Arneal, Rev John F (pastor, First Unit Presb Ch, Balto
                     1921-1957) notebook, loose papers, history of Montebello
                     Unit Presb Ch * MHS Mss Div
Meth Epis   Asbury Chapel SEE: Great Falls Circuit Meth Epis Ch
Luth   Ascension Luth Ch, 7601 York Rd, Balto 21204 (1940's) * ch
Cong   Assoc Cong Ch, Balto 1900-1926 minute book * MHS Mss Div
                     (formerly located at Maryland Ave & Preston Sts; affiliated
                     with Messiah Evan & Ref Ch in 1946)

Ref   Assoc Ref Cong, Maryland Ave & Preston St, Balto 1812-1865 #
       MHS LDS (formerly located Fayette St w of Charles St)
Cath   Associated Cath Charities, 320 Cathedral St, Balto 21201
       1812- * records of Cath orphan asylums & homes
Cong   Associated Cong Ch SEE; First Cong Ch, Balto
Ref   Associated Ref Ch of Balto 1803; 1824-1900 * MHS Mss Div (in
       1900 merged with First Cong Ch of Balto, became Associated
       Cong Ch)
Luth   Augustana Luth Ch, 3401 Mannasota Ave, Balto 21213 (1889)
       1889- * ch (formerly known as St Olaf's, estab in Fells
       Point by a Norwegian congregation)
Presb   Babcock Presb Ch, 8240 Loch Raven Blvd, Balto 21204 1888- *
       ch (Park Ch Mission started at North & Madison Aves)
Meth Epis Back River SEE: Great Falls Circuit Meth Epis Ch
Bap   Balto Chinese Bap Mission, 1313 York Rd, Lutherville 21093 *
       ch
Meth Epis Balto Circuit Meth Epis Ch 1794-1816 and 1858-1946 * and #
       MSA (includes Ames, Finksburg, Granite, Marcella, Meadow
       Dale, Mt Olive, Mt Pleasant, Owings Mills, Pimlico, Piney
       Grove, Pleasant Grove, Pleasant Hill, Quarries,
       Reisterstown, St Pauls, Stone Chapel, Sunny Hill,
       Tabernacle, Wards Chapel)
Epis   Balto City Mission 1926-1937 * MDA
Meth Epis Balto City Station 1836-1865 # MSA, 1821-1863 # MGS Bull.
       SEE ALSO: Meth Epis Ch
Ref Jud   Balto Hebrew Congregation, 7401 Park Heights Ave, Balto 21208
       1851- * syn
Friends   Balto Monthly & Preparative Meet 1776-1930 # MSA
Friends   Balto Monthly Meet, Orth 1769-1963 # MSA
Friends   Balto Preparative Meet for Eastern & Western Districts, Orth
       1828-1930 # MSA
Friends   Balto Quarterly Meet, Orth 1807-1956 # MSA
Swed   Balto Society of the General Ch of the New Jerusalem Hillside
       Chapel, 901 Dartmouth Rd, Balto 21212 (1794) 1794- * ch
Friends   Balto Yearly & Monthly Meet 1681-1963 # MSA, 1844 rules of
       discipline # LDS
R Cath   Basilica of the Assumption of the Blessed Virgin Mary,
       Cathedral & Mulberry Sts, Balto 21201 (1806) 1782-1976 #
       MSA (formerly St Peters 1775-1806) SEE ALSO: St Joseph
       Ch, Buckeystown, Frederick Co
Luth   Berea Luth Ch, 2200 E Oliver St, Balto 21213 (1958) 1958- *
       ch
Epis   Berger, Rev A J (Christ Ch, Western Run Parish) 1828-1891
       account books and papers * MHS Mss Div
Orth Jud   Beth Jacob Congregation, 5713 Park Heights Ave, Balto 21215
       1938- * syn
Orth Jud   Beth Tfiloh congregation, 3300 Old Court Rd, Balto 21208
       1921- * syn
Meth Epis Bethany Meth Epis Ch 1868-1928 * UMHS # MSA
Meth Prot Bethany Meth Prot Ch 1880-1933 * UMHS, 1891-1921 # MSA
Presb   Bethany Presb Ch SEE: Hope Presb Ch, Shelbourne & Ten Oaks
       Rd, Balto 21227

Ref	Bethany Ref Ch, Pennsylvania Ave & Cumberland, Balto 1893-1930 * Messiah UCC, 5615 The Alameda, Balto 21239 (in 1931 Bethany Ref Ch & Christ Ref Ch merged & chose name Messiah)
UCC	Bethany UCC, 1928 Gwynn Oak Ave, Balto 21207. A summary of their ch records # MGS Bull
Afric Meth Epis	Bethel Afric Meth Epis Ch, Druid Hill Ave & Lanvale St, Balto 21217. 1825-1964 # MSA (one of Baltimore's earliest black churches)
Evan Luth	Bethlehem Evan Luth Ch, Oliver St & Collington Ave, Balto. SEE: Bethlehem Luth Ch
Luth	Bethlehem Luth Ch, 4815 Hamilton Ave, Balto 21206 1886- * ch (organized as St Peter's, later known as Bethlehem Evan Luth Ch, Oliver St & Collington Ave)
Prim Bap	Black Rock Bap Ch, Black Rock 1828-1899 minutes * and # MSA
Meth Epis	Broadway Meth Epis Ch 1869-1960 # MSA
Meth Prot	Broadway Meth Prot Ch 1856-1920 # MSA (organized 1856 as Fells Point Mission)
Meth Epis	Broadway Station, Balto 1864-1918 # MSA (erected from E Balto Station 1864)
Bap	Brooklyn First Bap Ch, 3801 Fifth St., Balto 21225 (1916) 1916- * ch
Presb	Brown Memorial Presb (one ch, two locations: Park & Lafayette Aves, Balto 21217 (1870); 6200 N Charles St, Balto 21212 (1961) 1871- * ch Charles St address
Meth Epis S	Caernarvon Meth Epis Ch South 1900-1927 * UMHS
Bap	Calvary Bap Ch, 120 W Pennsylvania Ave, Balto 21204 1891- * ch
Evan Unit Breth	Calvary Evan Unit Breth Ch 1848-1969 * UMHS
Meth Epis S	Calvary Meth Epis Ch South 1867-1918 * UMHS # MSA
Meth Epis	Camp Chapel SEE: Great Falls Circuit Meth Epis Ch
Meth Epis	Canton SEE: Great Falls Circuit Meth Epis Ch
Bap	Canton Bap Mission Center, 3302 Toone St, Balto 21224 (1908) * ch
R Cath	Carmelite Sisters of Balto, 1318 Dulany Valley Rd, Balto 21204. 1640's; 1792- * (oldest community of R Cath Sisters, estab in Port Tobacco, in 1790)
Meth Epis	Caroline Street Meth Ch, 12 S Caroline St, Balto 21231 1851-1960 # MSA
Prot Epis	Cathedral Ch of the Incarnation, 4 E University Pkwy, Balto 21218. 1907-1969 # MSA (formed from merger of St Barnabas Ch & St George's Ch)
R Cath	Cathedral of Mary Our Queen, 5300 N Charles St, Balto 21210 (1959) 1959- * ch
Bap	Caton Hills Bap Ch, Nelway & Smith Aves, Lansdowne SEE: First Bap Ch of Lansdowne
Bap	Catonsville Bap Ch, 1004 Frederick Ave., Balto 21228 (1924) 1930's- * ch
UCC	Catonsville Immanuel UCC, 1905 Edmondson Ave, Balto 21228 (1866) 1866- * ch (formerly Immanuel Evan & Ref Ch located on Saratoga St, moved to Catonsville about 1959)

Presb	Catonsville Presb Ch, 1400 Frederick Rd, Balto 21228 1900- * ch
Meth Epis S	Central Meth Epis Ch South 1915-1920 * UMHS (merged with Summerfield located at Wildwood Pkwy & Gelston Dr; renamed Wildwood Parkway Unit Meth Ch c.1983)
Presb	Central Presb Ch, 7308 York Rd, Balto 21204 1949- * ch
Prot Epis	Chapel of Ease (1755) (from St John's Parish, Joppa) SEE: St James Epis Ch, My Lady's Manor
Prot Epis	Chapel of the Holy Cross, Freeland 1911-1928 (defunct) 1888-1923 # MSA
Prot Epis	Chapel of the Nativity, Cedarcroft 1912-1921 # MSA
Meth Epis	Charles Street Meth Epis Ch SEE: Mt Vernon Place Unit Meth Ch, 10 E Mt Vernon Pl, Balto 21202
Meth Epis	Chatsworth Meth Epis Ch (1861) 1861-1910 # MSA (1864-1898 known as Chatsworth Indep Meth Ch; 1898-1914 Chatsworth Meth Epis Ch; 1914 merged with Fulton Avenue Meth Epis Ch) SEE ALSO: Hillsdale-Chatsworth Unit Meth Ch
Jud	Chizuk Amuno Congregation, 8100 Stevenson Rd, Balto 21208 (1871) 1871- * syn
Prot Epis	Christ Ch, St John's Parish SEE: Keech, Rev John Reeder
Epis	Christ Ch, Western Run Parish SEE: Berger, Rev A J
Luth	Christ Eng Luth Ch. SEE: Christ Luth Ch
Evan Luth	Christ Evan Luth Ch, 5700 Edmondson Ave, Balto 21228. 1908- * ch (formerly located at Payson & Saratoga Sts)
Luth	Christ Luth Ch, 701 S Charles St (Charles & Hill Sts) Balto 21230 (1898) 1887- * ch (formerly called Christ Eng Luth Ch)
Meth Prot	Christ Meth Prot Ch 1913-1920 * UMHS
Prot Epis	Christ Prot Epis Ch 1828-1903 * MHS Mss Div
Ref	Christ Ref Ch, North Ave & Druid, Balto 1909-1931 * Messiah UCC, 5615 The Alameda, Balto 21239 (in 1931 Bethany Ref Ch & Christ Ref Ch merged & chose name Messiah)
Disc	Christian Temple, Edmondson Ave & Academy Rd, Balto 21228 (1904) 1889- * ch
Epis	Christ's Ch, 1110 St Paul St, Balto 21202 (1794) 1794- * ch, 1828-1871 # MHS, 1829-1870 # LDS, June 23, 1855 vestry # MGS Bull (also known as Christ Epis Ch, founded 1794 from St Paul's Ch, Charles & Saratoga Sts)
Luth	Christus Victor Evan Luth Ch, 9833 Harford Rd, Balto 21234 1958- * ch
R Cath	Ch of All Saints, 4408 Liberty Heights Ave, Balto 21207 1912- * ch
Cath	Ch of Ascension, Potomac & Poplar Aves, Halethorpe 21227 (1913) 1913- * ch
Prot Epis	Ch of Our Saviour, Broadway & McElderry Sts, Balto 1844-1870 * MDA, 1844-1865 # MSA (formerly known as Cranmer Chapel)
Epis	Ch of St Katherine of Alexandria 1892-1968 * MDA
Epis	Ch of St Mary, 5610 Dogwood Rd, Woodlawn 21207 (c.1871) * ch
Epis	Ch of St Stephen the Martyr 1900-1979 * MDA
Presb	Ch of Soldiers' Delight SEE: Mt Paran Presb Ch
Epis	Ch of the Advent, 1301 S Charles St, Balto 21230 (1869) 1880- * ch

R Cath   Ch of the Annunciation, 5212 McCormick Ave, Balto 21206
                (1968) 1968- * ch
Prot Epis   Ch of the Ascension and Prince of Peace, 8334 Liberty Rd,
                Balto 21207 (1838) * ch; 1883-1906 * MDA; 1838-1951 # MSA;
                1838-1860, 1878-1884 * MHS Mss Div (Ch of the Ascension,
                Lafayette Ave & Arlington St, and Prince of Peace, Walbrook
                Ave & Ellamont St merged in 1931)
Epis   Ch of the Holy Apostles, 4922 Leeds Ave, Balto 21227 (1884)
                1884- * ch (formerly located on Sulphur Spring Rd, then
                1913-1950 on Arbutus Ave, 1950 on Leeds Ave)
Prot Epis   Ch of the Holy Comforter, Rossville 1896-1927 (defunct)
                1896-1910 * MDA # MSA
Epis   Ch of the Holy Cross 1905-1910 * MDA
Prot Epis   Ch of the Holy Innocents 1858-1925 (defunct) 1899-1925 *
                MDA # MSA, 1888-1895 * MHS Mss Div (last located at Chase &
                Eden Sts)
Prot Epis   Ch of the Holy Nativity, 3811 Egerton Rd, Balto 21204
                1911-1961 # MSA
Epis   Ch of the Holy Trinity, 2300 W Lafayette Ave, Balto 21216
                (1953) 1953- * ch (This is a black ch, prior to 1953 it
                was a white ch also called Holy Trinity. Their records are
                at St Bartholomew's Ch, 4711 Edmondson Ave, Balto 21229)
Cath   Ch of the Immaculate Conception, Mosher St & Druid Hill Ave,
                Balto 21217 (1850) 1850- * ch, 1852-1981 # MSA
Cath   Ch of the Immaculate Conception, Balto & Ware Aves, Towson,
                Balto 21204 (1883) 1886-1979 # MSA
R Cath   Ch of the Immaculate Heart of Mary, 8501 Loch Raven Blvd,
                Balto 21204 (1948) 1948- * ch
Epis   Ch of the Messiah, Harford Rd & White Ave, Balto 21214.
                1873-1966 * MDA # MSA. SEE ALSO: St Andrews Ch
Epis   Ch of the Nativity, 419 Cedarcroft Rd, Balto 21212. 1911-1947
                * MDA
Prot Epis   Ch of the Prince of Peace, Walbrook Ave & Ellamont St, Balto
                1899-1938 # MSA (merged with Ch of the Ascension in 1931)
Prot Epis   Ch of the Redeemer, N Charles St & Melrose Ave (5603 N Charles
                St) Balto 21210. 1849-1950 * MHS Mss Div, 1854-1920 # MSA
Epis   Ch of the Redemption, Towson & Clement Sts, Balto 21230
                (1902) 1902 * ch
Meth Epis   City Station, Balto 1799-1881 # MSA (later First Meth)
Meth Epis   Clifton Avenue Meth Epis Ch 1897-1951 * UMHS, 1888-1922 # MSA
Friends   Clifts Monthly Meet 1649-1945 # MSA SEE ALSO: West River &
                Clifts Monthly Meet
Meth   Clynmalira Unit Meth Ch, 15100 Old York Rd, Monkton 21131
                (1845) (records were destroyed in parsonage fire; minutes
                of Ladies Aid Society are in a safe depsit box)
Evan & Ref   Coblentz, Rev Lloyd E (St Paul's Ch) 1893-1899 * E&RA
S Bap   Colgate Bap Ch, 502 Fairview Ave, Balto 21224. 1983- * ch #
                MBHS
Prot Epis   Colmen, Rev John 1789-1807 # LDS (Rev John Coleman)
Meth   Columbia Avenue Meth Ch. SEE: Columbia Station Meth Epis Ch

Meth Epis	Columbia Station Meth Epis Ch 1842-1947 # MSA (in 1939 name changed from Columbia Avenue Meth Epis Ch to Columbia Avenue Meth Ch, in 1947 merged with Northwood Meth Ch)
Jud	Congregation Shomrei Emunah, 6213 Greenspring Ave, Balto 21209. 1970- * syn
Cath	Corpus Christi Ch, 110 W Lafayette Ave (Mt Royal & Lafayette Aves) Balto 21217 (1881) 1881- * ch, 1881-1982 # MSA (Jenkins Memorial)
Evan & Ref	Cort, Rev Cyrus 1881-1914 * E&RA # LDS
Prot Epis	Cranmer Chapel 1844-1870 * MDA. SEE ALSO: Ch of Our Saviour
Meth Epis S	Deer Park. SEE: Freedom Circuit
Luth	Derr, Rev S J of Hampstead 1887-1919 # MGS Bull
Presb	Dickey Memorial Presb Ch, 5112 Wetheredsville Rd, Dickeyville 21207 (1872) 1877- * ch
Luth	Divinity Luth Ch, Providence Rd at Stags Head, Towson 21204. 1960- * ch
Unit Breth	Dorguth Memorial Unit Breth Ch 1855-1923 * LL # MSA (also known as Dorguth Memorial Ch of the Unit Breth in Christ, formerly Otterbein Chapel, Conway St now Scott St)
Bap	Druid Park Ch SEE: Fuller Memorial Bap Ch
Bap	East Balto Bap Ch 1821-1951 * MBHS (formed in 1916 by merger of two earlier Bap churches, the Second & Fourth churches, was located at the Second Bap Ch bldg on Orleans & Luzerne Sts)
Meth Epis	East Balto Station. SEE: Broadway Station, Balto
Meth Epis	East Balto Station Meth Epis Ch 1800-1958 # MSA. SEE ALSO: Jackson Square Meth Epis Ch
Meth Prot	East Balto Station Meth Prot Ch 1833-1943 * Northwood-Appold Unit Meth Ch, Loch Raven Blvd & Cold Spring Ln, Balto 21239 # MSA. SEE ALSO: Mt Lebanon Indep Meth Ch
Meth Epis	Ebenezer. SEE: Great Falls Circuit Meth Epis Ch
Afric Meth Epis	Ebenezer Afric Meth Epis Ch, 18-20 W Montgomery St, Balto 21230 1850- * Thomas M Boone, 929 E 43rd St, Balto 21212 (one of Baltimore's early black churches)
Prim Bap	Ebenezer Bap Ch (1821) 1826-1899 * and # MSA
Unit Meth	Elderslie-St Andrews Unit Meth Ch, 5601 Pimlico Rd, Balto 21209. 1928- * ch
Prot Epis	Emmanuel Ch, Cathedral & Read Sts (811 Cathedral St) Balto 21201 (1852) 1854-1959 # MSA
Evan Luth	Emmanuel Eng Evan Luth Ch, 3131 E Balto St, Balto 21224 1905- * ch
Meth Epis	Emmanuel Meth Epis Ch South 1869-1910 * UMHS, 1903-1925 # MSA (in 1907 name changed to St John's Emmanuel Ch South)
Ref Epis	Emmanuel Ref Epis Ch, 3517 Harford Rd, Balto 21218. 1876- * ch (formerly located at Eden & Hoffman Sts)
Meth	Emory Grove Camp Meet 1878-1882 minutes * MHS Mss Div
Evan & Ref	Engelbrecht, Rev Jacob 1849-1851 * E&RA
Eng Luth	Eng Luth Ch of Balto, Charles & 39th Sts, Balto 21218. 1824-1826, 1860-1924 # MHS
Luth	Epiphany Luth Ch, 4302 Raspe Ave, Balto 21206 (1908) 1908- * ch
Meth Epis	Epworth. SEE: Oxford Meth Epis Ch

Meth	Epworth League 1910-1917 minutes, 1894-1915 Appold Chapter * MS Mss Div
Meth Epis S	Epworth Meth Epis Ch South 1896-1934 * UMHS
Bap	Eutaw Place Bap Ch. SEE: Woodbrook Bap Ch
Meth Epis	Eutaw Street Meth Epis Ch 1869-1921 # MSA (until 1869 part of Balto City Station, in 1924 merged with Mt Vernon) SEE ALSO: Meth Epis Ch
Evan Luth	Evan Luth Ch of the Ascension. SEE: Third Evan Luth Ch
Luth	Evan Luth Ch of the Prince of Peace, 8212 Phila Rd, Balto 21237 (1928) 1928- * ch (separated from Zion Evan Luth Ch on Golden Ring Rd, then called Stemmers Run Rd)
Meth Prot	Evergreen Meth Prot Ch. SEE: Roland Avenue Evergreen Unit Meth Ch
Meth	Exeter Memorial Meth Ch 1959-1971 * UMHS
Unit Meth	Fairview Unit Meth Ch, 13916 Jarrettsville Pike, Phoenix 21131. 1909- * ch
Evan Luth	Faith Evan Luth Ch, 1900 E North Ave at Wolfe St, Balto 21213. 1893- * ch
Presb	Faith Presb Ch, Loch Raven Blvd & Woodbourne Ave, Balto 21239 (1876) 1876- * ch
--	Federal Hill Male Sun Sch 1818-1819 * MHS Mss Div
Friends	Federal Hill Mission Meet 1879-1909 # MSA
Meth Prot	Fells Point Mission. SEE: Broadway Meth Prot Ch
Unit Meth	Fells Point Parish (organized in 1965 from East Balto Station, Caroline Street and Broadway Meth churches
Presb	Fifth Presb Ch 1833-1858 minutes * MHS Mss Div
Meth Epis	Finksburg. SEE: Balto Circuit Meth Epis Ch
Presb	First & Franklin Street Presb Ch, 808 Park Ave, Balto 21202. 1764 * ch (in 1973 First Presb Ch & Franklin Street Presb Ch merged)
UCC	First & St Stephens UCC of Balto 1716-1851 # MGS Bull (formerly First Ref Ch of Balto)
Bap	First Bap Ch of Balto, 4200 Liberty Heights Ave, Balto 21207 (1773) 1786-1965 * MBHS, 1784-1869 * MHS Mss Div
Bap	First Bap Ch of Lansdowne, 2320 Alma Rd, Lansdowne 21227 (1944) 1934- * ch (prior to 1947 known as Caton Hills Bap Ch, Nelway & Smith Aves, Lansdowne; from Fulton Avenue Bap Ch, the mother ch)
Disc	First Chris Ch, 5802 Roland Ave, Balto 21210. 19th century- * ch, 1810-1892 # MHS (1834 on North St nr Market St (now Guilford Ave nr Balto St); 1869 at Dolphin & Etting Sts)
Evan & Ref	First Ch 1750-1874 # E&RA
Chris Sci	First Ch of Christ, Scientist, 102 W University Pkwy, Balto 21210. 1894- * FHL
Ch of God	First Ch of God of Balto, 4801 Sipple Ave, Balto 21206. 1915- * ch
Bap	First Colored Bap Ch, 525 N Caroline St, Balto 21205 (1836) 1908- * ch
Cong	First Cong Ch of Balto 1865-1900 # MHS (in 1900 merged with Associated Ref Ch of Balto to become Associated Cong Ch)
Luth	First Eng Evan Luth Ch, 3807 N Charles St, Balto 21218 (1825) 1825- * ch, 1860-1924 # MHS

Ref   First Ger Ref Ch (Otterbein) (1798) 1798-1850 # MHS. SEE
       ALSO Old Otterbein...)
Ref   First Ger Ref Congregation 1769-1851 # MHS LDS
Unit Evan First Ger Unit Evan Ch 1849-1853, 1911-1921, 1936-1965 # MSA.
       SEE ALSO: First Unit Evan Ch
Unitar   First Indep Ch of Balto, Charles & Franklin Sts, Balto 21201
       (1818) 1818-1925 * ch # MHS
Luth   First Luth Ch of Govans. SEE: Luth Ch of the Holy Comforter
Meth   First Meth. SEE: City Station, Balto
Meth Epis First Meth Epis Ch, St Paul & 22nd Sts, Balto 21218. * ch,
       1882-1915 # MSA, 1799-1866 # MHS (formerly Old Light Street
       Ch, now known as Lovely Lane Unit Meth Ch)
Bap   First Mt Cavalry Bap Ch, 1142 N Fulton Ave, Balto 21217.
       1921- * ch
Presb   First Presb Ch 1767-1879 # MHS (First Presb Ch & Franklin
       Street Ch merged in 1973 to form First & Franklin Street
       Presb Ch)
Ref   First Ref Ch, Second St, Balto 1821-1899 # MGS Bull (The Ger
       Ref Ch)
Unitar   First Unitar Ch. SEE: First Indep Ch of Balto
UCC   First Unit Evan Ch, 1728 Eastern Ave, Balto 21231. 1850- *
       ch, 1850-1978 # MSA (Formerly known as First Ger Unit Evan
       Ch)
Unit Presb First Unit Presb Ch, 1908 E 30th St, Balto 1826-1962 * and #
       MSA (now Montebello Presb Ch)
Meth Epis Fork. SEE: Great Falls Circuit Meth Epis Ch, Long Green
       Circuit Meth Epis Ch
Meth Epis Fort Avenue Meth Epis Ch. SEE: Good Shepherd Unit Meth Ch
Cath   Fourteen Holy Martyrs Ch, 101 S Mount St nr Lombard St, Balto
       (1870-1964) * St Martin's Ch, 31 N Fulton Ave, Balto 21223
       # MSA
Bap   Fourth Bap Ch (1835-1916) * MBHS (began as High Street Bap
       Ch, merged with Second Bap Ch in 1916 to become E Balto Bap
       Ch--locations of Fourth Bap Ch: Calvert St nr Saratoga
       1835, High St bet Fayette & Low Sts 1844, Broadway &
       Jefferson St 1891-1916)
Presb   Franklin Street Ch. SEE: First & Franklin Street Presb Ch
Meth   Franklin Street Meth Ch (1860-1927) * UMHS
Presb   Franklinville Presb Ch, Bradshaw 21021 * ch (dates not
       given)
Prot Epis Free Ch of St Barnabas 1872-1882 # MSA. SEE ALSO: Cathedral
       Ch of the Incarnation, St Barnabas Ch
Meth Epis S Freedom Circuit 1876-1925, 1940 # MSA (includes Deer Park
       and West Point, Balto Co)
Evan Luth Friedens Evan Luth Ch, 219 N Chester St, Balto * LCA (ch no
       longer at this address)
Friends   Friends Sch of Balto, 5114 N Charles St, Balto 21210. 1784- *
       FHL
Bap   Fuller Memorial Bap Ch 1880-1947 * MBHS (merged with Druid
       Park Ch)
Meth Epis Fulton Avenue & Chatsworth Meth Epis Ch 1900-1926 # MSA. SEE
       ALSO: Chatsworth Meth Epis Ch

Bap	Fulton Avenue Bap Ch, 3 N Fulton Ave, Balto 21223. 1883 * ch
Breth	Fulton Avenue Ch of the Breth. SEE: Woodberry Ch of the Breth
Meth Epis	Fulton Avenue Meth Epis Ch 1897-1914 # MSA (organized in 1889 as Lafayette Avenue Meth Epis Ch, merged in 1914 with Chatsworth Meth Epis Ch) SEE ALSO: Hillsdale-Chatsworth Unit Meth Ch
Meth Epis	Furnace. SEE: Great Falls Circuit Meth Epis Ch
Bap	Garrison Forest, 2 Tahoe Circle, Balto 21117. 1980 * Temple Bap Ch, 6916 Dogwood Rd, Balto 21207
Unit Meth	Gatch Memorial Unit Meth Ch, 5738 Belair Rd, Balto 21206. 1916 * ch (estab in 1772 as Gatch Ch) SEE ALSO: Great Falls Circuit Meth Epis Ch
Ref & Luth	Ger Ch in Balto Co 1760-1836 # LDS (first record book for Ref & Luth congregations at Manchester, Balto Co, now Carroll Co; known as Zion Ch)
Evan Luth	Ger Evan Luth St Peters Congregation, Randallstown 1850-1873 # LDS
Luth	Ger Immanuel Luth Ch. SEE: Our Saviour Luth Ch
Prot Ref	Ger Prot Ref Ch 1785-1965 # MHS Mss Div
Ref	Ger Ref Ch. SEE: First Ref Ch
Unit Evan	Ger Unit Evan Ch. SEE: Unit Evan Ch of UCC
Meth	Gibson, Rev Alexander 1853-1896 * MDA
Unit Meth	Good Shepherd Unit Meth Ch, 301 E Fort Ave, Balto 21230 1856- * ch (Fort Avenue Meth Epis Ch (1890-1958), S Balto Station Meth Epis Ch (1871-1958), Light Street Meth Prot Ch (1856-1958), Patterson Memorial Meth Epis Ch (1856-1958) & Lowe Memorial Meth Prot Ch (1875-1958) merged in 1958 to form Good Shepherd...)
Presb	Govans Presb Ch, 5828 York Rd, Balto 21212 (1839) 1940 * ch, prior to 1940 * PHS
Epis	Grace & St Peter's Ch, 707 Park Ave (Park Ave & Monument St) Balto 21201. 1803- * ch, 1900-1936 # MHS Mss Div (Grace Ch (1852) and St Peter's Ch (1803) merged in 1912)
Bap	Grace Bap Ch, Alameda & 32nd St, Balto 21218. 1870- * ch
Prot Epis	Grace Chapel, Mt Winans 1909-1929 * MDA # MSA
Epis	Grace Ch. SEE: Grace & St Peter's Ch
Meth Prot	Grace Clifton Park Meth Prot Ch 1921-1958 * UMHS
Evan Luth	Grace Eng Evan Luth Ch, 8601 Valleyfield Rd, Lutherville 21093 1885- * ch (formerly located at Broadway & Gough St, Balto)
Luth	Grace Evan Luth Ch, 5205 Harford Rd, Balto 21214. 1903- * ch
Unit Meth	Grace-Hampden Unit Meth Ch. (1890-1980) SEE: Roland Avenue-Evergreen Unit Meth Ch
Meth Epis	Grace Meth Epis Ch. SEE: Grace Unit Meth Ch
UCC	Grace UCC, 1404 S Charles St, Balto 21230 (1895) 1897- * ch
Unit Meth	Grace Unit Meth Ch, 5407 N Charles St, Balto 21210. 1868- * ch (formerly Grace Meth Epis Ch, Roland Park Meth Epis Ch, & N Balto Meth Prot Ch)
Meth	Granite. SEE: Balto Circuit Meth Epis Ch, Stone Chapel
Meth Epis	Great Falls Circuit Meth Epis Ch 1851-1931 # MSA (includes Asbury Chapel, Back River, Camp Chapel, Canton, Ebenezer, Fork, Furnace, Gatch, Highland Avenue, Hiss, Hisses,

	Loreley, Orems, Patapsco, Piney Grove, Providence, Salem, Waugh, Wilson)
Greek Orth	Greek Orth Cathedral of the Annunciation, 24 W Preston St, Balto 21201. (1906) 1911- * ch (first meeting held at Fayette & Gay Sts)
Meth Epis	Greenmount Meth Epis Ch 1867-1901 * UMHS
Bap	Gregory Memorial Bap Ch 1924-1956 * MBHS
Meth Epis	Guilford Avenue Meth Epis Ch 1886-1936 * UMHS, 1886-1911 # MSA
Bap	Gunpowder Bap Ch, Freeland 1806-1966 # MSA MHS
Friends	Gunpowder Monthly Meet # MHS (copies of cards, Hinshaw's notes for a work that was never published)
Presb	Hamilton Presb Ch, 5532 Hamilton Ave, Balto 21218 (1901) 1901 * ch
Unit Presb	Hampden Unit Presb Ch (1875) 1886-1973 * PHS (in 1973 merged with Wa2erly Presb Ch)
Meth Epis	Hanover Street Meth Epis Ch 1858-1894 * UMHS, 1858-1876 # MSA
Jud	Har Siani Congregation, 6300 Park Heights Ave, Balto 21215. 1842 * syn
Meth Epis	Harford Avenue Meth Epis Ch (1858) 1858-1939 * UMHS # MSA
Bap	Harford Bap Ch, 4906 Harford Rd, Balto 21214. 1957- * ch
Meth	Harford Circuit Meth Ch 1832-1842 * MHS Mss Div
Bap	Hazelwood Bap Ch, 5310 Hazelwood Ave, Balto 21206 (1959) 1962- * ch
UCC	Heritage UCC, 3106 Liberty Heights Ave, Balto 21215 (1965) 1963- * ch
Bap	High Street Bap Ch. 1875-1898 * MHS Mss Div. SEE ALSO: Fourth Bap Ch
Meth Epis	High Street Meth Epis Ch 1844-1927 * UMHS, 1844-1896 # MSA
Meth Epis	Highland Avenue. SEE: Great Falls Circuit Meth Epis Ch
Breth	Hill Street Ch of the Breth. SEE: Woodberry Ch of the Breth
Unit Meth	Hillsdale-Chatsworth Unit Meth Ch, 5114 Windsor Mill Rd, Balto 21207. 1861-1953 # MSA (Chatsworth Meth Epis Ch (1861) merged with Fulton Avenue Ch in 1914, later with Hillsdale Ch)
Meth	Hillsdale Circuit Meth Ch 1945-1954 # MSA
Meth Epis	Hillsdale Circuit Meth Epis Ch 1919-1960 # MSA. SEE ALSO: Chatsworth Meth Epis Ch
Unit Meth	Hiss Church, Parkville 1842-1958 # MSA (known as Hiss Memorial Meth Ch (Hysses Chapel), Hiss (Memorial) Meth Epis Ch, Hiss Meth Epis Ch, & Hiss Meth Ch) SEE ALSO: Great Falls Circuit Meth Epis Ch
Meth Epis	Hisses. SEE: Great Falls Circuit Meth Epis Ch
Cath	Holy Cross, 110 E West St, Balto 21230 (1858) 1858- * ch, 1858-1979 # MSA (developed from St Alphonsus)
Epis	Holy Cross Chapel, Freeland 1888-1923 * MDA
Luth	Holy Cross Luth Ch, 8516 Loch Raven Blvd, Balto 21204 (1951) 1950- * ch
Cath	Holy Cross Parish of the Polish Natl Cath Ch, 208 S Broadway, Balto 21231 1898- * ch
Cath	Holy Family, 9533 Liberty Rd, Randallstown 21133 (1876) 1876- * ch

Baltimore City and Baltimore County

Epis   Holy Nativity Epis Ch, 3811 Egerton Rd, Balto 21215.
            1911-1961 # MSA
Cath   Holy Redeemer Chapel, 800 S Oldham St, Balto 21224 (1944)
            1944- * ch (developed by Sacred Heart Parish)
R Cath   Holy Rosary Ch, 408 S Chester St, Balto 21231 (1887) 1887- *
            ch, 1887-1985 # MSA
Epis   Holy Trinity Epis Ch, 2300 W Lafayette Ave, Balto (1875)
            1875-1953 * St Bartholomew's Ch, 4711 Edmondson Ave, Balto
            21229 # MSA (in 1953 merged with St Bartholomew's Ch)
Rus Orth   Holy Trinity Rus Orth Ch, 1725 E Fairmount Ave, Balto 21231
            1918- * ch
Evan Luth   Hope Evan Luth Ch, 1901 Middleborough Rd, Balto 21221. 1955 *
            ch
Presb   Hope Presb Ch, Shelbourne & Ten Oaks Rd, Balto 21227. 1880- *
            ch (in 1969 Relay Presb Ch & Bethany Presb Ch merged)
Unit Meth   Howard Park Unit eth Ch, 5024 Gwynn Oak Dr, Balto 21207
            (1910) 1910- * ch
Presb   Hunting Ridge Presb Ch, 4640 Edmondson Ave, Balto 21229
            (1880) * ch (formerly Lafayette Square Presb Ch, moved to
            present address in 1929)
Bap   Huntingdon Bap Ch, 31st & Barclay Sts, Balto 21218 (1846) *
            ch
Meth Epis   Huntington Avenue Meth Epis Ch 1861-1885 * UMHS # MSA
Meth   Hysses Chapel. SEE: Hiss Ch
Unit Meth   Idleywlde Unit Meth Ch, 1000 Regester Ave, Balto 21239 1917-
            * ch
Evan & Ref Immanuel Evan & Ref Ch, Saratoga St, Balto. SEE: Catonsville
            Immanuel UCC
Luth   Immanuel Luth Ch, Loch Raven Blvd & Belvedere Ave, Balto 21239
            1864- * ch (formerly at Caroline & Balto Sts)
Unit Meth   Immanuel Unit Meth Ch, Annabel Ave & 5th St, Balto 21225.
            1840- * ch
Meth Prot   Israel Colored Meth Prot Ch 1849-1884 * UMHS
Evan Luth   Jackson Square Evan Luth Ch. SEE: Our Saviour Luth Ch
Meth Epis   Jackson Square Meth Epis Ch 1865-1889 * UMHS (merged with E
            Balto Station Meth Epis Ch
Meth Epis   Jefferson Street Meth Epis Ch 1854-1919 * UMHS, 1854-1915 #
            MSA
Cath   Jenkins Memorial. SEE: Corpus Christi Ch
Luth   Jerusalem Luth Ch, 4605 Belair Rd, Balto 21206. 1800's- * ch
            (originally served a Ger speaking congregation)
Prot Epis   Keech, Rev John Reeder 1819-1864 * MDA, 1819-1861 # LDS,
            1819-1861 # MGS Bull
Unit Presb Knox Presb Ch, 1300 N Eden St, Balto 21213 (1930) 1969- * ch
Bap   Korean of Balto, c/o Colonial Bap, 4619 Old Court Rd, Balto
            21208 (1951) 1951- * ch
Presb   Korean Presb Ch of Balto, 3426 Bank St, Balto 21224 1974- *
            ch
Unit Meth   Korean Unit Meth Ch of Balto, N Charles St & University Pkwy,
            Balto 21218 1975- * ch
Meth Epis   Lafayette Avenue Meth Epis Ch. SEE: Fulton Avenue Meth Epis
            Ch

17

Meth Prot	Lafayette House Meth Prot Ch 1883-1912 # MSA. SEE ALSO: W Balto Station
Presb	Lafayette Square Presb Ch. SEE: Hunting Ridge Presb Ch
Unit Meth	Lauraville Unit Meth Ch, Harford Rd & Southern Ave, Balto 21214. 1904- * ch, 1904-1962 # MSA (until union in 1939 Lauraville was a Meth Prot ch)
Bap	Lee Street Memorial Bap Ch, 111 Warren Ave, Balto 21230 (1855) 1921- * ch
Unit Breth	Liberty Heights Unit Breth in Christ Ch, Liberty Heights & Montgomery Ave, Balto 1925-1927 * UMHS # MSA (Little Gray Stone Ch)
Meth Epis	Light Street. SEE: Meth Epis Ch
Meth Epis	Light Street Ger Meth Epis Ch 1869-1943 * UMHS, 1870-1942 # MSA
Meth Epis	Light Street Meth Epis Ch 1823-1833 # MHS
Meth Prot	Light Street Meth Prot Ch 1856-1958. SEE ALSO: Good Shepherd Unit Meth Ch
Presb	Light Street Presb Ch, 809 Light St, Balto 21230 1854 * ch (first Presb ch in Federal Hill)
Unit Breth	Little Gray Stone Church. SEE: Liberty Heights Unit Breth in Christ Ch
Bap	Loch Raven Bap Ch, 8600 Loch Raven Blvd, Balto 21204 * ch (dates not given)
Bap	Long Green Bap Ch, 13010 Manor Rd, Long Green 21047. 1960- * ch
Unit Meth	Long Green Circuit Meth Epis Ch 1836-1941 # MSA (includes Fork, Salem, Union, Waugh, Wilson)
Meth Epis	Loreley. SEE: Great Falls Circuit Meth Epis Ch
Meth Epis	Lovely Lane Unit Meth Ch, 2200 St Paul St, Balto 21218. 1795- * ch (formerly First Meth Epis Ch)
Meth Prot	Lowe Memorial Meth Prot Ch 1875-1958. SEE: Good Shepherd Unit Meth Ch
Luth	Luther Memorial Luth Ch, 5401 Eastern Ave, Balto 21224 (1917) 1917- * ch
Luth	Lutheran Ch of the Holy Comforter, 5513 York Rd, Balto 21212 1911- * ch (formerly First Luth Ch of Govans; fire in 1955 destroyed some records)
Luth	Lutheran Ch of the Messiah, Cross & Cleveland Sts, Balto. SEE: Martini Evan Luth Ch
Meth Epis	Lutherville Meth Epis Ch. SEE: St John's Meth Epis Ch, Lutherville
Meth	Madison Avenue Meth Ch 1864-1927 * Mt Vernon Place Unit Meth Ch, 10 E Mt Vernon Pl, Balto 21202
Meth Epis	Madison Avenue Meth Epis Ch 1870-1949 * UMHS
Presb	Madison Avenue Presb Ch, 2100 Madison Ave, Balto 21217. 1868- *·ch (originally at Madison Ave & Ploy Al; Baltimore's first black Presb ch)
Meth Epis	Madison Square Centenary Meth Epis Ch 1866-1923 # MSA
Meth Epis	Madison Square Meth Epis Ch 1869-1931 * UMHS, 1922-1931 # MSA (merged with North Avenue Meth Epis Ch)
Meth Epis	Madison Square Station Meth Epis Ch 1876-1889 # MSA
Evan & Ref	Manchester Evan & Ref Ch 1760-1836, 1884, 1908 * MHS Mss Div

Meth Epis	Marcella. SEE: Balto Circuit Meth Epis Ch
Evan Luth	Martin Luther Evan Luth Ch, 401 N Patterson Park Ave (Orleans St & Patterson Park Ave) Balto 21231. 1890- * ch. SEE ALSO: St Paul Luth Ch, 141 S. Clinton St, Balto 21224
Evan Luth	Martini Evan Luth Ch, Hanover & Henrietta Sts, Balto 21230. 1868- * ch, 1886-1976 # MSA
Luth	Martini Luth Ch 1868-1900 # MSA
Cath	Mary Star of the Sea, 1419 Riverside Ave, Balto 21230 (1868) 1868- * ch
Presb	Md Presb Ch, 1105 Providence Rd, Towson 21204. 1957-1965 * PHS, 1967- * ch
Luth	Md Synod of the Lutheran Ch in Amer, 7604 York Rd, Balto 21204. 1820 * and # records, proceedings, reports
Meth Epis	McKendree Meth Epis Ch 1856, 1872, 1878-1943 * Arlington Unit Meth Ch, 5268 Reisterstown Rd, Balto 21215
Meth Epis	Meadow Dale. SEE: Balto Circuit Meth Epis Ch
Prot Epis	Memorial Ch, Bolton St & Lafayette Ave, Balto 1859-1971 # MSA
Prot Epis	Memorial Ch of the Holy Comforter, Pratt & Chester Sts, Balto 1875-1922 * MDA # MSA
Epis	Memorial Epis Ch, 1407 Bolton St, Balto 21217. 1864- * ch
Unit Meth	Memorial Unit Meth Ch, 3412 Frederick Ave, Balto 21229. 1884- * ch (known as Mt Olivet Meth Epis Ch 1867-1889)
Meth	Meredith Meet House. SEE: West Liberty Meth Ch
Luth	Messiah Eng Luth Ch, Potomac & O'Donnell Sts, Balto 21224 (1889) 1889- * ch
Evan & Ref	Messiah Evan & Ref Ch 1934-1956 * Messiah UCC
Ref	Messiah Ref Ch 1931-1933 * Messiah UCC (in 1931 Bethany Ref Ch & Christ Ref Ch merged & chose the name Messiah)
UCC	Messiah UCC, 5615 The Alameda, Balto 21239. 1957- * ch. SEE ALSO: Bethany Ref Ch, Christ Ref Ch, Messiah Ref Ch, Messiah Evan & Ref Ch
Meth	Meth Ch in Md 1770-1912 * MHS Mss Div (manuscript history of the Meth Ch, never published)
Meth Epis	Meth Epis Ch (receipts for building materials, ground rents, labor, and advertising for Baltimore City Station 1824-1856, Light Street 1830-1869, Eutaw Street 1832-1858, and First Meth Epis Ch 1895-1905 * MHS Mss Div)
Bap	Middle River Bap Ch, 610 Middle River Rd, Balto 21220. 1945- * ch
Meth	Milton Avenue Meth Ch 1905-1959 * UMHS
Presb	Montebello Unit Presb Ch. SEE: Arneal, Rev John F, also First Unit Presb Ch
Meth	Monument Street Meth Ch 1858-1861 minutes of Taylor Mission Bible & Sun Sch Soc * UMHS (merged with Northwood-Appold)
Evan	Morrell Park Ger Evan Ch. SEE: St Mark's UCC, 1805 Wickes Ave, Balto 21230
Epis	Mt Calvary Ch, 816 N Eutaw St, Balto 21201. 1955 * ch, 1842-1975 # MSA
Bap	Mt Lebanon Bap Ch, 2320 Reisterstown Rd, Balto 21217. 1924- * ch
Meth	Mt Lebanon Indep Meth Ch (united with E Balto Station Meth Prot Ch in 1880)

Meth Prot	Mt Lebanon Meth Prot Ch 1892-1897 * UMHS (merged with Northwood Appold)
Meth	Mt Olive. SEE: Balto Circuit Meth Epis Ch, Stone Chapel
Luth	Mt Olive Luth Ch, 2999 Belair Rd, Balto 21214. 1949 * ch
Meth Epis	Mt Olivet Meth Epis Ch (1867-1889) SEE: Memorial Unit Meth Ch
Presb	Mt Paran Presb Ch, 10308 Liberty Rd, Randallstown 21133 (1715) 1841- * ch (the second oldest Presb ch in Amer, on Lyons Mill Rd, Harrisonville, known under three names: Patapsco Ch, Ch of Soldiers' Delight, Mt Paran)
Meth Epis	Mt Pleasant. SEE: Balto Circuit Meth Epis Ch
Cath	Mt St Joseph's Ch. SEE: St Mary's Industrial Sch
Meth Epis	Mt Vernon Place Meth Epis Ch 1872, 1880-1889 pew cert & rentals * MHS Mss Div. SEE ALSO: Mt Vernon Place Unit Meth Ch
Unit Meth	Mt Vernon Place Unit Meth Ch, 10 E Mt Vernon Pl, Balto 21202. 1843- * ch (known as Charles Street Meth Epis Ch (1843-1872) and Mt Vernon Place Meth Epis Ch (1872-1939)
Unit Meth	Mt Washington Unit Meth Ch, 5800 Cottonworth Ave, Balto 21209 (prior to 1822) * ch (records destroyed in flood of 1979)
Luth	Nativity Luth Ch c/o 14 Ratna Ct, Balto 21236. 1984- * ch
Luth	Nazareth Luth Ch, 3401 Bank St, Balto 21224 (1905) 1905- * ch
Swed	New Jerusalem (Swedenborgen) Ch 1793-1862 # MHS
Bap	New Shiloh Bap Ch, 823 W Lanvale St (Fremont Ave & Lanvale St) Balto 21217 (1902) 1959- * ch
Bap	North Avenue Bap Ch 1891-1933 * MBHS
Meth	North Avenue Meth Ch 1890-1975 * UMHS
Meth Epis	North Avenue Meth Epis Ch, North Ave & Caroline St, Balto (1892) 1892-1975 # MSA (in 1888 developed as a chapel from Madison Square Meth Epis Ch)
Meth Prot	North Balto Meth Prot Ch. SEE: Grace Unit Meth Ch
Meth Epis	North Balto Station Meth Epis Ch 1837-1943 * Northwood Appold Unit Meth Ch, Loch Raven Blvd & Cold Spring Ln, Balto 21239, 1836-1943 # MSA (merged with Northwood Appold)
Bap	Northside Bap Ch, 1100 E Northern Pkwy, Balto 21239 (1958) 1954- * ch
Bap	Northwest Bap Ch, P.O.Box 372 Reisterstown 21136 (1971) 1971- * ch
Meth Epis	Northwest Mission Meth Epis Ch 1881-1886 * UMHS, 1882-1886 # MSA
Unit Meth	Northwood Appold Unit Meth Ch, Loch Raven Blvd & Cold Spring Ln, Balto 21239. 1943- * ch, 1943-1974 # MSA (also records of churches that merged in 1943: N Balto Station Meth Epis Ch (1837-1943), E Balto Station Meth Prot Ch (1833-1943), and Appold Meth Epis Ch (1877-1948)
Meth	Northwood Meth Ch. SEE: Columbia Station Meth Epis Ch
--	Norwegian Seaman's Ch, 300 S Patterson Pk Ave, Balto 21231 1919- * ch
Friends	Nottingham Quarterly, Monthly and Preparative Meet 1679-1955 # MSA
Meth	Old Light Street Ch. SEE: First Meth Epis Ch

Baltimore City and Baltimore County

Unit Meth	Old Otterbein Unit Meth Ch, 112 W Conway St, Balto 21201 (1771) 1785-1960 # MSA MHS (formerly Ger Evan Ref, Unit Breth, Evan Unit Breth, now Unit Meth) SEE ALSO: First Ger Ref Ch (Otterbein)
Meth Epis	Orems. SEE: Great Falls Circuit Meth Epis Ch
Unit Meth	Orems Unit Meth Ch, 1020 Orems Rd, Balto 21220 1951- * ch
--	Otterbein Chapel. SEE: Dorguth Memorial Unit Breth Ch
Prot Ref	Otterbein Ch 1785-1960 # E&RA. SEE ALSO: Ger Prot Ref Ch
Unit Meth	Otterbein Memorial Unit Meth Ch, 38th St & Roland Ave, Balto 21211. 1871-1910 # MSA (formerly Union Ave)
R Cath	Our Lady of Fatima, 6400 E Pratt St, Balto 21224. 1951- * ch (originally a mission of Sacred Heart of Jesus)
Cath	Our Lady of Good Counsel, Fort Ave & Towson St, Balto 21230 (1859) 1850's- * ch, 1860-1981 # MSA (formerly a ch at Cooksey St & Fort Ave known as St Laurence, served as a mission chapel of St Brigid's Parish, name changed to Our Lady of Good Counsel bet 1873-1889)
Cath	Our Lady of Grace, 18310 Middletown Rd, Parkton 21120. 1974- * ch
Cath	Our Lady of Lourdes, Liberty Heights Ave & Edgewood Rd, Balto 21215 (1925) 1925- * ch
Cath	Our Lady of Mt Carmel, Middle River. SEE: Our Lady Queen of Peace Ch
Cath	Our Lady of Perpetual Help, 6950 Dogwood Rd (nr Rolling Rd) Balto 21207 (1936) 1938- * ch
R Cath	Our Lady of Pompeii Ch, Claremont & Conkling Sts, Balto 21224. 1924- * ch
R Cath	Our Lady of Sorrows Ch, West Hill St, Balto (1925-1935) * Holy Cross, 110 E West St, Balto 21230, 1922-1934 # MSA
Cath	Our Lady of Victory, 4416 Wilkens Ave, Arbutus, Balto 21229 (1952) 1952- * ch
Cath	Our Lady Queen of Peace Ch, 10003 Bird River Rd, Balto 21220. 1953- * ch (Our Lady of Mt Carmel, Middle River, is the parent ch)
Luth	Our Saviour Luth Ch, 3301 The Alameda, Balto 21218 (1892) 1892- * ch (estab by members of Ger Immanuel Luth Ch who wanted Eng language services; called Jackson Square Evan Luth Ch, Fairmount Ave & Jackson Sq (1892-1919), in 1973 merged with St Matthew Luth Ch, Druid Hill Ave & Robert St)
Bap	Overlea Bap Ch, 4016 Overlea Ave, Balto 21206. 1919- * ch
Unit Meth	Overlea Unit Meth Ch, 3900 Overlea Ave, Balto 21206. 1925- * ch
Meth Epis	Oxford Meth Epis Ch 1889-1957 * UMHS, 1889-1941 # MSA
Cath	Paca Street Chapel. SEE: Sulp Arc
Meth Epis	Park Heights Avenue Meth Epis Ch 1907-1914 * Arlington Unit Meth Ch, 5268 Reisterstown Rd, Balto 21215
Unit Meth	Parkside Unit Meth Ch, 4400 Parkside Dr, Balto 21206 (1932) 1932- * ch
Meth Epis	Patapsco Chapel. SEE: Great Falls Circuit Meth Epis Ch
Presb	Patapsco Ch. SEE: Mt Paran Presb Ch
Friends	Patapsco Preparative Meet 1776-1807 # MSA

Meth Epis	Patterson Memorial Meth Epis Ch. SEE: Good Shepherd Unit Meth Ch
Bap	Patterson Park Bap Ch, 3115 Eastern Ave, Balto 21224 (1911) 1911- * ch
Bap	Perkins Square Bap Ch, 2500 Edmondson Ave, Balto 21223. 1881- * ch (a black ch formerly at George & Ogle Sts)
Presb	Perry Hall Presb Ch, 8848 Belair Rd, Balto 21236 (1957) 1957- * ch
Meth Epis	Piney Grove. SEE: Great Falls Circuit Meth Epis Ch
Meth	Pleasant Hill. SEE: Stone Chapel
Meth Epis	Powhatan Meth Epis Ch. SEE: St Luke's Unit Meth Ch of Woodlawn
Prot Epis	Prince of Peace Ch, Walbrook. SEE: Church of the Ascension and Prince of Peace
Meth Epis	Providence. SEE: Great Falls Circuit Meth Epis Ch
Unit Meth	Providence Unit Meth Ch, 10 E Seminary Ave, Lutherville 21093 (1858) 1956- * ch
S Bap	Ranelagh Road Bap Ch, 5700 Ranelagh Rd, White March 21161. 1986- * ch, 1954-1986 * MBHS (organized as Grace Bap Ch in 1954, name changed in 1986)
Prot Epis	Raspeburg Mission 1907 * MDA. SEE ALSO: St Matthias Ch
Luth	Redeemer Luth Ch, Gwynn Oak Ave, Balto 1927-1962 * LCA
Luth	Reformation Luth Ch, 6200 Loch Raven Blvd, Balto 21239 (1890) 1890- * ch (formerly at 1700 N Caroline St)
Ref & Luth	Ref & Luth Congregations, Manchelter 1760-1836 # MHS (called the German Churche in Baltymore County)
Bap	Reisterstown Bap Ch, Chestnut Hill Ln, Reisterstown 21136 (1962) 1962- * ch
Presb	Relay Presb Ch. SEE: Hope Presb Ch
Meth	Roberts, Rev George C M 1828-1868 # MHS Mss Div
Meth	Rognel Heights Meth Ch 1914-1958 * UMHS
Unit Meth	Roland Avenue-Evergreen Unit Meth Ch, 4228 Falls Rd, Balto 21211 (1887) 1891- * ch (Roland Avenue Meth Ch & Evergreen Meth Prot Ch merged in 1971; Grace Hampden Unit Meth Ch merged in 1980)
Meth	Roland Avenue Meth Ch. SEE: Roland Avenue-Evergreen Unit Meth Ch
Cath	Roland Park Chapel. SEE: Sulp Arc
Meth Epis	Roland Park Meth Epis Ch. SEE: Grace Unit Meth Ch
Presb	Roland Park Presb Ch, 4801 Roland Ave, Balto 21210 (1901) 1901 * ch
Unit Presb	Roland Park Presb Ch 1900-1957 # MSA
Meth Epis	Royers Hill Meth Epis Ch, 24th St, Balto 1885-1903 # MSA
R Cath	Sacred Heart of Jesus R Cath Ch, 600 S Conkling St, Balto 21224 (1873) 1873-1977 # MSA
Cath	Sacred Heart Parish. SEE: Holy Redeemer Chapel, Shrine of the Sacred Heart
Indep Meth	Sailor's Union Bethel Indep Meth Ch, 454 E Cross St, Balto 21230. 1890's- * ch
Cath	St Adrian Ch (1948-1967) * Our Lady of Hope Rectory, 1727 Lynch Rd, Balto 21222

Baltimore City and Baltimore County

Cath	St Agnes, Rt 10 at St Agnes Ln, Catonsville 21229 (1852) 1852- * ch, 1852-1978 # MSA
R Cath	St Alphonsus Ch, Park Ave & Saratoga St, Balto 21201 (1887) 1845-1977 # MSA (founded to serve Ger catholics, in 1917 began to serve the Lithuanian community) SEE ALSO: Holy Cross, 110 E West St, Balto 21230
R Cath	St Alphonsus Rodriguez R Cath Ch, 10800 Old Court Rd, Woodstock 21163. 1870 * ch
Cath	St Ambrose, 4502 Park Heights Ave, Balto 21215 (1902) 1902- * ch
Cath	St Andrew (1878-1974) * Cath Cen
Epis	St Andrew's Chapel, Lauraville 1891-1907 * MDA
Prot Epis	St Andrew's Ch, 6010 Harford Rd, Balto (1874-1920) 1891-1907 * MDA # MSA, 1909-1920 * Church of the Messiah, Harford Rd & White Ave, Balto 21214
Cath	St Andrews, Johns Hopkins Hospital Apostolate, Washington & Monument Sts, Balto 21205 1878-1979 # MSA
Prot Epis	St Andrews Prot Epis Ch, Balto 1837-1859 * MHS Mss Div (previously called Trinity)
R Cath	St Ann, 2201 Greenmount Ave, Balto 21218 (1873) 1873- * ch, 1873-1982 # MSA
R Cath	St Anthony of Padua R Cath Ch, 4420 Frankford Ave, Balto 21206 (1884) 1885-1983 # MSA (congregation composed of immigrants from Bavaria & Hesse Darmstadt, became parent of parishes: St Dominic 1906, St Michael 1914, Shrine of the Little Flower 1926, St Francis of Assisi 1927, and St Ursula 1933)
Cath	St Athanasius, Prudence & Cypress St, Curtis Bay, Balto 21226 (1890) 1890- * ch
Luth	St Augustine Luth Ch, Broadway & Gough Sts, Balto (1967-1977) * LCA
Prot Epis	St Barnabas Chapel 1853-1872 # MSA
Prot Epis	St Barnabas Ch 1883-1911 # MSA. SEE ALSO: Cathedral Ch of the Incarnation, Free Ch of St Barnabas
Cath	St Barnabas Ch, Biddle & Argyle Ave, Balto (1908-1931) * St Pius V, 521 N Schroeder St, Balto 21223
Prot Epis	St Barnabas Ch, Sykesville 1843-1929 * and # MSA
Epis	St Barnabas Memorial Ch, Curtis Bay, Balto 1892-1898 * MDA
Prot Epis	St Bartholomew's Ch (Ten Hills), 4711 Edmondson Ave, Balto 21229. 1872-1972 # MSA (formerly located at North & Madison Aves)
Cath	St Benedict, 2612 Wilkens Ave, Balto 21223 (1893) 1893- * ch
Cath	St Bernadine, Edmondson Ave & Mt Holly St, Balto 21229 (1928) 1928- * ch
R Cath	St Bernard, 928 Gorsuch Ave, Balto 21218 (1891) 1891- * ch, 1891-1979 # MSA
R Cath	St Brigid, 911 S Ellwood Ave (Ellwood Ave & Hudson St) Balto 21224 (1854) 1858- * ch, 1858-1978 # MSA
Cath	St Casimir's Ch, 2736 O'Donnell St, Balto 21224 (1902) 1903- * ch
Cath	St Cecilia, Windsor Ave & Hilton St, Balto 21216 (1902) 1902- * ch

23

Baltimore City and Baltimore County

Cath	St Charles Borromeo, 101 Church Ln, P.O.Box 5783, Pikesville 21208 (1848) 1848- * ch, 1848-1981 # MSA
R Cath	St Charles Villa, 603 Maiden Choice Ln, Balto 21228 (1971) * St Martin's Home, Little Sisters of the Poor, 601 Maiden Choice Ln, Balto 21228 or Provincial House, Soc of St Sulpice, 5408 Roland Ave, Balto 21210 or Sulp Arc at Balto, 711 Maiden Choice Ln, Balto 21228
Cath	St Clement, 2700 Washington Ave, Lansdowne 21227 (1891) 1918- * ch, prior to 1910 * St Jeromes, 775 W Hamburg St, Balto 21230 (baptismal records 1910-1918 were destroyed by fire)
Cath	St Clement Mary Hofbauer Cath Ch, 1220 Chesaco Ave, Rosedale, Balto 21237. 1924-1933 * Sacred Heart of Jesus Ch, 600 S Conkling St, Balto 21224
Prot Epis	St Clement's Chapel, Phila Rd nr Rosedale (1877-1909) * MDA. SEE ALSO: St Andrew's Ch, 6010 Harford Rd, Balto
Epis	St David's Ch, 4700 Roland Ave (Roland Ave & Oakdale Rd) Balto 21210. 1906- * ch, 1904-1967 # MSA
Greek Orth	St Demetrios Greek Orth Ch, 2504 Cub Hill Rd, Balto 21234. 1969- * ch (formerly Suburban Greek Orth Com Ch)
Cath	St Edward, Popular Grove & Prospect Sts, Balto 21216 (1880) 1880- * ch
R Cath	St Elizabeth of Hungary Ch, 2638 E Balto St, Balto 21224 (1895) 1895- * and # Parish Center, 2 N Belnord Ave, Balto 21224
Cath	St Francis Xavier Ch, 1501 E Oliver St, Balto 21213 (1863) 1871-1979 # MSA (the nation's first black Cath parish (1793) known as Chapelle Basse (the parish for coloreds) on Paca St, moved to Calvert St in the 1860's, acquired the former St Paul Cath Ch at Caroline & Oliver Sts in 1968)
Epis	St George's & St Matthews, 2900 Dunleer Rd, Dundalk, Balto 21222. * ch (dates not given)
R Cath	St George's Cath Ch, Valley Lee 20692 (1855) 1952- * ch
Prot Epis	St George's Ch 1887-1918 # MSA (In 1911 Cathedral Ch of the Incarnation was formed from merger of St Barnabas Ch and St George's Ch)
Prot Epis	St George's Parish 1681-1799 # MHS, 1681-1850 # LDS. SEE ALSO: St John's Ch, Kingsville, and St John's Parish, Joppa
R Cath	St Gregory the Great, 1542 N Gilmor St, Balto 21217 (1884) 1883- * ch, 1884-1982 # MSA
R Cath	St Ignatius R Cath Ch, 740 N Calvert St (Calvert & Madison Sts) Balto 21202 (1856) 1853-1978 # MSA
R Cath	St Isaac Jogues, 9215 Old Harford Rd, Balto 21234 (1968) 1968- * ch
Luth	St James. SEE: St Stephen & St James Evan Luth Ch
Cath	St James, Aisquith & Eager Sts, Balto 21202 (1833) 1840-1977 # MSA (a predominantly Ger parish) SEE ALSO: St James & St John Cath Ch, 1225 E Eager St, Balto 21202
Cath	St James & St John Cath Ch, 1225 E Eager St, Balto 21202. 1840- * ch (includes St James 1840-1966, St John 1853-1966, St James & St John 1967-)

24

Epis   St James Ch, 801 N Arlington Ave, Balto 21217. middle 1800's
            * ch (a black congregation)
Epis   St James Ch, 205 S Augusta Ave, Irvington 21229 (1910) 1910-
            * ch, 1908-1955 # MSA
Epis   St James Epis Ch (St James Parish, My Ladys Manor), 3100
            Monkton Rd, Monkton 21111. 1819-1861 * MDA, 1783-1815 * MHS
            Mss Div, 1787-1815 # MSA, 1767-1883 # MHS, 1819-1861 # MGS
            Bull, dates not given # LDS (began as Chapel of Ease 1755
            from St John's Parish, Joppa, erected as parish 1777)
Epis   St James Epis Ch, 1005 Lafayette Ave, Balto 21217. 1841- * ch
            (Baltimore's oldest black Epis ch)
Evan Luth   St James Evan Luth Ch, Hanover & Hamburg Sts, Balto 1894-1962
            # MSA MHS
Evan Luth   St James Evan Luth Ch, Liberty Rd, Randallstown # MHS LDS
            (dates not given)
Prot Epis   St James Parish 1807, 1809, 1812 # MSA. SEE ALSO: St James
            Epis Ch; St John's Ch, Kingsville; St John's Parish, Joppa
Prot Epis   St James Prot Epis Parish 1787-1885 # LDS
Cath   St Jerome, 775 W Hamburg St (Scott & Hamburg St) Balto 21230
            (1887) 1888- * ch, 1882-1983 # MSA
Luth   St John Luth Ch, 224 Washburn Ave, Brooklyn 21225 (1914)
            1929- * ch
Cath   St John the Evangelist, Valley & Eager Sts, Balto (1853-1966)
            1853-1966 * St James & St John Cath Ch, 1225 E Eager St,
            Balto 21202 # MSA (a predominantly Irish parish)
Cath   St John the Evangelist, 13305 Long Green Pike, Hydes 21082
            (1822) 1857- * ch (originally on Carroll Manor Rd)
Prot Epis   St John's & St George's Parishes 1696-1851 # MHS, 1735-1782 #
            LDS
Prot Epis   St John's & St James' Parishes 1819-1821 # MHS
Epis   St John's Chapel, Relay 1928-1968 * MDA
Epis   St John's Ch, 3001 Old York Rd (Greenmount Ave & Old York Rd)
            Balto 21218 (Huntingdon, Waverly) 1844- * ch, 1843-1961 #
            MSA
Epis   St John's Ch, South Rd & Kelly Ave, Balto 21218 (Mt
            Washington) 1869- * ch
Prot Epis   St John's Ch, Kingsville 1696-1960 # MSA, 1792-1899 # MHS
Prot Epis   St John's Ch, Western Run Parish 1893-1898 # MHS 1810-1885 #
            LDS
Prot Epis   St John's Ch-in-the-Valley (Worthington Valley) 1820-1899 *
            MDA, 1782-1899 # MHS
Meth Epis S St John's Emmanuel Meth Epis Ch South 1888-1928 * UMHS
Evan Luth   St John's Evan Luth Ch, 4403 Pimlico Rd, Balto 21215. 1911 *
            ch
Evan & Ref St John's (Fourth Ger) Ch, Balto 1854-1923 * and # E&RA
Cath   St John's Ger Cath Ch (1799) 1840-1845 * St James & St John
            Cath Ch, 1225 E Eager St, Balto 21202, 1845-1917 * St
            Alphonsus Ch, Park Ave & Saratoga St, Balto 21201
Meth Prot   St John's Indep Meth Prot Ch 1802-1945 * MHS Mss Div
Luth   St John's Luth Ch, 3d St & Washburn Ave, Balto 21225 (1927)
            1927- * ch

Luth	St John's Luth Ch of Blenheim, 13300 Manor Rd, Long Green 21092 (1949) 1949- * ch
Luth	St John's Luth Ch of Essex, 518 Franklin Ave, Balto 21221 (1913) 1913- * ch
Meth Epis	St John's Meth Epis Ch, Lutherville (1869) 1880-1933 # MSA (formerly Lutherville Meth Epis Ch)
Meth Prot	St John's Meth Prot Ch. SEE: W Balto Station
Epis	St John's, Mt Washington, 1700 South Rd, Balto 21209 late 1800's * ch
Unit Meth	St John's of Hamilton Unit Meth Ch, 5315 Harford Rd, Balto 21214. 1903- * ch
Prot Epis	St John's Parish 1796-1815 # MSA
Prot Epis	St John's Parish, Joppa 1696-1788 # MHS LDS. SEE ALSO: St John's Ch, Kingsville; St James Ch (St James Parish, My Ladys Manor)
Ch of Eng	St John's Parish, Kingsville 1696-1788 # LDS
Prot Epis	St John's Parish, Reisterstown Parish 1694-1891 # LDS
UCC	St Johns UCC, 1000 S Rolling Rd, Balto 21228. 1867- * ch
Unit Meth	St John's Unit Meth Ch, 214 W Seminary Ave, Lutherville 21093 (1869) 1855- * ch
Cath	St Joseph, 8420 Belair Rd, Balto 21236 (Fullerton) (1850) 1855- * ch, 1842-1981 # MSA
Cath	St Joseph, 101 Church Ln, Balto 21030 (1852) 1905- * ch (many records lost in fire)
Cath	St Joseph Passionate Monastery Ch, 3800 Frederick Ave (Old Frederick Rd & Monastery Ave) Balto 21229 (1867) 1890's- * ch, 1872-1979 # MSA
Cath	St Joseph Soc of the Sacred Heart, 1130 N Calvert St, Balto 21201. 1871- * Soc
Cath	St Joseph's Ch, 199 W Lee St, Balto (1829-1962) * Holy Cross Rectory, 110 E West St, Balto 21230, 1839-1962 # MSA
R Cath	St Katharine of Sienna, 1222 N Luzerne Ave, Balto 21213 (1902) 1903- * St Wenceslaus Ch, 2100 Ashland Ave, Balto 21205 (merged with St Wenceslaus Ch in 1986)
Cath	St Laurence. SEE: Our Lady of Good Counsel
Cath	St Lawrence Ch, 5801 Security Blvd, Balto 21207 (1912) 1912-1962 * St Agnes, 5422 Old Frederick Rd, Balto 21229, 1962- * ch (mission ch on grounds of Kernans Hospital, in a barn, became St Lawrence Ch in 1962)
Cath	St Leo, 227 S Exeter St (Stiles & Exeter Sts) Balto 21202 (1881) 1881- * ch, 1881-1982 # MSA (Formerly called St Leo the Great, carved out of St Vincent de Paul for the Italian & Irish members, by mid 1890's, exclusively Italian)
Evan Luth	St Luke Evan Luth Ch, 7001 Harford Rd, Balto 21234. 1928- * ch
Epis	St Luke's Chapel, Harrisonville 1879-1911 * MDA
Epis	St Luke's Ch, 217 N Carey St, Balto 21223 (1847) * ch
Evan & Ref	St Luke's Ch, Balto 1908-1926 * and # E&RA
Luth	St Luke's Ch, 36th St & Chestnut Ave, Balto 21211 1884- * ch
Evan & Ref	St Luke's Evan & Ref Ch. SEE: St Luke's UCC
Evan	St Luke's Evan Congregation 1923-1953 # MSA
Evan Luth	St Luke's Evan Luth Congregation. SEE: St Luke's UCC

Ref	St Luke's Ref Ch 1908-1926 * E&RA # LDS
R Cath	St Luke's R Cath Ch, 7517 N Point Rd, Balto 21219 (1888) 1888- * ch
UCC	St Luke's UCC, 1301 W Fayette St (Fayette & Carey Sts) Balto 21223 (abt 1864) * ch, 1866-1977 # MSA (formerly St Luke's Evan Luth Congregation, St. Luke's Evan & Ref Ch, originally at Henrietta & Eutaw Sts)
Unit Meth	St Luke's Unit Meth Ch of Woodlawn, 2119 Gwynn Oak Ave, Balto 21207 (1856) * ch (formerly known as Powhatan Meth Epis Ch, Woodlawn Meth Epis Ch; merged with St Luke's)
Luth	St Mark. SEE: St Paul Luth Ch, 141 S Clinton St, Balto 21224
Cath	St Mark's, 30 Melvin Ave, Balto 21228 (Catonsville) (1888) 1889- * ch, 1889-1978 # MSA
Prot Epis	St Mark's Ch, Lombard St bet Fremont Ave & Pendleton St, Balto (1847-1917) 1847-1917 * MDA # MSA
Luth	St Marks Estonian Luth Ch, 1900 St Paul St, Balto 21218 (1951) 1951- * ch
Evan Luth	St Mark's Evan Luth Ch, 1900 St Paul St, Balto 21218 (1860) 1860- * ch (formerly on Eutaw St)
UCC	St Marks UCC, 1805 Wickes Ave, Balto 21230 (1915) 1915- * ch (in 1916 known as Morrell Park Evan Ch, 1926 St Mark's Evan Luth Ch of Morrell Park, 1934 St Mark's Evan & Ref Ch of Morrell Park, 1952 St Mark's Evan & Ref Luth Ch of Morrell Park, 1954 St Mark's Evan & Ref Ch, Morrell Park, 1957 St Mark's UUC of Morrell Park)
Cath	St Martin, 31 N Fulton Ave (Fulton Ave & Fayette St) Balto 21223 (1865) 1876- * ch, 1867-1981 # MSA
R Cath	St Mary of the Assumption, 5502 York Rd, Balto 21212 (Govans) (1850) 1850- * ch, 1850-1981 # MSA
Epis	St Mary's Ch, 3900 Roland Ave, Balto 21211 (Hampden) (1855) 36th St)
Cath	St Mary's Ch. SEE: Sulp Arc
Cath	St Mary's Industrial Sch 1905-1949 # MSA, SEE ALSO: Associated Cath Charities
R Cath	St Mary's Star of the Sea, 1419 Riverside Ave, Balto 21230 (1868) 1896-1919 * MHS Mss Div, 1868-1981 # MSA (served Irish community)
Evan Luth	St Matthew Evan Luth Ch, 3620 Red Rose Farm Rd, Balto 21220 1961- * ch
Epis	St Matthew's Chapel 1875-1922 * MDA
Cath	St Matthews Ch, 5401 Loch Raven Blvd (Loch Raven Blvd & Woodbourne) Balto 21239 (1949) 1951-1982 # MSA
Meth Epis	St Matthew's Meth Epis Ch 1911-1923 * UMHS
UCC	St Matthews UCC, 3400 Norman Ave, (Mayfield, Norman & Lake Aves) Balto 21213 (1852) 1852- * ch (formerly St Matthews Evan Luth Ch, originally at 6 Central Ave below Fayette St, 1873-1930 Fayette St & Central Ave)
Epis	St Matthias Ch, 6400 Belair Rd, (Belair Rd & C donia Ave) Balto 21206 (1906) 1907- * ch, 1907-1945 # MSA (formerly at Belair Rd & Springwood Ave, originally called Raspeburg Mission)

Prot Epis	St Mich el & All Angels Epis Ch, 2013 St Paul St (St Paul & 20th Sts) Balto 21218 (1876) 1877-1966 # MSA
Luth	St Michael Luth Ch, 9534 Belair Rd, Balto 21236. 1862- * ch
Cath	St Michael the Archangel Ch, 2 Willow Ave (Belair Rd & Willow Ave) Balto 21206 (Overlea) (1914) 1913-1979 # MSA
Cath	St Michael's Ch, 7 S Wolfe St (Lombard & Wolfe Sts) Balto 21231 (1852) 1852-1977 # MSA (served Ger community in Fells Point)
Epis	St Michael's Ch, Balto Co. 1909-1972 * MDA
Cath	St Michael's Ukrainian Cath Ch of the Byzantine Rite, 524 S Wolfe St, Balto 21231. 1893- * ch
Orth	St Michael's Ukrainian Orth Ch, 2019 Gough St, Balto 21231. 1950- * ch
Cath	St Mildred Ch (1948-1967) * Our Lady of Hope Rectory, 1727 Lynch Rd, Balto 21222
Cath	St Monica, 421 Henrietta St (Henrietta & Eutaw Sts), Balto (1883--1959) * Cath Cen # MSA
Greek Orth	St Nicholas Greek Orth Ch, 520 S Ponca St, Balto 21224 (1953) 1953- * ch
Luth	St Olaf's. SEE: Augustana Luth Ch
R Cath	St Patrick, 317 S Broadway (Broadway & Bank St) Balto 21231 (1792) 1806-1977 # MSA
Cath	St Paul, Caroline & Oliver Sts, Balto (1888) * St Francis Xavier Ch, 1501 E Oliver St, Balto 21213 (combined with St Francis Xavier; St Pauls first black Cath parish in US)
Evan Luth	St Paul Evan Luth Ch, 2001 Old Frederick Rd, Catonsville 21228. 1868- * ch (formerly at Fremont Ave & Saratoga St)
Luth	St Paul Luth Ch, 141 S Clinton St (Pratt & Clinton Sts), Balto 21224 (1900) 1913- * ch (organized by members of Martin Luther (Orleans St & Patterson Park Ave), St Mark (Broadway & Fairmount Ave), and St Peter (North Ave & Payson St, but since relocated in Northwood) who had moved into the Highlandtown area)
Meth Epis	St Pauls. SEE: Balto Circuit Meth Epis Ch
Luth	St Pauls Ch 1857-1945 # CHI
Evan Luth	St Paul's Evan Luth Ch, Arcadia # LDS (dates not given)
Evan Luth	St Paul's Evan Luth Ch, 2111 Hollins Ferry Rd, Balto 21230 * ch (dates not given)
Evan Luth	St Paul's Evan Luth Ch, 1609 Kurtz Ave, Lutherville 21093 (1853) 1869- * ch
Luth	St Paul's Luth Ch, 12022 Jerusalem Rd, Kingsville 21087 * ch (no dates given)
Meth Epis	St Paul's Meth Epis Ch 1879-1887, 1914-1924 * MHS Mss Div
Meth Epis S	St Paul's Meth Epis Ch South 1891-1923 # MSA (merged into Trinity Meth Epis Ch South)
Prot Epis	St Paul's Parish 1806, 1814 # MSA
Prot Epis	St Paul's Prot Epis Ch, Charles & Saratoga Sts, Balto 21202. 1710-1935 * MHS Mss Div # MSA, 1710-1837 # LDS
Epis	St Paul's Parish (1692) 1774, 1877-1926 * MHS Mss Div
Prot Epis	St Paul's Parish, Patapsco River 1805 * MDA, 1710-1836, 1878-? # MHS (Old St Paul's Ch)
Ref	St Paul's Ref Ch, Balto 1878-1954 * E&RA # LDS

Ukra Cath	St Peter & Paul's Ukrainian Cath Ch, 1506 Church St, Balto 21226. 1940- * ch
Cath	St Peter Claver Ch, 1546 N Fremont Ave, Balto 21217 (1888) 1888- * ch
Luth	St Peter Evan Luth Ch, 7834 Eastern Ave, Balto 21224 (1903) 1911- * ch
R Cath	St Peter the Apostle R Cath Ch, 848 Hollins St (Poppleton & Hollins Sts) Balto 21201 (1838) 1843-1968 # MSA, 1843-1901 # MHS, 1843-1853 # MGS Bull
Luth	St Peters # CHI (dates not given)
R Cath	St Peters. SEE: Bascilica of the Assumption of the Blessed Virgin Mary
Epis	St Peter's Ch, Balto 1850-1853 * MDA, 1817-1885 # LDS. SEE ALSO: Grace & St Peter's Ch
Evan Luth	St Peter's Congregation. SEE: Ger Evan Luth St Peter's Congregation, Randallstown
Evan Luth	St Peter's Evan Luth Ch, North Ave & Payson St, Balto. SEE: St Peter's of Northwood, St Paul Luth Ch, 141 S Clinton St, Balto
Evan Luth	St Peter's Evan Luth Ch. SEE: Bethlehem Luth Ch
Evan Luth	St Peter's Evan Luth Ch, 7910 Belair Rd, Balto 21236 (1865) 1865- * ch
Luth	St Peter's of Northwood, 4215 Loch Raven Blvd, Balto 21218 (1861) 1854- * ch (began in 1856 as St Peter's Evan Luth Ch of the Unaltered Augsburg Confession, congregation worshipped at Newton Univ on Lexington St, in 1865 disbanded, re-estab 1874 at Fayette St & Rogers Ave (now East St), 1906 at North Ave & Aiken St, 1942 in Northwood)
Prot Epis	St Peter's Prot Epis Ch, Sharp & German Sts, Balto 1803-1885 # MHS
Cath	St Pius V Ch, Schroeder St & Edmondson Ave, Balto 21223 (1878) 1878- * ch, 1878-1980 # MSA (congregation of St Barnabas (1907) moved to St Pius V Ch in 1931)
Cath	St Rose of Lima, 4th St & Washburn Ave, Balto 21225 (1915) 1915-* ch
R Cath	St Stanislaus Kostka (Polish) 700 S Ann St, Balto 21231 (1879) 1879-1977 # MSA
Evan Luth	St Stephen & St James Evan Luth Ch, Hanover & Hamburg Sts, Balto 21230. 1851-1975 # MSA (two Luth churches merged in 1962)
Luth	St Stephen Luth Ch, Wilkens Ave & Courtney Rd, Balto 21228 * ch
Epis	St Stephen's Ch, Balto 1900-1962, 1975-1979, 1982 * MDA
Prot Epis	St Stephen's Ch, Hanover St & Welcome Al, Balto 1857-1892 * MDA & MSA
Evan Luth	St Stephens Evan Luth Ch 1851-1962 # MSA (formerly on Light St bet West & Ostend) SEE ALSO: St Stephen & St James Evan Luth Ch
R Cath	St Thomas Aquinas R Cath Ch, 1008 W 37th St, Balto 21211 (1867) 1867-1981 # MSA
Meth Prot	St Thomas Colored Meth Prot Ch 1867-1868 * UMHS
Luth	St Thomas Luth Ch, 339 S Pulaski St, Balto 21223. 1890- * ch

R Cath	St Thomas More, 6806 McClean Blvd, Balto 21234 (1961) 1961- * ch
Prot Epis	St Thomas Parish 1813-1815 # MSA
Prot Epis	St Thomas Parish, Garrison Forest 1726-1824 # MSA, 1728-1891 # MHS LDS. SEE ALSO: St John's Ch, Kingsville
Prot Epis	St Thomas Prot Epis Ch 1729-1800, 1824 # MGS Bull
--	St Thomas's Ch 1763-1771 * MHS Mss Div
Epis	St Timothy's Ch, 200 Ingleside Ave, Catonsville 21228 (1844) 1844- * ch, 1844-1962 # MSA
Luth	St Timothy's Evan Luth Ch, 2120 Dundalk Ave, Balto 21222. 1929- * ch
Cath	St Veronica, 804 Cherry Hill Rd, Balto 21225 (1945) 1945- * ch
R Cath	St Vincent de Paul, 120 N Front St (Front St & the Fallsway), Balto 21202 (1840) 1840- * ch, 1834-1978 # MSA (one of Baltimore's early R Cath churches)
Cath	St Wenceslaus Ch, 2111 Ashland Ave (Collington & Ashland Aves), Balto 21205 (1872) 1872- * ch, 1912 reports, history, Czech Bible published in 1916 * MHS Mss Div, 1868-1979 # MSA (Bohemian, Czechoslovakian) SEE ALSO: St Katharine of Sienna
R Cath	St William of York, Edmondson Ave & Cooks Ln, Balto 21229 (1914) 1914- * ch
R Cath	SS Philip & James R Cath Congregation, 2801 N Charles St, Balto 21218 (1898) 1898- * ch, 1898-1978 # MSA
Meth Epis	Salem. SEE: Great Falls Circuit Meth Epis Ch, Long Green Circuit Meth Epis Ch
Evan	Salem Evan Ch, Catonsville 1852-1904 # MHS (Salems Gemeinde)
Evan Luth	Salem Evan Luth Ch, 905 Frederick Rd, Catonsville 21228 (1849) 1849- * ch, 1848-1969 # MSA, 1849-1901 # MHS
Luth	Salem Luth Ch, 216 E Randall St, Balto 21230. 1885- * ch
Evan	Salems Gemeinde. SEE: Salem Evan Ch, Catonsville
Unit Meth	Scandinavian Meth Epis Ch 1915-1942 # MSA
Bap	Second & Fourth Bap Ch, Luzerne Ave & Orleans St, Balto 21224 * ch (prior to 1972 called E Balto Ch)
Bap	Second Bap Ch (1797) * MBHS, 1797-1822 # LDS (at Fells Point 1795, Aliceanna & Broadway 1795, Bank & Eden 1797, Fleet St nr Ann 1811, 210 S Broadway 1853, and Orleans & Luzerne 1899-1916)
Luth	Second Eng # CHI (dates not given)
Luth	Second Luth Ch, 5010 Briarclift Rd, Balto 21229. 1840- * ch (formerly on Lombard St w of Greene)
Presb	Second Presb Ch, 2 Stratford Rd (St Paul St & Stratford Rd), Balto 21218 (1803) 1803-1964 # MSA, 1803-1939 # MHS
Bap	Sharon Bap Ch, 1373 Stricker St, Balto 21217. 1882- * ch (a black church)
Unit Meth	Sharp Street Memorial Unit Meth Ch, Dolphin & Etting Sts, Balto 21217. 1787- * ch, 1872-1927 # MSA (one of Baltimore's oldest black congregations)
Bap	Shelbourne Ch, Shelbourne & Courtney Rd, Balto 21227 (1916) 1904- * ch (started as a mission in 1904, disbanded & resurrected as a church in 1916)

Baltimore City and Baltimore County

Prot Epis	Sherwood Ch, Cockeysville (1835) 1876-1966 # MSA
Bap	Shiloh Bap Ch. SEE: New Shiloh Bap Ch
Cath	Shrine of the Little Flower, 2854 Brendan Ave, Balto 21213 (1926) 1927- * ch
R Cath	Shrine of the Sacred Heart, 1701 Regent Rd, Balto 21209 (1855) 1869- * ch, 1869-1981 # MSA (in Mt Washington, formerly known as Sacred Heart of Jesus)
Meth Prot	South Balto Meth Prot Ch 1865-1871 * LL
Meth Epis	South Balto Station Meth Epis Ch 1850-1918 * UMHS. SEE ALSO: Good Shepherd Unit Meth Ch
Meth Prot	Starr Meth Prot Ch 1865-1966 * UMHS
Meth	Stone Chapel, 9 Walker Ave, Pikesville 21208. 1862-1908 # MSA (includes Ames Chapel, Granite, Mt Olive, Pleasant Hill, Stone Chapel, Wards) SEE ALSO: Balto Circuit Meth Epis Ch
Friends	Stony Run Friends Meet, 5116 N Charles St, Balto 21210. 1677- * FHL
Meth Epis	Strawbridge Meth Epis Ch 1843-1954 # MHS Mss Div
Greek Orth	Suburban Greek Orth Com Ch. SEE: St Demetrios Greek Orth Ch
Unit Meth	Sudbrook Unit Meth Ch, 503 Reisterstown Rd, Pikesville 21208 (1894) 1894- * ch
Sulp Arc	Sulpician Archives, 711 Maiden Choice Ln, Balto Md 21228. 1783- * arc
Meth Epis S	Summerfield Ch, Wildwood Pkwy & Gelston Dr, Balto. SEE: Central Meth Epis Ch South
Meth Epis	Summerfield Circuit Meth Epis Ch 1849-1922 # MSA
Meth Epis	Sunny Hill. SEE: Balto Circuit Meth Epis Ch
Jud	Szold, Rabbi Benjamin of Oheb Shalom Congregation 1853-1893 papers * MHS Mss Div. SEE ALSO: Temple Oheb Shalom
Meth Epis	Tabernacle. SEE: Balto Circuit Meth Epis Ch
Meth	Taylor Mission Bible & Sun Sch Soc. SEE: Monument Street Meth Ch
Meth	Taylor's Chapel, 6001 Hillen Rd, Balto 21239 (1853) 1853- * St John's of Hamilton Unit Meth Ch, # MGS Bull (began in 1770 as a Quaker Meet House, became Meth in 1853)
Bap	Temple Bap, 6916 Dogwood Rd, Balto 21207 (1899) 1899- * ch
Jud	Temple Oheb Shalom, 7310 Park Heights Ave, Balto 21208. 1853- * syn. SEE ALSO: Szold, Rabbi Benjamin
Evan & Ref	Third Ch 1853-1937 * E&RA
Evan Luth	Third Evan Luth Ch, 3000 Hillen Rd, Balto 21218. 1880- * ch (formerly known as Evan Luth Ch of the Ascension)
Evan Unit Breth	Third Evan Unit Breth Ch, Fulton Ave & Lombard St, Balto (1867) 1867-1960 # MSA (a Ger ch)
Prot Epis	Thomas, Rev George W 1890-1911 * MHS Mss Div
Unit Meth	Timonium Unit Meth Ch, Pot Spring & Chantry Rds, Timonium 21093 (1902) 1913- * ch
Unitar Univ	Towson Unitar Univ Ch, 1710 Dulaney Valley Rd, Lutherville 21093. 1960- * ch
Prot Epis	Trinity. SEE: St Andrews Prot Epis Ch
Bap	Trinity Bap Ch, 1601 Druid Hill Ave, Balto 21217 (1887) 1897- * ch (a black ch)
Prot Epis	Trinity Chapel (1924) * St Bartholomew's Ch, 1924-1960 # MSA (merged with St Bartholomew's (Ten Hills) in 1953)

Prot Epis	Trinity Ch, Broadway & Pratt Sts, Balto 1802-1904 * MDA, 1845-1904 # MSA
Prot Epis	Trinity Ch, Polly, now Trinity St w of Exeter OT, Balto 1802-1818 # MHS, 1796-1819 # LDS
Prot Epis	Trinity Ch, Towson 1859-1951 # MSA
Epis	Trinity Epis Ch, 12400 Manor Rd, Long Green 21092 (1820) 1878- * ch
Evan Luth	Trinity Evan Ger Luth Ch, McElderry St, Balto 1853-1878 # MSA MHS (formerly on Trinity St nr High St)
Evan Luth	Trinity Evan Luth Ch, 109 Main St, Reisterstown 21136 (1855) 1855- * ch
Luth	Trinity Luth Ch, Balto & Pulaski Sts, Balto (1893) 1893-1919 * St Stephen Luth Ch, Wilkens Ave & Courtney Rd, Balto 21228
Meth Epis S	Trinity Meth Epis Ch South, Madison & Preston Sts, Balto (1865) 1862-1963 * UMHS, 1862-1956 # MSA (relocated in 1927 to Liberty Heights Ave & Wabash, formerly known as St John Emmanuel, merged with Calvary in 1906, called Trinity-Calvary, St Pauls merged in 1927)
Presb	Trinity Presb Ch, 3200 Walbrook Ave, Balto 21216 (1959) 1959- * ch (original name: Walbrook Unit Presb Ch, changed to Walbrook-Trinity Unit Presb Ch in 1959, later name was shortened to Trinity Presb Ch (USA)
Prot Epis	Trinity Prot Epis Ch 1815-1836, 1860-1873 * MHS Mss Div
UCC	Trinity UCC. SEE: Ref & Luth Congregations, Manchester, Balto Co, now Carroll Co
Meth Epis	Twenty Fourth Street Meth Epis Ch, Royer's Hill, Balto 1880-1936 * LL (merged with Huntington Avenue Meth Epis Ch)
Meth Epis	Union. SEE: Long Green Circuit Meth Epis Ch
Bap	Union Bap Ch, 1219 Druid Hill Ave, Balto 21217 (1852) 1930- * ch (serving the black community)
Bap	Unit Bap Ch, 932 N Broadway, Balto 21205. 1922- * ch
UCC	Unit Evan Ch of UCC, 3200 Dillon St (East Ave & Dillon St), Balto 21224 (1873) 1873- * ch (formerly known as Zion Evan Ch and Ger Unit Evan Ch)
Unit Meth	Unit Meth His Soc, City Station 1816-1901 # MSA
Evan & Ref	Unit (St Luke & St John) Ch 1927-1967 * E&RA
--	Unity Center of Christianity, 2901 N Charles St, Balto 21218. 1962- * Center
Bap	University Bap Ch, 3501 N Charles St, Balto 21237. 1916- * ch
Ref	Vierten Deutsch Ref St Johannis Gemeinde, Balto 1906-1925 # LDS
Unit Meth	Violetville Unit Meth Ch, 3646 Coolidge Ave, Balto 21229 (1896) 1896- * ch
Presb	Walbrook-Trinity Unit Presb Ch. SEE: Trinity Presb Ch
Presb	Walbrook Unit Presb Ch. SEE: Trinity Presb Ch
Meth	Wards. SEE: Stone Chapel
Meth Epis	Wards Chapel. SEE: Balto Circuit Meth Epis Ch
Meth Epis	Waugh. SEE: Great Falls Circuit Meth Epis Ch, Long Green Circuit Meth Epis Ch
Meth Epis	Waverly Meth Epis Ch. SEE: Waverly Unit Meth Ch
Presb	Waverly Presb Ch. SEE: Hampden Unit Presb Ch, Waverly Unit Presb Ch

Unit Meth	Waverly Unit Meth Ch, 33rd & Frisby Sts, Balto 21218 (1873) 1873- * ch (formerly Waverly Meth Epis Ch)
Presb	Waverly Unit Presb ch, Old York Rd & 34th St, Balto 21218 (1888) 1888- * ch (formerly Waverly Presb Ch)
Unitar	Weld, Rev Charles R 1891-1895 clippings & sermons * MHS Mss Div (of First Indep Christ Ch (Unitarian), Balto)
Meth Epis	Wesley Chapel Meth Epis Ch 1859-1906 # MSA
Meth Prot	West Balto Station (1843) 1872-1937 # MSA (estab by male members of St John's Meth Prot Ch). SEE ALSO: Lafayette House Meth Prot Ch
Meth Epis	West Balto Station Meth Epis Ch 1920-1943 * Arlington Unit Meth Ch, 5268 Reisterstown Rd, Balto 21215 (on outside of register is written name "Whatcoat Church")
Unit Meth	West Balto Unit Meth Ch, Charing Cross & Greenwich Ave, Balto 21229 1843- * ch (formerly at Lafayette Ave & Gilmor St)
Meth	West Liberty Meth Ch, 20400 West Liberty Rd, White Hall 21161 (early 1700's) 1871 Sun Sch children * ch, * LL (originally called Meredith Meet House)
Meth Epis S	West Point. SEE: Freedom Circuit
Friends	West River & Clifts Monthly Meet 1662-1814? # MHS
Epis	Western Run Parish 1820-1899 * MDA. SEE ALSO: Thomas, Rev George W
Meth	Whatcoat Ch. SEE: West Balto Station Meth Epis Ch
Unit Meth	Wildwood Pkwy Unit Meth Ch. SEE: Central Meth Epis Ch South
Chris	Wilhelm Park Chris Ch, Wilmington & Cowan Aves, Balto 21223 (1908) 1923- * ch
Meth Epis	Wilson. SEE: Great Falls Circuit Meth Epis Ch, Long Green Circuit Meth Epis Ch
Meth Prot	Wilton Heights Meth Prot Ch 1923-1924 * UMHS
Bap	Women's Missionary Union of Md 1872- * MBHS
Meth Epis	Woodberry Avenue Meth Epis Ch (1844) 1862-1955 (also known as Woodberry Meth Epis Ch, Woodberry First Meth Epis Ch, Woodberry Station Meth Epis Ch, Woodberry Unit Meth Ch)
Breth	Woodberry Ch of the Breth, 36th & Poole sts, Balto 21211. 1907- * ch (formerly Fulton Avenue Ch of the Breth, Hill Street Ch of the Breth)
Unit Meth	Woodberry Unit Meth Ch, 2054 Druid Park Dr, Balto 21211. SEE: Woodberry Avenue Meth Epis Ch
Bap	Woodbrook Bap Ch, 25 Stevenson Ln, Balto 21212 (1871) 1871- * ch (formerly Eutaw Place Bap Ch 1871-1969)
Meth Epis	Woodlawn Meth Epis Ch. SEE: St Luke's Unit Meth Ch of Woodlawn
Luth	Zion 1840 * CHI
Ref & Luth	Zion Ch, Manchester, Balto Co 1760-1836 # LDS
Evan & Ref	Zion Evan & Ref Ch. SEE: Zion UCC, Harford Rd & Iona Ter, Balto 21214
Evan	Zion Evan Ch. SEE: Unit Evan Ch of UCC
Luth	Zion Evan Luth Ch, Grindon & Mainfield Aves, Balto 21214. 1913- * ch
Evan Luth	Zion Evan Luth Ch, Stemmers Run Rd, Balto Co. SEE: Evan Luth Ch of the Prince of Peace, 8218 Phila Rd, Balto 21237
Evan Ref &	Zion Ger Ch, Manchester 1760-1836 * and # MSA

Luth	
Luth	Zion Ger Luth Ch, Gay St, Balto 1784-1849 # MHS, 1784-1855 # LDS
Luth	Zion Luth Ch, Holliday & Lexington Sts (City Hall Plaza) Balto 21202 1785- * ch, 1785-1977 # MSA (Baltimore's oldest Ger Luth ch)
Ref	Zion Ref Ch. SEE: Zion UCC, Harford Rd & Iona Ter, Balto 21214
UCC	Zion UCC, P.O.Box 3615, Balto 21214. 1886- * ch
UCC	Zion UCC, Harford Rd & Iona Ter, Balto 21214 (1874) 1874- * ch (formerly Zion Ref Ch, later Zion Evan & Ref Ch)

Calvert County

Epis	All Saints, Sunderland 20689. 1840- * ch, 1703-1717, 1720-1753 * and # MSA, 1859-1958 # MSA, 1702-1753 # MHS LDS
Bap	Asbury Com Ch, 219 Barstow Rd, Prince Frederick 20678 (no records)
Meth	Asbury Meth Ch. SEE: Trinity Unit Meth Ch
Unit Meth	Brooks Unit Meth Ch, Rt 264, Box 22, Port Republic 20676 (1846) 1891- * ch
Bible	Calvary Bible Ch, Box 307, Lusby 20678 (abt 1955) * ch
Meth Epis S	Calvert Circuit Meth Epis Ch, South 1923-1955 # MSA
Meth	Central Meth Ch. SEE: Trinity Unit Meth Ch
Epis	Christ Ch, Rt 264 Box 3, Port Republic 20676 (1672) 1902 * ch, 1685-1902 * and # MSA, 1688-1847 # LDS
Prot Epis	Christ Ch Parish 1896-1899 * MDA, 1688-1847 # MHS
Friends	Clifts Meet 1677-1780 # MGS Bull
Luth	First Luth Ch, P.O.Box 129, Sunderland 20689 (1974) 1974- * ch
Assem of God	Full Gospel Assem of God, Rt 4 South, P.O.Box 850, Prince Frederick 20678 (1935) 1935- * ch (formerly Full Gospel Tabernacle)
Pent	Greater Bibleway Ch, P.O.Box 806, Prince Frederick 20678 (1952) 1952- * ch (some records damaged by water)
Unit Meth	Huntingtown-Emmanuel Unit Meth Charge, P.O.Box 115, Huntingtown 20639 (1870) 1870- * ch
Unit Meth	Huntingtown Unit Meth Ch, P.O.Box 216, Huntingtown 20639 (1840) 1868-1894, 1923- * ch
Jeh Wit	Jehovah's Wit, Prince Frederick Congregation, P.O.Box 471, Prince Frederick 20678 (no records)
Epis	Middleham Chapel, Box 188, Solomons 20688 (1684) 1849-1946, 1958-1968 * Middleham-St Peter's Parish House, Lusby (St Peter's & Middleham Chapel joined into a single congregation)
Prot Epis	Middleham Chapel, Lusby 1900-1957 # MSA (originally a chapel in Christ Ch Parish)
Friends	Monthly Meet at the Clifts 1649-1945 # MSA

34

Bap	Mt Gethsemane Bap Ch, Rt 1 Box 391, Pond Woods Rd, Huntingtown 20639 (1964) 1965- * ch
Unit Meth	Mt Harmony Unit Meth Ch. SEE: Smithville Unit Meth Ch
Meth	Olivet Ch 1893-1924 # MSA
R Cath	Our Lady Star of the Sea, Box 560, Solomons 20688 (1888) 1901- * ch (prior records at St Francis deSales, Benedict 20612)
Friends	Quarterly Meet for the Western Shore 1680-1951 # MSA
Cath	St John Mary Bap Vianney, SR 1, Box 264, Prince Frederick 20678 (1965) 1965- * ch (prior records at Our Lady Star of the Sea, P.O.Box 560, Solomons 20688; began as a mission 1939)
R Cath	St John Vianney Ch, Prince Frederick 20678 (1939) 1965- * ch
Meth	St John's Ch 1882-1892 # MSA
Epis	St Paul, Prince Frederick (1841) 1841-1900 # Peabody
Unit Meth	St Paul Unit Meth Ch, P.O.Box 203, Lusby 20657 (1866) 1945- * ch (prior records at Solomons Charge which originally included Olivet, Solomons & St Paul churches)
Epis	St Paul's, P.O.Box 99, Prince Frederick 20678 (1841) 1841- * ch, 1841-1950 * and # MSA
Meth	St Paul's Ch 1923-1955 # MSA
Prot Epis	St Peter's Chapel, Solomons 1900-1957 # MSA (estab as chapel of Christ Ch Parish) SEE ALSO: Middleham Chapel, Lusby
Unit Meth	Smithville Unit Meth Ch, P.O.Box 175, Dunkirk 20754 (1838) mid 1800's * ch (Mt Harmony Unit Meth Ch & Smithville Unit Meth Ch formerly Smithville Unit Meth charge)
Meth Epis	Solomon's Isl Charge Meth Epis Ch 1882-1943 # MSA
Unit Meth	Trinity Unit Meth Ch, P.O.Box 171, (corner Md 231 & 765), Prince Frederick 20678 (1955) 1882- * ch (merger of Asbury, Central & Wesley Meth churches)
Meth	Wesley Meth Ch. SEE: Trinity Unit Meth Ch
Meth	Wesleyan Ch, Box 95, Broomes Isl 20615 (1904) 1904- * ch
Friends	West River & Clifts Monthly Meet 1662-1814? # MHS

Caroline County

Meth	American Corner. SEE: Grove Circuit Meth Prot Ch
Meth Epis S	Antioch Meth Ch, Templeville 1953-1963 # MSA
Unit Meth	Bloomery Unit Meth Ch, 109 Park Lane, Federalsburg 21632. 1953- * Christ Unit Meth Ch, Federalsburg. SEE ALSO: Denton Circuit Meth Epis Ch, Concord Meth Epis Circuit
Meth	Burrsville Meth Ch 1932-1959 # MSA (Union, Wesley, Thawley & White churhes)
Meth	Calvary Meth Ch in Marydel 1952-1967 # MSA
Meth Prot	Caroline Charge Meth Prot Ch. SEE: St Luke's Meth Ch
Meth	Caroline Circuit 1836-1866 # MSA (1850 renamed Greensboro Circuit)
Meth Prot	Caroline Circuit Meth Prot Ch 1865-1905 # MSA

Meth	Central Ch 1915-1925 # MSA. SEE ALSO: Denton Circuit Meth Epis Ch
Meth	Chestnut Grove. SEE: Concord Meth Epis Circuit
Meth	Chestnut Grove Unit Meth Ch, Chipman's Ln, Federalsburg 21632. 1953- * Christ Unit Meth Ch, Federalsburg
Prot Epis	Christ Ch, Denton 1871-1951 * MSA, 1871-1956 # MSA
Meth Prot	Christ Meth Prot Ch, Federalsburg 1902-1967 # MSA
Meth	Christ Unit Meth Ch, Main St & Maple Ave, Federalsburg 21632. 1902- * ch
Prot Epis	Ch of the Holy Trinity, Greensboro 1888-1950 * and # MSA
Meth	Concord Circuit. SEE: Grove Circuit Meth Prot Ch
Meth Epis	Concord Meth Epis Circuit 1909-1915 # MSA (in 1945 this Circuit with churches at Concord, Bloomery, Chestnut Grove & Harmony united with Grove Circuit, now part of Harmony Charge Meth Ch)
Meth	Concord Unit Meth Ch, Rt 313 & Dion Rd, Federalsburg 21632. 1886- * Union Unit Meth, N Main St & Greenridge Rd, Federalsburg 21632
Evan & Ref	Cort, Rev Cyrus 1881-1914 # LDS
Meth Epis	Deal's Isl Charge Meth Epis Ch 1917-1921 # MSA
Meth Epis	Denton Circuit Meth Epis Ch 1857-1924 (includes Potter's Landing, Harris' Landing, Sheppard, Bloomery, Central & Denton congregations)
Meth Prot	Denton Meth Prot Charge. SEE: St Luke's Meth Ch
Meth Epis	Farmington Circuit Meth Epis Ch 1916-1948 # MSA (Prospect Ch)
Presb	Federalsburg Presb Ch, 109 Park Ln, Federalsburg 21632. 1872-1896 * Christ Unit Meth Ch, Federalsburg
Meth	First & Grace. SEE: St Luke's Meth Prot Ch
Bap	First B p Ch, P.O.Box 66, 401 Sunset Ave, Greensboro 21369 (1920) 1920- * ch
Ch of God	First Ch of God, N Main St & Bloomingdale Ave, Federalsburg 21632. 1970's- * ch
Unit Meth	Goldsboro Charge 1885-1914 # MSA (includes Hartley, Marydel, Templeville, Thomas Chapel)
Meth Epis	Goldsboro Charge Meth Epis Ch, South 1903-1916 # MSA (includes Goldsboro, Irving's, Moore's, Trinity)
Meth	Grace Meth Ch. SEE: St Luke's Meth Ch
Meth Epis	Greensboro Charge Meth Epis Ch 1861-1892, 1921-1925 # MSA (prior to 1904 Greensboro Meth Epis Ch)
Meth	Greensboro Circuit. SEE: Caroline Circuit
Meth Epis	Greensboro Meth Epis Ch. SEE: Greensboro Charge Meth Epis Ch
Meth	Grove Circuit. SEE: Concord Meth Epis Circuit
Meth Prot	Grove Circuit Meth Prot Ch 1920-1956 # MSA (includes American Corner, Grove & Harmony congregations; after 1945 united with Concord Circuit, now part of Harmony Charge Meth Ch)
Meth	Grove Meth Ch 1947-1963 # MSA
Meth	Harmony Charge Meth Ch. SEE: Concord Meth Epis Circuit, Grove Circuit Meth Prot Ch
Meth	Harmony Meth Ch 1951-1965 # MSA
Meth Epis	Harris' Landing. SEE: Denton Circuit Meth Epis Ch

Meth	Hartley. SEE: Goldsboro Charge, Marydel Charge Meth Epis Ch, Marydel Circuit Meth Epis Ch
Meth	Hawkins. SEE: Marydel Circuit Meth Epis Ch
Meth	Henderson Meth Charge 1895-1965 # MSA
Meth Epis	Hickman Meth Epis Ch 1913-1928 # MSA
Meth Epis	Hillsboro Circuit Meth Epis Ch, South 1866-1909 # MSA
Cath	Immaculate Conception Cath Ch, Marydel 21649 (1914) 1914- * ch
Meth	Irving's. SEE: Goldsboro Charge Meth Epis Ch, South
Meth Epis	Johns Meth Epis Ch, Ellwood (1895) 1895-1912 # MHS Mss Div (merged with Mt Pleasant Ch & Zoar Ch to form Mt Calvary Ch, Preston, in 1968)
Meth	Marydel. SEE: Goldsboro Charge, Marydel Circuit Meth Epis Ch
Meth Epis	Marydel Charge Meth Epis Ch 1914-1952 # MSA (includes Hartley, Marydel, Templeville, Thomas Chapel)
Meth Epis	Marydel Circuit Meth Epis Ch 1869-1909 # MSA (includes Hartley Chapel, Hawkins, Marydel, Thomas Chapel)
Meth	Moore's. SEE: Goldsboro Charge Meth Epis Ch, South
Meth Epis	Mt Calvary Ch, Preston. SEE: Johns Meth Epis Ch
Meth Epis	Mt Pleasant Ch. SEE: Johns Meth Epis Ch
Ch of God	Park Lane Ch of God, 209 Park Ln, Federalsburg 21632. 1955- * ch
Meth Epis	Potter's Landing. SEE: Denton Circuit Meth Epis Ch
Meth	Prospect Ch. SEE: Farmington Circuit Meth Epis Ch
Meth Epis	Queen Anne Charge Meth Epis Ch, South 1913-1940 # MSA
Meth Epis	Ridgely Circuit Meth Epis Ch 1901-1932 # MSA
Prot Epis	St John's Parish 1747-1853 # MHS, 1749-1858 # LDS
Meth	St Luke's Meth Ch, Denton 1869-1962 # MSA (Caroline Charge Meth Prot Ch, after 1940 Grace Meth Ch, formerly Denton Meth Prot Charge)
Meth Prot	St Luke's Meth Prot Ch, Denton 1931-1965 # MSA (First & Grace merged to form St Luke's)
Prot Epis	St Paul's Ch, Hillsboro (prior to 1717) 1752-1782, 1858-1952 * and # MSA (now under Christ Ch, Denton, St Mary's Whitechapel Parish)
Meth	St Paul's Meth Ch, Greensboro 1917-1964 # MSA
Meth Epis	St Paul's Meth Epis Ch, Greensboro 1896-1964 # MSA
Meth Epis	Sheppard. SEE: Denton Circuit Meth Epis Ch
Friends	Southern QuarterlyMeet 1755-1893 # MSA
Meth	Templeville. SEE: Goldsboro Charge, Marydel Charge Meth Epis Ch
Meth	Thawley Ch. SEE: Burrsville Meth Ch
Meth	Thomas Chapel. SEE: Goldsboro Charge, Marydel Charge Meth Epis Ch, Marydel Circuit Meth Epis Ch
Meth	Trinity. SEE: Goldsboro Charge Meth Epis Ch, South
Meth Epis S	Trinity Meth Epis Ch, South, Goldsboro 1917-1967 # MSA
Meth	Union Ch. SEE: Burrsville Meth Ch
Meth Epis	Union Meth Epis Ch, Federalsburg 1859-1956 * MSA, 1859-1961 # MSA
Unit Meth	Union Unit Meth Ch, N Main St & Greenridge Rd, Federalsburg 21632 (1785) 1961- * ch, 1859-1961 # ch
Meth	Wesley Ch 1886-1932 # MSA. SEE ALSO: Burrsville Meth Ch

Caroline County

Meth	Westville Lodge 1868-1875 # MSA
Meth	White Ch. SEE: Burrsville Meth Ch
Ref	Wilhemena Ref Ch, Preston 1896-1908 # LDS
Unit Meth	Wye Mills 1885-1962 # MSA
Unit Meth	Zion Unit Meth Ch, Old Denton Rd, Federalsburg 21632. 1905- * ch (some records lost in floods)
Meth Epis	Zoar Ch. SEE: Johns Meth Epis Ch

Carroll County

Free Meth	Alesia Free Meth Ch, 4250 Alesia-Lineboro Rd, Millers 21107 (abt 1935) 1935- * ch
Epis	Ascension Epis Ch, 23 N Court St, Westminster 21157 (1847) 1846 * ch (first mission of Holy Trinity, Eldersburg)
Ref	Bachman's Ch. SEE: Jerusalem Luth Ch, 1372 Bachman's Valley Rd, Westminster 21157
Bap	Bap Ch of Taneytown, Baptist & Emmitsburg Rds, Taneytown 21787 (1791) no records located (building completely gone, cemetery remains)
Bible	Barkhill Bible Ch, Glenn Hill Ct & Barkhill Rd, Union Bridge 21791 (1887) 1984- * ch, 1866-1901 * CCHS (founded as Barkhill Ch of God, became Bible Ch in 1981)
Ch of God	Barkhill Ch of God. SEE: Barkhill Bible Ch
Meth	Barnes Chapel, Linganore. SEE: Linganore Circuit
UCC	Baust Emmanuel UCC, 2940 Old Taneytown Rd, Westminster 21157 (1784) 1851- * ch, 1792-1872 # MHS LDS, # SL LTS DAR CCHS CCPL
Jud	Beth Shalom Congregation, 437 W Old Liberty Rd (197-) * syn (moving to 2020 Liberty Rd, 8 mi w of Eldersburg)
Meth	Bethany Ch, Franklinville. SEE: Linganore Circuit
Meth Epis	Bethany Meth Epis Ch, Hooper Rd & Rt 26, Franklinville 1872-1889 # MSA
Meth	Bethel. SEE: New Windsor Circuit Meth Epis Ch, Westminster Circuit Meth Epis Ch
Bible	Bethel Bible Ch, High St, Manchester (1962) (no longer exists)
Unit Breth	Bethel Unit (also Manchester Ch of Breth), Maiden Ln & High St, Manchester 21102 (1845 or 1839, closed abt 1898) 1870-1898 # CCHS
Unit Meth	Bethel Unit Meth Ch, Buffalo & Sam's Creek Rd, New Windsor 21776 (1801) 1856- * ch, 1874-1947 # MSA, # CCHS
Meth	Bethesda. SEE: New Windsor Circuit Meth Epis Ch, West Falls Circuit Meth Epis Ch, Westminster Circuit Meth Epis Ch
Unit Meth	Bethesda Unit Meth Ch, 328 Klees Mill Rd, Sykesville 21784 (1810) * ch, 1843-1872 # MSA (in present building since 1880)
Unit Breth	Biggs Chapel, Manchester Circuit 1875-1890 # CCHS

Carroll County

Unit Meth	Bixler Unit Meth Ch, Bixler Church & Back Woods Rds, Manchester 21102. 1870- * ch # CCHS (formerly Breth, became Meth 1968)
--	Bowen's Chapel, Back Hill Rd & Raywell Ave, Union Bridge (1892) (no information)
Ref	Bowers Ch. SEE: Jerusalem Luth Ch, 1372 Bachman's Valley Rd, Westminster 21157
Unit Meth	Brandenburg Unit Meth Ch, Streaker Rd & Rt 97, Mt Airy 21771 (1883) * Taylorsville Unit Meth Ch, 4360 Ridge Rd, Mt Airy 21771
Meth	Brick Ch. SEE: Pipe Creek Unit Meth Ch, 3403 Uniontown Rd, Westminster 21157
Breth	Browns, Manchester Circuit # CCHS
Meth Epis	Brown's Meet House, nr Houcksville (1800-1879) (changed name to Wesley Chapel 1879, to Wesley Meth 1922) SEE: Wesley Unit Meth Ch, 3239 Carrollton Rd, Hampstead 21074
Bap	Calvary. SEE: Liberty Bap Ch, 2127 Old Liberty Rd, New Windsor 21776
Bap	Calvary Bap Ch, 2000 Liberty Rd, Westminster 21157 (1980) 1980- * ch
Bible	Calvary Bible Ch, 2447 Mexico Rd, Westminster 21157 (1957) 1957- * ch
Luth	Calvary Luth Ch, Rt 94 just n of RR, Woodbine 21797 (1889) 1891- * ch, # MHS (early records fragmentary, Messiah Luth Ch in Berrett could have some; moving to Howard Co, Old Frederick & Woodbine Rds)
Unit Meth	Calvary Unit Meth Ch, 3939 Gamber Rd, Finksburg 21048 (1943) 1943- * ch, early records at LL (founded as Providence Meth 1807, merged with Mt Pleasant 1943 and took name Calvary)
Unit Meth	Calvary Unit Meth Ch, 403 S Main St, Mt Airy 21771 (1890) 1890- * ch, 1872-1920 # MSA
Prim Bap	Carroll Prim Bap Ch, North Watersville Rd, Sykesville 21784 (1857) (no records found)
Ch of God	Carrollton Ch of God, Carrollton Rd, Finksburg 21048 (1850) 1982- * ch (early records destroyed by fire)
Meth Epis	Carrollton Circuit Meth Epis Ch 1870-1949 # MSA (after 1939 Carrollton Circuit Meth Ch) (includes Carrollton, Finksburg, Patapsco, Pleasant Grove, Tannery, Thomas Chapel) SEE ALSO: Westminster Circuit Meth Epis Ch
Breth	Cedar Grove (1871) # CCHS (merged with Pine Grove, Balto Co 1873)
Meth Epis	Centenary Meth Epis Ch. SEE: Westminster Unit Meth Ch, 165 E Main St, Westminster 21157
LDS	Ch of Jesus Christ Latter Day Saints, 4117 Lower Beckleysville Rd, Hampstead 21074. 1971- * ch # LDS
Prot Epis	Ch of the Ascension, Westminster 1842-1956 # MSA
Indep	Ch of the Open Door, 550 Balto Blvd, Westminster 21157 (1967) 1967- * ch
Bible	Clearfield Bible Ch, 1303 Old Westminster Pike, Westminster 21157 (1967) 1967- * ch
Meth	Cooks Sch House. SEE: Westminster Circuit Meth Epis Ch

Bible	Deer Park Bible Ch, 1950 Deer Park Rd, Finksburg 21048. 1965?- * ch
Cath	Deer Park Chapel, Deer Park Rd, S of Gamber (1866) (no records)
Unit Meth	Deer Park Unit Meth Ch, 2200 Sykesville Rd, Westminster 21157 (1853) recent records * ch (early records lost)
Breth	DeHoffs Meet House, Inter Rt 30 & Greenmount Church Rd e/s Hanover Pike. SEE: Greenmount Unit, Hampstead 21074
Luth	Derr, Rev S J, Hampstead 1887-1919 # MGS Bull (a Luth minister at St Paul's Luth Ch, Arcadia, Upperco, Balto Co, and St Mark's Luth Ch, Hampstead)
Meth	Ebenezer. SEE: New Windsor Circuit Meth Epis Ch, West Falls Circuit Meth Epis Ch, Westminster Circuit Meth Epis Ch, Winfield Circuit Meth Epis Ch
Unit Meth	Ebenezer Unit Meth Ch, 4901 Woodbine Rd, Sykesville 21784 (1858) 1927- * ch, 1874-1947 # MSA
Breth	Edgewood Ch of Breth, Rt 2, New Windsor 21776 (1941) 1941- * ch
Bap	Elders Bap Ch, 1216 Liberty Rd, Sykesville 21784 (1965) 1965- * ch
Meth	Emanuel. SEE: Westminster Unit Meth Ch, 165 E Main St, Westminster 21157
Luth & Ref	Emanuel Ch. SEE: Baust Emmanuel UCC
Bap	Emmanuel Bap Ch, 4150 Sykesville Rd, Finksbug 21048 (1961) 1956- * ch (formerly Mt Pleasant Meth Ch; has merged with Calvary Meth Ch)
Meth	Emory Meth Ch, 1600 Emory Rd, Upperco 21155 (1841) 1980- * ch, prior to 1980 * Pleasant Grove Unit Meth Ch or Wesley Unit Meth Ch, 3239 Carrollton Rd, Hampstead 21074
Meth	Fair View Meth Ch, Old Rt 26, Buffalo Rd, Mt Airy 21771 (1851) (no records located, first organized black congregation in Carroll Co)
Bible	Faith Com Bible Ch, 3819 Old Hanover Rd, Westminster 21157 (1981) 1981- * ch
Luth	Faith Luth Ch, Johnsville Sr Center Eldersburg, Sykesville 21784 (1977) 1977- * ch
Meth	Finksburg. SEE: Carrollton Circuit Meth Epis Ch
Meth	Finksburg Charge Patapsco Meth Ch 1948-1968 # MSA
Bible	Finn Foundation Bible Fellowship, meets in Westminster High, Westminster 21157 (1984) 1984- * home of pastor, Tom DiMaggio
Assem of God	First Assem of God, Cranberry Rd & Rt 140, Westminster 21157 (1959) 1959- * ch
Chris Sci	First Ch of Chris Sci, 346 Old New Windsor Rd, Westminster 21157 (1971)
Presb	First Unit Presb Ch, 65 Washington Rd, Westminster 21157. 1960- * ch
Unit Meth	Flohsville Unit Meth Ch, 6620 Church St, Sykesville 21784 (1911) 1911- incomplete * ch
Meth Epis S	Freedom Circuit 1876-1925, 1940 # MSA (includes Freedom (1866), Oakland (1866), Stony Ridge (1867)

Carroll County

Bible	Frizzellburg Bible Ch, 1905 Frizzellburg Rd, Westminster 21157 (1842) records fragmentary * ch (began as Ch of God) SEE ALSO: St Lucas Ref Ch, Uniontown
Meth	Gaither Unit Meth Ch, 7701 Gaither Rd, Gaither 21735 (1911) 1911 * ch
Ref & Luth	Ger Ch in Balto Co. SEE: Ref & Luth Congregations at Manchester, Balto Co, now Carroll Co
Bible	Grace Bible Ch, 3250 Charmil Dr, Manchester 21102 (1967) 1967- * ch
Luth	Grace Luth Ch, 21 Carroll St, Westminster 21157 (1842) 1878- * ch (early records burned)
UCC Ref	Grace UCC, 49 W Balto St, Taneytown 21787 (1770) 1770- * ch (records fragmentary before 1890)
UCC Ref	Grace UCC, 2049 Keysville-Bonceville Rd, Keymar 21757 (1820) * ch (was Log Chapel (Union) Luth Meth Breth, Ref ch since 1919)
Unit Meth	Grace Unit Meth Ch, 4618 Black Rock Rd, Hampstead 21074 (1866) 1866- * ch (partial records)
Ch of God	Greenmount. SEE: St Lucas Ref Ch, Uniontown
Breth	Greenmount Unit, Rt 30 & Greenmount Church Rd, e/s Hanover Pike, Hampstead 21074 (1851) recent records * ch, # CCHS
Unit Meth	Greenmount Unit Meth Ch, 2001 Hanover Pike, Hampstead 21074 (1871) 1871- * ch (founded as Ch of Breth, became Meth 1966)(DeHoffs Meet House, Manchester, became Unit Meth in 1966)
Breth	Greenwood, nr New Windsor, e/s Greenwood Rd (1737) records not located (became Eng Presb 1838, later New Windsor Assoc Ref Presb)
Bap	Hampstead Bap Ch, 328 Hanover Pike, Hampstead 21074 (1956) 1956- * ch
Meth	Harmony Grove, Klees Mill Rd, Sykesville 21784 (1840) no records located
Luth	Harney. SEE: St Paul's Luth Ch, 5918 Conover Rd, Taneytown 21787
Meth	Harrisville Meth Ch (no longer in existence)
Bap	Heritage Bap Ch, 1641 Old Westminster Rd, Westminster 21157 (1963) 1963- * ch (started as Warfieldsburg Bible Ch)
Luth	Holy Spirit Luth Ch, 2205 Old Liberty Rd, Sykesville 21784 (1967) 1967- * ch
Epis	Holy Trinity, Liberty Rd, Eldersburg (1771-1923) * MDA # MHS (estab fr St Thomas Parish, Balto Co)
Naz	Hope Naz Ch, Balto & Frederick St, Taneytown 21784 (1979) 1979- * ch
Breth	Hoshalls (1870-1898) # CCHS
Breth	Houcksville (1877-1878) # CCHS
Evan Luth	Immanuel Evan Luth Ch, 3184 Church St, Manchester 21102 (1760) 1760-1850 # MHS, 1760-1784 # CCHS, 1783-1939 # CCPL, 1760-1836 # LDS (formerly Zion Luth Ch, until 1863 Zion Union (Luth & Ref), oldest Luth congregation in Carroll Co, named Immanuel (Emmanuel) in 1863 when union was dissolved) SEE ALSO: Ref & Luth Congregations at Manchester, Balto Co, now Carroll Co

41

Evan Luth	Jerusalem Ch # LDS (Eng Luth congregation)
Luth	Jerusalem Luth Ch, 1372 Bachman's Valley Rd, Westminster 21157 (1797) 1797-1860 * ch, 1799-1880 # MHS, 1797-1910 # CCHS, 1797-1911 # HPL (known as Bowers Ch and Bachman's Ch, was a union ch with Ref; in 1970 Ref group went to Krider's UCC leaving Jerusalem as Luth)
UCC Ref	Jerusalem UCC, 1372 Bachman Valley Rd, Westminster 21157 (1797) records not located, may be at Krider's (founded Union with Luth, joined Krider's in 1970, Jerusalem UCC now inactive)
Meth	Johnsville Unit Meth Ch, Johnsville Rd & Lawrence Dr, Sykesville 21784 (1920) 1950- * ch
Evan Chris	Keymar Evan Chris Ch, 1011 Francis Scott Key Hwy, Keymar 21757 (1940) 1940- * ch
Luth	Keysville Luth Ch, 7301 Keysville Rd, Keysville 21757 (1872) 1872- * ch, 1863-1900 # MHS
Jeh Wit	Kingdom Hall Jeh Wit, Rt 32 just s of Eldersburg (1938) 1938- * ch
Evan Luth	Kirchen-Ordnung der Evan Luth Zions Gemeinde in Md # LDS
Evan Luth	Krider's Evan Luth Ch, Pipe Creek 1766-1837 # MHS DAR CCHS. SEE ALSO: Jerusalem Luth Ch, 1372 Bachman's Valley Rd, Westminster 21157, St Benjamin's Evan Luth Ch, Pipe Creek
Breth	Lawsons 1871-1879 # CCHS
Luth	Lazarus Luth Ch, Church St, Lineboro 21088 (1853) 1854-1960 # CCHS
UCC	Lazarus UCC, Box 64, Lineboro 21102 (1853) 1853- * Trinity UCC, Manchester, 1853-1960 # CCHS
Bap	Liberty Bap Ch, 2127 Old Liberty Rd, New Windsor 21776. 1980- * ch (Calvary, met in Winfield Elem Sch)
Breth	Liberty Ch of Md, 135 E Main St, Westminster 21157 (1980) 1980- * ch (moving to 613 Uniontown Rd, Westminster 21157)
Meth	Linganore Circuit # MSA (includes Barnes Chapel; Bethany Ch; Franklinville (1867); Linganore (1866); Marvin Chapel, Plane # 4 (1888); Mt Airy Ch, Mt Airy; New Market Ch, New Market (1867); Pearre Chapel; St James Ch, Dennings (1878); Sidney Ch, Sidney Grove (1869))
Breth	Linwood Breth Ch, 575 McKenstry Mill Rd, P.O.Box 27, Linwood 21764 (1903) 1903- * ch
Meth	Log Chapel. SEE: Stone Chapel Unit Meth Ch, Stone Chapel & Bowersox Rd, Westminster 21157
Bap	Manchester Bap Ch, 2933 Bap Church Rd, Manchester 21102 (1950) 1950- * ch
Unit Breth	Manchester Ch of Breth, Maiden Ln & High St, Manchester 21102. SEE: Bethel Unit
Meth	Marvin Chapel, Plane # 4. SEE: Linganore Circuit
Ch of God	Mayberry (Bethel) Ch of God, 2428 Mayberry Rd, Westminster 21157 (1880) no records (Uniontown Ch of God joined Mayberry in 1973) SEE: St Lucas Ref Ch, Uniontown
Breth	Meadow Branch Ch of Breth, 818 Old Taneytown Rd, Westminster 21157 (1825) 1825- * ch
Luth	Messiah Luth Ch, 5600 Old Washington Rd, Sykesville 21784 (1872) 1872- * ch

Unit Meth	Messiah Unit Meth Ch, 24 Middle St, Taneytown 21787 (1894) 1837- * ch
Ch of God	Middleburg. SEE: St Lucas Ref Ch, Uniontown
Meth	Middleburg Unit Meth Ch, Johnsville & Middleburg Rds, Keymar 21757 (1859) (some records in Union Bridge Circuit Register at Union Bridge Unit Meth Ch)
Meth	Millers Unit Meth Ch, Wereheine Rd, Millers 21107 (1884) 1946- * ch, 1870-1898 # CCHS
Inter	Miracle Valley Ch, Rt 91 & Lawndale Rd, Finksburg 21048 (1971) 1971- * ch
Bap	Misssionary Bap Ch (Salem), Arrington & Stoney Ridge Rds, Marriottsville 21104 (1867) no records located (founded as Salem Meth South, now Missionary Bap)
Meth	Morgan Chapel, Rt 94 & Hook Mill Rd, Woodbine 21797 (1871) 1871- * ch. SEE ALSO: West Falls Circuit Meth Epis Ch
Bap	Mt Airy Bap Ch, Rt 808 & Ellis Rd, P.O.Box 447, Mt Airy 21771 (1972) 1972- * ch
Meth	Mt Airy Ch, Mt Airy. SEE: Linganore Circuit, Mt Airy Circuit
LDS	Mt Airy Ch of LDS, Beck's Corner, Mt Airy 21771 (1979) 1979- * ch # LDS
Meth Epis	Mt Airy Circuit 1894-1939 # MSA (includes Mt Airy Ch, New Market Ch, Prospect Ch)
Menn	Mt Airy Menn Ch, 7101 Watersville Rd, Mt Airy 21771 (1961) 1961- # ch
Meth	Mt Olive Meth Ch, 2927 Gillis Falls Rd, Mt Airy 21771 (1871) 1871- * ch. SEE ALSO: West Falls Circuit Meth Epis Ch
Meth	Mt Pleasant. SEE: Calvary Unit Meth Ch, 3939 Gamber Rd, Finksburg 21048
Unit Breth	Mt Pleasant Unit Breth Ch. SEE: Taneytown Unit Breth Ch
Breth	Mt Union (1872-1926) 1872-1899 # CCHS
Luth	Mt Union Luth Ch, Hapes Mill & Middleburg Rd, Taneytown 21787 (1857) 1958- * ch, prior to 1958 * LTS
Meth	Mt Zion. SEE: Westminster Circuit Meth Epis Ch
Unit Breth	Mt Zion Unit Breth in Christ, Harney nr Harney & Conover Rds nr Penn State Line (1866-1889) records not located
Unit Meth	Mt Zion Unit Meth Ch, 3006 Old Westminster Pike, Finksburg 21048 (1896) 1896- * ch
Meth Epis	New Market Ch, New Market. SEE: Linganore Circuit, Mt Airy Circuit
Meth	New Windsor. SEE: Westminster Circuit Meth Epis Ch
Presb	New Windsor Assoc Ref Presb Ch, Church & High St, New Windsor 21776 (1838) * PHS
Ch of God	New Windsor Ch of God, 1400 New Windsor Rd, New Windsor 21776 (1964) 1964- * ch
Meth Epis	New Windsor Circuit Meth Epis Ch 1874-1888 # MSA (includes Bailes Sch House, Bethel, Bethesda, Cook's Sch House, Ebenezer, Gist Sch House, New Windsor, Salem, Stone Chapel, Stone Market Sch House, Union Bridge)
Assem of God	North Carroll Assem of God, P.O.Box 720, Manchester Elem Sch, Manchester 21102 * pastor's files
Meth Epis S	Oakland. SEE: Freedom Circuit

Unit Meth	Oakland Unit Meth Ch, 5969 Mineral Hill Rd, Sykesville 21784 (1852) partial records * ch, possibly others at LL, 1876-1908 # MSA. SEE ALSO: Freedom Circuit
Meth	Patapsco. SEE: Carrollton Circuit Meth Epis Ch
Bap	Patapsco Bap Ch, 2203 Old Liberty Rd, Sykesville 21784 (1810-1921) no records located
Meth Epis	Patapsco Circuit 1893-1923, 1932-1937 # MSA
Unit Meth	Patapsco Unit Meth Ch, Finksburg 21048. 1866- * ch
Meth	Pearre Chapel. SEE: Linganore Circuit
Presb	Pine Grove Presb Ch, s/s Main St, Mt Airy (1846) records not located
Presb	Piney Creek Presb Ch, Piney Creek & Harney Rds, Harney 21787 (1763) * ch PHS (oldest Presb ch in Carroll Co)
Friends	Pipe Creek 1730-1895 # WMG
Meth	Pipe Creek. SEE: Stone Chapel Unit Meth Ch, Stone Chapel & Bowersox Rd, Westminster 21157
Breth	Pipe Creek Ch of Breth (1758) * ch, # CCHS (first colonial ch of Breth east of Blue Ridge Mtns, mother ch of Carroll Co Breth churches)
Friends	Pipe Creek Meet House, P.O.Box 277, Union Bridge 21791 (1764) 1773-1909 # MSA DAR
Friends	Pipe Creek Monthly & Preparative Meet 1737-1921 # MSA
Friends	Pipe Creek Monthly Meet 1964-1978 # MSA, # MHS
Unit Meth	Pipe Creek Unit Meth Ch, 3403 Uniontown Rd, Westminster 21157 (1829) 1882- * ch (Brick Ch)
Meth	Pleasant Grove. SEE: Carrollton Circuit Meth Epis Ch, Westminster Circuit Meth Epis Ch
Breth	Pleasant Valley Union, Rt 7, Westminster (1872) closed, records not found
Meth	Poulson's. SEE; Stone Chapel Unit Meth Ch, Stone Chapel & Bowersox Rd, Westminster 21157
Presb	Presb Ch at New Windsor 1839-1939 # LDS
Meth Epis	Prospect Ch. SEE: Mt Airy Circuit
Meth	Providence Meth Ch. SEE: Calvary Unit Meth Ch
Ref & Luth	Ref & Luth Congregations at Manchester, Balto Co, now Carroll Co 1760-1836 # SSGL LDS (these congregations have been known as Zion Ch, Ger Ch in Balto Co, later the Luth congregation was known as Immanuel Ch & the Ref congregation as Trinity UCC)
Meth	Reisterstown: Deer Park 1866-1969 # MSA (formerly Meth Epis Ch, South; Meth 1939-1965; Unit Meth 1965-)
Presb	Ridge Presb Ch, Ridgeville Ave bet Parrsville & Mt Airy 21771 (1849 or 1846) not active, no records located (since 1934 used as non-sectarian funeral chapel, called Pine Grove Chapel, no longer Presb)
Unit Meth	Ridgeville Unit Meth Ch, Ridgeville Blvd, Mt Airy 21771 (1851) * ch
Prot Epis	St Barnabas Ch, Sykesville. misc papers * MSA, 1843-1954 # MSA
Epis	St Barnabas Epis Ch, 13125 Forsythe Rd, Sykesville 21784 * ch
R Cath	St Bartholomew, Park Ave, Manchester 21102 (1865) 1965- * ch, prior to 1965 * St Johns, Westminster

Epis	St Bede's Chapel, Westminster 1962-1966 * MDA
Evan Luth	St Benjamins (Krider's) Evan Luth Ch, Pipe Creek, Westminster (1761) 1754-1837 * ch # LDS, 1754-1836 # MSA, 1763-1836 # MHS, # CCHS CCPL (Jerusalem Ref Congregation joined Krider's 1970), SEE ALSO: Krider's Evan Luth Ch
Ref	St Benjamins (Kreider's) Ref Ch, Pipe Creek 1754-1836 # LDS, 1763-1836 # WMG
Luth	St Benjamin's Luth Ch, Rt 140, Westminster 21157 (1761) 1771-1800 * ch
Epis	St George's Epis Ch, Cape Horn Rd, P.O.Box 339, Manchester 21102 (1957) 1957- * ch
Meth	St James Ch, Dennings. SEE: Linganore Circuit
Epis	St James Epis Ch, 206 N Main St, Mt Airy 21771 (1888) * ch, early records * Grace Ch, New Market
Luth	St James Luth Ch, 14 S Benedum St, Union Bridge 21791 (1883) 1885- * ch (started by Mt Union Middleburg Ch)
Meth	St James Unit Meth Ch, Marston Rd, nr Dennings 21157 (1870) 1940- * ch
R Cath	St Johns, Monroe St, P.O.Box 546, Westminster 21157 (1853) 1805- * ch (founded as Christs Ch 1789-1866)
Luth	St John's (Leisters), 827 Leister's Church Rd, Westminster 21157 (1776) 1834- * ch, # CCHS
Unit Meth	St John's Unit Meth Ch, 1205 N Main St, Hampstead 21074 (1800) 1853- * ch, prior to 1853 not known
R Cath	St Joseph's, P.O.Box 384, Sykesville 21784. 1892- * ch, prior to 1892 * GUL (Bldg # 1, Mellor Ave, Sykesville (1867); Bldg # 2, Liberty Rd & Freedom Ave, Eldersburg (1977))
R Cath	St Joseph's, 44 Frederick St, Taneytown 21787 (1802) 1802- * ch
Ch of God	St Lucas Ref Ch, Uniontown (1814) 1829-1901 # MSA (became Uniontown Ch of God 1836, Mother Ch of God, Middleburg; Mayberry, Frizzellburg; Warfield, Greenmount)
Luth	St Lukes (Winters) Luth Ch, 701 Green Valley Rd, New Windsor 21776 (1783) recent records * ch, prior records * LTS, 1783-1884 # MHS, 1768-1885 # LDS, # CCHS CCPL
Luth	St Mark's Luth Ch, 1373 N Main St, Hampstead 21074 (1883) 1877- * ch
Luth	St Marks Luth Ch, Snydersburg Rd, Snydersburg 21157 (1878) 1880-1905 # CCHS (Union with Ref, Snydersburg)
Prot Epis	St Mark's Prot Epis Ch, McKinstry Mill Rd, Westminster (1861-1880)
UCC	St Marks UCC, Box 64, Snydersburg 21102 (1878) 1880-1905 * Trinity UCC, Manchester, # CCHS
R Cath	St Mary's Chapel, Shriver Estate, Union Mills 21157 (1868) no records
Evan Ref & Luth	St Mary's Ch, Silver Run 1812-1866 # MSA, 1784-1863 # MHS, 1759-1873 # LDS
UCC	St Mary's UCC, Mayberry Rd, Westminster 21157 (1762) 1812- * ch, 1784-1866 # LDS, # CCHS CCPL
Luth	St Mathew's Luth Ch (1879) # YCHS (union with UCC)
UCC	St Mathew's UCC, Pleasant Valley Rd, Westminster 21157 (1879) 1882- * ch (founded as union ch with Luth)

Breth	St Paul (1885) 1885-1899 # CCHS
Luth	St Paul's Luth (Harney), 5918 Conover Rd, Taneytown 21787 (1890) 1890- * ch
Luth	St Pauls Luth (Uniontown), 3330 Uniontown Rd, Westminster 21157 (1870) 1876- recent records * ch, prior records * LTS
UCC	St Paul's UCC, Green & Bond St, Westminster 21157 (1868) 1868- * ch (St Benjamin's (Krider's) was mother ch)
Unit Meth	St Paul's Unit Meth Ch, 408 High St, New Windsor 21776 (1844) 1946- * ch, 1876-1947 # MSA
Unit Meth	St Paul's Unit Meth Ch, 7538 Main St, Sykesville 21784 (1878) 1880-1891 # CCHS
Meth	Salem. SEE: Missionary Bap Ch, Arrington & Stony Ridge Rds, Marriottsville 21104, New Windsor Circuit Meth Epis Ch, West Falls Circuit MeOh Epis Ch, Westminster Circuit Meth Epis Ch, Winfield Circuit Meth Epis Ch
Meth S	Salem Meth, South. SEE: Missionary Bap Ch (Salem)
Meth	Salem-Stoney Ridge, Arrington & Stoney Ridge Rds, Marriottsville 21104 (1867) 1876-1911 # MSA (became Missionary Bap Ch c1911)
Unit Meth	Salem Unit Meth Ch, 3322 Salem Bottom Rd, Westminster 21157 (1832) 1940- * ch, 1843-1872 # MSA
Breth	Sam's Creek Ch of Breth, 2736 Marston Rd, New Windsor 21776 (1836) 1873-1903 # CCHS
Meth	Sam's Creek Meth Ch * Bethel Ch parsonage, 408 High St, New Windsor 21776. SEE ALSO: Stone Chapel Unit Meth Ch, Stone Chapel & Bowersox Rd, Westminster 21157
Meth Prot	Sandymount Meth Prot Ch 1857-1867, 1910-1947 # MSA
Unit Meth	Sandymount Unit Meth Ch, 2101 Old Westminster Pike, Finksburg 21048 (1827) 1860- * ch, 1877- # CCHS (first Meth Prot ch in Carroll Co)
Unit Meth	Shiloh Unit Meth Ch, Shiloh Rd nr Brodheek Rd, Hampstead 21074 (1811) 1900- * ch, prior to 1900 * St Johns Meth Ch, Hampstead
Meth	Sidney Ch, Sidney Grove. SEE: Linganore Circuit
Bahai	Spiritual Assem Faith of Bahai of Balto, P.O.Box 362, Westminster 21157 (1977) 1977- * ch
Presb	Springfield Presb Ch, Sykesville (1835) 1835-1940 # MSA (first Presb ch in Carroll Co)
Meth	Stone Chapel. SEE: New Windsor Circuit Meth Epis Ch, Westminster Circuit Meth Epis Ch
Unit Meth	Stone Chapel Unit Meth Ch, Stone Chapel & Bowersox Rd, Westminster 21157 (1783) 1874-1946 # MSA (first Meth chapel in America, also called Log Chapel, Strawbridge, Sam's Creek, Pipe Creek, Poulson's)
--	Stoner, Elder Solomon, January 1866- August 1901 marriages # MGS Bull (the "marrying preacher")
Meth Epis S	Stony Ridge. SEE: Freedom Circuit
Meth	Stony Ridge-Salem, Arrington & Stoney Ridge Rds, Sykesville 21784. 1876-1940 # MSA (Freedom Circuit, now a Missionary Bap Ch)

Meth	Strawbridge. SEE: Stone Chapel Unit Meth Ch, Stone Chapel & Bowersox Rd, Westminster 21157
Unit Meth	Strawbridge Unit Meth Ch, Rt 31 & Wakefield Valley Rd, New Windsor 21776 (1868) records not located
Bap	Sykesville Bap Chapel, 7609 Main St, P.O.Box 312, Sykesville 21784 (1984) no records kept (met in St Barnabas Epis Parish Hall, now meets in Sykesville Middle Sch)
Bap	Taneytown Bap Ch, 4150 Sells Mills Rd, Taneytown 21787 (1980) 1980 * ch
Presb	Taneytown Presb Ch, 30 York St, Taneytown 21787 (1828) 1920- * ch
Unit Breth	Taneytown Unit Breth Ch, Taneytown (abt 1850-?) no records located (known as Mt Pleasant Unit Breth)
Meth	Tannery. SEE: Carrollton Circuit Meth Epis Ch
Meth	Taylorsville. SEE: West Falls Circuit Meth Epis Ch, Westminster Circuit Meth Epis Ch, Winfield Circuit Meth Epis Ch
Unit Meth	Taylorsville Unit Meth Ch, 4360 Ridge Rd, Mt Airy 21771 (1876) 1876- * ch (records fragmentary)
Meth	Thomas Chapel, Tannery Rd, nr Carrollton (1876) (ch destroyed by fire c1982) SEE: Carrollton Circuit Meth Epis Ch, Westminster Bible Ch
Luth	Trinity Luth Ch, 38 W Balto St, Taneytown 21187 (1750) 1788- * ch, 1788-1862 # MHS LDS, # LTS CCPL ACPHS
Luth	Trinity Luth Ch, 821 Deer Park Rd, Westminster 21157 (1866) 1866-1901, 1929- * ch, # CCHS (1901-1928 records destroyed by fire)
UCC	Trinity UCC, York St, Manchester 21102 (1760) 1760-1836 # MHS HPL CCHS LDS (formerly Zion Luth Ch, until 1863 Zion Union (Luth & Ref), oldest Luth congregation in Carroll Co, named Immanuel (Emmanuel) in 1863 when union was dissolved, MHS records under Zion). SEE ALSO: Ref & Luth Congregations, Manchester, Balto Co, now Carroll Co
Meth	Union Bridge. SEE: New Windsor Circuit Meth Epis Ch
Bap	Union Bridge Bap Ch, Broadway St, Union Bridge (1877) no records located (ch now a funeral home)
Breth	Union Bridge Ch of Breth, Main & Church St, Union Bridge 21791 (1954) 1945- * ch (Pipe Creek Ch of Breth was mother ch, early records at Pipe Creek to 1945)
Unit Meth	Union Bridge Unit Meth Ch, 7 S Main St, Union Bridge 21791 (1879) 1901- * ch, 1874-1888 # MSA
--	Union Meet House, Westminster (1760-1891) no records located
Unit Meth	Union Street Unit Meth Ch, 26 Union St, Westminster 21157 (1869) 1920- * ch
Bible	Uniontown Bible Ch, Uniontown 21157 (1815) 1967- * ch (started as Ger Ref 1815, became Bible Ch 1967, part went to Uniontown Ch of God after fire 1976, part to Mayberry)
Ch of God	Uniontown Ch of God, Uniontown (1836) 1870-1890 # MSA, 1840-1930 # CCHS
Meth	Uniontown Meth Ch, 3405 Uniontown Rd, Westminster 21157 (1829) 1933- * ch

Bible	Wakefield Valley Bible Ch, 2214 Old New Windsor Rd, New Windsor 21776 (1903) 1903- * ch (began as Ch of God)
Ch of God	Warfield. SEE: St Lucas Ref Ch, Uniontown
Bible	Warfieldsburg Bible Ch. SEE: Heritage Bap Ch
Unit Meth	Watersville Unit Meth Ch, Watersville Rd, Mt Airy 21771 (1866) 1886-1898, 1906-1928, 1944-1953 # MSA. SEE ALSO: West Falls Circuit Meth Epis Ch
Meth	Wesley Chapel. SEE: Wesley Unit Meth Ch, 3239 Carrollton Rd, Hampstead 21074
Meth	Wesley-Freedom Unit Meth Ch, 1011 Liberty Rd, Sykesville 21784 recent records * ch, older records * LL, 1876-1925, 1940- # MSA (combination of Wesley Chapel (1822) and Freedom (1866))
Unit Meth	Wesley Unit Meth Ch (St John's), 3239 Carrollton Rd, Hampstead 21074 (1797) 1951- * ch, # LL (Brown's Meet House 1800-1877, Wesley Chapel 1879)
Meth	West End. SEE: Westminster Circuit Meth Epis Ch
Meth Epis	West Falls Circuit Meth Epis Ch 1886-1898, 1906-1928, 1944-1953 # MSA (includes Bethesda, Ebenezer, Morgan Chapel, Mt Olive, Salem, Taylorsville, Watersville, West Falls; West Falls Circuit became Winfield Circuit in 1910)
Bap	Westminster Bap Ch, 354 Crest Ln, Westminster 21157 (1963) 1963- * ch
Bible	Westminster Bible Ch, 310 Gorsuch Rd, Westminster 21157 (1962) 1962- * ch (began as Thomas Chapel)
Ch of Christ	Westminster Ch of Christ, 114 Liberty St, Westminster 21157 (1977) 1977- * ch
Ch of God	Westminster Ch of God, Rt 27 & 640 Lucabaurgh Mill Rd, P.O.Box 444, Westminster 21157 (1967) 1967- * ch
Breth	Westminster Ch of the Breth, Park & Bond St, Westminster 21157 (1877) 1877- * ch
Naz	Westminster Ch of the Naz, 61 Madison St, Westminster 21157 (1941) 1941- * ch
Meth Epis	Westminster Circuit Meth Epis Ch 1865-1872 # MSA (includes Bethel, Bethesda, Carrollton, Cooks Sch House, Ebenezer, Mt Zion, New Windsor, Pleasant Grove, Salem, Stone Chapel, Taylorsville, West End, Westminster)
Unit Meth	Westminster Unit Meth Ch, 165 E Main St, Westminster 21157 (1837) 1837- * ch (Centenary Meth Epis 1870, meetings held in homes as early as 1769, first building 1839, merged with Emanuel to become Westminster 1941)
Unit Meth	White Rock Unit Meth Ch, 6300 White Rock Rd, Sykesville 21784 (1974) 1974- * ch
Bible	Winfield Bible Ch, 5407 Woodbine Rd, Woodbine 21797 (1860) 1974- * ch (founded as a Ch of God)
Meth Epis	Winfield Circuit Meth Epis Ch 1933-1945 # MSA (includes Ebenezer, Salem, Taylorville)
Luth	Winters. SEE: St Lukes Luth Ch, 701 Green Valley Rd, New Windsor 21776
Ref & Luth	Zion Ch. SEE: Ref & Luth Congregations at Manchester, Balto Co, now Carroll Co
Evan Luth	Zion Evan Luth Ch, Manchester 1784-1853 # MHS

Carroll County

Ref & Luth   Zion Luth Ch, Manchester 1760-1836 # MSA, 1782-1870 # MHS,
                1760-1836 # LDS
Unit Meth   Zion Unit Meth Ch, 2716 Old Washington Rd, Westminster 21157
                (1882) 1905- * ch

Cecil County

Meth   Asbury. SEE: Charlestown Charge Meth Epis Ch
R Cath   Bohemia Parish 1789-1882 # MSA
Meth Epis   Cecil Circuit Meth Epis Ch, New Castle Co. Del 1849-1869 #
                LDS (includes Andora, Cherry Hill, Chesapeake City,
                Christiana, Flint Hill, Glasgow, McClellandville, Newark,
                Newport, Summit Bridge)
Meth   Cecilton Charge Meth Ch 1942-1968 # MSA
Meth   Cecilton-St Paul's Charge Meth Ch 1934-1941, 1955-1964 # MSA
Meth Epis   Cecilton-St Paul's Charge Meth Epis Ch 1865-1958 # MSA
Meth Epis   Cecilton-St Paul's Circuit. SEE: Millington Circuit Meth
                Epis Ch
Meth Epis   Charlestown Charge Meth Epis Ch 1858-1881 # MSA (includes
                Asbury, Charlestown, Harts, Hebron Sch House, Perryville,
                Principio, Wesley Chapel)
Prot Epis   Ch of the Good Shepherd. SEE: St Augustine Ch & Ch of the
                Good Shepherd
Meth   Harts. SEE: Charlestown Charge Meth Epis Ch
Meth   Hebron Sch House. SEE: Charlestown Charge Meth Epis Ch
Presb   Lower West Nottingham Presb Ch, Colora 1838-1894 # LDS (also
                known as West Nottingham Presb Ch)
Meth Epis   Millington Circuit Meth Epis Ch 1851-1919 # MSA (became
                Cecilton-St Paul's Circuit)
Meth   North East Meth Ch 1940-1968 # MSA
Meth Epis   North East Meth Epis Ch 1908-1938 # MSA
Friends   Nottingham Monthly & Quarterly Meet 1801-1978 # MSA
Friends   Nottingham Quarterly, Monthly & Preparative Meet 1679-1955 #
                MSA
Meth   Perryville. SEE: Charlestown Charge Meth Epis Ch
Meth Epis   Perryville Charge Meth Epis Ch 1912-1931 # MSA
Meth Epis   Perryville Meth Epis Ch 1859-1881 # MHS
Presb   Presb Ch, Zion 1849-1861, 1882-1899 # LDS
Meth   Principio. SEE: Charlestown Charge Meth Epis Ch
Prot Epis   St Augustine Ch & Ch of the Good Shepherd 1838-1923,
                1964-1981 * and # MSA
Prot Epis   St James Ch, Port Deposit 1931-1961 # MSA
Prot Epis   St Mary Anne's Ch, North East 1711-1799, 1824-1931 # MSA
Prot Epis   St Mary Ann's Parish 1713-1799 # MHS, 1718-1799 # LDS
Prot Epis   St Stephen's, Earleville 1693-1899, 1905-1949 # MSA,
                1693-1804 # LDS
Epis   St Stephen's Parish 1693-1913 * MHS Mss Div, 1687-1837 # MHS
                LDS
Prot Epis   Schouler, Rev William 1864-1932 diaries * MHS Mss Div

49

Cecil County

Meth Epis	Tome Memorial Meth Epis Ch, Port Deposit (1872) 1873-1891 # MHS
Prot Epis	Trinity Ch, Elkton 1833-1957 * and # MSA
Bap	Welch Tract Bap Ch, Iron Hill 1804-1899 # LDS
Meth	Wesley Chapel. SEE: Charlestown Charge Meth Epis Ch
Presb	West Nottingham Presb Ch # LDS. SEE ALSO: Lower West Nottingham Presb Ch
Meth	Zion Ch, Cecilton 1851-1929 # MSA

Charles County

Epis	Accokeek Ch 1824-1843, 1863-1876 # DAR (originated as Chapel of Ease) SEE ALSO: Christ Ch, Accokeek, St Johns Parish, both Prince George's Co.
Meth	Cedar Point. SEE: St Mary's Circuit Meth Epis Ch
Meth	Charles Circuit Meth Epis Ch. SEE: Leonardtown and Charles Circuit Meth Epis Ch
Prot Epis	Christ Ch, Accokeek 1824-1934 * and # MSA, 1941-1977 # MSA, 1843-1863, 1876-1908 # DAR (also called Accokeek Ch)
Prot Epis	Durham Parish 1666-1724, 1774-1824, 1842-? # MHS, 1774-1824, 1776 Oath of Fidelity # LDS DAR (known as Nanjemoy)
Meth	Ebenezer. SEE: St Mary's Circuit Meth Epis Ch
Bap	First Bap Ch, General Delivery, Welcome 20693 (1947) 1947- * ch
Meth	Friendship. SEE: St Mary's Circuit Meth Epis Ch
Presb	Good Samaritan Presb Ch, P.O.Box 925, Waldorf 20601 (1978) 1978- * ch
Bap	Grace Bap Ch, Bryan's Rd, Rt 1 Box 23, Bryan's Road 20616 (1958) 1958- * ch
Meth	Joy Chapel, Hollywood. SEE: Leonardtown Charge Meth Epis Ch
Unit Meth	LaPlata Unit Meth Ch, Box 216, LaPlata 20646 (1890) 1890- * ch
Meth Epis	Leonardtown & Charles Circuit Meth Epis Ch 1849, 1873-1883 # MSA
Meth	Leonardtown Charge Meth Ch 1933-1968 # MSA (includes St Paul's Ch with members from Mt Zion & St George's Isl churches)
Meth Epis	Leonardtown Charge Meth Epis Ch 1883-1943 # MSA (includes St Paul's at Leonardtown, Joy Chapel at Hollywood, Mt Zion at Laurel Grove and Sand Gates)
R Cath	Mattawoman 1793-1861 # LDS
Meth	Mt Zion Ch, Laurel Grove. SEE: Leonardtown Charge Meth Ch, Leonardtown Charge Meth Epis Ch
Epis	Nanjemoy. SEE: Durham Parish
Prot Epis	Old Durham Ch, Ironsides 1774-1824, 1843 * and # MSA
Friends	Patuxent Monthly Meet, Orth 1809-1950 # MSA
Meth	Pisgah. SEE: St Mary's Cirʔuit Meth Epis Ch
Prot Epis	Prot Epis Ch. early records # LDS

Charles County

Meth	St George's Isl churches. SEE: Leonardtown Charge Meth Ch, St Mary's Circuit Meth Epis Ch
R Cath	St Ignatius, Upper Zachius, 1852-1870 # MSA. SEE ALSO: St Peter's, Waldorf
Prot Epis	St John's Chapel, Pomonkey. SEE: Christ Ch, Accokeek, Prince George's Co
Epis	St Johns Parish 1701-1878 # LDS (Piscataway, commonly called King George's Parish)
Meth Epis	St Mary's Circuit Meth Epis Ch 1875-1895, 1902-1929 # MSA (includes Cedar Point, Ebenezer, Friendship, Pisgah, St George's Isl)
Meth	St Paul's Ch, Leonardtown 1962-1967 # MSA. SEE ALSO: Leonardtown Charge Meth Ch, Leonardtown Charge Meth Epis Ch
R Cath	St Peter's, Waldorf 1870-1896 # MSA (before 1869 known as St Ignatius, Upper Zachiah)
Meth	Sand Gates. SEE: Leonardtown Charge Meth Epis Ch
Prot Epis	Trinity Ch, Newport 1729-1922 * and # MSA # DAR
Prot Epis	Trinity Parish 1729-1803 # MHS, 1830-1906 # DAR, 1729-1857 # LDS (Chapel called Old Fields, completed 1769)
Prot Epis	Zachiah St Mary's Maltawoman Parish, Bryantown 1793-1861 # MHS

District of Columbia

Unit Meth	Douglas Memorial, 11th & H Sts NE, Washington DC 1881-1952 # MSA
Epis	Epis Ch of the Transfiguration, 14th & Galliton Sts NW, Washington, DC 1890-1957 * Epis Ch House, Mt St Alban, Washington, DC 20016
Presb	Northminster Presb Ch, Alaska Ave & Kalmia Rd NW, Washington DC 20012. 1943-1984 # MSA
Prot Epis	St Paul's Ch, Washington DC 1695-1959 # MSA (until 1727 part of St John's Parish, Piscataway; in that year included in newly erected Prince George's Parish, 1856 erected as separate parish & called Rock Creek Parish)
Presb	Wallace Memorial Presb Ch, 7201 16th Pl, Hyattsville 20783 (1910) 1950- * ch

Meth	Beulah. SEE: Unity Meth Prot Ch
Meth	Brookview. SEE: East New Market Charge Meth Ch
Meth Prot	Cambridge Circuit Meth Prot Ch 1881-1917 # MSA (Chateau & St Pauls churches)
Meth	Chateau. SEE: Cambridge Circuit Meth Prot Ch
Prot Epis	Christ Ch, Cambridge 1788-1926 * and # MSA (includes Dorchester Parish, Bishop Kemp records 1796-1812), 1743-1760, 1788-1904 # MHS (includes Dorchester Parish, Great Choptank Parish)
Meth Epis	Christ Rock Meth Epis Ch 1956-1962 # MSA
Unit Meth	Christ Unit Meth Ch, P.O.Box 275, Cambridge 21613 (1914) (church burned, records destroyed)
Unit Meth	Ch Creek Unit Meth Charge, Box 46, Church Creek 21622 (1800's) 1800's * ch (includes Joppa, Milton, Taylor's, White Haven)
R Cath	Ch of Our Lady of Good Counsel, Secretary 21664 (1891) 1964- * ch, prior records * St Mary Refuge of Sinners, Cambridge
Epis	Dorchester Parish 1790-1806 * MDA, 1743-1760, 1790-1904 # MHS 1743-1903 # LDS (includes Christ Ch, Cambridge, Dorchester Parish, Great Choptank Parish)
Meth	East New Market Charge Meth Ch 1949-1968 # MSA (includes Brookview, Eldorado, Trinity)
Meth	Eldorado. SEE: East New Market Charge Meth Ch, Unity Meth Epis Ch
Meth	Friendship. SEE: Williamsburg Circuit Meth Epis Ch
Prot Epis	Grace Ch, Taylors Isl. SEE: Trinity Ch, Church Creek
Epis	Great Choptank Parish, Cambridge 1791-1802 # MHS, 1790-1893 # LDS. SEE ALSO: Christ Ch, Cambridge
Meth	Hurlock & McKendree Meth Epis Ch 1892-1950 # MSA
Meth	Hynson. SEE: Williamsburg Circuit Meth Epis Ch
Meth Epis	Johns Meth Epis Ch, Ellwood 1895-1912 # MHS Mss Div MSA, 1895-1912, 1970-1983 # MHS (merged with Mt Pleasant Ch & Zoar Ch to form Mt Calvary Ch, Preston, Caroline Co)
Meth	Joppa. SEE: Church Creek Unit Meth Charge, Box 46, Church Creek 21622)
Meth	McKendree. SEE: Hurlock & McKendree Meth Epis Ch
Prot Epis	Kemp, Bishop. SEE: Christ Ch, Cambridge
Meth	Milton. SEE: Church Creek Unit Meth Charge, Box 46, Church Creek 21622
Meth Epis	Mt Calvary Ch, Preston, Caroline Co. SEE: Johns Meth Epis Ch
Bap	Mt Olive Bap Ch, 601 Douglas St, Cambridge 21613 * ch (dates not given)
Meth Epis	Mt Pleasant Ch. SEE: Johns Meth Epis Ch
Meth	St Luke's, Secretary. SEE: Unity Meth Prot Ch
Unit Meth	St Lukes Unit Meth Ch 1956-1959 # MSA
Meth	St Paul's. SEE: Cambridge Circuit Meth Prot Ch, Williamsburg Circuit Meth Epis Ch
Prot Epis	St Paul's Ch, Vienna 1866-1957 # MSA
Meth	St Paul's Meth Ch, Cambridge 1946-1967 # MSA
Meth	St Paul's Meth Prot Ch 1917-1927 # MSA
Prot Epis	St Stephen's Ch, East New Market 1904-1953 # MSA
Meth Epis	St Thomas Meth Epis Ch, Bishop's Head 1935 history # MSA

Meth	Taylor's. SEE: Church Creek Unit Meth Charge, Box 46, Church Creek 21622
Meth	Trinity. SEE: East New Market Charge Meth Ch
Prot Epis	Trinity Ch, Church Creek 1737-1948 * and # MSA (built prior to 1690, includes Grace Ch, Taylor's Isl)
Meth Epis	Trinity Meth Epis Ch 1849-1887 * MSA
Meth	Unity Meth Epis Ch 1891-1944 # MSA (includes churches at Beulah, Eldorado & St Luke's, Secretary)
Meth	Unity-Washington Ch 1891-1897, 1953-1963 # MSA
Unit Meth	Vienna-Elliotts Unit Meth Charge, Box 278, Vienna 21869 (c1900) 1900- * ch
Meth	Washington Chapel 1800-1928 * and # MSA
Unit Meth	Waters Unit Meth Ch (Fork Neck), P.O. box 275, Cambridge 21613 * ch (dates not given)
Meth	White Haven. SEE: Church Creek Unit Meth Charge, Box 46, Church Creek 21622
Meth Epis	Williamsburg Circuit Meth Epis Ch 1897-1943 # MSA (includes Friendship, Hynson, St Paul's, Williamsburg)
Meth	Zion Meth Ch 1942-1969 # MSA
Meth Epis	Zion Meth Epis Ch, Cambridge 1800-1967 # MSA
Unit Meth	Zion Unit Meth Ch, 610 Locust St, Cambridge 21613 (1780) 1780- * ch, 1855-1866 # LDS
Meth Epis	Zoar Ch. SEE: Johns Meth Epis Ch

Frederick County

Prot Epis	All Saints' Ch, Frederick 1727/8-1781, 1804-1960 # MSA. SEE ALSO: Allen, Rev Ethan
Prot Epis	All Saints' Parish 1746-1775 # MSA, 1727/8-1862 # MHS, 1727-1863 # LDS
Prot Epis	Allen, Rev. Ethan 1797-1879 writings & notes # MHS Mss Div (includes St John's Parish, Prince George's Co; Prince George's Parish, Montgomery Co; All Saints' Parish & St Mark's, Frederick Co; Washington & Allegany Co parishes)
Ref	Apples' Congregation of the Ref Ch nr Mechanicstown 1884-1962 # LDS
Luth & Ref	Apples' Luth & Ref Ch, Thurmont 1773-1849 # LDS
Ref	Assoc of Ref Congregations. SEE: St Benjamin's (Kreider's) Ch, Pipe Creek
Meth Epis S	Barnes' Chapel, Linganore (1866). SEE: Linganore Circuit
Meth Epis S	Bethany Ch, Franklinville (1867). SEE: Linganore Circuit
Meth	Bethany, Flint Hill. SEE: Trinity Charge Meth Ch
--	Bethel. SEE: Glade Charge
Afric Meth Epis	Bethel Congregation. SEE: Quinn Chapel
Evan Luth	Bethel Evan Luth Ch, 9664 O'Possumtown Pike, Frederick 21701. 1941- * ch, 1840-1941 * Bethel Luth Ch, c/o Margaret Myers, 317 E Third St, Frederick 21710

--	Bossler, David 1822-1852, 1860-1870 (marriage book, Emmitsburg, Md & Adams Co, Harrisburg, Cumberland Co, York, Pa)
Meth	Brook Hill. SEE: Trinity Charge Meth Ch
Evan Ref	Brunner book. SEE: Evan Ref Ch
--	Bucher, John C 1828-1843 # WMG (register, Middletown Valley)
Unit Meth	Calvary Unit Meth Ch, W 2nd & Bentz Sts, Frederick 21701 (1770) 1861- * ch
Unit Meth	Catoctin Unit Meth Ch, Kelly Store Rd, Thurmont 21788 1946- * ch. SEE ALSO: Trinity Charge Meth Ch
Evan & Ref	Cort, Cyrus 1881-1914 # LDS
Luth & Ref	Creagerstown Luth & Ref Congregations. SEE: St John Luth & Ref Congregations
Unit Meth	Deerfield Unit Meth Ch, 16405 Foxville-Deerfield Rd, Sabillasville 21780. 1934- * ch (mailing address: 101 Dogwood Ave, Thurmont 21788) SEE ALSO: Weller's-Deerfield Unit Meth Charge, 101 Dogwood Ave, Thurmont 21788)
Afric Meth Epis	East Third Street Ch. SEE: Quinn Chapel
Luth	Elias Luth Ch, Emmitsburg 1850-1950 # MHS
Evan Luth & Ref	Evan Luth & Ref Ch, Woodsboro 1803-1873 # LDS
Evan Luth	Evan Luth Ch, Frederick 1742-1751 # MSA, 1742-1859 # MHS, 1737-1887 # LDS
Evan Luth	Evan Luth Ch, Woodsboro 1803-1861 # MHS
Evan Luth	Evan Luth Congregation, Frederick 1743-1811 # LDS (includes Monocacy Ch)
Evan Luth	Evan Luth Congregation, Middletown 1743-1887 # LDS
Evan Luth	Evan Luth Congregation, Mitteldaun 1781-1825 # LDS
Evan Luth	Evan Luth Krauter's Ch 1766-1837 # SSGL
Evan Ref	Evan Ref Ch, Frederick (c1753) 1746-1875 Brunner Book * and # MSA, 1753-1840 Schlatter Book * and # MSA, 1835-1892 Kirchen Buch * and # MSA, 1779-1866 * MHS Mss Div, 1770-1795 # MMG, 1746-1833 # LDS (known as Ger Ref, Ref Presb, Ger Presb Ch)
Meth	Eyler's Valley. SEE: Weller Unit Meth Ch, 101 N Altamont Ave, Thurmont 21788
UCC	Faith UCC, 9333 O'Possumtown Pike, Frederick 21701. 1839-1908, 1915- * ch (St Paul's Ref UCC, Utica & Zion Ref UCC, Charlesville merged in 1964 to form Faith UCC)
Bap	First Bap Ch, 3 A St, P.O.Box 277, Prunswick 21716 (1905) 1905- * ch
Ref	First Ger Ref Ch, Frederick 1753-1897 # MHS # LDS
UnitBreth	Frederick Circuit Unit Breth in Christ 1857-1912 # MSA (includes Georgetown Chapel)
Meth Epis S	Frederick City Appointment Meth Epis Ch, South 1866-1940 # MSA
Evan Luth	Frederick Evan Luth Ch, Frederick 1743-1811 # MHS
Presb	Frederick Presb Ch, 115 W Second St, Frederick 21701 * ch (dates not given)
Ref	Frederick Ref Ch, Frederick 1788-1802 # MGS Bull

Frederick County

Meth	Garfield Ch, Wolfsville. SEE: Myersville Circuit Unit Breth in Christ
Unit Breth	Georgetown Chapel. SEE: Frederick Circuit Unit Breth in Christ
Ref	Ger Ref Ch, Frederick 1746–1900 # LDS
--	Glade Charge 1563–1865 # MHS (consists of 4 churches: Glade, Bethel, Utica & Woodsboro)
Ref	Glade Ref Ch, Walkersville 1772–1873 # MHS, 1768–1857 # LDS
Evan Luth	Grace Evan Luth Ch nr Woodsboro 1767–1889 # MHS LDS (formerly St Peter's Ch, Rocky Hill)
Ref	Grace Ref Congregation, Pleasant Hill 1885–1955 # MHS
Meth Epis	Israels Creek Meth Epis Ch. SEE: Walkersville Meth Charge
Evan & Ref	Krebs, Walter E 1859–1862 # LDS (pastor's records, Emmitsburg)
Ref	Kreider's Ch. SEE: St Benjamin's (Kreider's) Ch
Meth Epis	Liberty Circuit Meth Epis Ch. SEE: Walkersville Meth Charge
Meth Epis S	Linganore Circuit * Calvary Meth Ch, 401 S Main St, Mt Airy 21771, 1872–1920 # MSA (includes Barnes' Chapel, Linganore (1866); Bethany Ch, Franklinville (1867); New Market Ch, New Market (1867); Sidney Ch, Sidney Grove (1869); St James Ch, Dennings (1878); Marvin Chapel, Plane # 4 (1888); Pearre Chapel; Mt Airy Ch, Mt Airy)
Meth Epis S	Marvin Chapel, Plane # 4 (1888). SEE: Linganore Circuit
Evan Luth	Monocacy Ch. SEE: Evan Luth Congregation, Frederick
Luth	Monocacy Congregation 1730–1779 # MHS
Ref	Monocacy Ref Ch 1742–1811 # LDS (includes Monocacy Ch & Evan Luth Congregation, both in Frederick)
Morav	Morav Com & Congregation, Graceham 1759–1871 # MSA, 1745–1937 # MHS, 1759–1871 # LDS
Meth Epis S	Mt Airy Ch, Mt Airy. SEE: Linganore Circuit, Mt Airy Circuit
Meth Epis	Mt Airy Circuit 1894–1939 # MSA (includes Mt Airy Ch, Mt Airy; New Market Ch, New Market; Prospect Ch)
Luth	Mt Bethel Ch, Frederick 1836–1926 # MSA
Meth Epis	Mt Pleasant Meth Epis Ch. SEE: Walkersville Meth Charge
Ref	Mt Tabor Ref Ch, Rocky Ridge 1875–1942 # LDS
Unit Breth	Myersville Circuit Unit Breth in Christ (in 1905 Pleasant Valley, Garfield & Salem churches at Wolfsville estab from Myersville Circuit)
Meth Epis S	New Market Ch, New Market (1867) SEE: Linganore Circuit, Mt Airy Circuit
Luth	Peace in Christ Luth Ch, 8325 Yellow Springs Rd, Frederick 21701 (1975) 1975– * ch
Meth Epis S	Pearre Chapel. SEE: Linganore Circuit
Meth	Pleasant Valley Ch, Wolfsville 1889–1924 # MSA. SEE ALSO: M8ersville Circuit Unit Breth in Christ
Prot Epis	Prince Georges' Parish, Rock Creek 1711–1832 # MHS, # LDS
Meth Eis	Prospect Ch. SEE: Mt Airy Circuit
Afric Meth Epis	Quinn Chapel, 106 E Third St, Frederick 21701 (1835) (a black ch; also known as Bethel Congregation)
Ref	Ref Ch, Frederick 1747–1758 # LDS
Ref	Ref Congregation, Frederick 1756–1834 # MHS, 1749–1801 # LDS
Ref	Rocky Hill Ref Ch nr Woodsboro 1768–1851 # LDS

Frederick County

Cath	St Anthony Shrine, Emmitsburg (1897) 1871-1981 # MSA (successor to St Mary's of the Mount)
Evan Ref & Luth	St Benjamin's (Kreider's) Ch, Pipe Creek 1754-1836 # MSA, 1763-1836 SSGL (includes minutes of the Assoc of Ref Congregations & classes in Md at Big Pipe Creek, Little Pipe Creek, Baltimore, Sam's Creek, Frederick, Antietam, Conewago Pa, Sharpsburg, Funkstown, Hagerstown, the Kemp's nr Frederick, Peter Reittmauer's, Beaver Dam & Germantown 1774-1776)
Meth Epis S	St James Ch, Dennings (1878). SEE: Linganore Circuit
Luth	St John Luth & Ref Congregations, Creagerstown 1789-1862 # MSA
Cath	St John the Evangelist, Second St, Frederick 1811-1981 # MSA. SEE ALSO: St Joseph Ch, Buckeystown
R Cath	St John's Cath Ch, Frederick 1811-1822 # MHS
Evan Luth	St Johns Evan Luth Ch, Creagerstown 1733-1941 # MSA, 1789-1941 # MHS LDS
Evan Luth	St John's Evan Luth Ch, 15 N Church St, Thurmont 21788. 1877-* ch
Evan Luth	St John's Evan Luth Congregation 1832-1921 # MSA
Evan Ref	St John's Evan Ref Ch, Frederick (1843-1912) 1846-1918 * MSA, 1787-1918 # MSA
Ref	St John's (fourth) Ref Ch, Buckeystown 1882-1917 # LDS
Prot Epis	St John's Parish 1878-1898 # LDS. SEE ALSO: Allen, Rev Ethan
UCC	St John's UCC, 8 N Second St, Woodsboro 21798 (abt 1747) 1892- * ch (in early years named Evan Luth & Ref Ch)
Cath	St Joseph 1812-1843 # MSA
R Cath	St Joseph Ch, Buckeystown 1902-1982 # MSA (includes Basilica of the Assumption, Balto & St John the Evangelist, Frederick)
R Cath	St Joseph Ch, Emmitsburg 1795-1979 # MSA (Poplar Fields became Emmitsburg in 1786)
Prot Epis	St Marks. SEE: Allen, Rev Ethan
Prot Epis	St Mark's Ch, Petersville 1789-1801, 1806-1917 # MSA
Luth	St Marks Luth Ch, 5132 Doubs Rd, Adamstown 21710 (1883) 1904- * ch
Epis	St Mark's Parish 1806-1916 * MDA
Evan Ref & Luth	St Mary's Ch, Silver Run 1812-1866, 1873 # MSA, 1784-1863 # MHS, 1812-1866 # SSGL, 1759-1873 # LDS
R Cath	St Mary's of the Mount, Emmitsburg 1815-1871, 1885 # MSA. SEE ALSO: St Anthony Shrine, Emmitsburg
Ref & Luth	St Paul & St Matthias Ref & Luth Congregations, Ladiesburg 1798-1834 # LDS
Evan Luth	St Paul Evan Luth Ch, Utica 1862-1941 # MHS, 1862-1942 # LDS
Prot Epis	St Pauls Parish # MHS (records of Rev George W Thomas while rector in Western Run Parish, St John's Ch, Balto Co. 1893-1898 & St Paul's Parish, Frederick Co 1899-1911)
UCC	St Paul's Ref UCC, Utica nr Lewistown. SEE: Faith UCC, 9333 O'Possumtown Pike, Frederick 21701
Evan Luth	**St Peter's Ch 1767-1854 # LDS**
Evan Luth	**St Peter's Ch, Rocky Hill. SEE: Grace Evan Luth Ch**

56

Luth	St Peter's Ch, Woodsboro 1767-1857 # MHS LDS
Meth	Salem Ch, Wolfsville. SEE: Myersville Circuit Unit Breth in Christ
Evan Ref	Schlatter Book. SEE: Evan Ref Ch, Frederick
Meth Epis S	Sidney Ch, Sidney Grove (1869). SEE: Linganore Circuit
Prot Epis	Thomas, Rev. George W. SEE: St Paul's Parish
Unit Meth	Tom's Creek Unit Meth Ch, Tom's Creek & Simmons Rd, Emmitsburg 21727 * ch (dates not given)
Meth	Trinity Charge Meth Ch 1866-1965 # MSA (includes Bethany at Flint Hill, Brook Hill, Catoctin, Trinity)
Meth	Trinity Meth Ch 1956-1963 # MSA
Meth Epis S	Trinity Meth Epis Ch, South 1880-1884, 1925-1926, 1964-1971 # MSA
Ref	Trinity Ref Congregation, Thurmont 1860-1952 # LDS
Unit Meth	Trinity Unit Meth Ch, W Main St, Emmitsburg 21727 * ch & Thurmont Unit Meth Ch (dates not given), 1880-1884, 1925-1974 # MSA
Ref	Union Chapel Ref Ch, Libertytown 1862-1930 # LDS
Evan Luth & Ref	Union Evan Luth & Ref Congregations, Woodsboro. SEE: Evan Luth Ch, Woodsboro
--	Utica 1862-1941 # MSA. SEE ALSO: Glade Charge
Luth	Utica Congregation, Utica 1862-1941 # MSA
Meth Epis	Walkersville Circuit Meth Epis Ch. SEE: Walkersville Meth Charge
Luth	Walkersville Glade Charge 1763-1833 # MSA
Meth	Walkersville Meth Charge 1856-1958 # MSA (includes Israels Creek Meth Epis Ch, Liberty Circuit Meth Epis Ch, Mt Pleasant Meth Epis Ch, Walkersville Circuit Meth Epis Ch)
Unit Meth	Weller Unit Meth Ch, 101 N Altamont Ave, Thurmont 21788. 1883- * ch (was Unit Breth in Christ, then Evan Unit Breth, now Unit Meth; includes Eyler's Valley; mailing address: 101 Dogwood Ave, Thurmont 21788)
Unit Meth	Weller's-Deerfield Unit Meth Charge, 101 Dogwood Ave, Thurmont 21788 1870- * ch (Weller Unit Meth Ch (1830) & Deerfield Unit Meth Ch (1879))
--	Woodsboro. SEE: Glade Charge
Evan Luth & Ref	Woodsboro Ch 1805-1852 # MHS LDS
Ref & Luth	Woodsboro Ref & Luth Ch 1803-1873 # LDS
Luth	Zion Ch, Middletown 1779-1853 # MSA MHS, 1779-1827 # LDS, 1781-1827 # SSGL (the Evan Luth Congregation in & around Mitteldaun)
Prot Epis	Zion Ch, Urbana 1820-1911 # MSA
Luth	Zion Ch, Urbana 1847-1873 # MSA
Epis	Zion Parish 1820-1961 * MDA
UCC	Zion Ref UCC, Charlesville nr Frederick. SEE: Faith UCC, 9333 O'Possumtown Pike, Frederick 21701
UCC	Zion UCC. SEE: Faith UCC

Prot Epis	Emmanuel Ch, Corunna (1889-1908) 1889-1908 * MDA, 1889-1898, 1904, 1908 # MSA (includes communicants from towns of Bayard, Davis & Elkins, W.Va.)
Unit Meth	Emmanuel Unit Meth Ch, Rt 40 & Pocohontas Rd, 4 mi w of Frostburg 1965- * ch (mailing address: Rt 2, Box 447, Frostburg 21532)
R Cath	Immaculate Conception, Rt 38 & Maple St, Kitzmiller 21538 1945-1983 # MSA
Meth Epis	Mountain Lake Park Auxiliary of the Woman's Foreign Missionary Society of the Meth Epis Ch 1894-1904 minute book * MHS Mss Div
Cath	St Ann, Avilton (1837) (merged with St Stephen, Grantsville, both missions forming a new parish: St Ann, Grantsville)
Cath	St Ann, Grantsville (formed by merger of St Ann, Avilton & St Stephen, Grantsville)
R Cath	St Peter the Apostle, 402 E Oak St, Oakland 21550. 1858-1983 # MSA
Cath	St Stephen, Grantsville (St Ann, Avilton, merged with St Stephen, Grantsville, both missions forming a new parish: St Ann, Grantsville)
Luth	Zion, Box 171, Accident 21520. 1854-1982 * CHI

Harford County

Meth Epis	Aberdeen. SEE: East Harford Charge Meth Epis Ch
Meth	Abington Ch. SEE: Bel Air Charge Meth Prot Ch, Deer Creek Charge Meth Prot Ch, East Harford Charge Meth Ch, East Harford Charge Meth Epis Ch
Prot Epis	Allen, Rev John of St George's Parish 1795-1815 * and # MSA
Meth	Asbury. SEE: West Harford Charge Meth Epis Ch
Meth	Asbury at Jarrettsville. SEE: West Harford charge Meth Epis Ch
Meth	Bel Air. SEE: West Harford Charge Meth Epis Ch
Meth Epis	Bel Air Charge Meth Epis Ch 1869-1936 # MSA (Bel Air & Mt Zion churches)
Meth Prot	Bel Air Charge Meth Prot Ch 1861-1931 # MSA (includes Abington, Bel Air, Deer Creek, Grace Ch, Mt Carmel, Mt Tabor, Providence, Union Chapel, Yingling Chapel)
Meth	Bel Air Circuit Meth Ch 1925-1948 # MSA (prior to 1940 a Meth Prot ch; includes Grace Ch)
Meth	Belle Air. SEE: Deer Creek Charge Meth Prot Ch
Presb	Bethel Presb Ch, Madonna 1750-1940 # LDS
Epis	Brand, Rev William Francis. SEE: St Mary's Epis Ch, Emmorton
Friends	Broad Creek Preparative Meet 1871-1900 # MSA
Meth Epis	Bush Chapel. SEE: East Harford Charge Meth Epis Ch
Meth	Calvary Ch. SEE: East Harford Charge Meth Ch, East Harford Charge Meth Epis Ch, Jarrettsville Charge Meth Epis Ch, South, West Harford Charge Meth Epis Ch, South
Meth Epis	Calvary Meth Epis Ch 1880-1942 # MSA

58

Unit Meth	Calvary Unit Meth Ch 1821-1984 # MSA
Meth	Cambria Ch. SEE: Mt Nebo Charge Meth Prot Ch, Whiteford Charge Meth Ch
Meth	Centre. SEE: West Harford Charge Meth Epis Ch
Meth	Centre School House. SEE: West Harford Charge Meth Epis Ch
Prot Epis	Christ Ch 1819-1842 * and # MSA
Meth	Cokesbury. SEE: East Harford Charge Meth Ch
Meth	Cokesbury Memorial Ch, Abingdon 1784-1984 # MSA
Prot Epis	Coleman, Rev John 1779-1809 * and # MSA
Prot Epis	Colmen, Rev John 1789-1807 # LDS
Meth	Cooptown. SEE: West Harford Charge Meth Epis Ch
Prot Epis	Copley Parish. SEE: St John's Ch, Kingsville
Meth	Darlington. SEE: West Harford Charge Meth Epis Ch
Meth	Darlington Charge Meth Ch 1946-1964 # MSA (includes Darlington & Rock Run churches)
Meth Epis	Darlington Charge Meth Epis Ch 1868-1887, 1891-1944 # MSA (includes Darlington, Rock Run, Thomas Run)
Meth	Dean's Sch House. SEE: West Harford Charge Meth Epis Ch
Meth Prot	Deer Creek. SEE: Bel Air Charge Meth Prot Ch
Friends	Deer Creek 1761-1823 # MGS Bull
Meth Prot	Deer Creek Charge Meth Prot Ch 1829-1842, 1844-1866 # MSA (includes Abington, Belle Air, Deer Creek, Union Chapel, Wesley Chapel)
Presb	Deer Creek Harmony Presb Ch, Darlington 1842-1978 # LDS
Friends	Deer Creek Monthly Meet 1760-1966 # MSA
Friends	Deer Creek Monthly Meet, Orth, Darlington 1801-1949 # MSA
Meth	Deet's Sch House. SEE: West Harford Charge Meth Epis Ch
Meth	Dublin. SEE: North Harford Charge Meth Ch, North Harford Charge Meth Epis Ch, West Harford Charge Meth Epis Ch
Meth	East Harford Charge Meth Ch 1916-1967 # MSA (includes Abington, Calvary, Cokesbury churches, Smith's Chapel)
Meth Epis	East Harford Charge Meth Epis Ch 1856-1929 # MSA (includes Aberdeen, Abington, Bush, Calvary, Garrettson's, Gunpowder, Magnolia, Rock Run, Smith's)
Meth	Ebenezer. SEE: West Harford Charge Meth Epis Ch
Meth	Eden. SEE: West Harford Charge Meth Epis Ch, William Watters Memorial
Meth	Edgewood Ch. SEE: Magnolia-Edgewood Charge Meth Ch
Meth	Emory. SEE: North Harford Charge Meth Ch, North Harford Charge Meth Epis Ch
Evan Meth	Evan Meth Ch of Dublin (1953) 1953- * ch (mail address Street 21154)
Meth	Fairview Ch. SEE: Jarrettsville Charge Meth Epis Ch South, West Harford Charge Meth Epis Ch South
Meth	Fallston Charge Meth Ch 1949-1966 # MSA (includes Friendship Ch, Providence Ch, Union Chapel)
Presb	Fallston Presb Ch, 600 Fallston Rd, Box 54, Fallston 21047 (1874) 1953- * ch
Meth Prot	Fawn Grove Charge Meth Prot Ch 1920-1955 # MSA (includes St Paul's Ch)
Meth	Fellowship. SEE: West Harford Charge Meth Epis Ch
Friends	Forrest Preparative Meet 1851-1927 # MSA

Meth	Franklin. SEE: North Harford Charge Meth Epis Ch
Meth	Friendship Ch. SEE: Fallston Charge Meth Ch, West Harford Charge Meth Epis Ch
Meth Epis	Garrettson's. SEE: East Harford Charge Meth Epis Ch
Presb	Good Shepherd Presb Ch, P.O.Box 57, Joppa 21085 (1965) 1965- * ch
Meth	Grace Ch. SEE: Bel Air Charge Meth Prot Ch, Bel Air Circuit Meth Ch
Presb	Grove Presb Ch, 50 E Bel Air Ave, Aberdeen 21001 1862- * ch, 1868-1976 # MSA
Meth Epis	Gunpowder. SEE: East Harford Charge Meth Epis Ch
Friends	Gunpowder Monthly Meet 1716-1955 # MSA, 1656-1818 # MHS Mss Div
Prot Epis	Gunpowder Parish. SEE: St John's Ch, Kingsville
Friends	Gunpowder Preparative Meet, Orth 1829-1852 # MSA
Meth Epis	Harford Charge Meth Epis Ch 1889-1891 # MSA (later Bel Air Charge)
Meth	Harford Circuit 1795-1876 # MHS, 1782-1862 # LDS
Epis	Havre de Grace Parish 1809-1916 history, 1832-1858 * MDA, 1809-1813 # MSA
Unit Meth	Havre de Grace Unit Meth Ch 1849-1976 # MSA
--	Hayes, Rev Charles W 1878-1899 # MHS
Meth	Henderson. SEE: West Harford Charge Meth Epis Ch
Meth	Jarrettsville. SEE: West Harford Charge Meth Epis Ch
Meth Epis S	Jarrettsville Charge Meth Epis Ch South 1918-1940 # MSA (includes Calvary & Fairview churches)
Prot Epis	Keech, Rev John R 1819-1861 * and # MSA
Prot Epis	Larmour, Rev John Worrall 1884-1922 * and # MSA
Meth	LeGrange Furnace. SEE: West Harford Charge Meth Epis Ch
Friends	Little Falls Monthly Meet 1738-1927, 1959-1979 # MSA, 1815-? # MHS
Meth Epis	Magnolia. SEE: East Harford Charge Meth Epis Ch
Meth	Magnolia-Edgewood Charge Meth Ch 1928-1964 # MSA
Meth	McKendree Chapel. SEE: West Harford Charge Meth Epis Ch
Meth	Mt Carmel. SEE: Bel Air Charge Meth Prot Ch
Meth Prot	Mt Nebo Charge Meth Prot Ch 1893-1950 # MSA (includes Cambria Ch)
Meth	Mt Tabor. SEE: Bel Air Charge Meth Prot Ch
Meth	Mt Zion. SEE: West Harford Charge Meth Epis Ch
Meth	Mt Zion Charge Meth Ch 1948-1959 # MSA
Meth	Mt Zion Ch. SEE: Bel Air Charge Meth Epis Ch
Bap	North Harford Bap Ch, 4008 Old Federal Hill Rd, Jarrettsville 21084 (1954) 1954- * ch
Meth	North Harford Charge Meth Ch 1950-1956 # MSA (includes Dublin, Emory, Vernon congregations)
Meth Epis	North Harford Charge Meth Epis Ch 1882-1936 # MSA (includes Dublin, Emory, Franklin, Vernon congregations)
Prot Epis	Pindell, Rev A Y 1875-1876 * and # MSA
Meth	Providence Ch. SEE: Bel Air Charge Meth Prot Ch, Fallston Charge Meth Ch
Friends	Quarterly Meet for the Western Shore 1680-1951 # MSA

Meth	Rock Run Ch. SEE: Darlington Charge Meth Ch, Darlington Charge Meth Epis Ch, East Harford Charge Meth Epis Ch
Prot Epis	St George's Ch, Perryman 1681-1958 * and # MSA, 1681-1903 # MHS (Spesutia Ch)
Prot Epis	St George's Parish, Perryman 1795-1816, 1846-1851 # MSA, 1681-1952 # MHS, 1681-1850 # LDS. SEE ALSO: St John's Parish, Joppa
R Cath	St Ignatius, Hickory 1817-1981 # MSA
Prot Epis	St Jame's Parish, Baltimore. SEE: St John's Parish, Joppa
Prot Epis	St John's & St George's Parishes, Baltimore 1696-1851 # MHS, 1735-1782 # LDS
Prot Epis	St John's & St Jame's Parishes 1819-1861 * and # MSA
Prot Epis	St John's Ch, Kingsville 1696-1960 * and # MSA, 1787-1899 # MHS
Prot Epis	St John's Parish, Joppa 1796-1815 # MSA, 1789-1883 # LDS. SEE ALSO: St John's Ch, Kingsville
Epis	St Mary's Epis Ch, Emmorton 1848-1963 # MHS Mss Div (Rev William Francis Brand, rector 1848-1907)
Meth	St Paul's Ch. SEE: Fawn Grove Charge Meth Prot Ch, Whiteford Charge Meth Ch
Prot Epis	St Paul's Parish, Baltimore. SEE: St John's Parish, Joppa
Meth Epis	Smith's Chapel. SEE: East Harford Charge Meth Ch, East Harford Charge Meth Epis Ch
Unit Meth	Smith's Chapel Unit Meth Ch, 3111 Churchville Rd, Churchville 21028 (1858) 1858-1935 * ch
Prot Epis	Spesutia Ch. SEE: St George's Ch, Perryman
Meth	Thomas Run Ch. SEE: Darlington Charge Meth Epis Ch, West Harford Charge Meth Epis Ch
Meth	Tredway. SEE: West Harford Charge Meth Epis Ch
Meth	Union Chapel. SEE: Bel Air Charge Meth Prot Ch, Deer Creek Charge Meth Prot Ch, Fallston Charge Meth Ch
Unit Meth	Union Chapel Unit Meth Ch, 203 Idlewild St, Bel Air 21014 (1822) 1952- * ch
Meth	Vernon. SEE: North Harford Charge Meth Ch, North Harford Charge Meth Epis Ch, West Harford Charge Meth Epis Ch
Meth	Watters Ch. SEE: West Harford Charge Meth Epis Ch
Meth	Wesley Chapel. SEE: Deer Creek Charge Meth Prot Ch
Meth Epis	West Harford Charge Meth Epis Ch 1830-1960 # MSA (includes Asbury, Bel Air, Centre, Centre School House, Cooptown, Darlington, Dean's Sch House, Deet's Sch House, Dublin, Ebenezer, Eden, Fellowship, Friendship, Henderson, Jarrettsville. LeGrange Furnace, McKendree, Mt Zion, Thomas Run, Tredway, Vernon, Watters Ch, William Watters Memorial)
Meth Epis S	West Harford Charge Meth Epis Ch South 1866-1918 # MSA, 1866-1889 # MGS Bull (includes Calvary & Fairview churches)
Meth	Whiteford Charge Meth Ch 1950-1957 # MSA (includes Cambria Ch, St Paul's Ch)
Meth	William Watters Memorial (formerly Eden). SEE: West Harford Charge Meth Epis Ch
Meth	Yingling Chapel. SEE: Bel Air Charge Meth Prot Ch

Prot Epis	All Saints Chapel, Annapolis Junction. SEE: Grace Ch, Elkridge
Meth	Ballou Springs. SEE: Melville Chapel Unit Meth Ch
Meth Epis	Browns Chapel. SEE: Howard Circuit or Howard Charge
Luth	Calvary Luth Ch, 16151 Old Frederick Rd, P.O.Box 215, Woodbine 21797 (1899) 1899- * ch (ch on Newport Hill dedicated Oct. 1890, joined with St Paul's & Messiah to form Freedom Charge, destroyed by fire 1904, rebuilt in Woodbine; in 1915 St Paul's Ch went out of business, the parish which included Calvary & Messiah was named Woodbine; in 1967 parish dissolved and each ch stood separately; in Nov. 1984 ch moved to Old Frederick Rd)
Prot Epis	Christ Ch nr Guilford 1712-1939 * MDA # MSA, 1711-1857 # MHS LDS
Epis	Christ Epis Ch, 6800 Oakland Mills Rd, Columbia 21045 1720s-1880s * MDA, 1880s- * ch, 1711-1880s # MHS (was a Chapel of Ease of St Anne's Parish, Anne Arundel Co, in 1727 called Queen Caroline Parish Ch, in 1811 named Christ Ch; also known as Old Brick Ch)
Presb	Christ Memorial Presb Ch, 6410 Amherst Ave, Columbia 21046 (1960) 1959- * ch
Meth Epis S	Concord. SEE Freedom Circuit
Meth	Elkridge Circuit. SEE: Melville Chapel Unit Meth Ch
Friends	Elkridge Preparative Meet 1795-1800 # MSA
Unit Meth	Elkridge Unit Meth Charge, 6166 Lawyers Hill Rd, Balto 21227 (1772) * ch (Melville Chapel Unit Meth Ch; dates of records not given)
Meth	Emory Chapel. SEE: Emory Unit Meth Ch
Unit Meth	Emory Unit Meth Ch, 3810 Church Rd, Ellicott City 21043 (1837) 1859- * ch (name changes: Emory Meth Epis Ch 1837-1939, Emory Meth Ch 1939-1969, Emory Unit Meth Ch 1969-; records include Emory chapel, Patapsco Station)
Evan Luth	Evan Luth St Johanne's Ch, Pfeiffer's Corner. SEE: St John Evan Luth Ch, 6004 Waterloo Rd, Columbia 21945
Naz	First Ch of the Nazarene, 8801 Rogers Ave, Ellicott City 21043. 1938- * ch (organized in 1910 in Balto, moved to Howard Co in 1974)
Evan Luth	First Evan Luth Ch, 3604 Chatham Rd, Ellicott City 21034 (1875) 1883- * ch, 1883-1974 # MSA (originally known as First Ger Evan Luth Ch located on Church Rd, changed name in 1915, moved to Chatham & Frederick Rds in 1956)
Evan Luth	First Ger Evan Luth Ch. SEE: First Luth Ch of Ellicott City
Luth	First Luth Ch of Ellicott City 1883-1979 # MSA (incorporated 1875 as First Ger Evan Luth Ch of Ellicott City, a daughter ch of Salem Luth Ch in Catonsville)
Presb	First Presb Ch of Howard Co, 9325 Old Annapolis Rd, Columbia 21045 (1839) 1833- * ch
Meth Epis S	Freedom Circuit 1876-1925, 1940 # MSA (includes Concord (1884), Harmony (1866), Linden (1866), Lisbon (1877), Mt Zion (1894), Pindells (1866), Providence (1888?)
Unit Meth	Glen Mar Unit Meth Ch, 8430 Glen Mar Rd, Ellicott City 21043 (1955) 1955- * ch

Unit Meth	Glenelg Unit Meth Ch, 13900 Burnt Woods Rd, Glenelg 21737 (1859) 1961- * ch (began as Westwood Chapel Meth Epis Ch)
Prot Epis	Grace Ch, 6725 Montgomery Rd, Elkridge 21227. 1840- * ch, 1845-1973 # MSA MHS (includes service record for All Saints Chapel, Annapolis Junction 1904-1927; also known as Grace Prot Epis Ch, St John's Mission, Relay)
Meth	Green Mount. SEE: Melville Chapel Unit Meth Ch
Meth	Guilford. SEE: Melville Chapel Unit Meth Ch
Meth	Harmony. SEE: Freedom Circuit; Mt Zion Unit Meth Ch, 12367 Rt 216, P.O.Box 44, Highland 20777
Meth	Harmony Charge 1925-1940 * St James Unit Meth Ch, 12450 Rt 99, West Friendship 21794
Presb	Harmony Presb Ch, Lisbon (1843) (records prior to 1914 destroyed by fire; no records kept since then)
Meth Prot	Howard Chapel (1859-1936) SEE: Lisbon Circuit Meth Prot Ch
Meth Epis	Howard Circuit or Howard Charge 1876-1886, 1896-1954 # MSA (includes Browns Chapel, Mt Zion Ch, Pine Orchard Ch, West Liberty Ch)
Meth Prot	Jennings Chapel (1868-1936) SEE: Lisbon Circuit Meth Prot Ch, Poplar Springs Charge Meth Prot Ch
Bap	Liberty Bap Ch, Lisbon 21765 (1942) 1942- * ch
Meth	Liberty Circuit 1866-1886 * St James Unit Meth Ch, 12450 Rt 99, West Friendship 21794
Meth	Linden: SEE: Mt Zion Unit Meth Ch
Unit Meth	Linden-Linthicum Unit Meth Ch, Box 63, Clarksville 21029 1849- * ch (two churches merged in 1959, they had both organized bet 1800-1829)
Meth	Linden Meth Ch, Dayton (1866) 1899-1925 * Mt Zion Unit Meth Ch, 12367 Rt 216, Highland 21777. SEE ALSO: Freedom Circuit
Meth Prot	Linden Meth Prot Ch, Dayton (1866) 1835- * Linden-Linthicum Unit Meth Ch, 12175 Rt 108, P.O.Box 63, Clarksville 21029
Meth Epis S	Lisbon. SEE: Freedom Circuit
Meth Prot	Lisbon. SEE: Poplar Springs Charge Meth Prot Ch
Meth Prot	Lisbon Circuit Meth Prot Ch 1886-1936 # MSA (includes Howard Chapel, Jennings Chapel, Poplar Springs Ch, Ridgeville, Union Chapel)
Meth	Lisbon Meth Ch 1868-1943 * St James Unit Meth Ch, 12450 Rt 99, West Friendship 21794
Meth	Locust. SEE: Melville Chapel Unit Meth Ch
Unit Meth	Locust Unit Meth Ch, Martin (Guilford) & Freetown Rds, Columbia 21044 (1869) 1948- * ch (mail address: P.O. Box 248, Simpsonville 21150; a black ch)
Meth	McKendree Meth Ch 1868-1954 * St James Unit Meth Ch, 12450 Rt 99, West Friendship 21794
Unit Meth	Melville Chapel Unit Meth Ch, 5660 Furnace Ave, Elkridge 21227 (1772) 1860-1960 * ch (includes Ballou Springs, Elkridge, Elkridge Circuit, Green Mount, Guilford, Locust, Orange Grove, Patapsco, Savage, Thistle, Timber Ridge; formerly Meth Epis; merged with Evan Unit Breth in 1968 & changed name to Unit Meth) SEE ALSO: Elkridge Unit Meth Charge, 6166 Lawyers Hill Rd, Baltimore 21227

Prot Epis	Mt Calvary Ch, Glenwood 1842-1940 * MDA, 1842-1923, 1936, 1940 # MSA
Presb	Mt Hebron Presb Ch, 2330 Mt Hebron Dr, Ellicott City 21043 (1961) 1960- * ch
Meth Epis S	Mt Zion. SEE: Freedom Circuit
Meth Epis	Mt Zion Ch. SEE: Howard Circuit or Howard Charge
Meth	Mt Zion Unit Meth Ch, 12367 Rt 216, P.O.Box 44, Highland 20777 (1888) 1899- * ch (includes Harmony, Linden, Mt Zion, Providence; many of this congregation came from Pindell's Sch House (1866))
Meth	Orange Grove. SEE: Melville Chapel Unit Meth Ch
Meth	Patapsco. SEE: Melville Chapel Unit Meth Ch
Meth	Patapsco Circuit 1862-1904 minutes * St James Unit Meth Ch, 12450 Rt 99, West Friendship 21794, 1893-1923 # MSA
Meth	Patapsco Station. SEE: Emory Unit Meth Ch
Meth	Pindell's Sch House. SEE: Freedom Circuit; Mt Zion Unit Meth Ch, 12367 Rt 216, P.O.Box 44, Highland 20777
Meth Epis	Pine Orchard Ch. SEE: Howard Circuit or Howard Charge
Meth Prot	Poplar Springs Charge Meth Prot Ch 1878-1969 (includes Jennings Chapel, Lisbon, Poplar Springs, Union Chapel)
Meth Prot	Poplar Springs Ch (1871-1936) SEE: Lisbon Circuit Meth Prot Ch, Poplar Springs Charge Meth Prot Ch
Meth Epis S	Providence Ch, Triadelphia & Sharp Rds (1889) 1899-1925 * Mt Zion Unit Meth Ch, 12367 Rt 216, Highland 21777, 1925- * Glenelg Unit Meth Ch, 13900 Burnt Woods Rd, Glenelg 21737 (Providence Ch & Westwood Ch merged in 1962 to form Glenelg Meth Ch) SEE ALSO: Freedom Circuit
Meth	Providence Meth Ch 1868-1951 * St James Unit Meth Ch, 12450 Rt 99, West Friendship 21794
Epis	Queen Caroline Parish 1771, 1855-1864 * MDA. SEE ALSO: St John's Ch, Kingsville, Balto & Harford counties
Meth Prot	Ridgeville. SEE: Lisbon Circuit Meth Prot Ch
Unit Meth	Rockland Unit Meth Ch, 8971 Chapel Ave, Ellicott City 21043 1901- * ch (by merger with Trinity Evan Unit Breth Ch of Rockland)
Bap	Rolling Hills Bap Ch, 11510 Johns Hopkins Rd, Clarksville 21029 (1969) 1969- * ch
Prot Epis	St Alban's Chapel, Alberton 1894-1918 * MDA # MSA
Cath	St Augustine, 5976 Old Washington Rd, Elkridge 21227 (1844) 1844- * ch, 1844-1981 # MSA
Prot Epis	St Barnabas Ch, Sykesville 1843-1954 # MSA
Unit Meth	St James Unit Meth Ch, 12450 Rt 99, West Friendship 21794 (1792) 1868- * ch
Evan Luth	St John Evan Luth Ch, 6004 Waterloo Rd, Columbia 21945 (1897) 1896- * ch (Evan Luth St Johanne's Ch, Pfeiffer's Corner)
Luth	St John Luth Ch of Wilde Lake, Wilde Lake Interfaith Center, 10431 Twin Rivers Rd, Columbia 21044 (1970) 1970- * ch
R Cath	St John the Evangelist, Columbia 1967-1984 # MSA
Epis	St John's, 9120 Frederick Rd, Ellicott City 21043 1834- * ch, 1834-1957 # MSA
Prot Epis	St Johns Mission, Relay. SEE: Grace Ch, Elkridge

Howard County

R Cath	St Louis Ch, Clarksville 1856-1981 # MSA (includes St Louis Parish, St Mary Chapel, Doughoregan Manor)
R Cath	St Louis Parish. SEE: St Louis Ch, Clarksville
Epis	St Mark's, Hall Shop Rd & Rt 216, Highland 20777. 1859- * ch, 1872-1898 # MSA
R Cath	St Mary Chapel, Doughoregan Manor. SEE: St Louis Ch, Clarksville
R Cath	St Paul's, 3755 St Paul St, Ellicott City 21043 (1838) 1838- * ch, 1838-1981 # MSA
Epis	St Paul's Epis Ch, 16457 Old Frederick Rd, Poplar Springs 21771 (1883) 1953- * ch, prior to 1953 * Grace Epis Ch, New Market, or St James Epis Ch, Mt Airy
Evan Luth	St Paul's Evan Luth Ch, Fulton 1870-? # MHS
Luth	St Paul's Luth Ch, 11795 Rt 216, Fulton 20759 (1870) 1870- * ch (formerly Evan Ref & Luth Ch of Howard Co, St Paul Evan Luth Ch)
Meth	Savage. SEE: Melville Chapel Unit Meth Ch
Luth	Shepherd of the Glen Luth Ch, 14551 Burnt Woods Rd, Glenwood 21738 (1980) 1980- * ch
Meth	Thistle. SEE: Melville Chapel Unit Meth Ch
Meth	Timber Ridge. SEE: Melville Chapel Unit Meth Ch
Prot Epis	Trinity Ch, 2 mi n of Waterloo 1866-1909 # MSA
Meth	Trinity Evan Unit Breth Ch of Rockland. SEE: Rockland Unit Meth Ch
Meth	Union Chapel 1849-1892 * Linden-Linthicum Unit Meth Ch, 12175 Rt 108, P.O.Box 63, Clarksville 21029. SEE ALSO: Lisbon Circuit Meth Prot Ch, Poplar Springs Charge Meth Prot Ch
Bap	Unity Bap Ch, 7204 Montgomery Rd, Elkridge 21227 (1915) 1960's- * ch (records destroyed in 1972 flood)
Meth Epis	West Liberty Ch. SEE: Howard Circuit or Howard Charge
Unit Meth	West Liberty Unit Meth Ch, Sand Hill Rd, Marriottsville 21104 (1880) 1957- * ch, some early records * LL
Meth Epis	Westwood Chapel Meth Epis Ch, Triadelphia Rd (1859) 1894-1961 * Glenelg Unit Meth Ch, 13900 Burnt Woods Rd, Glenelg 21737 (Westwood Ch & Providence Ch merged in 1962 to form Glenelg Meth Ch)
Meth	Westwood Meth 1943-1951 * St James Unit Meth Ch, 12450 Rt 99, West Friendship 21794

Kent County

Meth	Asbury Ch. SEE: Millington Charge Meth Epis Ch
Meth	Bellair. SEE: Kent Circuit Meth Epis Ch
R Cath	Bohemia Parish. 1789-1882 # MSA
Friends	Cecil Monthly Meet 1698-1913 # MHS LDS
Meth Prot	Chesapeake Circuit Meth Prot Ch 1866-1955 # MSA (includes Kesley, Raum & Wesley Chapels)
Epis	Chester Parish 1766-1867 * MDA, 1766-1897 # MHS
Meth	Chestertown. SEE: Kent Circuit Meth Epis Ch

65

Kent County

Meth Epis	Chestertown Sta Meth Epis Ch 1869-1918 # MSA
Meth Epis S	Chesterville. SEE: Kent Circuit Meth Epis Ch, South
Prot Epis	Christ Ch, Worton (1765) 1861-1957 # MSA (includes St John's by the Bay, Betterton)
Meth	Christ Meth Ch, Chestertown 1941-1952 # MSA
Meth Prot	Christ Meth Prot Ch, Chestertown 1858-1965 # MSA
Meth Epis	Cross Roads. SEE: Kent Circuit Meth Epis Ch
Prot Epis	Emmanuel Ch, Chestertown 1766-1970 * and # MSA
Meth	First Meth Ch, Chestertown 1952-1969 # MSA
Unit Meth	First Unit Meth Ch, P.O.Box 227, Chestertown 21620 (1780) * ch (dates not given)
Meth Epis	Galena Circuit Meth Epis Ch 1871-1902 # MSA
Meth Epis	Georgetown. SEE: Kent Circuit Meth Epis Ch
Meth Epis	Harmony. SEE: Kent Circuit Meth Epis Ch
Meth Epis	Holdens. SEE: Kent Circuit Meth Epis Ch
Prot Epis	Holy Cross Ch, Millington. SEE: St Clement's Ch, Massey
Meth Epis	Hynsons. SEE: Kent Circuit Meth Epis Ch
Meth Epis	I U. SEE: Kent Circuit Meth Epis Ch
Meth	Kennedyville. SEE: Kent Circuit Meth Prot Ch
Meth Epis	Kent Circuit 1853-1869 # MHS LDS
Meth Epis	Kent Circuit Meth Epis Ch 1833-1898 # MSA, 1853-1869 # MHS (includes Bellair, Chestertown, Cross Roads, Georgetown, Harmony, Holdens, Hynsons, I U, Millington, New Market, Olivet, Piney Neck, Quaker Neck, Rock Hall, St John's, Salem, Still Pond, Union, Urievlle, Walton Chapel, Worton)
Meth Epis S	Kent Circuit Meth Epis Ch, South (1867) 1867-1890, 1933-1937 # MSA (includes Chesterville, called Emmanuel & Millington)
Meth Prot	Kent Circuit Meth Prot Ch 1856-1934 # MSA (includes Kennedyville, Waters Chapel)
Meth	Kesley Chapel. SEE: Chesapeake Circuit Meth Prot Ch
Meth	Millington. SEE: Kent Circuit Meth Epis Ch; Kent Circuit Meth Epis Ch, South; Millington-Pondtown Charge Unit Meth Ch
Meth Epis	Millington Charge Meth Epis Ch 1855-?, 1918-1960 # MSA (includes Asbury, Millington)
Meth Epis	Millington Circuit Meth Epis Ch 1859-1870 # MSA
Meth	Millington-Pondtown Charge Meth Ch 1944-1947, 1960 # MSA
Unit Meth	Millington-Pondtown Charge Unit Meth Ch 1958-1969 # MSA (includes Millington, Pondtown)
Meth Epis	New Market. SEE: Kent Circuit Meth Epis Ch
Meth	Olivet. SEE: Kent Circuit Meth Epis Ch
Meth Epis	Piney Neck Meth Epis Ch 1892-1952 # MSA. SEE ALSO: Kent Circuit Meth Epis Ch
Meth	Pondtown. SEE: Millington-Pondtown Charge Unit Meth Ch
Meth	Quaker Neck. SEE: Kent Circuit Meth Epis Ch
Meth	Raum Chapel. SEE: Chesapeake Circuit Meth Prot Ch, Wesley Chapel Meth Prot Charge
Meth Epis	Rock Hall. SEE: Kent Circuit Meth Epis Ch
Meth	Rock Hall Charge Meth Ch 1953-1977 # MSA (includes Wesley Chapel)
Unit Meth	Rock Hall Charge Unit Meth Ch 1956-1978 # MSA (includes Wesley Chapel)
Meth Epis	Rock Hall Meth Epis Ch 1902-1968 # MSA

66

Kent County

Prot Epis	St Clement's Ch, Massey (1748) 1856-1859, 1874-1957 # MSA (originated as Shrewsbury Chapel in Shrewsbury Parish; consecrated as St Clement's Ch in North Kent Parish 1855; includes Holy Cross Ch, Millington)
Meth Epis	St John's. SEE: Kent Circuit Meth Epis Ch
Prot Epis	St John's by the Bay, Betterton. SEE: Christ Ch, Worton
Prot Epis	St Paul's Ch, Fairlee 1679-1956 * and # MSA
Prot Epis	St Paul's Parish 1650-1818 # MHS LDS
Meth Epis	Salem. SEE: Kent Circuit Meth Epis Ch
Prot Epis	Shrewsbury Chapel. SEE: St Clement's Ch, Massey
Prot Epis	Shrewsbury Parish 1692-1882 # LDS
Prot Epis	Shrewsbury Prot Epis Ch, Kennedyville (prior to 1691) 1699-1945 * and # MSA, 1701-1882 # MHS
Friends	Southern Quarterly Meet 1755-1893 # MSA
Meth Epis	Still Pond Meth Epis Ch 1772-1912 history & directory # MSA. SEE ALSO: Kent Circuit Meth Epis Ch
Meth Epis	Thomas Chapel Meth Epis Ch 1867-1879 # MSA
Meth Epis	Union. SEE: Kent Circuit Meth Epis Ch
Meth Epis	Urieville. SEE: Kent Circuit Meth Epis Ch
Meth Epis	Walton Chapel at Quaker Neck & Piney Neck. SEE: Kent Circuit Meth Epis Ch
Meth	Waters Chapel. SEE: Kent Circuit Meth Prot Ch
Meth	Wesley Chapel. SEE: Chesapeake Circuit Meth Prot Ch, Rock Hall Charge Meth Ch, Rock Hall Charge Unit Meth Ch
Meth	Wesley Chapel Meth Ch 1941-1972 # MSA
Meth Prot	Wesley Chapel Meth Prot Charge 1919-1975 # MSA (includes Raum Chapel)
Unit Meth	Wesley Chapel Unit Meth Ch 1978 Heritage of Faith # MSA
Meth Prot	Wesleyan Chapel Meth Prot Ch 1829-1962 # MSA
Meth	Worton. SEE: Kent Circuit Meth Epis Ch

Montgomery County

Prot Epis	Allen, Rev Ethan 1797-1879 articles # MHS Mss Div (notes on St John's Parish, Prince George's Co.; Prince George's Parish, Montgomery Co.; All Saints' Parish & St Mark's, Frederick Co., 1792; Washington & Allegany Co parishes 1777-1806)
Prot Epis	Ascension Chapel, Gaithersburg. SEE: Christ Ch, Rockville; Church of the Ascension, 202 S Summit Ave, Gaithersburg 20879
Friends	Ashton Monthly Meet, Orth 1887-1950 # MSA
Unit Meth	Ashton Unit Meth Ch, 801 Tucker Ln, Ashton 20861 (1865) 1947- * ch (on Spencerville Circuit until 1948)
Meth	Barnesville. SEE: Montgomery Circuit Meth Epis Ch
Meth	Beltsville. SEE: Emmanuel Unit Meth Ch
Meth	Bennett's Creek. SEE: Montgomery Circuit Meth Epis Ch
Meth	Bethesda nr Browningsville. SEE: Montgomery Circuit Meth Epis Ch

Disc	Bethesda Chris Ch, 6050 Wisconsin Ave, Chevy Chase 20815. 1940- * ch, # Disc HS
Meth Epis S	Bethesda Meth Ch 1916-1941 # MSA
Friends	Bethesda Monthly & Preparative Meet 1962-1979 # MSA
Presb	Bethesda Presb Ch # LDS (dates not given)
Presb	Bethesda-Rockville Presb Ch 1818-1962 # MSA (includes Bethesda, Cabin John, Rockville; originally on Cedar Ln, including cemetery, on Rock Pike)
Unit Meth	Bethesda Unit Meth Ch, 8300 Old Georgetown Rd, Bethesda 20817 (1916) 1916- * ch (in 1922 called Central Meth Ch on St Elmo Ave, in 1949 moved to Huntington Pkwy & Old Georgetown Rd)
Presb	Boyds Presb Ch, 19901 White Ground Rd, Boyds 20841 (1876) 1931- * ch
Meth	Branchville (later named North Ch) SEE: Emmanuel Unit Meth Ch
Presb	Cabin John. SEE: Bethesda-Rockville Presb Ch
Meth	Cedar Grove (later became Salem) SEE: Montgomery Circuit Meth Epis Ch
Meth	Chapel. SEE: Montgomery Circuit Meth Epis Ch
Unit Meth	Chevy Chase Unit Meth Ch, 7001 Connecticut Ave, Chevy Chase 20815. 1912- * ch
Prot Epis	Christ Ch, Rockville 1711-1845 * and # MSA (includes Ascension Chapel, Gaithersburg)
LDS	Ch of Jesus Christ of Latter-Day Saints, Washington Temple, 9900 Stoneybrook Dr, Kensington 20895-3199 * and # LDS, 50 E North Temple, Salt Lake City UT 84150
Cath	Ch of St Mary, 520 Veirs Mill Rd, Rockville 20852. 1814- * ch, # MCHS
Epis	Ch of the Ascension, 202 S Summit Ave, Gaithersburg 20879. 1885- * ch (known as Ascension Chapel to 1965)
Meth	Clarksburg. SEE: Montgomery Circuit Meth Epis Ch
Meth	Colesville. SEE: Emmanuel Unit Meth Ch
Unit Meth	Colesville Unit Meth Ch, Colesville 20904. SEE: Marvin Memorial Unit Meth Ch, 33 University Blvd E, Silver Spring 20901
Unit Meth	Concord-St Andrews Unit Meth Ch, River & Goldsboro Rds, Bethesda 20817. 1819- * ch
Meth	Damascus (formerly known as Mt Lebanon) SEE: Montgomery Circuit Meth Epis Ch
Unit Meth	Damascus Unit Meth Ch, Church St, Damascus 20872. 1822-1890 * Bethesda Unit Meth Ch, 1890-1921 * Laytonsville Meth Ch, 1921- * ch, 1922-1890 # MSA
Meth	Darnestown. SEE: Montgomery Circuit Meth Epis Ch
Unit Meth	Emmanuel Unit Meth Ch, 11416 Cedar Ln, Beltsville 20705. 1886-1961 # MSA (prior to 1893 called Worthington Chapel; includes Beltsville, Branchville, Colesville, Four Corners, Lay Hill)
Unit Meth	Epworth Unit Meth Ch, 9008 Rosemont Dr, Gaithersburg 20877. 1890- * ch
Unit Meth	Fairhaven Unit Meth Ch, 224 Cedar Ave, Gaithersburg 20877. 1965- * ch

Friends	Fairhill Boarding Sch 1815-1927, 1949-1976 # MSA (Balto Yearly Meet--Hicksite)
Chris Sci	First Ch of Christ Sci, 7901 Connecticut Ave, Chevy Chase 20815 (no records kept)
Ch of God	First Ch of God, 1011 Maple Ave, Rockville 20851 (1916) no records kept (originally on Montgomery Ave, purchased land on Maple Ave in 1949, at that time ch was known as Rockville Com Ch of God, moved to Maple Ave in 1960)
Unit Meth	First Unit Meth Ch, Hyattsville. SEE: Marvin Memorial Unit Meth Ch, 33 University Blvd E, Silver Spring 20901
Breth	Flower Hill Ch of the Breth, 7412 Muncaster Mill Rd, Gaithersburg 20877. 1930- * ch
Meth	Four Corners Meth Ch. SEE: Emmanuel Unit Meth Ch, Marvin Memorial Unit Meth Ch, 33 University Blvd E, Silver Spring 20901
Presb	Fourth Presb Ch, 5500 River Rd, Bethesda 20816 (1828) 1828- * ch
Meth Epis S	Francis Asbury Meth Epis Ch, South. SEE: Francis Asbury Unit Meth Ch
Unit Meth	Francis Asbury Unit Meth Ch, 2181 Balto Rd, Rockville 20851. 1972- * ch (stems from congregation on 16th St SW, founded 1909; from Twinbrook Meth Ch organized in 1959 at Meadow Hall Sch, later name changed to St Mark's Meth Ch; in 1962 present sanctuary completed; in 1968 Francis Asbury Ch, downtown, & St Mark's (Twinbrook) Ch merged)
Unit Presb	Geneva Unit Presb Ch, 11931 Seven Locks Rd, Rockville 20854 (1964) 1964- * ch
Bap	Georgia Avenue Bap Ch, 12525 Georgia Ave, Wheaton 20906 (1951) 1951- * ch (associated ch: Olney Bap Chapel)
Unit Meth	Glenmont Unit Meth Ch, 2801 Weller Rd, Wheaton 20906 (1957) 1957- * ch
Meth	Grace Meth Ch, Takoma Park 1944-1969 # MSA
Unit Meth	Grace Unit Meth Ch, 119 N Frederick Ave, Gaithersburg 20877. 1865- * ch
Disc	Heritage Chris Ch, 15250 New Hampshire Ave, Silver Spring 20904 (1964) 1964- * ch (the old Ninth Street Chris Ch in DC was the parent ch)
Friends	Hopewell Monthly & Preparative Meet, Orth 1828-1934 # MSA
Meth	Hyattstown. SEE: Montgomery Circuit Meth Epis Ch
Inter	Inter Ch of God, 14 Brookes Ave, Gaithersburg 20877 * ch (dates not given)
Orth Presb	Knox Orth Presb Ch, Granville Dr & Sutherland Rd, Silver Spring 20901 (1936) 1936-1950 * William Campbell, 9924 Markham St, Silver Spring 20901; 1950- * Dr Leonard Miller, 4310 Puller Dr, Kensington 20895 (originally called Knox Presb Ch of Amer, 1000 block of Vermont Ave NW, Washington DC, name changed (date unknown), moved to Sutherland & Forest Glen Rds 1943, to Granville Dr 1950)
Presb	Knox Presb Ch of Amer. SEE: Knox Orth Presb Ch
Meth	Lay Hill. SEE: Emmanuel Unit Meth Ch
Meth Epis S	Lay Hill Meth Epis Ch, South (1886) SEE: Oak Chapel Unit Meth Ch, 14503 Argyle Club Rd, Silver Spring 20906

Meth Epis	Laytonsville Charge Meth Epis Ch 1866-1950 # MSA
Meth	Laytonsville Meth Ch. SEE: Damascus Unit Meth Ch, Church St, Damascus 20872
Unit Meth	Liberty Grove Unit Meth Ch, 15118 Liberty Grove Dr, Burtonsville 20866. 1887- * ch (1859 Spencerville Circuit, 1863 Liberty Grove)
Epis S	Marvin Epis Ch, South. SEE: Marvin Memorial Unit Meth Ch, 33 University Blvd E, Silver Spring 20901
Unit Meth	Marvin Memorial Unit Meth Ch, 33 University Blvd E, Silver Spring 20901 (1872) 1872-1904 * First Unit Meth Ch, Hyattsville; 1904-1941 * Colesville Unit Meth Ch, C'lesville; 1893-1941 * Marvin Epis Ch, South, now Marvin Memorial Unit Meth Ch; 1945- * ch (began as Wesley Chapel Meth Epis Ch, South, at Four Corners, Silver Spring; became known as Four Corners Meth Ch)
Unit Meth	Memorial Unit Meth Ch, 9226 Colesville Rd, Silver Spring 20910 (1890) 1900- * ch (began on N Capitol & R Sts, Washington DC; in 1946 became known as Memorial Evan Unit Breth Ch; moved to Silver Spring in 1958)
Unit Meth	Mill Creek Unit Meth Ch, 17825 Cliffbourne Ln, Rockville 20855 (1968) 1968- * ch
Meth Epis	Montgomery Circuit Meth Epis Ch 1856-1874, 1879-1910 # MSA (includes Barnesville, Bennett's Creek, Bethesda nr Browningsville, Cedar Grove, Chapel, Clarksburg, Darnestown, Hyattstown, Mt Lebanon, Pleasant Plains, Poolesville, Sugar Loaf Mountain; Cedar Grove later became Salem, Mt Lebanon became Damascus)
Unit Meth	Montgomery Unit Meth Ch, 28325 Kemptown Rd, Damascus 20872. 1893- * ch
Meth	Mt Lebanon (became Damascus) SEE: Montgomery Circuit Meth Epis Ch
Presb	Neelsville Presb Ch, 20701 Frederick Rd, Germantown 20767 (1845) 1845- * ch
Unit Meth	Oak Chapel Unit Meth Ch, 14503 Argyle Club Rd, Silver Spring 20906 (1886) 1940- * ch (originally called Lay Hill Meth Epis Ch, South, changed name in 1967)
Bap	Olney Bap Chapel. SEE: Georgia Avenue Bap Ch, 12525 Georgia Ave, Wheaton 20906
Cath	Our Lady of Lourdes, 7500 Pearl St, Bethesda 20814. 1926- * ch
Meth	Pleasant Plains. SEE: Montgomery Circuit Meth Epis Ch
Meth	Poolesville. SEE: Montgomery Circuit Meth Epis Ch
Presb	Poolesville Presb Ch, Box 68, Poolesville 20837. 1962- * ch (early records have been lost)
Presb	Potomac Presb Ch, 10301 River Rd, Potomac 20854 (1963) 1963- * ch
Unit Meth	Potomac Unit Meth Ch, 9908 S Glen Rd, Potomac 20854 * ch (dates not given)
Prot Epis	Prince George's Parish 1719-1845 # MHS, 1711-1845 (includes Rock Creek Parish) # DAR, 1792-1845 # LDS
Luth	Resurrection Luth Ch, 3101 University Blvd W, Kensington 20895 (1951) 1951- * ch

Epis	Rock Creek Parish. SEE: Prince George's Parish
Prot	Rockville Chris Ch, 301 Adclare Rd, Rockville 20850. 1878 * ch
Presb	Rockville Presb Ch, 215 W Montgomery Ave, Rockville 20850 * ch (dates not given). SEE ALSO: Bethesda-Rockville Presb Ch
Epis	St John's Ch, Norwood Parish, 6701 Wisconsin Ave, Chevy Chase 20815. 1895- * ch
Epis	St John's Epis Ch, 3427 Olney-Laytonsville Rd, Olney 20832. 1910- * ch (1842-1909 records were burned in rectory fire)
Evan Luth	St Luke Evan Luth Ch, 9100 Colesville Rd, Silver Spring 20904. 1940- * ch
Luth	St Luke Luth Ch, 17740 Muncaster Rd, Derwood 20855. 1901- * ch
Meth	St Marks Meth Ch. SEE: Francis Asbury Unit Meth Ch
R Cath	St Martin's, 201 S Frederick Ave, Gaithersburg 20877 (1920) 1920- * ch
Unit Meth	St Paul Unit Meth Ch, 21720 Laytonsville Rd, Laytonsville 20879. 1890- * ch
Meth	St Paul's Meth Ch, Laytonsville 1944-1964 # MSA
R Cath	St Peter's, 2900 Sandy Spring Rd, Olney 20832 (1898) 1938- * ch
Prot Epis	St Peter's Ch, Poolesville 1799-1966 # MSA, 1799-1830 # WMG
Epis	St Peter's Parish, P.O.Box 387, 20100 Fisher Ave, Poolesville 20837. 1790s- * ch, 1797-1854 # MHS, MHS Mss Div, 1822-1854 # LDS
Cath	St Rose of Lima Cath Ch, 11811 Clopper Rd, Gaithersburg 20760 (1884) * ch (dates not given)
Meth	Salem (formerly known as Cedar Grove) SEE: Montgomery Circuit Meth Epis Ch
Friends	Sandy Spring Monthly Meet, Sandy Spring 20860. 1730-?, 1824-1985 * Haverford, Swarthmore, 1736-1979 # MSA
Meth	Spencerville Circuit. SEE: Ashton Unit Meth Ch, 801 Tucker Ln, Ashton 20861, Liberty Grove Unit Meth Ch, 15118 Liberty Grove Dr, Burtonsville 20866
Meth	Sugar Loaf Mountain. SEE: Montgomery Circuit Meth Epis Ch
Meth	Twinbrook Meth Ch (1959) SEE: Francis Asbury Unit Meth Ch
Unit Meth	Washington Grove Unit Meth Ch, 305 Chestnut Rd, P.O.Box 115, Washington Grove 20880. 1911- * ch
Meth Epis S	Wesley Chapel Meth Epis Ch, South, Four Corners, Silver Spring. SEE: Marvin Memorial Unit Meth Ch, 33 University Blvd E, Silver Spring 20901
Unit Meth	Woodside Unit Meth Ch, 8900 Georgia Ave, Silver Spring 20910. 1899- * ch
Meth	Worthington Chapel. SEE: Emmanuel Unit Meth Ch, 11416 Cedar Ln, Beltsville 20705

Epis   Accokeek Ch   1824-1843, 1863-1876 # DAR   (originated as Chapel
                of Ease built by parishoners of Piscataway Parish) SEE
                ALSO: St Johns Parish or Piscataway Parish
Prot Epis   Addison Parish 1919-1974 # MSA
Prot Epis   Allen, Rev Ethan 1797-1879 articles # MHS Mss Div (includes
                notes on St John's Parish, Prince Georges Co; Prince Georges
                Parish, Montgomery Co; All Saints Parish & St Marks,
                Frederick Co, 1792; Washington & Allegany Co parishes
                1777-1806)
Unit Meth   Bell's Unit Meth Ch, 6016 Allentown Rd, Camp Springs 20031
                (1813) 1876-1913 * Forestville Charge Meth Epis Ch (name
                also spelled Beall's, Beale's; known as Tolson's Camp Ground
                Meet; was on Bladensburg Circuit 1842-1862)
Meth   Beltsville. SEE: Emmanuel Unit Meth Ch, 11416 Cedar Ln,
                Beltsville 20705
Presb   Berwyn Presb Ch, 6301 Greenbelt Rd, College Park 20740 (1914)
                1942- * ch
Meth Epis S   Bladensburg Charge Meth Epis Ch, South 1867-1883 # MSA
                (prior to 1861 a Meth Epis ch; includes Bladensburg, Emory
                Chapel, Forest Grove, McKendree Ch, Scagg's Chapel, Upper
                Marlborough, Whitfield Ch) SEE ALSO: Forest Grove Charge
                Meth Epis Ch, South
Meth   Bladensburg Circuit 1867-1883 # MSA
Meth Epis, S   Bladensburg-Emory Charge Meth Epis Ch, South 1883-1896
                (includes Colesville, Four Corners, Hyattsville, Lay Hill,
                Piney Grove)
Cath   Boone's Cath Chapel, Van Brady Rd, Rosaryville (1735-1844?)
                (replaced by Church of the Holy Rosary)
Meth   Bowie Sta Meth Epis Ch (1880) (now Bowie Unit Meth Ch, 6th
                St, Bowie 20715) SEE: Lanham Unit Meth Ch, 5512 Whitfield
                Chapel Rd, Lanham 20754
Meth   Bradbury Heights Ch. SEE: Forestville Charge Meth Ch,
                Forestville Charge Meth Epis Ch
Meth   Branchville. SEE: Emmanuel Unit Meth Ch, 11416 Cedar Ln,
                Beltsville 20705
Meth   Brentwood. SEE: Hyattsville Charge Meth Epis Ch, South
Prot Epis   Broad Creek Ch. SEE: St John's Ch, Broad Creek
Bap   Broadview Bap Ch, 5757 Temple Hills Rd, Temple Hills 20748
                (1960) 1960- * ch
Meth   Brookfield Ch. SEE: Prince George's Circuit Meth Ch, Prince
                George's Circuit Meth Epis Ch, South
Meth   Calvary, Waldorf. SEE: Prince George's Circuit Meth Ch
Bap   Calvary Bap Ch, 8330 Crain Hwy, Upper Marlboro 20772 * ch
                (dates not given)
Meth   Calvary-Cheltenham Circuit Meth Ch 1951-1958 # MSA
Meth   Calvary Ch. SEE: Prince George's Circuit Meth Epis Ch, South
Meth   Cedarville. SEE: Forestville Charge Meth Epis Ch
Prot Epis   Chapel of Ease, Croome. SEE: St Paul's Parish
Meth   Cheltenham Ch. SEE: Forestville Charge Meth Epis Ch, Prince
                George's Circuit Meth Ch
Prot Epis   Christ Chapel, Clinton (formerly Surratsville) (1875) SEE:
                Epiphany Epis Ch, 3111 Richie Rd, Forestville 20747

Epis	Christ Epis Ch, Bryan Pt & Farmington Rds, Accokeek 20607. 1824-1934 * MSA, 1843-1863, 1876-1908 # DAR
Presb	Chris Com Presb Ch, 3120 Belair Dr, Bowie 20715 (1962) 1962- * ch
LDS	Ch of Jesus Christ of Latter-Day Saints, Greenbelt Branch 1940-1948 # LDS
Meth	Colesville. SEE: Bladensburg-Emory Charge Meth Epis Ch, South; Emmanuel Unit Meth Ch, 11416 Cedar Ln, Beltsville 20705; Hyattsville Charge Meth Epis Ch, South
Unit Meth	Emmanuel Unit Meth Ch, 11416 Cedar Ln, Beltsville 20705. 1886-1969 # MSA (includes Beltsville, Branchville, Colesville, Four Corners, Lay Hill)
Meth	Emory chapel. SEE: Bladensburg Charge Meth Epis Ch, South
Prot Epis	Epiphany Epis Ch, 3111 Richie Rd, Forestville (1862) 1880-1926 * ch, before 1880 * Trinity Ch, Upper Marlboro, 1870-1964 # MSA (Includes Christ Chapel, Clinton (formerly Surratsville))
Evan Luth	Evan Luth Ch of the Abiding Presence, 11310 Montgomery Rd, Beltsville 20705 (1959) 1959- * ch
Meth	First Meth Ch, Hyattsville 1938-1957 # MSA
Ref	First Ref Ch, 6th & N Sts NW & 13th & Monroe Sts, Washington DC. SEE: Trinity UCC, 7300 New Hampshire Ave, Takoma Park 20912
Meth Epis S	Forest Grove Charge Meth Epis Ch, South 1854-1943 (includes Bladensburg, Forest Grove, Marlboro)
Meth	Forest Grove Ch. SEE: Bladensburg Charge Meth Epis Ch, South, Forestville Charge Meth Ch, Prince George's Circuit Meth Epis Ch, South
Meth Epis S	Forest Grove Circuit Meth Epis Ch, South 1900-1903, 1909-1918 # MSA (includes Forest Grove & Mt Oak churches)
Meth	Forest Memorial Ch. SEE: Forestville Charge Meth Ch
Meth Epis S	Forestville & Cheltenham Charge Meth Epis Ch 1912-1921 # MSA
Meth	Forestville Charge Meth Ch 1937-1964 # MSA (includes Bradbury Heights, Forest Grove, Forest Memorial, Forestville churches)
Meth Epis	Forestville Charge Meth Epis Ch 1876-1913, 1920-1943 # MSA (includes Bells, Bradbury Heights, Cedarville, Cheltenham, Forestville, Garners, Grace, House of Reformation, Oxon Hill, Pine Grove Chapel, Pyles, Scaggs, Suitland, Westwood)
Meth	Four Corners. SEE: Bladensburg-Emory Charge Meth Epis Ch, South, Emmanuel Unit Meth Ch, 11416 Cedar Ln, Beltsville 20705, Hyattsville Charge Meth Epis Ch, South
Meth	Garners. SEE: Forestville Charge Meth Epis Ch
Unit Meth	Gibbons Unit Meth Ch, 14107 Gibbons Church Rd, Brandywine 20613 (1884) * ch (dates not given; a black ch)
Meth	Grace. SEE: Forestville Charge Meth Epis Ch
Meth	Grace Meth Ch, Takoma Park 1944-1969 # MSA
Epis	Henderson Chapel. SEE: Holy Trinity Epis Ch, Rt 450 bet Highbridge & Hillmeade Rds, Collington, Bowie 20715
Cath	Holy Family Cath Ch, 12010 Woodmore Rd, Mitchellville 20716 (1890) * ch (dates not given)

Luth	Holy Trinity Luth Ch, 7607 Sandy Spring Rd, Laurel 20707 (1956) 1958- * ch
Prot Epis	Holy Trinity Parish, Collington 1826-1973 # MSA, 1844-1899 # MHS
Meth	House of Reformation. SEE: Forestville Charge Meth Epis Ch
Meth	Hyattsville. SEE: Bladensburg-Emory Charge Meth Epis Ch, South
Meth Epis S	Hyattsville & Brentwood Charge Meth Epis Ch, South 1914-1924 # MSA
Meth Epis S	Hyattsville Charge Meth Epis Ch, South 1894-1932 # MSA (includes Brentwood, Colesville, Four Corners, Hyattsville, Landover, Lay Hill)
Meth	Immanuel Ch. SEE: Prince George's Circuit Meth Ch, Prince George's Circuit Meth Epis Ch, South
Unit Meth	Immanuel Unit Meth Ch, 17400 Aquasco Rd, cor Rt 381 & Horsehead Rd, Brandywine 20613 (1794) 1876-1899 * ch (founded as Smith's Meet House)
Epis	King George's Parish (1692) 1689-1878 # MHS. SEE ALSO: St John's Ch, Broad Creek
Unit Meth	Korean First Unit Meth Ch, 11334 Evans Trail, Beltsville 20705 (1973) 1973- * ch
Meth	Landover. SEE: Hyattsville Charge Meth Epis Ch, South
Unit Meth	Lanham Unit Meth Ch, 5512 Whitfield Chapel Rd, Lanham 20754 (1837) 1863-1881 * ch # PGCGS Bull (first known as Whitefield Chapel)
Presb	Laurel Presb Ch, 7610 Sandy Spring Rd, Laurel 20707 (1865) 1860- * ch
Meth	Lay Hill. SEE: Bladensburg-Emory Charge Meth Epis Ch, South, Emmanuel Unit Meth Ch, 11416 Cedar Ln, Beltsville 20705, Hyattsville Charge Meth Epis Ch, South
Meth Epis S	Marlboro Charge Meth Epis Ch, South. SEE: Forest Grove Charge Meth Epis Ch, South
Meth	McKendree Ch. SEE: Bladensburg Charge Meth Epis Ch, South; Prince George's Circuit Meth Epis Ch, South; Waldorf-Calvary Circuit Meth Ch
Meth	Mt Oak Ch. SEE: Forest Grove Circuit Meth Epis Ch, South
Unit Meth	Mowatt Memorial Unit Meth Ch, 40 Ridge Rd, Greenbelt 20770 (1946) 1946- * ch
Unit Meth	North College Park Unit Meth Ch. SEE: Haddaway Chapel Meth Epis Ch, 60th St & Cunningham Dr, Berwyn Heights 20740
Meth Epis S	Oakland Charge Meth Epis Ch, South 1902-1905 # MSA
Meth	Oakland Ch. SEE: Prince George's Circuit Meth Epis Ch, South
Luth	Our Savior Luth Ch, 13611 Bowie Rd, Laurel 20708 (1969) 1969- * ch
Meth	Oxon Hill Charge Meth Ch 1946-1968 # MSA. SEE ALSO: Forestville Charge Meth Epis Ch
Meth	Pine Grove Chapel. SEE: Forestville Charge Meth Epis Ch
Meth	Piney Grove. SEE: Bladensburg-Emory Charge Meth Epis Ch, South
Prot Epis	Piscataway Parish 1693-? # LDS. SEE ALSO: St Johns Parish
Meth	Pomonkey Ch. SEE: Prince George's Circuit Meth Epis Ch, South

Prince Georges County

Meth	Prince George's Circuit Meth Ch 1943-1953 # MSA (includes Brookfield, Calvary at Waldorf, Cheltenham, Immanuel churches)
Meth Epis S	Prince George's Circuit Meth Epis Ch, South 1876-1946 # MSA (includes Brookfield, Calvary, Forest Grove, Immanuel, McKendree, Oakland, Pomonkey, Providence, Shiloh, Woodville churches & Waldorf Aux book)
Prot Epis	Prince George's Parish 1711-1845 # MHS
Meth	Providence Ch. SEE: Prince George's Circuit Meth Epis Ch, South
Meth	Pyles. SEE: Forestville Charge Meth Epis Ch
Prot Epis	Queen Anne's Parish 1690-1770 # MHS, 1689-1777 # LDS, 6 July 1762 list of batchelors # MGS Bull (includes St Barnabas Ch)
Prot Epis	St Barnabas Chapel, Oxon Hill (1830) SEE: St John's Ch, Broad Creek
Prot Epis	St Barnabas Ch, Leeland (1700) 1686-1777 * and # MSA, 1705-1773 # DAR, 1689-1777 # LDS (registers 1773-1905 destroyed by fire)
Luth	St John Luth Ch, 5820 Riverdale Rd, Riverdale 20737 (1922) 1922- * ch
Cath	St John the Evangelist Cath Ch, 8908 Old Branch Ave, Clinton 20735 (1875) 1879- * ch
Prot Epis	St John's Ch, Broad Creek 1689-1878 * and # MSA (originally called Broad Creek Ch; records 1823-1890 believed destroyed in Baltimore fire 1904)
Prot Epis	St John's Parish 1691-1805 # MHS, 1701-1878 # LDS (known as Piscataway Parish 1692-1726, St John's Parish 1726-1902, King George's Parish 1902-) SEE ALSO: Allen, Rev Ethan
R Cath	St Mary's, Laurel. SEE: St Lawrence, Jessup, Anne Arundel Co
Cath	St Mary's Cath Ch, 13401 Piscataway Rd, Rt 223, Clinton 20735 (1830) 1874- * ch
R Cath	St Mary's Chapel, Laurel Factory. SEE: St Mary's of the Mills Parish, Laurel
R Cath	St Mary's of the Mills Parish, 114 8th St, Laurel 20707 (1843) 1841-1871 # MSA (includes St Mary's Chapel, Laurel Factory)
Prot Epis	St Matthew's Ch, Seat Pleasant 1896-1965 # MSA
Epis	St Matthew's Parish 1828-1845 * MDA, 1915-1953 # MSA
--	St Matthew's Parish, Hyattsville Md 1834-1926 # LDS
Prot Epis	St Paul's Ch, Baden (1682) 1733-1966 * and # MSA (includes St Mary's Chapel, Aquasco, originally called Woodville)
Prot Epis	St Paul's Parish 1733-1885 # MHS, 1733-1823 # LDS (includes Chapel of Ease, Croome)
Prot Epis	St Philip's Ch, Laurel (1845) 1846-1970 # MSA
Prot Epis	St Philips, 13801 Baden-Westwood Rd, Baden (1876) 1907-1980 # MSA (a black ch)
Epis	St Phillips Parish, Laurel 1846-1868 # MHS LDS
Prot Epis	St Simon's Chapel, Croome 1902-1963 # MSA (a black ch)
Epis	St Thomas Epis Ch, St Thomas Church Rd, off Rt 382, Croome (1733) 1850-1956 # MSA

Meth	Scaggs Chapel. SEE: Bladensburg Charge Meth Epis Ch, South; Forestville Charge Meth Epis Ch
Meth	Seat Pleasant Meth Ch (1910) 1910-1968 # MSA (formerly Meth Epis)
Meth	Siloh Ch. SEE: Prince George's Circuit Meth Epis Ch, South
Meth	Suitland. SEE: Forestville Charge Meth Epis Ch
Prot Epis	Trinity Ch, Upper Marlboro (1810) 1847-1969 # MSA
UCC	Trinity UCC, 7300 New Hampshire Ave, Takoma Park 20912 1867- * ch (Trinity UCC also has records of First Ref Ch, 6th & N Sts NW & 13th & Monroe Sts, Washington DC)
Meth	Upper Marlborough. SEE: Bladensburg Charge Meth Epis Ch, South
Meth	Waldorf Aux book. SEE: Prince George's Circuit Meth Epis Ch, South
Meth	Waldorf-Calvary Circuit Meth Ch 1921-1925, 1953-1954 # MSA (includes McKendree Ch)
Presb	Wallace Memorial Presb Ch, 7201 16th Pl, Hyattsville 20783 (1910) 1950- * ch
Unit Meth	West Hyattsville Ager Road Unit Meth Ch 1957-1969 # MSA
Meth	Westwood. SEE: Forestville Charge Meth Epis Ch
Meth	Whitefield Chapel. SEE: Lanham Unit Meth Ch
Meth	Whitfield Ch. SEE: Bladensburg Charge Meth Epis Ch, South
Meth	Woodville Ch. SEE: Prince George's Circuit Meth Epis Ch, South

Queen Anne's County

Meth	Antioch. SEE: Meth Epis Ch
Meth	Barclay. SEE: Ingleside Charge Meth Epis Ch, South; Queen Anne's Charge Meth Epis Ch, South
Meth	Beaver Dam. SEE: Meth Epis Ch; Queen Anne's Charge Meth Epis Ch, South; Queen Anne's Circuit Meth Epis Ch, South; St Paul's Unit Meth Ch, Ingleside
Meth	Bethany Ch. SEE: Church Hill Charge Meth Ch, Church Hill Charge Meth Epis Ch
Meth	Busick. SEE: Meth Epis Ch
Meth	Centerville-Gouldtown Charge Meth Ch 1953-1967 # MSA (includes Charles Wesley Ch, Centerville; Metropolitan, Gouldtown)
Unit Meth	Centreville Unit Meth Ch, P.O.Box 447, Centreville 21617 (has records: * Centreville 1856-1879, Centreville Ch 1880-1900, Centreville Meth Ch 1892-1974, Centreville Meth Epis Ch 1869-1891, 1902-1946, Centreville Meth Prot Ch 1837-1910, Centreville Unit Meth Ch 1901-)
Meth	Charles Wesley Ch, Centerville. SEE: Centerville-Gouldtown Charge Meth Ch
Prot Epis	Christ Ch, Stevensville (1652) 1801-1909, 1912-1954 # MSA, 1801-1908 # MHS
Meth	Church Hill. SEE: Queen Anne's Circuit Meth Epis Ch, South

Queen Anne's County

Meth Epis S	Church Hill & Millington Circuit Meth Epis Ch, South 1924-1950 # MSA
Meth Epis S	Church Hill & Stevens Circuit Meth Epis Ch, South 1881-1924 # MSA
Meth	Church Hill Charge Meth Ch 1921-1957 # MSA (includes Bethany Ch at Price; formerly Price Sta Meth Epis Ch)
Meth Epis	Church Hill Charge Meth Epis Ch 1866-1917 # MSA (includes Church Hill, Price (later Bethany), Salem, Spainard Neck, Union)
Meth	Church Hill Circuit 1836-1853 # MSA
Meth	Crumpton. SEE: Meth Epis Ch
Meth	Double Creek. SEE: Meth Epis Ch
Meth	Dudley's. SEE: Meth Epis Ch
Meth Epis	Dudley's Chapel Meth Epis Ch 1782-1980 # MSA
Meth Epis	Ebenezer Meth Epis Ch (1917-1938) * Centreville Unit Meth Ch
Meth	Epworth Meth Ch, Liberty St, Centreville 1954-1959 * Centreville Unit Meth Ch
Meth Epis	Epworth Meth Epis Ch 1900-1954 * Centreville Unit Meth Ch
Luth	Galilee Luth Ch, Harbor View, Chester 21619 (1961) 1961- * ch
Meth	Goldsborough. SEE: Ingleside & Goldsborough Charge Meth Epis Ch, South; Queen Anne's Charge Meth Epis Ch, South; Queen Anne's Circuit Meth Epis Ch, South
Meth	Grasonville. SEE: Queenstown Charge Meth Epis Ch
Meth	Grasonville Meth Ch 1944-1966 # MSA
Meth Epis S	Hillsboro Circuit Meth Epis Ch, South 1866-1909 # MSA
Meth	Holdens. SEE: Meth Epis Ch
Meth	Ingleside. SEE: Queen Anne's Charge Meth Epis Ch, South; Queen Anne's Circuit Meth Epis Ch, South
Meth Epis S	Ingleside & Goldsborough Charge Meth Epis Ch, South 1903-1907 # MSA (includes Ingleside & Goldsborough)
Meth Epis S	Ingleside Charge Meth Epis Ch, South 1907-1958 # MSA (includes Ingleside & Barclay)
Meth Prot	Kent Isl Charge Meth Prot Ch 1894-1944 # MSA (called Kent Isl-Wye Charge; includes Trinity Ch & Murray's Chapel)
Meth Prot	Kent Isl Mission Meth Prot Ch 1864-1898 # MSA (includes Trinity Ch & Murray's Chapel)
Unit Meth	Kent Isl Unit Meth Ch, Harbor View Dr, Chester 21619 (1778) 1925 * ch
Meth	Kent Isl-Wye Charge. SEE: Kent Isl Charge Meth Prot Ch
Meth	Marvin Chapel, Barclay. SEE: Queen Anne's Circuit Meth Epis Ch, South
Meth	Mary Del. SEE: Queen Anne's Circuit Meth Epis Ch, South
Meth Epis	Meth Epis Ch 1836-1876 conference minutes # MSA (includes Antioch, Beaver Dam, Busick, Crumpton, Double Creek, Dudley's, Holdens, Roseville, Sudlersville, Templeville, Union)
Meth Epis S	Meth Epis Ch, South 1936-1939 # MSA (Eastern Shore Preacher's Meet)
Meth	Metropolitan, Gouldtown. SEE: Centerville-Gouldtown Charge Meth Ch

Meth	Millington Ch. SEE: Church Hill & Millington Circuit Meth Epis Ch, South
Meth	Moore's Chapel. SEE: Queen Anne's Charge Meth Epis Ch, South; Queen Anne's Circuit Meth Epis Ch, South
Meth	Murray's Chapel. SEE: Kent Isl Charge Meth Prot Ch, Kent Isl Mission Meth Prot Ch
Prot Epis	Old Chester Ch. SEE: St Paul's Ch, Centreville
Prot Epis	Old Wye Ch, Wye Mills (1717) 1859-1957 # MSA (originated as St Luke's Chapel in St Paul's Parish)
Meth	Perry's Corner. SEE: Queenstown Charge Meth Epis Ch
Meth	Piney Neck Ch. SEE: Queenstown Charge Meth Epis Ch
Meth	Piney Neck Circuit, Centreville 1853-1903 * Centreville Unit Meth Ch
Meth	Price Ch. SEE: Church Hill Charge Meth Epis Ch
Meth	Price Sta Meth Epis Ch. SEE: Church Hill Charge Meth Ch
Meth Epis S	Queen Anne's Charge Meth Epis Ch, South 1884-1899, 1913-1940 # MSA (includes Barclay, Beaver Dam, Goldsborough, Ingleside, Moore's Chapel, Sudlersville)
Meth Epis S	Queen Anne's Circuit Meth Epis Ch, South 1868-1953 # MSA (includes Beaver Dam, Church Hill, Ingleside, Goldsborough, Marvin Chapel at Barclay, Mary Del, Moore's Chapel, St Paul's at Beaver Dam, Stevens Chapel at Barclay, Stevens Chapel at Roseville, Sudlersville, Wesley Chapel at Sudlersville,
Meth Prot	Queen Anne's Co Circuit 1852-? annual conference * Centreville Unit Meth Ch, P.O.Box 447, Centreville 21617
Meth Epis S	Queenstown Charge Meth Epis Ch 1876-1948 # MSA (includes Grasonville, Perry's Corner, Piney Neck, Queenstown, Simpers Ch)
Meth	Roseville. SEE: Meth Epis Ch
Meth Prot	Ruthsburg/Calvary, Hayden * Centreville Unit Meth Ch, P.O.Box 447, Centreville 21617 (dates not given)
Meth Prot	Ruthsburg/Church Hill--Centreville Sta 1851-1875 * Centreville Unit Meth Ch, P.O.Box 447, Centreville 21617
Prot Epis	St John's Parish 1747-1853 # MHS, 1754-1809 # MGS Bull
Prot Epis	St John's Parish, Hillsboro 1749-1858 # LDS
Prot Epis	St Luke's Chapel. SEE: Old Wye Ch, Wye Mills
Prot Epis	St Luke's Ch, Church Hill (1728) 1722-1957 * and # MSA
Prot Epis	St Luke's Parish (or Church Hill) 1722-1850 # MHS
Prot Epis	St Luke's Prot Epis Parish, Church Hill 1722-1847 # LDS
Meth	St Paul's, Beaver Dam. SEE: Queen Anne's Circuit Meth Epis Ch, South
Prot Epis	St Paul's Ch, Centreville (1640) 1694-1819, 1837-1940 * and # MSA (Old Chester Ch)
Prot Epis	St Paul's Ch, Hillsboro (prior to 1717) 1752-1782, 1856-1952 * and # MSA
Prot Epis	St Paul's Parish 1694-1819 # MHS, 1694-1852 # LDS
Unit Meth	St Paul's Unit Meth Ch, Ingleside 1868-1968 * MSA (formerly Beaver Dam)
Meth	Salem Ch. SEE: Church Hill Charge Meth Epis Ch
Meth	Simpers Ch. SEE: Queenstown Charge Meth Epis Ch
Meth	Spainard Neck Ch. SEE: Church Hill Charge Meth Epis Ch

Meth	Stevens Chapel, Barclay. SEE: Queen Anne's Circuit Meth Epis Ch, South
Meth	Stevens Chapel, Roseville. SEE: Queen Anne's Circuit Meth Epis Ch, South
Meth	Sudlersville Ch. SEE: Church Hill & Millington Circuit Meth Epis Ch, South; Meth Epis Ch; Queen Anne's Circuit Meth Epis Ch, South
Meth	Sudlersville Circuit 1853-1876 # MSA
Meth	Templeville. SEE: Meth Epis Ch
Meth	Trinity Ch. SEE: Kent Isl Charge Meth Prot Ch, Kent Isl Mission Meth Prot Ch
Meth	Union. SEE: Meth Epis Ch
Meth	Union Ch. SEE: Church Hill Charge Meth Epis Ch
Meth	Wesley Chapel, Sudlersville. SEE: Queen Anne's Circuit Meth Epis Ch, South
Meth	Wye Meth Ch, Carmichael 1945-1948 # MSA
Meth Prot	Wye Meth Prot Ch 1879-1944 # MSA
Meth	Wye Mills 1885-1962 # MSA

St. Mary's County

Prot Epis	All Faith Ch, Huntersville (1675) 1692-1960 * and # MSA (includes Chapel of Ease, Mechanicsville (1887) & Dent Memorial Chapel, Charlotte Hall (1884))
Prot Epis	All Faith Parish 1893-1960 # MSA, 1692-1775? # MHS, 1720-1892 # DAR
Epis	All Faith Parish, Huntersville 1692-1824 # LDS (includes chapels of ease at Four Mile Run Ch (later part of St Andrew's Parish), Red Ch & Dent Memorial Chapel
Prot Epis	All Faith Parish, Mechanicsville 1905-1975 # LDS
Epis	All Saints' Epis Ch 1893-1976 # LDS
Meth Epis	Bell's. SEE: Forestville Circuit Meth Epis Ch
Meth	Bladensburg Circuit. SEE: Forest Grove Circuit Meth Epis Ch, South
Meth	Bradbury Heights. SEE: Forestville Charge Meth Ch
Meth	Cedar Point. SEE: St Mary's Circuit Meth Epis Ch
Meth Epis	Cedar Point Meth Epis Ch 1889-1891 Young People's Chris Assoc Record Book * MHS Mss Div
Meth	Cedarville. SEE: Forestville Circuit Meth Epis Ch
Prot Epis	Chapel of Ease, Mechanicsville. SEE: All Faith Ch, Huntersville
Meth Epis	Charles Circuit Meth Epis Ch. SEE: Leonardtown & Charles Circuit Meth Epis Ch
Meth	Cheltenham. SEE: Forestville Circuit Meth Epis Ch
Prot Epis	Christ Ch, Chaptico (1692) 1788-1881 * and MSA
Prot Epis	Dent Memorial Chapel, Charlotte Hall. SEE: All Faith Ch, Huntersville; All Faith Parish, Huntersville
Meth	Ebenezer. SEE: St Mary's Circuit Meth Epis Ch
Cath	First Cath Brick Chapel 1637/8 # MGS Bull

Meth	Forest Grove Ch. SEE: Forest Grove Circuit Meth Epis Ch, South; Forestville Charge Meth Ch
Meth Epis S	Forest Grove Circuit Meth Epis Ch, South 1854-1943 # MSA (includes Forest Grove Ch history & history of Bladensburg, Marlboro & Forest Grove Circuits)
Meth	Forest Memorial Ch. SEE: Forestville Charge Meth Ch
Meth Epis	Forestville & Cheltenham Charge Meth Epis Ch 1912-1921 # MSA
Meth	Forestville Charge Meth Ch 1937-1947, 1955-1964 # MSA (includes Bradbury Heights, Forest Grove, Forest Memorial, Forestville)
Meth Epis	Forestville Charge Meth Epis Ch 1920-1943 # MSA
Meth Epis	Forestville Circuit Meth Epis Ch 1876-1913 # MSA (includes Bell's; Forestville; Garners; Grace, Cedarville; House of Reformation; Oxen Hill; Pine Grove Chapel; Pyles; Scaggs; Suitland; Westwood or Cheltenham)
Unit Meth	Forestville Unit Meth Ch 1887-1899 # MSA
Epis	Four Mile Run Ch. SEE: All Faith Parish, Huntersville
Meth	Friendship. SEE: Lexington Park Charge, St Mary's Circuit Meth Epis Ch
Meth	Garners. SEE: Forestville Circuit Meth Epis Ch
Meth	Grace. SEE: Forestville Circuit Meth Epis Ch
Meth	House of Reformation. SEE: Forestville Circuit Meth Epis Ch
R Cath	Immaculate Heart of Mary Cath Ch, P.O.Box 6, Lexington Park 20653. 1852- * ch
Meth	Joy Chapel, Hollywood. SEE: Leonardtown Charge Meth Epis Ch
Epis	King & Queen Parish 1772-1792 * MDA, 1799-1838 # DAR, 1799-1906 # LDS
Meth Epis	Leonardtown & Charles Circuit Meth Epis Ch 1849, 1873-1883 # MSA
Meth	Leonardtown Charge Meth Ch 1933-1968 # MSA (includes Mt Zion, St George's Isl, St Paul's churches)
Meth Epis	Leonardtown Charge Meth Epis Ch 1883-1943 # MSA (includes Joy Chapel at Hollywood,, Mt Zion at Laurel Grove, St Paul's at Leonardtown, Sand Gates)
Unit Meth	Leonardtown Charge Unit Meth Ch 1968 minutes # MSA (St Paul's Ch)
Bap	Lexington Park Bap Ch, 100 S Shangri-La Dr, Lexington Park 20653 (1949) 1949- * ch
Meth	Lexington Park Charge 1960-1969 # MSA (Friendship Ch)
Meth	Marlboro Circuit. SEE: Forest Grove Circuit Meth Epis Ch, South
Meth	Mt Zion Ch, Laurel Grove. SEE: Leonardtown Charge Meth Ch, Leonardtown Charge Meth Epis Ch
Meth Epis	Oxen Hill. SEE: Forestville Circuit Meth Epis Ch
Meth	Pine Grove Chapel. SEE: Forestville Circuit Meth Epis Ch
Meth	Pisgah. SEE: St Mary's Circuit Meth Epis Ch
Prot Epis	Poplar Hill Ch. SEE: St George's Epis Ch, Valley Lee
Meth	Pyles. SEE: Forestville Circuit Meth Epis Ch
Epis	Red Ch. SEE: All Faith Parish, Huntersville
R Cath	St Aloysius Ch, Leonardtown 1869-1907 # MHS

St. Mary's County

Prot Epis	St Andrew's Epis Ch (1703) 1753-1895, 1917-1944 * and # MSA 1700's-1900's # LDS (includes St Peter's Chapel, Leonardtown)
Prot Epis	St Andrew's Parish, Leonardtown 1736-1886 # MHS LDS. SEE ALSO: All Faith Parish, Huntersville
R Cath	St George's Cath Ch, Valley Lee 20692 (1855) 1952 * ch
Prot Epis	St George's Epis Ch, Valley Lee (1642) 1798-1903, 1914 * and # MSA; 1798-1923 # DAR; 1787-1875, 1798-1914 # LDS (known as Poplar Hill Ch) SEE ALSO: William & Mary Parish
Meth	St George's Isl Ch. SEE: Leonardtown Charge Meth Ch, St Mary's Circuit Meth Epis Ch
-	St Inigoes # MHS (dates not given), 1766-1794 # LDS
Cath	St Joseph's Cath Ch, Morganza 20660 (1700) 1914- * ch
Meth Epis	St Mary's Circuit Meth Epis Ch 1859-1920 * MHS Mss Div, 1857-1929 # MSA (includes Cedar Point, Ebenezer, Friendship, Pisgah, St George's Isl)
Epis	St Mary's Epis Ch, New Market 1906-1965 # LDS
Meth	St Paul's Ch, Leonardtown. SEE: Leonardtown Charge Meth Ch, Leonardtown Charge Meth Epis Ch
Prot Epis	St Peter's Chapel, Leonardtown (1870) 1753-1895, 1917-1944 * and # MSA. SEE ALSO: St Andrew's Epis Ch
Meth	Sand Gates. SEE: Leonardtown Charge Meth Epis Ch
Meth	Scaggs. SEE: Forestville Circuit Meth Epis Ch
Meth	Suitland. SEE: Forestville Circuit Meth Epis Ch
Epis	Trinity Ch, St Mary's City 1893 * ch
R Cath	Walton, Father James E 1766-1794 baptisms # LDS
Meth	Westwood. SEE: Forestville Circuit Meth Epis Ch
Epis	William and Mary Parish, Valley Lee 1650-1903 * and # MHS Mss Div, 1798-1925 # LDS (St George's Ch known as Poplar Hill Ch) SEE ALSO: St George's Epis Ch

Somerset County

Prot Epis	All Saint's Ch, Monie (1694) 1689-1956 # MSA
Meth	Antioch. SEE: Princess Anne Charge Meth Ch, Princess Anne Charge Meth Epis Ch, St Paul's Meth Epis Ch, South
Meth	Antioch Charge 1828-1900 # LDS
Meth	Antioch Charge Meth Ch 1962-1967 # MSA (until 1964 Princess Anne Charge)
Meth	Antioch Meth Ch 1962-1963 # MSA
Meth Epis	Antioch Meth Epis Ch, Princess Anne 1881-1948 # MSA
Meth	Asbury, Mt Vernon. SEE: Princess Anne Charge Meth Epis Ch
Meth	Back Creek. SEE: Princess Anne Charge Meth Epis Ch
Meth	Bethel. SEE: Princess Anne Charge Meth Epis Ch
Meth	Calvary Ch, Rhodes Pt. SEE: Smith Isl Charge Meth Ch
Epis	Coventry Parish 1724-1891 # LDS. SEE ALSO: Somerset Parish
Meth	Dames Quarter. SEE: Princess Anne Charge Meth Epis Ch
Meth	Deal's Isl. SEE: Princess Anne Charge Meth Epis Ch
Meth	Delaware Conference Meth Epis Ch 1925-1954 # MSA

Meth	Ewell Ch. SEE: Smith Isl Charge Meth Ch, Smith Isl Charge Meth Epis Ch
Meth Epis	Fairmount Charge Meth Epis Ch 1877-1946 # MSA
Meth Epis	Fairmount Sta Meth Epis Ch 1860-1877 # MSA
Meth	Grace. SEE: Quindocqua Sta Meth Epis Ch
Meth	Holland's Isl. SEE: Princess Anne Charge Meth Epis Ch
Meth	Hopewell. SEE: Princess Anne Charge Meth Epis Ch
Meth	Hungary Neck. SEE: Princess Anne Charge Meth Epis Ch
Meth	John Wesley. SEE: Princess Anne Charge Meth Epis Ch
Ref	Kampen Ref Ch 1900-1902 # LDS
Meth	Kingston Charge Meth Ch 1939-1958 # MSA (later Marion Sta Marmumsco Meth Ch
Presb	Manokin Presb Ch, Princess Anne (1683) 1737-1964 # MSA, 1747-1869 # MHS
Meth	Mariners Meth Ch, Crisfield 1941-1964 # MSA (until 1967 part of Mt Pleasant Charge, Crisfield)
Meth Prot	Mariners Meth Prot Ch 1897-1941 # MSA
Meth	Marion Charge 1954-1966 # MSA (includes Phoenix, Quindocqua, Trinity)
Meth	Marion Sta Marmumsco Meth Ch 1965-1966 # MSA. SEE ALSO: Kingston Charge Meth Ch
Meth	Marmumsco Meth Ch. SEE: Marion Sta
Meth	Metropolitan Meth Ch 1926-1967 # MSA (prior to 1940 a Meth Epis ch)
Meth Epis	Metropolitan Meth Epis Ch 1875-1928 # MSA
Meth	Mt Pleasant Charge, Crisfield. SEE: Mariners Meth Ch
Meth	Mt Pleasant Meth Ch, Crisfield 1876-1967 # MSA (prior to 1940 a Meth Prot ch)
Meth	New Bethel Meth Ch 1957 roll of constituents # MSA
Meth	Phoebus. SEE: Princess Anne Charge Meth Epis Ch
Meth	Phoenix Meth Ch 1956-1962 # MSA. SEE ALSO: Marion Charge, Trinity Sta Meth Prot Ch
Meth	Princess Anne Charge Meth Ch 1941-1968 # MSA (includes Antioch & St Paul's in Westover)
Meth Epis	Princess Anne Charge Meth Epis Ch 1856-1940 # MSA (includes Antioch, Asbury in Mt Vernon, Back Creek, Bethel, Dames Quarter, Deal's Isl, Holland's Isl, Hopewell, Hungary Neck, John Wesley, Phoebus, Princess Anne, Rock Creek, St Peter's Smith's Isl, Trappe, Upper Trappe, Zion)
Meth Epis	Princess Anne Circuit Meth Epis Ch 1857-1898, 1917-1925, 1929-1931 # MSA
Meth	Quindocqua Ch 1906-1947 # MSA
Meth	Quindocqua Meth Ch 1950-1963 # MSA. SEE ALSO: Marion Charge
Meth Epis	Quindocqua Sta Meth Epis Ch 1892-1946 # MSA (Quindocqua & Grace congregations)
Presb	Rehoboth by the River, Rehoboth # LDS (dates not given)
Prot Epis	Rehoboth Ch 1734?-1791?, 1821-1868 # MHS
Meth	Rhodes Pt. SEE: Smith Isl Charge Meth Epis Ch
Presb	Rocawakin Presb Ch 23 April 1759 pew rentals # MGS Bull
Meth	Rock Creek. SEE: Princess Anne Charge Meth Epis Ch
Meth Epis	St Andrew's Charge Meth Epis Ch, Upper Hill 1932-1955 # MSA
Prot Epis	St Andrew's Ch, Princess Anne (1771) 1771-1956 # MSA

Somerset County

Meth	St Andrew's Meth Ch 1955 marriages # MSA. SEE ALSO: Upper Hill Charge Meth Ch
Meth Epis	St Andrew's Meth Epis Ch, Upper Hill 1913-1921, 1946-1949 # MSA
Prot Epis	St Mark's Ch, Kingston 1745-1915 # MSA
Meth	St Paul's, Westover. SEE: Princess Anne Charge Meth Ch
Meth Epis	St Paul's Meth Epis Ch, South 1920-1963 # MSA (after 1940 a Meth ch; closed 1963 & majority of members joined Antioch)
Meth	St Peter's Meth Ch 1940-1965 # MSA
Meth Epis	St Peter's Meth Epis Ch 1867-1884, 1899-1909, 1926-1952 # MSA. SEE ALSO: Princess Anne Charge Meth Epis Ch
Meth	Smith Isl Charge Meth Ch 1907-1967 # MSA (includes Calvary Ch at Rhodes Pt, Ewell Ch, Union Ch at Tylerton)
Meth Epis	Smith Isl Charge Meth Epis Ch 1884-1940 # MSA (includes Ewell, Rhodes Pt, Tylerton)
Meth	Smith's Isl. SEE: Princess Anne Charge Meth Epis Ch
Prot Epis	Somerset Parish # MHS LDS (dates not given; includes Coventry Parish)
Prot Epis	Stepney Parish, Green Hill 1799, 1809-1812, 1820-1822, 1833 * MHS Mss Div, 1703-1890 # MHS LDS
Meth	Trappe. SEE: Princess Anne Charge Meth Epis Ch
Meth	Trinity Meth Ch 1916-1956 # MSA. SEE ALSO: Marion Charge
Meth Prot	Trinity Sta Meth Prot Ch 1880-1955 # MSA (includes Trinity & Phoenix congregations)
Prot Epis	Turner, Rev C H B -- genealogical abstracts of Somerset & Coventry Parish # MHS (dates not given)
Meth	Tylerton. SEE: Smith Isl Charge Meth Epis Ch
Meth	Union Ch, Tylerton. SEE: Smith Isl Charge Meth Ch
Meth	Upper Fairmount Charge Meth Ch 1912-1958 # MSA
Meth	Upper Hill Charge Meth Ch 1944-1964 # MSA (includes St Andrew's Meth Ch)
Meth	Upper Trappe. SEE: Princess Anne Charge Meth Epis Ch
Meth	Zion. SEE: Princess Anne Charge Meth Epis Ch

Talbot County

Prot Epis	All Faith Prot Epis Ch, Longwood 1875-1946 # MSA
Prot Epis	All Faith's Ch, Tunis Mills. SEE: St John's Ch
Prot Epis	All Saints' Ch, Longwoods (1875) 1875-1950 # MSA
Meth	Asbury. SEE: Bayside Meth Ch
Meth	Bambury. SEE: Talbot Circuit Meth Prot Ch
Meth	Bayside. SEE: Talbot Circuit Meth Epis Ch, Talbot Circuit Meth Prot Ch
Meth Epis	Bayside & Tilghman Charge Meth Epis Ch. SEE: Bayside Meth Ch
Meth	Bayside Charge Meth Ch. SEE: Bayside Meth Ch
Meth	Bayside Meth Ch 1892-1964 # MSA (includes Asbury, Bayside, Bozman, Sherwood congregations; after 1940 called Bayside & Tilghman Charge Meth Ch, after 1943, Bayside Charge Meth Ch)
Meth	Bolingbroke. SEE: Easton Circuit Meth Epis Ch

Meth	Bozman. SEE: Bayside Meth Ch
Meth	Bozman & Neavett Charge Meth Epis Ch. SEE: Bozman Meth Ch
Meth	Bozman Meth Ch 1902-1967 # MSA (formerly Bozman & Neavett Charge Meth Epis Ch)
Meth	Broad Creek Neck. SEE: Talbot Circuit Meth Epis Ch
Meth	Calvary Ch. SEE: St Mark's Meth Ch
Meth	Calvary Meth Ch 1949-1950 # MSA
Meth Prot	Calvary Meth Prot Ch 1828-1949 # MSA (includes Easton Sta Meth Prot Ch, Talbot Circuit Meth Prot Ch)
Meth	Chapel. SEE: Easton Circuit Meth Epis Ch, Talbot Circuit Meth Prot Ch
Prot Epis	Christ Ch, Easton 1681-1957 * and # MSA
Prot Epis	Christ Ch, St Michael's (1672) 1672-1704, 1731-1933 * and # MSA
--	Christ Ch I U Families Assoc 1949-1961 * MHS Mss Div
Meth	Claiborne Meth Ch 1941-1964 # MSA
--	Coventry Parish. SEE: Somerset Parish
Meth	Easton. SEE: Talbot Circuit Meth Prot Ch
Meth Epis	Easton Charge Meth Epis Ch 1894-1921 # MSA
Meth Epis	Easton Circuit Meth Epis Ch 1835-1894 # MSA (includes Bolingbroke, Chapel, Easton, Kings Creek, Lansing Neck, Oxford Neck, Trappe)
Meth Prot	Easton Sta Meth Prot Ch 1828-1949 # MSA (includes Calvary Meth Prot Ch, Talbot Circuit Meth Prot Ch)
Meth	Ebenezer Ch. SEE: St Mark's Meth Ch
Meth	Ebenezer Meth Ch 1936-1953 # MSA
Meth Epis	Ebenezer Meth Epis Ch 1829-1936 # MSA
Meth	Ferry Neck. SEE: Talbot Circuit Meth Epis Ch
Meth	Grasonville. SEE: Queenstown Charge Meth Epis Ch
Meth	Grasonville Meth Ch 1944-1966 # MSA
Prot Epis	Holy Trinity Ch, Oxford? Greensboro? 1850-1853, 1898-1951 # MSA (for earlier records see St Peter's Parish)
Meth	John Wesley Meth Ch, Oxford Rd, Oxford 1967 history # MSA. SEE ALSO: Waters & John Wesley Meth churches
Meth Prot	Kent Isl Charge Meth Prot Ch 1894-1944 # MSA (called Kent Isl-Wye Charge; includes Murray's Chapel & Trinity Ch)
Meth Prot	Kent Isl Mission Meth Prot Ch 1864-1898 # MSA (includes Murray's Chapel & Trinity Ch)
Meth Prot	Kent Isl-Wye Charge. SEE: Kent Isl Charge Meth Prot Ch
Meth	Kings Creek. SEE: Easton Circuit Meth Epis Ch
Meth	Lansing Neck. SEE: Easton Circuit Meth Epis Ch
Meth	Lebanon Chapel 1828-1938 # MSA
Meth	Longwoods. SEE: Talbot Circuit Meth Prot Ch
Meth Epis	Meth Epis Ch, Easton 1875-1883, 1891-1907 # MSA
Meth Prot	Meth Prot Ch, Easton 1828-1949 (includes Calvary Meth Prot Ch, Easton Sta Meth Prot Ch, Talbot Circuit Meth Prot Ch)
Meth	Miles River. SEE: Talbot Circuit Meth Epis Ch
Meth Prot	Murray's Chapel. SEE: Kent Isl Charge Meth Prot Ch, Kent Isl Mission Meth Prot Ch
Friends	North West Fork Monthly Meet 1800-1904 # LDS
Meth	Oxford. SEE: Talbot Circuit Meth Prot Ch
Meth	Oxford Neck. SEE: Easton Circuit Meth Epis Ch

Talbot County

Meth	Perry's Corner. SEE: Queenstown charge Meth Epis Ch
Meth	Piney Neck Ch. SEE: Queenstown Charge Meth Epis Ch
Meth Epis	Queenstown Charge Meth Epis Ch 1876-1948 # MSA (includes Grasonville, Perry's Corner, Piney Neck, Queenstown, Simpers)
Meth	Royal Oak. SEE: Talbot Circuit Meth Epis Ch
Prot Epis	St John's Ch 1880-1956 # MSA (includes All Faith's Ch, Tunis Mills, All Saints' Parish)
R Cath	St Joseph's Mission, Cordova 1803-1879 # MSA
Meth Epis	St Lukes Ch. SEE: Sardis Meth Epis Ch, St Michaels
Meth	St Luke's Meth Ch, Front St, Bellevue 1903-1967 # MSA
Unit Meth	St Lukes Unit Meth Ch 1651-1889 # MSA
Meth	St Mark's Meth Ch 1952-1966 # MSA (formed from Trinity, Ebenezer & Calvary churches, Easton 1953)
Meth	St Michael's. SEE: Talbot Circuit Meth Epis Ch, Talbot Circuit Meth Prot Ch
Prot Epis	St Michael's Parish 1747-1805, 1852-1929 # MSA, 1672-1859 # MHS LDS
Prot Epis	St Paul's Ch, Hillsboro 1752-1952 * and # MSA
Prot Epis	St Paul's Ch, Trappe 1857-1954 # MSA
Prot Epis	St Paul's Parish 1694-1819 # MHS
Prot Epis	St Peters Parish 1681-1855 # MHS, 1672-1859 # LDS. See Also: Holy Trinity Ch
Meth Epis	Sardis Meth Epis Ch, St Michaels 1875-1949 # MSA
Meth	Sherwood. SEE: Bayside Meth Ch
Meth	Sherwood Meth Ch 1964-1967 # MSA
Meth	Simpers Ch. SEE: Queenstown Charge Meth Epis Ch
--	Somerset Parish # LDS (dates not given; includes Coventry Parish)
Friends	Southern Quarterly Meet 1755-1893 # MSA
Meth Epis	Southland Ch. SEE: Sardis Meth Epis Ch, St Michaels
Meth Epis	Talbot Circuit Meth Epis Ch 1838-1875 # MSA (includes Bayside, Broad Creek Neck, Ferry Neck, Miles River, Royal Oak, St Michaels, Tilghmans Isl, Trappe)
Meth Prot	Talbot Circuit Meth Prot Ch 1828-1951 # MSA (includes Bambury, Bayside, Calvary, Chapel, Easton, Longwoods, Oxford, St Michael's, Trappe, Windy Hill) SEE ALSO: Meth Prot Ch, Easton
Friends	Third Haven Monthly Meet (Tred-Avon), Easton 1664-1973 # MSA. SEE ALSO: Tread Avon
Meth	Tilghmans Isl. SEE: Talbot Circuit Meth Epis Ch
Meth	Trappe. SEE: Easton Circuit Meth Epis Ch, Talbot Circuit Meth Epis Ch, Talbot Circuit Meth Prot Ch
Meth	Trappe Charge Meth Ch 1870-1963 # MSA
Meth	Trappe Charge Meth Epis Ch 1855-1916 # MSA (prior to 1866 called Easton Circuit; includes Union Ch at Landing Neck)
Friends	Tread Avon (Tred Avon) Friends Meet 1676-1797 # MHS. SEE ALSO: Third Haven Monthly Meet
Prot Epis	Trinity Cathedral, Easton (1876) 1869-1956 # MSA
Meth	Trinity Ch. SEE: Kent Isl Charge Meth Prot Ch, St Mark's Meth Ch
Meth	Trinity Meth Ch 1944-1953 # MSA

Talbot County

Meth Epis S	Trinity Meth Epis Ch, South 1873-1944 # MSA
Meth	Union Ch, Landing Neck. SEE: Trappe Charge Meth Epis Ch
Meth	Waters & John Wesley Meth churches 1883, 1956-1964 # MSA
Meth	Waters Meth Ch, Banks & Market St, Oxford 1967 history # MSA
Meth	Windy Hill. SEE: Talbot Circuit Meth Prot Ch
Meth	Wittman Meth Ch 1921-1951, 1963-1967 # MSA (formerly Wittman Meth Epis Ch)
Meth	Wittman Meth Epis Ch. SEE: Wittman Meth Ch
Meth	Wye Meth Ch, Carmichael 1945-1948 # MSA
Meth Prot	Wye Meth Prot Ch 1879-1944 # MSA

Washington County

Prot Epis	Allen, Rev Ethan 1777-1806 # MHS Mss Div (notes on St John's Parish, Prince George's Co; Prince George's Parish, Montgomery Co; All Saints' Parish & St Mark's, Frederick Co; Washington & Allegany Co parishes)
Luth	Beard's-St Peter's Luth Ch 1828-1906 # MHS
Unit Meth	Benevola & Mt Lena Unit Meth churches, Rt 1 Box 138, Boonsboro 21713 * ch (Benevola (1858) Mt Lena (1879), formerly Unit Breth then Evan Unit Breth, currently Unit Meth)
Unit Meth	Bethel Unit Meth Charge, Box 37, Chewsville 21721 (1805) 1920- * ch
Evan Luth	Christ's Evan Luth Ch, Funkstown 1852-1900 # MHS
Luth	Concordia Luth Ch, 1799 Garden Ln, Hagerstown 21740 (1960) 1960- * ch
Evan & Ref	Cort, Cyrus 1881-1914 # LDS
Ref	Deyshere's. SEE: Salem Ref Ch
Evan Luth & Ref	Evan Luth & Ref Ch Congregations, Provinz 1788-1853 # MHS
Luth	Evan Luth Ch, Elizabethtown 1768-1967 # MSA
Disc	First Chris Ch, St Paul St, Boonsboro 21713 early 1900's * ch
Disc	First Chris Ch, 1345 Potomac Ave, Hagerstown 21740. 1876- * ch
Unit Evan	First Unit Evan Ch. SEE: St Matthews Unit Meth Ch, 443 W Franklin St, Hagerstown 21740
Evan Ref	Ger Evan Ref Congregation. SEE: Salem Ger Ref Ch
Ref	Ger Ref Congregation, Cave Town 1853-1917 # MHS
Luth	Ger St John's Ch 1793-1818 # MSA. SEE ALSO: St John's Ch, Hagerstown
--	Goering, Jacob M 1788-1792 # LDS
Unit Meth	Grace Unit Meth Ch, 712 Church St (Church & Winter Sts), Hagerstown 21740 (1897) 1909- * ch
Bap	Greenbrier Bap Ch, Rt 2, Box 94W, Boonsboro 21713 (1977) 1977- * ch
Luth	Haven Luth Ch, 1035 Haven Rd, Hagerstown 21740 (1953) 1953- * ch
Luth	Jacobs Luth Ch, nr Leitersburg 1791-1860 # MHS LDS

86

Unit Meth	John Wesley Unit Meth Ch, 129 N Potomac St, Hagerstown 21740 1825- * ch (formerly St Paul's Meth Ch)
Luth	Luth Ch in Hagerstown 1860-1916 # MSA. SEE ALSO: St John's Ch, Hagerstown
Unit Meth	Mt Lena Unit Meth Ch, Rt 1 Box 1, Boonsboro 21713. 1902- * Benevola Unit Meth Ch, Benevola Church Rd, Rt 1 Box 1, Boonsboro 21713
Meth	Mt Zion Unit Meth Ch, RFD, Sabillasville 21780 1934- * Rev James L Fisher, 7912 Rocky Ridge Rd, Thurmont 21788
Evan Luth & Ref	Old Ger Evan Luth & Ref Ch, Funkstown 1788-1849 # MHS (Funkstown was originally called Jerusalem)
Luth & Ref	Old St Paul's Luth & Ref Ch. SEE: St Paul's Evan Luth & Ref Ch nr Clear Spring
Unit Meth	Otterbein Unit Meth Ch, 108 E Franklin St, Hagerstown 21740. 1807- * ch
Bap	Paramount Bap Ch, 2323 Marsh Pike, Hagerstown 21740 (1961) 1961- * ch
Presb	Presb Ch of Hagerstown, 20 S Prospect St, Hagerstown Md 21740. 1817- * ch, 1816- # ch, 1816-1873 # Western Md Room of Washington Co Library, Hagerstown
Ref	Ref Ch. SEE: Zion UCC
Ref	Ref Ch of Conocoheague. SEE: St Paul's Ref Congregation
Ref	Ref Congregation, Hagerstown 1766-1807 # MHS LDS. SEE ALSO: Zion UCC
Epis	St Alban's Ch, Halfway 1959-1965 * MDA
Epis	St Alban's Ch, Williamsport 1960-1971 * MDA
Prot Epis	St Andrew's Ch, Clear Spring (1839) 1912-1964 # MSA
Unit Meth	St Andrew's Unit Meth Ch, 1020 Maryland Ave, Hagerstown 21740. 1919- * ch
Prot Epis	St Anne's Ch, Smithsburg (1873) 1897-1964 # MSA
Prot Epis	St Clement's Chapel, Indian Springs (1900) 1951-1963 # MSA
Luth	St John's Ch, Hagerstown 1818-1967 # MSA (originated at Elizabethtown, after 1806 known as Ger St John's Ch then Luth Ch in Hagerstown; has records of St Mathew's Ger Eng Evan Luth Ch which closed 1917)
Prot Epis	St John's Ch, Hagerstown (1787) 1787-1963 # MSA
Evan Luth	St John's Evan Luth Ch, Hagerstown # LDS (dates not given)
Prot Epis	St John's Parish, Hagerstown 1787-1893 # MHS
UCC Ref	St John's UCC (Ref), Cumberland St, Clear Spring 21722. 1828- * ch
Prot Epis	St Mark's Ch, Lappan's Cross Rds (1849) 1849-1958 # MSA
Prot Epis	St Mark's Ch, Petersville (1806) 1806-1917 # MSA
Luth	St Mathew's Ger Eng Evan Luth Ch 1905-1917 * St John's Ch, Hagerstown # MSA
Evan Unit Breth	St Matthews Evan Unit Breth Ch. SEE: St Matthews Unit Meth Ch, 443 W Franklin St, Hagerstown 21740
Unit Meth	St Matthews Unit Meth Ch, 443 W Franklin St, Hagerstown 21740 (1884) 1916- * ch (1884- known as First Unit Evan Ch; 1922- St Pauls Evan Ch; 1946- St Matthews Evan Unit Breth Ch; 1968- St Matthews Unit Meth Ch)
Prot Epis	St Paul's Ch, Sharpsburg (1819) 1893-1958 # MSA
Evan Luth &	St Paul's Ch on the Western Pike (west of Conococheague

Ref	Creek) SEE: Evan Luth & Ref Ch Congregations, Provinz
Ref	St Pauls Congregation nr Clear Spring. SEE: St Paul's Evan Luth & Ref Ch nr Clear Spring
Evan	St Pauls Evan Ch. SEE: St Matthews Unit Meth Ch, 443 W Franklin St, Hagerstown 21740
Evan Luth & Ref	St Paul's Evan Luth & Ref Ch nr Clear Spring 1787-1829 # MHS (known as Old St Paul's Luth & Ref Ch)
Evan Luth	St Paul's Evan Luth Ch, Greensburg 1823-1930 # MHS
Luth	St Paul's Luth Ch, Leitersburg 21740 (1826) 1747-1911, 1941- * ch
Meth Epis	St Pauls Meth Epis Ch, Hagerstown 1825-1910 # LDS
Meth Epis	St Paul's Meth Epis Ch, Smithsburg (1831) 1868-1933 # MHS
Ref	St Paul's Ref Congregation nr Clear Spring 1846-1866 # MHS
Ref	St Paul's Ref Congregation of the Ref Ch of Concococheague 1883-1903 # MHS
UCC	St Paul's UCC, Rt 1 Box 407A, Clear Spring Md 21722. 1788- * ch
Unit Meth	St Paul's Unit Meth Ch, P.O.Box 205, 51 S Main St, Smithsburg 21783. 1869- * ch
Luth	St Peter's Luth Ch. SEE: Beard's-St Peters Luth Ch
Epis	St Thomas's Parish 1848-1850 * MDA
Ref	Salem Congregation, Ger Ref Ch, Hagerstown Charge 1862-1901 # MHS
Ref	Salem (Deyshere's) Ref Ch 1774-1900 # MHS
Ref	Salem Ger Ref Ch, Conococheague District 1771-1783 # LDS (also known as Evan Ref Congregation, Salem Ref Ch, Salem UCC)
Ref	Salem Ref Ch 1774-1800 # MHS. SEE ALSO: Salem Ger Ref Ch
UCC	Salem UCC. SEE: Salem Ger Ref Ch
Unit Meth	Salem Unit Meth Ch, 25 S Main St, Box 25, Keedysville 21756 (1774) 1830- * ch (followers of Otterbein named ch Getting Meet House; called Mt Hebron Ch of Unit Breth in Christ, 1946 became Evan Unit Breth, 1968 Unit Meth)
Luth	Trinity Luth Ch, SmithsbuOg 1872-1901 # MHS
Unit Meth	Washington Square Unit Meth Ch, 538 Washington Sq, Hagerstown 21740. 1890s- * ch
Evan & Ref	Zion Evan & Ref Ch, 201 N Potomac St, Hagerstown 21740. 1766 * ch
Evan Luth	Zion Evan Luth Ch, 35 W Potomac St, Williamsport Md 21795. 1791- * ch, 1791-1853 # MHS (formerly known as Zion's Ger Evan Luth Congregation)
Ref	Zion Ref Ch, Hagerstown 1807-1849 # MHS LDS. SEE ALSO: Zion UCC, Hagerstown
UCC	Zion UCC, Hagerstown 1766-1944 # LDS (known as Ref Ch & Zion Ref Ch)

Meth Epis S	Allen Charge (Circuit) Meth Epis Ch, South 1913-1935 # MSA (includes Allen, Eden, Trinity)
Bap	Allen Memorial Bap Ch, Salisbury (1859) 1859-1877, 1905-1950 # MSA
Meth	Asbury Ch. SEE: Allen Charge (Circuit Meth Epis Ch, South, Crisfield Stat Meth Epis Ch, Wicomico Circuit Meth Epis Ch, South
Meth	Asbury Meth Ch, Salisbury 1851-1965 # MSA
Meth Epis	Asbury Meth Epis Ch, Crisfield 1870-1939, 1950-1957 # MSA
Meth Epis	Asbury Meth Epis Ch, Sharptown 1904-1935 # MSA
Meth Epis S	Asbury Meth Epis Ch, South 1921-1923, 1933 # MSA
Meth	Asbury-Riverton Charge, Sharptown 1949-1967 # MSA
Meth Prot	Barren Creek Circuit Meth Prot Ch. SEE: Mardela Charge Meth Ch
Meth	Barren Creek Springs Ch. SEE: Union Circuit Meth Prot Ch
Meth	Barr's. SEE: Oriole Charge Meth Ch
Evan Luth	Bethany Evan Luth Ch, Camden Ave & South Blvd, Salisbury 21801 (1934) 1954- * ch
Meth	Bethel Ch. SEE: Oriole Charge Meth Ch, Parsonburg Circuit Meth Epis Ch, Quantico Circuit Meth Prot Ch, Wicomico Circuit Meth Epis Ch, South
Meth	Bethel eth Ch 1932-1966 # MSA (prior to 1940 a Meth Epis ch)
Meth	Bethesda. SEE: Salisbury-Bethesda Meth Ch
Meth Prot	Bethesda Meth Prot Ch 1864, 1898-1964 # MSA
Meth	Bivalve Meth Ch 1936-1959 # MSA (prior to 1940 a Meth Prot ch) SEE ALSO: Waltersville Charge Meth Prot Ch
Meth	Charity. SEE: Hebron Charge
Meth	Christ Meth Ch 1952-1967 # MSA
Meth Epis	Crisfield Sta Meth Epis Ch 1871-1887, 1901-1907 # MSA (later split into Asbury & Immanuel churches)
Meth	Dames Quarter Meth Ch 1951-1967 # MSA
Meth	Delmar Charge Meth Ch 1908-1953 # MSA (prior to 1940 a Meth Epis ch)
Meth Prot	Delmar Charge Meth Prot Ch 1909-1947 # MSA (includes Mt Olive Meth Ch)
Meth Epis	Delmar Circuit Meth Epis Ch 1867-1907 # MSA (includes Delmar, Mt Pleasant, King's, St George's)
Meth	Ebenezer Ch. SEE: Quantico Circuit Meth Prot Ch
Unit Meth	Ebenezer Unit Meth Ch of Rockawalkin, Rt 1 Box 78, Hebron 21830 (1839) 1839- * ch
Meth	Eden Ch. SEE: Allen Charge (Circuit) Meth Epis Ch, South, Wicomico Circuit Meth Epis Ch, South
Meth	Eden Meth Ch, Willards 1959-1967 # MSA
Meth	Emmanuel Meth Ch, Mardela Springs 1960-1967 # MSA
Meth	Emmanuel, Snethen, Mt Pleasant, Hebron & Riverson churches 1899-1962 # MSA
Meth	First Meth Ch 1961-1966 # MSA
Meth	First Meth Ch, Delmar DE 1940-1964 # MSA
Meth	First Meth-Quantico & Whitehaven Meth churches 1964-1967 # MSA
Meth	Friendship. SEE: Powellville Circuit Meth Epis Ch

Meth	Grace Meth Ch 1943-1967 # MSA
Meth Epis	Grace Meth Epis Ch 1907-1941 # MSA
Prot Epis	Green Hill Prot Epis Ch 1703-1824 # LDS
Meth	Hebron Charge 1869-1918 # MSA (includes Charity, Nelson's Memorial, St Paul, Union Circuit Meth Prot)
Meth	Hebron Ch. SEE: Emmanuel, Snethen, Mt Pleasant, Hebron & Riverson churches; also Quantico Circuit Meth Prot Ch
Meth	Immanuel Meth Ch, Crisfield 1904-1967 # MSA
Meth Epis	Immanuel Meth Epis Ch, Crisfield 1873-1904, 1907-1930, 1959-1961 # MSA. SEE ALSO: Crisfield Sta Meth Epis Ch
Meth	Jerusalem Ch. SEE: Parsonburg Circuit Meth Epis Ch
Meth	Jerusalem Meth Ch 1932-1967 # MSA (prior to 1940 a Meth Epis ch)
Meth	Jone's Ch. SEE: Nanticoke Circuit Meth Epis Ch, Parsonburg Circuit Meth Epis Ch, Quantico Circuit Meth Epis Ch
Meth	King's. SEE: Delmar Circuit Meth Epis Ch
Meth	Mardela Charge Meth Ch 1888-1941, 1946-1959 # MSA (before 1895 Barren Creek Circuit Meth Prot Ch)
Prot Epis	Mardela Springs. SEE: St Paul's Ch
Meth Epis	Marren Creek Meth Epis Ch. SEE: St Pauls Meth Ch
Meth	Melsons Ch. SEE: Parsonburg Circuit Meth Epis Ch
Meth	Melson's Meth Ch 1960-1967 # MSA (prior to 1966 part of Pittsville Charge)
Meth	Messick's Ch. SEE: Quantico Circuit Meth Epis Ch, Quantico Circuit Meth Prot Ch
Meth	Mills Ch. SEE: Quantico Circuit Meth Prot Ch
Meth	Moore's Ch. SEE: Quantico Circuit Meth Epis Ch
Meth	Morris Schoolhouse Congregation. SEE: Wicomico Circuit Meth Epis Ch, South
Meth	Mt Hermon Ch. SEE: Pittsville Circuit Meth Prot Ch, Union Circuit Meth Prot Ch
Meth	Mt Hermon Meth Ch 1922-1967 # MSA (includes Mt Hermon Meth Prot Ch)
Meth	Mt Olive Ch. SEE: Powellville Charge Meth Ch, Powellville Charge Meth Prot Ch, Powellville Circuit Meth Prot Ch
Meth	Mt Olive Meth Ch, Delmar DE 1943-1963 # MSA. SEE ALSO: Delmar Charge Meth Prot Ch
Meth	Mt Pleasant Ch. SEE: Delmar Circuit Meth Epis Ch; Emmanuel, Snethen, Mt Pleasant, Hebron & Riverson churches; Powellville Charge Meth Ch; Powellville Charge Meth Epis Ch; Powellville Circuit Meth Epis Ch
Meth	Mt Pleasant Meth Ch 1961-1965 # MSA
Meth	Mt Vernon Charge Meth Ch 1923-1959 # MSA. SEE ALSO: Sharptown-Mt Vernon Charge
Meth	Mt Zion Ch. SEE: Powellville Charge Meth Ch, Powellville Charge Meth Prot Ch, Powellville Circuit Meth Epis Ch, Powellville Circuit Meth Prot Ch, Quantico Charge Meth Ch
Meth	Mussey's Ch. SEE: Quantico Circuit Meth Epis Ch
Meth Epis	Nanticoke Circuit Meth Epis Ch 1885-1961 # MSA (includes Jones, Trinity, Tyaskin, Whitehaven)
Meth	Nanticoke Meth Ch 1900-1964 # MSA (prior to 1940 a Meth Epis ch)

Meth	Nelson's Memorial Meth Ch 1923-1966 # MSA. SEE ALSO: Hebron Charge
Meth	New Ch. SEE: Wicomico Circuit Meth Epis Ch, South
Meth	New Hope Ch 1939-1967 # MSA. SEE ALSO: Pittsville Circuit Meth Prot Ch, Whaleyville Circuit Meth Prot Ch
Meth	New Hope Meth Ch 1955-1958 # MSA
Bap	New Testament Bap Ch, P.O.Box 1509, Salisbury Md 21801 (1981) 1981- * ch
Meth	Oak Grove Ch. SEE: Waltersville Charge Meth Prot Ch
Prot Epis	Old Green Hill Ch. SEE: St Bartholomew's Ch, Green Hill
Meth	Oriole Charge Meth Ch 1885-1946 (includes Barr's, Bethel, Oriole, St Peter's, St Stephen's)
Meth	Parker's Chapel. SEE: Powellville Circuit Meth Epis Ch
Meth Epis	Parsonburg Circuit Meth Epis Ch 1876-1932 # MSA (includes Bethel, Jerusalem, Jones, Melsons, Parsonburg, St Johns, Wesley, Zion)
Meth	Pittsville Charge. SEE: Melson's Meth Ch
Meth Prot	Pittsville Circuit Meth Prot Ch 1914-1937 # MSA (Mt Hermon & New Hope)
Meth	Portsville Ch. SEE: Union Circuit Meth Prot Ch
Meth	Powellville Charge Meth Ch 1933-1967 # MSA (includes Mt Olive, Mt Pleasant, Mt Zion, Powellville, St John's, White's Chapel, Willards)
Meth Epis	Powellville Charge Meth Epis Ch 1916-1944 # MSA (includes Mt Pleasant & St John's)
Meth Prot	Powellville Charge Meth Prot Ch 1921-1933 # MSA (includes Mt Olive, Mt Zion, Powellville)
Meth Epis	Powellville Circuit Meth Epis Ch 1882-1916 # MSA (includes Friendship, Mt Pleasant, Parker's Chapel, Powellville, St John's, Wesley)
Meth Prot	Powellville Circuit Meth Prot Ch 1876-1914 # MSA (includes Mt Olive, Mt Zion, Powellville)
Meth	Providence Ch. SEE: Union Circuit Meth Prot Ch
Prot Epis	Quantico. SEE: St Paul's Ch
Meth	Quantico Charge Meth Ch 1942-1962 # MSA (includes Mt Zion, St Lukes, St Marks)
Meth	Quantico Ch. SEE: Quantico Circuit Meth Epis Ch
Meth Epis	Quantico Circuit Meth Epis Ch 1860-1881 # MSA (includes Jone's, Messick's, Moore's, Mussey's, Quantico, Sharptown)
Meth Prot	Quantico Circuit Meth Prot Ch 1880-1960 # MSA (includes Bethel, Ebenezer, Hebron, Messick, Mills, Quantico, Rockawalkin, Royal Oaks, Siloam)
Meth	Quantico Meth Ch. SEE: First Meth-Quantico & Whitehaven Meth churches
Meth	Rehoboth. SEE: Whaleyville Charge Meth Ch, Whaleyville Circuit Meth Prot Ch
Meth	Riverson Ch. SEE: Emmanuel, Snethen, Mt Pleasant, Hebron & Riverson churches
Meth	Riverton Charge. SEE: Asbury-Riverton Charge
Presb	Rocawakin Presb Ch 23 April 1759 pew rentals # MGS Bull
Meth	Rockawalkin Meth Ch 1957-1967 # MSA. SEE ALSO: Quantico Circuit Meth Prot Ch

Meth Prot	Royal Oaks Ch. SEE: Quantico Circuit Meth Prot Ch
Meth	Russum. SEE: Union Circuit Meth Prot Ch
Meth	St Andrews Ch. SEE: South Salisbury Circuit Meth Epis Ch, South
Meth	St Andrews Meth Ch 1936-1967 # MSA (prior to 1940 South Salisbury Meth Epis Ch, South)
Prot Epis	St Bartholomew's Ch, Green Hill (1698) 1721-1838, 1840-1845 * and # MSA (known as Old Green Hill Ch)
Meth	St George's. SEE: Delmar Circuit Meth Epis Ch
Meth	St John's. SEE: Parsonburg Circuit Meth Epis Ch, Powellville Charge Meth Ch, Powellville Charge Meth Epis Ch, Powellville Circuit Meth Epis Ch
Meth	St John's Com Meth Ch, Fruitland 1953-1967 # MSA
Meth	St John's Meth Ch, Fruitland 1938-1967 # MSA
Meth	St Lukes Ch. SEE: Quantico Charge Meth Ch
Meth	St Marks Ch. SEE: Quantico Charge Meth Ch
Meth	St Paul. SEE: Hebron Charge
Prot Epis	St Paul's Ch 1832-1954 * and # MSA (organized as Spring Hill Chapel in Stepney Parish; includes Mardella Springs, Quantico, Spring Hill)
Meth	St Paul's Meth Ch 1910-1962 # MSA
Meth	St Pauls Meth Ch 1949-1963 # MSA (formerly Marren Creek Meth Epis Ch)
Meth	St Peter's Ch. SEE: Oriole Charge Meth Ch
Prot Epis	St Peter's Chapel, Stepney Parish. SEE: St Peter's Ch, Salisbury
Prot Epis	St Peter's Ch, Salisbury (1768) 1879-1923 * and # MSA (organized as St Peter's Chapel, Stepney Parish)
Meth	St Peter's Meth Ch 1945-1967 # MSA
Meth	St Stephan's Ch. SEE: Oriole Charge Meth Ch
Meth	Salisbury-Bethesda Meth Ch 1934-1959 # MSA (prior to 1940 Salisbury Meth Prot Ch)
Meth Prot	Salisbury Circuit Meth Prot Ch 1842-1936 # MSA
Meth Prot	Salisbury Meth Prot Ch. SEE: Salisbury-Bethesda Meth Ch
Meth	Selbyville. SEE: Whaleyville Circuit Meth Prot Ch
Meth	Sharptown Ch. SEE: Quantico Circuit Meth Epis Ch, Union Circuit Meth Prot Ch
Meth Epis	Sharptown Circuit Meth Epis Ch 1862-1876 # MSA
Meth Epis	Sharptown Meth Epis Ch 1876-1910 # MSA
Meth	Sharptown-Mt Vernon Charge 1895-1905, 1916-1918 # MSA
Meth	Shiloh Meth Ch 1931-1967 # MSA
Meth	Siloam Ch. SEE: Quantico Circuit Meth Prot Ch
Meth	Snethan Meth Ch 1961-1967 # MSA. SEE ALSO: Emmanuel, Snethen, Mt Pleasant, Hebron & Riverson churches; Union Circuit Meth Prot Ch
Meth Epis S	South Salisbury Circuit Meth Epis Ch, South 1904-1939 # MSA (includes St Andrews Ch)
Meth Epis S	South Salisbury Meth Epis Ch, South. SEE: St Andrews Meth Ch
Prot Epis	Spring Hill Chapel. SEE: St Paul's Ch
Prot Epis	Stepney Parish 1676-1804 # LDS

Wicomico County

Meth	Trinity Meth Ch 1867-1958 # MSA. SEE ALSO: Allen charge (Circuit) Meth Epis Ch, South; Nanticoke Circuit Meth Epis Ch; Wicomico Circuit Meth Epis Ch, South
Meth Epis	Trinity Meth Epis Ch. SEE: White Haven & Trinity Meth Epis churches
Meth Epis S	Trinity Meth Epis Ch, South 1920-1921 # MSA
Meth	Tyaskin Ch. SEE: Nanticoke Circuit Meth Epis Ch
Meth Prot	Union Circuit Meth Prot Ch 1863-1905 # MSA (includes Barren Creek Springs, Mt Hermon, Portsville, Providence, Russum, Snethen, Sharptown) SEE ALSO: Hebron Charge
Meth Prot	Waltersville Charge Meth Prot Ch 1884-1932 # MSA (later became Bivalve; includes Waltersville & Oak Grove churches)
Meth	Washington Ch. SEE: Wicomico Circuit Meth Epis Ch, South
Meth	Wesley Ch. SEE: Parsonburg Circuit Meth Epis Ch, Powellville Circuit Meth Epis Ch
Meth	Whaleyville Charge Meth Ch 1938-1964 # MSA (prior to 1940 a Meth Prot ch; includes Rehoboth)
Meth Prot	Whaleyville Circuit Meth Prot Ch 1909-1948 # MSA (includes New Hope, Rehoboth, Selbyville, Whaleyville)
Meth Prot	Wheatley Meth Prot Ch 1887-1950 # MSA
Meth Epis	White Haven & Trinity Meth Epis churches 1924-1942 # MSA
Meth	Whitehaven Meth Ch 1962-1966 # MSA. SEE ALSO: First Meth, Quantico & Whitehaven Meth churches; Nanticoke Circuit Meth Epis Ch
Meth	White's Chapel. SEE: Powellville Charge Meth Ch
Meth Epis S	Wicomico Circuit Meth Epis Ch, South 1877-1939 (includes Asbury, Bethel, Eden, Morris Schoolhouse, New, Trinity, Washington)
Meth	Willards. SEE: Powellville Charge Meth Ch
Meth	Zion Meth Ch 1932-1966 # MSA (prior to 1940 a Meth Epis ch) SEE ALSO: Parsonburg Circuit Meth Epis Ch

Worcester County

Prot Epis	All Hallow's Ch, Snow Hill (1697) 1844-1957 # MSA
Meth	Annamessex. SEE: Newtown Circuit Meth Prot Ch
Meth	Atlantic Meth Ch, Ocean City 1934-1966 # MSA
Meth Epis	Atlantic Meth Epis Ch 1915-1932 # MSA (includes First Meth Epis Ch, Ocean City; Bethany Meth Epis Ch, Synepuxent)
Unit Meth	Atlantic Unit Meth Ch, P.O.Box 88, Ocean City Md 21842 * ch (dates not given)
Meth	Basket Town. SEE: Snow Hill Circuit Meth Prot Ch
Meth	Bates Memorial Ch. SEE: Snow Hill Circuit Meth Prot Ch
Meth	Bates Memorial Meth Ch, Snow Hill 1930-1967 # MSA (prior to 1940 a Meth Prot ch)
Meth Epis	Berlin Circuit Meth Epis Ch 1857-1875, 1891-1896 # MSA (includes Bethel, Friendship, Line, Poplartown, Sinepuxent, Stevenson, Whaleyville, Zion (in 1895 Berlin made a Sta with Stevenson Ch)

Worcester County

Meth Epis	Berlin sta Meth Epis Ch, Berlin 1895-1925 # MSA
Meth	Bethany Ch. SEE: Pocomoke City Charge Meth Prot Ch, Salem-Bethany Unit Meth Ch
Meth	Bethany Meth Ch, Synepuxent 1963-1967 # MSA
Meth Epis	Bethany Meth Epis Ch, Synepuxent 1915-1960 # MSA. SEE ALSO: Atlantic Meth Epis Ch
Unit Meth	Bethany Unit Meth Ch, P.O.Box 36, Newark 21841 (1942) 1963-* ch. SEE ALSO: Salem-Bethany Unit Meth Ch
Meth	Bethel. SEE: Berlin Circuit Meth Epis Ch
Meth	Bowen Meth Ch, Newark 1936-1967 # MSA (prior to 1940 a Meth Epis Ch)
Meth	Box Iron. SEE: Snow Hill Circuit Meth Prot Ch
Presb	Buckingham Presb Ch, Main St, Berlin 21811 (1683) 1793-1797, 1818-1864 * ch, # PHS (dates not given)
Meth	Cokesbury. SEE: Pocomoke (New Town) Circuit Meth Epis Ch
Meth	Conners. SEE: Girdletree Charge Meth Epis Ch
Meth	Cool Spring. SEE: Snow Hill Circuit Meth Prot Ch
Meth	Ebenezer. SEE: Snow Hill-Ebenezer Charge Meth Ch
Meth	First Meth Epis Ch, Ocean City. SEE: Atlantic Meth Epis Ch
Meth	Friendship. SEE: Berlin Circuit Meth Epis Ch, Newtown Circuit Meth Prot Ch, Powellville Circuit Meth Epis Ch
Meth Epis	Girdletree Charge Meth Epis Ch 1885-1935 # MSA (includes Conners, Girdletree, Goodwill, Grange, Klej, Remson)
Meth	Girdletree Ch. SEE: Girdletree Charge Meth Epis Ch, Snow Hill Circuit Meth Prot Ch
Meth	Girdletree-Stockton Charge Meth Ch 1927-1965 # MSA (includes Girdletree, Portersville, Remson, Stockton)
Meth	Goodwill. SEE: Girdletree Charge Meth Epis Ch, Pocomoke (New Town) Circuit Meth Epis Ch
Meth	Grange. SEE: Girdletree Charge Meth Epis Ch
Meth	Greenback. SEE: Pocomoke (New town) Circuit Meth Epis Ch
Meth	Holland. SEE: Pocomoke (New Town) Circuit Meth Epis Ch
Meth	Hopewell. SEE: Pocomoke (New Town) Circuit Meth Epis Ch
Meth Prot	Indian River Charge Meth Prot Ch 1920-1944 # MSA
Meth	Klej. SEE: Girdletree Charge Meth Epis Ch
Meth	Laurel Circuit. SEE: Berlin Circuit Meth Epis Ch
Meth	Liberty Town. SEE: Snow Hill Circuit Meth Prot Ch
Meth	Line. SEE: Berlin Circuit Meth Epis Ch
Presb	Makemie Memorial Presb Ch, Snow Hill. 1818-1833, 1895-1957 # MSA
Meth	Mt Olive Ch. SEE: Powellville Charge Meth Ch, Powellville Charge Meth Prot Ch, Powellville Circuit Meth Epis Ch
Meth	Mt Pleasant Ch. SEE: Powellville Charge Meth Ch, Powellville Charge Meth Epis Ch, Powellville Circuit Meth Epis Ch
Meth	Mt Wesley. SEE: Snow Hill-Ebenezer Charge Meth Ch
Meth	Mt Zion. SEE: Powellville Charge Meth Ch, Powellville Charge Meth Prot Ch, Powellville Circuit Meth Prot Ch
Meth	Nassawango. SEE: Snow Hill Circuit Meth Prot Ch
Meth	New Hope. SEE: Whaleyville Charge Meth Ch, Whaleyville Circuit Meth Prot Ch
Meth	New Hope Meth Ch 1954-1958 # MSA
Meth	New Town. SEE: Pocomoke (New Town) Circuit Meth Epis Ch

94

Meth Prot	Newtown Circuit Meth Prot Ch 1832-1909 # MSA (includes Annamessex, Friendship, Newtown, Quinton, Wesley Chapel)
Meth	Parker's Chapel. SEE: Powellville Circuit Meth Epis Ch
Meth	Pocomoke-Bethany Meth Ch 1942-1953 # MSA
Meth	Pocomoke Circuit Meth Ch 1940-1951 # MSA (after 1945 Pocomoke-Salem Charge)
Meth Epis	Pocomoke Circuit Meth Epis Ch 1881-1899 # MSA
Meth Epis	Pocomoke City Charge Meth Epis Ch 1899-1942 # MSA
Meth Prot	Pocomoke City Charge Meth Prot Ch 1886-1951 # MSA (includes Bethany, Quinton)
Meth Epis	Pocomoke (New Town) Circuit Meth Epis Ch 1871-1881 # MSA (includes Cokesbury, Goodwill, Greenback, Holland, Hopewell, New Town, Remson, Stockton, Williams)
Meth	Pocomoke-Salem Meth Ch 1930-1963 # MSA (prior to 1946 Pocomoke Circuit, until 1940 Pocomoke Circuit Meth Epis Ch)
Meth	Poplartown. SEE: Berlin Circuit Meth Epis Ch
Meth	Portersville (Porterville) Ch. SEE: Girdletree-Stockton Charge Meth Ch, Snow Hill Circuit Meth Prot Ch
Meth	Powell's Chapel. SEE: Snow Hill-Ebenezer Charge Meth Ch
Meth	Powellville Charge Meth Ch 1933-1967 # MSA (includes Mt Olive, Mt Pleasant, Mt Zion, Powellville, St John's, White's Chapel, Willards; prior to 1940 a Meth Prot ch)
Meth Epis	Powellville Charge Meth Epis Ch 1916-1944 # MSA (includes Mt Pleasant, St John's)
Meth Prot	Powellville Charge Meth Prot Ch 1911-1919, 1921-1933 # MSA (includes Mt Olive, Mt Zion, Powellville)
Meth Epis	Powellville Circuit Meth Epis Ch 1882-1916 # MSA (includes Friendship, Mt Pleasant, Parker's Chapel, St John's, Wesley)
Meth Prot	Powellville Circuit Meth Prot Ch 1876-1914 # MSA (includes Mt Olive, Mt Zion, Powellville)
Meth	Quinton Ch. SEE: Newtown Circuit Meth Prot Ch, Pocomoke City Charge Meth Prot Ch
Meth	Rehoboth. SEE: Whaleyville Charge Meth Ch, Whaleyville Circuit Meth Prot Ch
Meth	Remson (Remsons) Ch. SEE: Girdletree Charge Meth Epis Ch, Girdletree-Stockton Charge Meth Ch, Pocomoke (New Town) Circuit Meth Epis Ch, Stockton Charge Meth Epis Ch
Meth	St John's. SEE: Powellville Charge Meth Ch, Powellville Charge Meth Epis Ch, Powellville Circuit Meth Epis Ch
Prot Epis	St Martins Ch 1722-1840 # MHS
Prot Epis	St Martin's Ch, Showell (1756) 1722-1893 * and # MSA, 1722-1839 # LDS
Prot Epis	St Mary the Virgin Ch, Pocomoke City (formerly Newtown) (1845) 1855-1930 # MSA
Prot Epis	St Paul's by-the-Sea Ch, Ocean City (1881) 1918-1957 # MSA
Unit Meth	Salem-Bethany Unit Meth Ch * ch (organized: Salem 1808, Bethany 1834; dates of records not given)
Meth	Selbyville. SEE: Waleyville Circuit Meth Prot Ch
Meth	Sinepuxent. SEE: Berlin Circuit Meth Epis Ch
Meth Prot	Snow Hill Circuit Meth Prot Ch 1863-1953 # MSA (includes Basket Town, Bates Memorial, Box Iron, Cool Spring,

	Girdletree, Liberty Town, Nassawango, Porterville, Snow Hill, Trinity; after 1940 a Meth ch)
Meth	Snow Hill Circuit Meth Prot Ch 1904-1923 # MSA (Bates Memorial Ch)
Meth	Snow Hill-Ebenezer Charge Meth Ch 1869-1966 # MSA (includes Ebenezer, Mt Wesley, Powell's Chapel)
Meth	Stevenson Meth Ch, Berlin 1950-1967 # MSA. SEE ALSO: Berlin Circuit Meth Epis Ch
Meth	Stockton. SEE: Girdletree-Stockton Charge Meth Ch, Pocomoke (New Town) Circuit Meth Epis Ch
Meth	Stockton Charge Meth Epis Ch 1911-1945 # MSA (after union became Girdletree-Stockton Charge)
Meth	Trinity. SEE: Snow Hill Circuit Meth Prot Ch
Meth	Trinity Meth Ch, Newark 1936-1967 # MSA (prior to 1940 a Meth Prot ch)
Meth	Wesley Chapel. SEE: Newtown Circuit Meth Prot Ch, Powellville Circuit Meth Epis Ch
Meth	Whaleyville. SEE: Berlin Circuit Meth Epis Ch
Meth	Whaleyville Charge Meth Ch 1938-1967 # MSA (includes New Hope, Rehoboth, Whaleyville; prior to 1940 a Meth Prot ch)
Meth Prot	Whaleyville Circuit Meth Prot Ch 1909-1948 # MSA (includes New Hope, Rehoboth, Selbyville, Whaleyville)
Meth Epis	Whatcoat Meth Epis Ch, Snow Hill 1894-1922 # MSA
Meth	White's Chapel. SEE: Powellville Charge Meth Ch
Meth	Willards. SEE: Powellville Charge Meth Ch
Meth	Williams. SEE: Pocomoke (New Town) Circuit Meth Epis Ch
Meth	Zion. SEE: Berlin Circuit Meth Epis Ch

CHURCH ADDRESSES

African Methodist Episcopal

Allegany   Metropolitan Afric Meth Epis Ch, 309 Frederick St, Cumberland
              21502
Anne Arundel Ebenezer Afric Meth Epis Ch, Main St & Church Ln, Galesville
              20765
              Mt Moriah Afric Meth Epis Ch, 2204 Bay Ridge Ave, Annapolis
              21403
              Mt Olive Afric Meth Epis Ch, 2 Hicks Ave, Annapolis 21401
              Payne Memorial Afric Meth Epis Ch, 7901 Brockbridge Rd, Jessup
              20794
              St John Afric Meth Epis Zion Ch, 2993 Conway, Odenton 21113
              Wayman-Good Hope Afric Meth Epis Ch, 100 Hoyle Dr, Severna
              Park 21146
Baltimore   Adams Chapel Afric Meth Epis Ch, 3811 Egerton Rd, Balto 21215
              Allen Afric Meth Epis Ch, 1130 W Lexington St, Balto 21223
              Bazil Afric Meth Epis Ch, Sherwood Rd, Cockeysville 21030
              Bethel Afric Meth Epis Ch, Druid Hill Ave & Lanvale St, Balto
              21217
              Campfield Afric Meth Epis Ch, 7140 Walnut St, Balto 21208
              Cowdensville Afric Meth Epis Ch, 1100 Sulphur Spring Rd, Balto
              21227
              Davis Memorial Afric Meth Epis Ch, 2409 Roslyn Ave, Balto
              21216
              Ebenezer Afric Meth Epis Ch, 20 W Montgomery St, Balto 21230
              Evergreen Afric Meth Epis Ch, 3342 Old Frederick Rd, Balto
              21229
              Falls Road Afric Meth Epis Ch, 4627 Falls Rd, Balto 21209
              Grace Afric Meth Epis Ch, 67 1/2 Winters Ln, Catonsville 21228
              Hemingway Temple Afric Meth Epis Ch, 2701 Woodview Rd, Cherry
              Hill, Balto 21225
              John Wesley Afric Meth Epis Ch, 1923 Ashland Ave, Balto 21205
              Mt Calvary Afric Meth Epis Ch, 300 Eudowood Ln, Towson 21204
              Mt Gilboa Afric Meth Epis Ch, 2312 Westchester Ave, Balto
              21228
              Mt Joy Afric Meth Epis Ch, 17223 Troyer Rd, Monkton 2111
              Mt Pleasant Afric Meth Epis Ch, 235 Tollgate Rd, Owings Mills
              21117
              Mt Zion Afric Meth Epis Ch, 12728 Manor Rd, Long green 21092
              Oak Street Afric Meth Epis Ch, 2317 N Howard St, Balto 21218
              Patterson-Asbury Afric Meth Epis Ch, 2211 Division St, Balto
              21217
              Payne Memorial Afric Meth Epis Ch (Madison & Laurens Sts) 1716
              Madison Ave, Balto 21217
              Pennsylvania Avenue Afric Meth Epis Ch, 1124 Pennsylvania Ave,
              Balto 21201
              St John's Afric Meth Epis Ch, 810 N Carrollton Ave, Balto
              21217
              St Stephen's Afric Meth Epis Ch, 1601 Eastern Ave, Essex 21221
              St Stephen's Afric Meth Epis Ch, 7741 Mayfield Ave, Balto
              21227
              Shiloh Afric Meth Epis Ch, 2601 Lyndhurst Ave, Balto 21216

Star of Bethlehem Afric Meth Epis Ch, 2525 Ridgely Rd, Balto 21230

Stevenson Afric Meth Epis Ch, 811 E Quaker Bottom Rd, Sparks 21152

Trinity Afric Meth Epis Ch, 2130 E Hoffman St, Balto 21213

Union Bethel Afric Meth Epis Ch, 8502 Liberty Rd, Randallstown 21133

Union Chapel, c/o Theodore McPherson, 6827 Alter St, Balto 21207

Waters Afric Meth Epis Ch, 417 Aisquith St, Balto 21202

Wayman Afric Meth Epis Ch, 1236 Bayard St, Balto 21230

Caroline
Allen Afric Meth Epis Ch, Hillsboro 21641

Bells Chapel Afric Meth Epis Ch, Tuckahoe Rd, Deep Branch, Denton 21629

Bethel Afric Meth Epis Ch, Lincoln St, Denton 21629

Coppin Afric Meth Epis Ch, RFD 2, Preston 21655

Ross Chapel Afric Meth Epis Ch, RFD 2, Denton 21629

Trinity Afric Meth Epis Ch, Ridgely 21660

Cecil
Bethel Afric Meth Epis Ch, Charles St, Chesapeake City 21915

Bethel Afric Meth Epis Ch, 198 Main St, Port Deposit 21904

Ebenezer Afric Meth Epis Ch, St Augustine Rd, Chesapeake City 21915

Mt Zoar Afric Meth Epis Ch, Mt Zoar Rd, Conowingo 21918

Union Bethel Afric Meth Epis Ch, 161 Church St, Cecilton 21913

Wright Afric Meth Epis Ch, Booth & Bethel Sts, Elkton 21921

District of
Columbia
The Afric Meth Epis Ch (A.M.E.) The Maryland Conference, 1239 Vermont Ave, NW Washington DC 20005

Dorchester
Bethel Afric Meth Epis Ch, 621 Pine St, Cambridge 21613

Hughes Chapel Afric Meth Epis Ch, RFD 2 Box 262, Cambridge 21613

Frederick
Ceres Bethel Afric Meth Epis Ch, Burkittsville 21756

Ebenezer Afric Meth Epic Ch, Maple Ave, Brunswick 21716

Mt Zion Afric Meth Epis Ch, 202 Jefferson Pike, Knoxville 21758

Quinn Chapel Afric Meth Epis Ch, 106 E 3rd St, Frederick 21701

St James Afric Meth Epis Ch, 6001 Bartonsville Rd, Frederick 21701

St Stephens Afric Meth Epis Ch, Unionville 21792

Union Bethel Afric Meth Epis Ch (Petersville) 718 Maple Ave, Brunswick 21716

Wayman Afric Meth Epis Ch, Old Liberty Rd, Mt Pleasant 21701

Harford
Chestnut Grove Afric Meth Epis Ch, 828 Coen Rd, Street 21154

Fairview Afric Meth Epis Ch (Highpoint Rd & Jarretsville Pike) 2328 Highpoint Rd, Forest Hill 21050

Hosanna Afric Meth Epis Ch, Castleton Rd, Darlington 21034

St James Afric Meth Epis Ch, 4139 Gravel Hill Rd, Havre de Grace 21078

St James Afric Meth Epis Ch, 615 Green St, Havre de Grace 21078

Howard
Gaines Afric Meth Epis Ch, 7134 Montgomery Rd, Elkridge 21227

Mt Pisgah Afric Meth Epis Ch, 8651 Old Annapolis Rd, Columbia 21043

African Methodist Episcopal

St Luke Afric Meth Epis Ch, 8411 Main St, Ellicott City 21403
Kent   Bethel Afric Meth Epis Ch, 237 College Ave, Chestertown 21620
              Boardley Chapel Afric Meth Epis Ch, Pondtown Rd, Pondtown
              Holy Trinity Afric Meth Epis Ch, P.O.Box 275, Rockhall 21661
              Mt Olive Afric Meth Epis Ch, Worton 21678
              New Bethel Afric Meth Epis Ch, Golts 21637
Montgomery   Allen Chapel Afric Meth Epis Ch, Dayton Ave & Dotson Ln,
                 Wheaton 20902
              LeeMemorial Afric Meth Epis Ch, 4115 Plyers Mill Rd,
                 Kensington 20795
              St Paul Afric Meth Epis ch, 1135 Della Rd, Dickerson 20753
Prince   Adams Inspirational Chapel Afric Meth Epis Ch, 10590
  Georges   Piscataway Rd, Clinton 20735
              Ebenezer Afric Meth Epis Ch, 7806 Allentown Rd, Fort
                 Washington 20744
              Embry Afric Meth Epis Ch, 5101 Lakeland Rd, College Park 20740
              Good Shepherd Afric Meth Epis Ch, 3505 Silver Park Dr,
                 Suitland 20746
              Hunter Memorial Afric Meth Epis Ch, 5001 Holly Spring St,
                 Suitland 20746
              Mt Nebro Afric Meth Epis Ch, Queen Anne Rd, Mitchellville
                 20716
              Seaton Memorial Afric Meth Ch, 5503 Lincoln Ave, Lanham 20801
              Union Bethel Afric Meth Epis Ch, Floral Park Rd, Brandywine
                 20613
Queen Annes   Bethel Afric Meth Epis Ch, N Liberty St, Centreville 21617
              Bethel Afric Meth Epis Ch, Box 68, Church Hill 21623
              Robinson Afric Meth Epis Ch, Cemetery Rd, Grasonville 21638
St Marys   St John Afric Meth Epis Ch, Charlotte Hall 20622
              Union Bethel Afric Meth Epis Ch, Charlotte Hall 20622
Somerset   St Paul Afric Meth Epis Ch, 101 S 4th St, Crisfield 21817
Talbot   Bethel Afric Meth Epis Ch, 112 S Hanson St, Easton 21601
              Queen Esther-Ivytown Afric Meth Epis Ch (Manadier Rd, Ivytown)
                 RFD 2 Box 290, Easton 21601
              St Stephen Afric Meth Epis Ch, RFD 1 Box 631, Easton 21601
Washington   Ebenezer Afric Meth Epis Ch, 26 Bethel St, Hagerstown 21740
Wicomico   First Afric Meth Epis Ch, 323 Broad St, Salisbury 21810
              Mt Olive Afric Meth Epis Ch, 109 S Division St, Fruitland
                 21826
              St Paul Afric Meth Epis Zion Ch, 410 Delaware Ave, Salisbury
                 21801
Worcester   Collins Temple & Georgetown Afric Meth Epis Ch, RFD 4 Box 64,
                 Snow Hill 21863
              St James Afric Meth Epis Ch, RFD 1 Box 29-C, Newark 21841
              St John Afric Meth Epis Ch, 605 Laurel St, Pocomoke City 21851
              St John's Afric Meth Epis Ch, P.O.Box 357, Bishopville 21813
              Tyree Afric Meth Epis Ch, Germantown Rd, RFD 3 Box 279, Berlin
                 21811
Anne Arundel Antioch Apos Ch, 1535 Ritchie Hwy, Arnold 21012
              House of Prayer Ch, 5161 Sudley Rd, West River 20778
              Lighthouse Apos Ch, 616 Severn Ave, Annapolis 21403
              Mt Zion Apos Ch, 3421 Riva Rd, Riva 21140

St James Ch of Apos Faith, Howard Rd, Marley Park, Glen Burnie
21061

Apostolic

Baltimore

Apostal True Foundation Ch, 2111 Edmondson Ave, Balto 21223
Apos Bible Study Ch, 1106 N Wolfe St, Balto 21213
Bethlehem Temple, 2100 Eutaw Pl, Balto 21217
Christ Tabernacle, 1400 McCulloh St, Balto 21217
Christ Temple Apos Ch, 827 Cherry Hill Rd, Balto 21225
Ch of Christ Household of Faith, Pillow Ground of Truth, 3503
  Fairview Ave, Balto 21216
Ch of the Lord Jesus Christ of the Apos Faith, 717 S Sharp St,
  Balto 21230
Ch of the Redeemed, 5100 Liberty Heights Ave, Balto 21207
Ch of the Redeemed of the Lord, 519 N Chester St, Balto 21205
Eastern Star Tabernacle, 1918 N Collington Ave, Balto 21213
Emmanuel Apos Faith Ch, 1349 N Gay St, Balto 21213
Faith Tabernacle Apos Ch, 2613 Ashland Ave, Balto 21205
First Apos Faith Ch, 25 S Caroline St, Balto 21231
First Emmanuel Ch Apos, 4534 Reisterstown Rd, Balto 21215
First Unit Ch of Jesus Christ Apos, 5150 Balto Natl Pike,
  Balto 21229
Full Gospel True Mission, 2001 E Barkley Ave, Balto 21221
Gospel Tabernacle Ch, 1 Ash Ave, Balto 21222
Greater Ch of Our Lord Jesus Christ Apos, 12 S Stockton St,
  Balto 21223
Highway Ch of Christ, 3413 Hayward Ave, Balto 21215
Highway to Heaven Apos Faith Ch, 1650 N Patterson Park Ave,
  Balto 21213
Hiway Chris Ch, 1100 Homewood Ave, Balto 21202
Holy Name Ch of Jesus, 5345 Park Heights Ave, Balto 21215
Lord's House Apos Faith Ch, 1418 W Lafayette Ave, Balto 21217
Macedonia Apos Faith Ch, 2019 E Biddle St, Balto 21213
Memorial Insti Ch of God, 2016 Greenmount Ave, Balto 21218
Mt Olive Holy Evangelistic Ch, 3816 Edmondson Ave, Balto 21229
Mt Zion Apos Faith Ch of Jesus Christ, 5501 Liberty Heights
  Ave, Balto 21207
Naz Temple, 2312 Harford Rd, Balto 21218
New Galilee Ch of God in Christ Jesus, 3016 Oakley Ave, Balto
  21215
Orth Apos Faith Ch, 1800 N Gay St, Balto 21213
Outreach Temple for Christ Apos, 1105 N Gay St, Balto 21213
Pillar of Truth Ch of God of the Apos Faith, 2505 E Madison
  St, Balto 21205
Prayer Chapel Ch, 1752 N Gay St, Balto 21213
Redeemed Ch of Christ Apos, 2616 Harford Rd, Balto 21218
Refuge Way of the Cross Ch, 4301 Old York Rd, Balto 21212
Rehoboth Ch of God, 700 Poplar Grove St, Balto 21216

Apostolic

	St James Apos Faith Ch, 4240 Park Heights Ave, Balto 21215
	St James Apos Faith Ch II, 2720 Boarman Ave, Balto 21215
	St Matthews Gospel Tabernacle, 1907 N Rosedale St, Balto 21216
	St Paul Ch of God in Christ Jesus Apos, 2625 E Hoffman, Balto 21213
	Saints Pent Holiness Ch Apos Faith, 4113 Frederick Ave, Balto 21229
	Shiloh Apos Temple Ch, 1400 N Broadway, Balto 21213
	Shiloh Unit Ch, 1615 E Lafayette Ave, Balto 21207
	Stephens Ch of God Apos Faith, 3008 Independence Ave, Balto 21218
	Trinity Apos Faith Ch, 2819 Frederick Ave, Balto 21223
	True Tabernacle Ch of Jesus Christ Apos, 1404 N Gay St, Balto 21213
	True Way Apos Ch, 4318 Pimlico Rd, Balto 21215
	Unit Ch of Jesus Christ Apos, 2226 Park Ave, Balto 21217
	Unit House of Prayer, 600 W Preston St, Balto 21201
	Unit House of Prayer for All People, 1515 Ashland Ave, Balto 21205
	Victory Prayer Chapel, 4848 Reisterstown Rd, Balto 21215
Calvert	Apos Faith Ch of Jesus Christ, Adams Church Rd, Owings 20736
	Calvert Unit Apos Ch, Wayside Rd, Owings 20736
	Solid Rock Ch of Christ, Port Republic 20676
Charles	Apos New Life Center, Waldorf 20601
	Free Gospel Ch, 1 Bryans Rd, Bryans Road 20616
Dorchester	Unit Apos Ch, 513 Goldsborough Ave, Cambridge 21613
Harford	Apos Ch of Jesus Christ, 2510 Sandy Hook Rd, Bel Air 21014
	Highway Holiness Ch, 511 Edmund St, Aberdeen 21001
	Zion Temple Ch, 501 Legion Dr, Havre de Grace 21078
St Marys	House of Prayer Ch, Mechanicsville 20659
Talbot	Unit Apos Ch of Jesus Christ, Cordova Rd, Easton 21601
Worcester	Glorious Ch of the Lord Jesus Christ, 7th & Young St, Pocomoke City 21851

Assembly of God

Allegany	Central Assem of God, 2020 Bedford St, Cumberland 21502
	Cresaptown Assem of God, Church Warrior Dr, Cresaptown 21502
	First Assem of God, 21 Elder St, Cumberland 21502
	First Assem of God, Rt 36 South, Lonaconing 21539
	LaVale Chapel, 525 National Hwy, LaVale 21502
	New Life Assem of God, 861 Columbia Ave, Cumberland 21502
	Trinity Assem of God, Midlothian 21543
Anne Arundel	Annapolis Assem of God, 913 Cedar Park Rd, Annapolis 21401
	Assembly of God, Hanover Ridge & Ridge Chapel Rds, Hanover 21076
	Faith Assem of God, 250 W Bay Front Rd, Lothian 20711
	Glen Burnie Assem of God, 7305 E Furnace Branch Rd, Glen Burnie 21061

	Pasadena Assem of God, 206 Pleasant View, Pasadena 21122
Baltimore	Bethel Assem of God, Waldman Ave, Balto 21219
	Carney Assem of God, 3319 Summit Ave, Balto 21234
	Central Chris Assem of God, 7902 Belair Rd, Balto 21236
	Dayspring Assem of God, 3555 4th St, Balto 21225
	Eastern Assem of God, 7923 Wise Ave, Balto 21222
	Essex Assem of God, 406 Beck St, Balto 21221
	Hereford Assem of God, 1211 Mt Carmel Dr, Parkton 21120
	Highland Assem of God, 2235 Essex St, Balto 21231
	Temple of Prayer Holy Assem of God, 3108 Clifton Ave, Balto 21216
	Middle River Assem of God, 9620 Bird River Rd, Balto 21220
	Trinity Assem of God, 2122 W Joppa Rd, Balto 21204
Calvert	Full Gospel Assem of God, Prince Frederick 20678
Carroll	Faith Tabernacle Assem of God, 1134 Long Corner Rd, Mt Airy 21771
	First Assem of God, 30 N Cranberry Rd, Westminster 21157
Cecil	First Assem of God, 290 White Hall Rd, Elkton 21921
Charles	Calvary Grace Assem of God, Newtown Estates, LaPlata 20646
	Glymont Assem of God, Indian Head 20640
Frederick	Calvary Assem of God, 8234 Woodsboro Pike, Walkersville 21793
	Faith Assem of God, cor Souder Rd & Rt 17, Brunswick 21716
	Point of Rocks Assem of God, 1508 Bank St, Point of Rocks 21777
	Shookstown Assem of God, 7722 Edgewood Church Rd, Frederick 21701
Garrett	Maranatha Assem of God, 1000 Springs Rd, Grantsville 21536
	Mt Top Chris Assem of God, Rt 135, Mt Lake Park 21550
Harford	Bel Air Assem of God, 701 Henderson Rd, Bel Air 21014
	Edgewood Assem of God, 803 Edgewood Rd, Edgewood 21040
	Evangel Assem of God, 302 W Bel Air Ave, Aberdeen 21001
	New Covenant Assem of God, 15 Churchville Rd, Bel Air 21014
Howard	Bethel Assem of God, 8340 Woodward St, Savage 20763
	Calvary Assem of God, 10817 David Ave, Woodstock 21163
Kent	Trinity Assem of God, Rt 213 North, Chestertown 21620
Prince	First Assem of God, 6705 Good Luck Rd, Lanham 20706
Georges	First Assem of God, 1102 Montgomery St, Laurel 20707
Queen Annes	Barclay Assem of God, Barclay 21607
St Marys	Patuxent River Assem of God, St James, Lexington Park 20653
Washington	Bethel Assem of God, 515 E Wilson Blvd, Hagerstown 21740
	Evangel Assem of God, 1028 Salem Ave, Hagerstown 21740
	Hancock Assem of God, N Pennsylvania Ave Ext, Hancock 21750
	Williamsport Assem of God, Falling Waters Rd, Williamsport 21795
Wicomico	First Assem of God, Westchester St, Salisbury 21801
Worcester	Glad Tidings Assem of God, Market St & Payne Ave, Pocomoke City 21851

Allegany	Bedford Road Bap Ch, Bedford & Mill Rds, Rt 3 Box 243A, Cumberland 21502
	Calvary Bap Ch, 14513 McMullen Hwy, Cresaptown 21502
	Calvary Bible Bap Ch off Rt 35 on left, Ellerslie 21529
	Christ Memorial Bap Ch, 207 Roosevelt St, Westernport 21562
	Cornerstone Bap Ch, 930 Frederick St, Cumberland 21502
	Ebenezer Bap Ch, 211 Cumberland St, Cumberland 21502
	Faith Indep Bap Ch, 255 Shaw St, Frostburg 21532
	First Bap Ch, 212 Bedford St, Cumberland 21502
	First Bap Ch, Main St & Philos Ave, Westernport 21562
	First Eng Bap Ch, 136 E Main St, Frostburg 21532
	Grace Bap Ch, 211 Greene St, Cumberland 21502
	Grace Mission, Rt 3 Box 269X, Rawlings 21557
	Highland Bap Ch, Messick Rd, Cumberland 21502
	La Vale Bap Ch, 1115 Natl Hwy, La Valle 21502
	Memorial Heights Bap Ch, 1419 Oldtown Rd, Cumberland 21502
	Oldtown Bap Ch, P.O.Box 115, Oldtown 21555
	Second Bap Ch, 1 Grand Ave, P.O.Box 2215, Cumberland 21502
	Stoney Run Bap Ch, Rt 1, Westernport 21562
	Welsh Memorial Bap Ch, 17 Beall St, Frostburg 21532
Anne Arundel	Anchor Bap Ch, W Pasadena Rd, Millersville 21108
	Arundel Bap Ch, 886 Annapolis Rd, Gambrills 21054
	Berea Bap Ch, 8017 Crain Hwy, Glen Burnie 21061
	Bethlehem Korean Bap Ch, 7378 Furnace Branch Rd, Glen Burnie 21061
	Broadneck Bap Ch, P.O.Box 116, Arnold 21012
	Calvary Bap Ch, 407 Marley Sta Rd, Glen Burnie 21061
	College Parkway Bap Ch, 301 College Pkwy, P.O.Box 217, Arnold 21012
	Dorsey Road Bap Ch, P.O.Box 339, Severna Park 21146
	Elvaton Bap Ch, P.O.Box 1317, Glen Burnie 21061
	Elvaton Bap Ch, Elvaton Rd, Millersville 21108
	Emmanuel Mission, 1215 Waugh Chapel Rd, P.O.Box 223, Gambrills 21054
	Faith Bap Ch, 7378 Furnace Branch Rd, Glen Burnie 21061
	First Bap Ch, 31 W Washington St, Annapolis 21401
	First Bap Ch, 1690 Crofton Pkwy, P.O.Box 3425, Crofton 21114
	First Bap Ch, 38 W Central Ave, P.O.Box 418, Edgewater 21037
	First Bap Ch, 1320 Avalon Blvd, Rt 468 Box 134, Shady Side 20764
	First Bap Ch of Eastport, 208 Chesapeake Ave, Annapolis 21403
	Glen Burnie Bap Ch, 7524 Old Stage Rd, Glen Burnie 21061
	Grace Bap Ch (Sunset Beach) 18 Somerset Rd, Pasadena 21122
	Grace Indep Bap Ch, 1311 Generals Hwy, Crownsville 21032
	Granite Bap Ch, 7823 Oakwood Rd, Glen Burnie 21061
	Heritage Bap Ch, 1740 Forest Dr, Annapolis 21401
	Heritage Bap Ch, 2901 Telegraph Rd, Odenton 21113
	Jessup Bap Ch, P.O.Box 308, Jessup 20794
	Lake Shore Bap Ch, 4613 Mountain Rd, P.O.Box 1038, Pasadena 21122
	Linthicum Bap Ch, 611 S Camp Meade Rd, Linthicum Heights 21090
	New Hope Bap Ch, 968 Lower Pindell Rd, Lothian 20711

CHURCH ADDRESSES

North Glen Bap Ch, 512 Furnace Branch Rd NW, Glen Burnie 21061
Odenton Bap Ch, 450 Telegraph Rd, Odenton 21113
Second Bap Ch, 1808 Poplar Ave, Annapolis 21401
Severn Bap Ch (Donald Ave & Telegraph Rd) 1330 Donald Ave,
  Severn 21144
Severna Park Bap Ch, 506 Benfield Rd, P.O.Box 339, Severna
  Park 21146
Silas First Bap Ch, Earleigh Hts Rd, Severna Park 21146
South Shore Bap Ch, 725 Herald Harbor Rd, Crownsville 21032
Temple Bap Ch, 15 Old Stage Rd, Glen Burnie 21061
Van Buren Street Bap Ch, 911 Van Buren St, Annapolis 21403
Weems Creek Bap Ch, Best Gate Rd & Ridgeley Ave, Annapolis
  21401

Baltimore   All Saints Bap Ch, 1702 Laurens St, Balto 21217
Antioch Bap Ch, 1799 Merritt Blvd, Balto 21222
Antioch Memorial Bap Ch, 5008 Ivanhoe Ave, Balto 21212
Arbutus Bap Ch, 5709 Oakland Rd, Arbutus, Balto 21227
Arlington Bap Ch, 3030 N Rolling Rd, Balto 21207
Balto Bap Assn, 1717 York Rd, Lutherville 21093
Balto Co Bap Ch, 14010 Hanover Pike, Reisterstown 21136
Bap Convention of Md (Southern Bap) 1313 York Rd, Lutherville
  21093
Beacon Bap Ch, 400 Wilson St, Balto 21217
Belvedere Bap Ch, 1301 Cheverly Rd, P.O.Box 5520, Towson 21204
Berea Bap Ch, 7001 German Hill Rd, Balto 21222
Berean Bap Ch, 5200 Denmore Ave, Balto 21215
Bethany Bap Ch, 2616 Ridgely St, Balto 21230
Bethel Bap Ch, 4261 Montgomery Rd, Balto 21227
Bethel Missionary Bap Ch, 1031 N Calhoun St, Balto 21217
Bible Bap Ch of Balto, 454 E Cross St, Balto 21230
Bible Way Bap Ch, 2423 E Biddle St, Balto 21213
Bibleway Free Will Bap Ch, 4412 Maine Ave, Balto 21207
Brantly Bap Ch, 5007 Balto Natl Pike, Balto 21229
Bright Crown Bap Ch, 1506 N Fulton Ave, Balto 21217
Browns Memorial Bap Ch, 3215 W Belvedere Ave, Balto 21215
Calvary Bap Ch, 3911 Garrison Blvd, Balto 21215
Calvary Bap Ch, 7321 Manchester Rd, Balto 21222
Calvary Bap Ch, 120 W Pennsylvania Ave, Towson 21204
Cannan Bap Ch of Balto City, 713 Tessier St, Balto 21201
Canton Mission, 3302 Toone St, Balto 21224
Carrollwood Bap Ch, 222 Carroll Isl Rd, Middle River, Balto
  21220
Catonsville Bap Ch, 1004 Frederick Ave, Balto 21228
Ceaser Memorial Bap Ch, 416 E Eager St, Balto 21202
Central Bap Ch, 2035 W Balto St, Balto 21223
Central Bap Ch, 404 N Marlyn Ave, Balto 21221
Chinese Mission, 1313 York Rd, Lutherville 21093
Christ Institution Bap Ch, 704 Ensor St, Balto 21202
Chris Bap Ch, 4303 Park Hts Ave, Balto 21215
Chris Center Union Bap Ch, 714 N Fremont Ave, Balto 21217
Chris Life Fellowship Bap Ch, 5203 Bosworth Ave, Randallstown
  21207

Baptist

City Temple of Balto, Eutaw & Dolphin Sts, Balto 21217
Cockeysville Bap Ch, 232 Warren Ave, Cockeysville 21030
Colgate Bap Ch, 502 Fairview Ave, Balto 21224
Colonial Bap Ch, 4619 Old Court Rd, Balto 21208
Com Bap Ch, 5912 Belle Grove Rd, Balto 21225
Com Bap Ch, 219 N Mount St, Balto 21223
Com Bap Ch of Chase, 12029 Eastern Ave, Chase 21027
Community Bap Ch of Walbrook, 2311 Garrison Blvd, Balto 21216
Concord Bap Ch, 5204 Liberty Hts Ave, Balto 21207
Cookley's Com Bap Ch, 1208 Walnut Ave, Balto 21229
David Memorial Bap Ch, 1401 N Milton Ave, Balto 21213
Delmar Bap Ch, 2925 Delmar Ave, Edgemere 21219
Eastside Bap Ch, 2519 E Preston St, Balto 21213
Ebenezer Bap Ch, 306 E 23rd St, Balto 21218
Edgemere Bap Ch, 7601 North Point Rd, Balto 21219
Emmanuel Bap Ch, 7400 Linden Ave, Overlea 21206
Emmanuel Free Will Bap Ch, 1901 Druid Hill Ave, Balto 21217
Enon Bap Ch, Edmondson Ave & Schroeder St, Balto 21223
Evan Bap Ch, 4430 Reisterstown Rd, Balto 21215
Faith Bap Ch, 833 N Bond St, Balto 21205
Faith Tabernacle Bap Ch, 1626 Druid Hill Ave, Balto 21217
Fellowship Missionary Bap Ch of Christ, 319 N Schroeder St,
  Balto 21223
First Abyssinia Bap Ch, 2500 Arunah Ave, Balto 21216
First Bap Ch, 525 N Caroline St, Balto 21205
First Bap Ch, 4200 Liberty Hts Ave, Balto 21207
First Bap Ch of Brooklyn, 3801 5th St, Balto 21225
First Bap Ch of Cherry Hill, 823 Cherry Hill Rd, Balto 21225
First Bap Ch of Dundalk, Dundalk & St Helena Aves, P.O.Box
  8964, Balto 21222
First Bap Ch of Essex, 911 Mace St, Balto 21221
First Bap Ch of Hereford, 24 Mt Carmel Rd, Parkton 21120
First Bap Ch of Lansdowne, 2320 Alma Rd, Lansdowne, Balto
  21227
First Bap Ch of Mt Winans, 2417 Puget St, Balto 21230
First Bap Ch of Pimlico, 5329 Denmore Ave, Balto 21215
First Charity Bap Ch, 611 N Aisquith St, Balto 21202
First Corinthian Bap Ch, 3512 Powhatan Ave, Balto 21216
Fountain Bap Ch, 1215 E Monument St, Balto 21202
Freedom Bap Ch, 624 Eastern Blvd, Essex, Balto 21221
Friendship Bap Ch, 307 Avondale Rd, Balto 21222
Friendship Bap ch, 346 Denison St, Balto 21229
Galilee Bap Ch, 2440 Old North Point Rd, Dundalk 21222
Garden of Prayer Bap Ch, 1727 Carswell St, Balto 21218
Garrison Forest Bap Ch, 2 Tahoe Circle, Owings Mills 21117
Gethsemane Bap Ch, 2520 Francis St, Balto 21217
Good Shepherd Bap Ch, 3459 Park Hts Ave, Balto 21215
Gospel Tabernacle Bap Ch, 3100 Walbrook Ave, Balto 21216
Grace Bap Ch, 8612 Phila Rd, Balto 21237
Grace Bap Ch (Alameda & 32nd Sts) 1600 E 32nd St, Balto 21218
Grace Bap Ch (Ranelagh & Larch Rds) 5700 Ranelagh Rd, White
  Marsh 21162

CHURCH ADDRESSES

Grace Bible Bap ch, 1518 N Rolling Rd, Catonsville 21228
Gray Manor Bap Ch, 2705 Gray Manor Ter, Balto 21222
Greater Gethsemane Missionary Bap Ch, 4749 Wrenwood Ave, Balto
  21212
Greater Harvest Bap Ch, 1617 W Saratoga St, Balto 21223
Greater New Hope Bap Ch, 2720 W North Ave, Balto 21216
Greater St John's Bap Ch, 209 Walnut Ave, Balto 21222
Gregory Memorial Bap Ch, 5701 York Rd, Balto 21212
Guiding Light Bap Ch, 2621 Oswego Ave, Balto 21215
Gunpowder Bap Ch, 20074 Middletown Rd, Freeland 21053
Hampden Bap Ch (37th St & Roland Ave) 3645 Roland Ave, Balto
  21211
Harbor Heights Bap Ch, 1613 Charlotte Ave, Balto 21224
Harford Bap Ch, 4906 Harford Rd, Balto 21214
Harlem Park Com Bap Ch, 614 N Gilmor St, Balto 21217
Hazelwood Bap Ch, 5310 Hazelwood Ave, Balto 21206
Highlands Bap Ch, 2900 Illinois Ave, Balto 21227
Holy Temple Freewill Bap Ch, 30 S Hilton St, Balto 21229
Hope Chapel, 1423 Riggs Ave, Balto 21217
Hosanna Chapel, c/o Loch Raven Bap Ch, 8600 Loch Raven Blvd,
  Balto 21204
Huntingdon Bap Ch, 31st & Barclay Sts, Balto 21218
Immanuel Bap Ch, 5407 Frankford Ave, Balto 21206
Israel Bap Ch, 1220 N Chester St, Balto 21213
Joppa Road Bap Ch, 2413 E Joppa Rd, Balto 21234
Korean Bap Ch of Balto, 4619 Old Court Rd, Balto 21208
Leadenhall Bap Ch, 1021 Leadenhall St, Balto 21230
Lee Street Memorial Bap Ch, 111 Warren Ave, Balto 21230
Liberty Memorial Bap Ch, 5015 Gwynn Oak Ave, Balto 21207
Little Mt Sinai Bap Ch, 1108 E Preston St, Balto 21202
Loch Raven Bap Ch, 8600 Loch Raven Blvd, Balto 21204
Long Green Bap Ch (Manor Rd & Langtree Dr) 13010 Manor Rd,
  Long Green 21092
Long Memorial Bap Ch, 1300 W North Ave, Balto 21217
Lovely Hill Bap Ch, 1654 N Smallwood St, Balto 21216
Macedonia Bap Ch, 718 W Lafayette Ave, Balto 21217
Mallory Center Bap Ch, 1127 Riverside Ave, Balto 21230
Manna Bible Bap Ch, 3043 W Belvedere Ave, Balto 21215
Maranatha Bap Ch, 918 E Preston St, Balto 21202
Maranatha Bap Ch, c/o Seventh Bap Ch, 1901 St Paul St, Balto
  21218
Maranatha Memorial Bap Ch, 4109 Ridgewood Ave, Balto 21215
Mars Hill Bap Ch, 1400 Eastern Ave, Balto 21221
Middle River Bap Ch, 610 Middle River Rd, Balto 21220
Morning Star Bap Ch, 1063 W Fayette St, Balto 21223
Morningstar Bap Ch, 154 Winters Ln, Balto 21228
Mt Arart Bap Ch, Gwynns Falls Pkwy & Longwood Ave, Balto 21216
Mt Calvary Bap Ch, 1607 E Oliver St, Balto 21213
Mt Carmel Bap Ch, 2230 Harford Rd, Balto 21218
Mt Hebron Bap Ch, 2651 W North Ave, Balto 21216
Mt Hope Bap Ch, 1716 Gwynns Falls Pkwy, Balto 21217
Mt Lebanon Bap Ch, 2320 Reisterstown Rd, Balto 21217

Mt Moriah Bap Ch, 2201 Garrison Blvd, Balto 21216
Mt Nebo Bap Ch, 1302 N Calhoun St, Balto 21217
Mt Olive Bap Ch, Dundalk Ave Ext, Balto 21222
Mt Olive Bap Ch, York & Bosley Rds, Balto 21204
Mt Olive Freewill Bap Ch, 290 N Fremont Ave, Balto 21201
Mt Oliver Missionary Bap Ch, 1831 N Gay St, Balto 21213
Mt Pleasant Bap Ch, 1801 E Preston St, Balto 21213
Mt Sinai Bap Ch, 922 E Preston St, Balto 21202
Mt Tabor Bap Ch, 1719 E Oliver St, Balto 21213
Mt Zion Bap Ch, 2000 E Belvedere Ave, Balto 21239
Mt Zion Original Free Will Bap Ch, 1325 N Spring St, Balto
  21213
New Antioch Bap Ch, 1400 N Eden St, Balto 21213
New Bap Ch, 1840 E Biddle St, Balto 21213
New Bethlehem Bap Ch, 1354 N Carey St, Balto 21217
New Bethlehem Free Will Bap Ch, 1129 N Gilmor St, Balto 21217
New Carmel Star Bap Ch, 1847 W Balto St, Balto 21223
New Cornerstone Bap Ch, 1530 E Preston St, Balto 21213
New Elizabeth Bap Ch, 4901 Park Heights Ave, Balto 21215
New Friendship Bap Ch, 1515 E Eager St, Balto 21205
New Frontiers of Faith Bap Ch, 1100 Beaumont Ave, Balto 21228
New Horizon Bap Ch, 3000 Huntingdon Ave, Balto 21211
New Lebanon Calvary Bap Ch, 501 N Milton Ave, Balto 21205
New Life Bap Ch, 3202 Woodland Ave, Balto 21215
New Life Missionary Bap Ch, 1801 N Bond St, Balto 21213
New Metropolitan Bap Ch, McCulloh & Mosher Sts, Balto 21217
New Mt Carmel Bap Ch, 1907 Poplar Grove St, Balto 21216
New Mt Hebron Bap Ch, 2016 W North Ave, Balto 21217
New Mt Joy Missionary Bap Ch, 1725 Division St, Balto 21217
New Mt Zion Bap Ch, 817 N Mount St, Balto 21217
New Pilgrim Bap Ch, 629 N Washington St, Balto 21205
New Pleasant Grove Missionary Bap Ch, 3300 Elmora Ave, Balto
  21213
New Psalmist Bap Ch, 100 W Franklin St, Balto 21201
New Rehoboth Bap Ch, 2504 N Hilton St, Balto 21216
New St John Bap Ch, 1106 W Franklin St, Balto 21223
New St Mark Bap Ch, 3902 Springdale Ave, Balto 21207
New Shiloh Bap Ch, 105 East Ave, Balto 21222
New Shiloh Bap Ch, 823 W Lanvale St, Balto 21217
New Tabernacle Bap Ch, 2101 Frederick Ave, Balto 21223
New Testament Bap Ch, 1624 W Balto St, Balto 21223
New Union Bap Ch, 510 N Monroe St, Balto 21223
New Unity Bap Ch, 2654 Polk St, Balto 21218
North East Bap Ch, 2301 Mayfield Ave, Balto 21213
North Point Bap Ch, 4201 North Point Blvd, Balto 21222 .
Northeast Bap Ch, 1400 Horners Ln, Balto 21205
Northside Bap Ch, 1100 E Northern Pkwy, Balto 21239
Old Landmark Bap Ch, 814 N Broadway, Balto 21205
Olive Bap Ch, York & Bosley Rds, Balto 21204
Olivet Bap Ch, 3500 Edmondson Ave, Balto 21229
Open Bible Bap Ch, 5718 Bowleys Ln, Balto 21206
Parklane Bap Ch, 4601 Park Hts Ave, Balto 21215

Parkville Bap Ch, 3309 Taylor Ave, Balto 21234
Patterson Park Bap Ch, 3115 Eastern Ave, Balto 21224
Perkins Square Bap Ch, 2500 Edmondson Ave, Balto 21223
Perry Hall Bap Ch, 3919 Schroeder Ave, Balto 21236
Pleasant Grove Bap Ch, 214 S Loudon Ave, Balto 21227
Pleasant Hope Bap Ch, 430 E Belvedere Ave, Balto 21212
Pleasant Zion Bap Ch, 4317 North Point Blvd, Balto 21222
Prince of Peace Bap Ch, 610 N Linwood Ave, Balto 21205
Progressive Natl Bap Convention, 3200 Garrison Blvd, Balto
   21216
Providence Inspirational Bap Ch, 850 Edmondson Ave, Balto
   21228
Provident Bap Ch, 1401 Pennsylvania Ave, Balto 21217
Ray of Hope Bap Ch, 3000 Parkside Dr, Balto 21214
Reisterstown Bap Ch, 25E Chestnut Hill Ln, Reisterstown 21136
Remnant Bap Ch, 2000 E Chase St, Balto 21213
Rising Sun Bap Ch, 1901 N Regester St, Balto 21213
Riverside Bap Ch, 1602 Johnson St, Balto 21230
Rosedale Bap Ch, 9202 Philadelphia Rd, Balto 21237
St James Free Bap Ch, 1508 E Lafayette Ave, Balto 21213
St Johns Bap Ch, 2929 Dupont Ave, Balto 21215
St Mark U Bap Ch, 1238 N Eden St, Balto 21213
St Mark's Insti Bap Ch, 655 N Bentalou St, Balto 21216
St Mark's Spiritual Bap Ch, 1625 N Hilton St, Balto 21216
St Paul Bap Ch, 3101 The Alameda, Balto 21218
St Paul Com Bap Ch (Federal & Wolfe Sts) 1901 E Federal St,
   Balto 21213
St Paul Insti Bap Ch, 2010 W North Ave, Balto 21217
St Paul's Free Will Bap Ch, 406 E 23rd St, Balto 21218
St Timothy's Chris Bap Ch, 4007 Groveland Ave, Balto 21215
Salem Thessalonian Bap Ch, 1422 Druid Hill Ave, Balto 21217
Saters Bap Ch (Falls Rd & Saters Ln) 1200 Saters Ln,
   Lutherville 21093
Scott Street Bap Ch, Scott & Cross Sts, Balto 21230
Second & Fourth Bap Ch, Orleans St & Luzerne Ave, Balto 21224
Second Bap Ch, 214 E Lanvale St, Balto 21202
Seventh Bap Ch, St Paul St & North Ave, Balto 21218
Sharon Bap Ch, 1375 N Stricker St, Balto 21217
Shelbourne Bap Ch, Shelbourne & Courtney Rds, Balto 21227
Shepherd Com Bap Ch, 115 N Patterson Park Ave, Balto 21231
Shiloh Free Will Bap Ch, 2121 Jefferson St, Balto 21205
Shining Star Bap Ch, 1503 E North Ave, Balto 21213
Shining Star Bap Ch, Eastern Ave Ext nr Bowleys Quarter Rd,
   Chase 21027
Siloam Freewill Bap Ch, 501 N Fulton Ave, Balto 21223
Sinner's Friend Bap Ch, 1744 Gorsuch Ave, Balto 21218
Solid Rock Full Gospel Bap Ch, 1646 Thomas Ave, Balto 21216
South Broadway Bap Ch, 211 S Broadway, Balto 21231
Southern Bap Ch, 1701 N Chester St, Balto 21213
Southern Bap Convention of Md, 1313 York Rd, Lutherville 21093
Southwest Bap Ch, 26 S Calhoun St, Balto 21223
Sweet Hope Free Will Bap Ch, 3925 Dolfield Ave, Balto 21215

Tabernacle Bap Ch,   (Bennett & Langley Rds) 121 Bennett Rd,
  Balto 21221
Temple Bap Ch, 1800 N Wolfe St, Balto 21213
Temple Bap Ch, 6916 Dogwood Rd, Woodlawn, Balto 21207
Temple of Christ Bap Ch, 1519 Winchester St, Balto 21217
Timothy Bap Ch, 1214 W Saratoga St, Balto 21223
Townsend Avenue Bap Ch, 4200 Townsend Ave, Balto 21225
Trinity Bap Ch, 1601 Druid Hill Ave, Balto 21217
Trinity Bap Ch, 3011 Ross Ave, Balto 21219
Triumph Missionary Bap Ch, 1606 Greenmount Ave, Balto 21202
Union Bap Ch, 932 N Broadway, Balto 21205
Union Bap Ch, 1219 Druid Hill Ave, Balto 21217
Union Bap Ch, 2011 Linden Ave, Balto 21217
Union Temple Bap Ch, 1100 W North Ave, Balto 21217
Unit Bap Missionary Convention of Md, 3900 Garrison Blvd,
  Balto 21215
Unity Bap Ch, 7204 Montgomery Rd, Balto 21227
University Bap Ch, 3501 N Charles St, Balto 21218
Upper Cross Roads Bap Ch (Greene Rd & Upper Cross Rds) 2717
  Greene Rd, Baldwin 21013
Upper Room Bap Ch, 1314 Harlem Ave, Balto 21217
Valley Bap Ch, 1401 N York Rd, Lutherville 21093
Watersedge Bap Ch, (Liberty Pkwy & Sollers Pt Rd) 3483 Liberty
  Pkwy, Balto 21222
Wayland Bap Ch, 3200 Garrison Blvd, Balto 21216
West Balto Bap Ch, Monroe St & Frederick Ave, Balto 21223
White Stone Bap Ch, 3005 Baker St, Balto 21216
Woodbrook Bap Ch, 25 Stevenson Ln, Balto 21212
Woolford Memorial Bap Ch, 1710 Delvale Ave, Balto 21222
Yale Heights Bap Ch, 620 Beechfield Rd, Balto 21229
Zion Bap Ch, 1700 N Caroline St, Balto 21213
Zion Hill Bap Ch, 931 E Preston St, Balto 21202

Calvert — Emmanuel Bap Ch, Rt 4 Box 99, Huntingtown 20639
First Bap Ch of Calvert Co, Prince Frederick 20678
Landmark Bap Temple, 955 Wilson Rd, Huntingtown 20639
Mt Gethsemane Bap Ch, Ponds Wood Rd, Huntingtown 20639
Southern Calvert Bap Ch, Lake Drive, Box 345K, Lusby 20657

Caroline — Calvary Bap Ch, Hobbs Rd, Denton 21629
Greensboro Bap Ch, 401 Sunset Ave, P.O.Box 66, Greensboro
  21639
Harmony Missionary Bap Ch, Rt 404, Denton 21629
Marydel Bap Ch, Rt 1 Box 408, Marydel 21649

Carroll — Calvary Bap Ch, 2127 Old Liberty Rd, New Windsor 21776
Elders Bap Ch, 1216 Liberty Rd, P.O.Box 705, Sykesville 21784
Emmanuel Bap Ch, 4150 Sykesville Rd, Finksburg 21048
Hampstead Bap Ch, 328 Hanover Pike, Hampstead 21074
Heritage Bap Ch, 1641 Old Westminster Rd, Westminster 21157
Manchester Bap Ch, 2933 Manchester Baptist Church Rd,
  Manchester 21102
Mt Airy Bap Ch, P.O.Box 447, Mt Airy 21771
Taneytown Bap Ch, 4150 Sells Mill Rd, P.O.Box 436, Taneytown
  21787

Trinity Bap Ch, 4411 Bartholows Rd, Mt Airy 21771

Warfieldsburg Bible Bap Ch, 1641 Old Westminster Rd, Westminster 21157

Westminster Bap Ch, 354 Crest Ln, Westminster 21157

Cecil Bap Bible Ch, 144 Appleton Rd, Elkton 21921

Calvary Missionary Bap Ch, 47 Half Mile Turn Rd, Rising Sun 21911

Conowingo Bap Ch, 151 Rock Springs Rd, P.O.Box 428, Conowingo 21918

First Bap Ch, 607 Delaware Ave, Elkton 21921

First Bap Ch, 206 Mechanics Valley Rd, North East 21901

First Bap Ch, Aiken Ave, P.O.Box 342, Perryville 21903

Franklin Bap Ch, Franklin Church Rd, North East 21901

Joulwan Charles Bap Ch, 144 Appleton Rd, Elkton 21921

Mt Carmel Bap Ch, 17 Russell St, North East 21901

Newark Bap Ch, 6011 Telegraph Rd (1 mi w of Newark, Rt 273) Elkton 21921

Pine Grove Bap Ch, 24 Fox Chase Dr, Elkton 21921

Pleasant View Bap Ch, 7 Pleasant View Church Rd, Port Deposit 21904

Porters Grove Bap Ch, 638 Ragan Rd, Conowingo 21918

State Line Bap Ch, 540 Chrome Rd, Rising Sun 21911

Charles Berean Bap Ch, Church St, Waldorf 20601

Faith Bap Ch, White Plains 20695

First Bap Ch, 136 Stoddert Ave, Waldorf 20601

First Bap Ch, (Hwy 301 & Berry Rd) Rt 4 Box 289, Waldorf 20601

Grace Bap Ch, Rt 1 Box 23, Bryan's Road 20616

Hughesville Bap Ch, P.O.Box 40, Hughesville 20637

Indian Head Bap Ch, Raymond Ave, P.O.Box AA, Indian Head 20640

La Plata Bap Ch, Rt 301 & Old Stage Coach Rd, La Plata 20646

Macedonia Bap Ch, Marshall Hall Rd, Bryans Road 20616

Marbury Bap Ch, P.O.Box 49, Marbury 20658

Mt Hope Bap Ch, Ironsides 20643

Nanjemoy Bap Ch, Rt 1 Box 82FF, Nanjemoy 20662

Pleasant Grove Bap Ch, Marbury 20658

Potomac Bap Assn, Tri County Federal Bldg, P.O.Box 736, Waldorf 20601

Potomac Heights Bap Ch, Glymont Rd, Indian Head 20640

Trinity Bap Ch, Mattawoman-Beantown Rd, Waldorf 20601

Trinity Chapel, Rt 7, Box 212, Waldorf 20601

Welcome Bap Ch, General Delivery, Welcome 20693

White Plains Bap Ch, Rt 227, Pomfret 20675

White Plains Chapel, P.O.Box 57, White Plains 20695

Woodland Village Bap Ch, 106 Ellerby Dr, Indian Head 20640

Zion Bap Ch, Annapolis Woods Rd, Welcome 20693

Dorchester First Bap Ch, 714 Locust St, P.O.Box 711, Cambridge 21613

Frist Bap Ch, P.O.Box 64, East New Market 21631

First Bap Ch, S Main St, P.O.Box 388, Hurlock 21643

Grace Bap Ch, Academy St, Hurlock 21643

Mt Olive Bap Ch, 601 Douglas St, Cambridge 21613

Unit Missionary Bap Ch, 1006 Phillips St, Cambridge 21613

Zion Bap Ch, 600 Cross St, Cambridge 21613

Frederick   Calvary Bap Ch, P.O.Box 112, Middletown 21769
               Faith Bap Ch (nr Jefferson) P.O.Box 217, Brunswick 21716
               First Bap Ch, 3 A St, P.O.Box 277, Brunswick 21716
               First Bap Ch, 217 Dill Ave, Frederick 21701
               First Bap Ch of Green Valley, Rt 75, Monrovia 21770
               First Bap Ch (Weverton) Rt 2 Box 29, Knoxville 21758
               Frederick Bap Temple, 5305 Mt Zion Rd, Frederick 21701
               Frederick Korean Bap Ch, 55 Winchester St, Frederick 21701
               Frederick Ref Bap Ch, 1336 Hillcrest Dr, Frederick 21701
               Fredericktowne Bap Ch, 8798 Adventure Ave, Walkersville 21793
               Mt Olivet Bap Ch, 27 West J St, Brunswick 21716
               Myersville Bap Ch, Rt 40 Box 67, Myersville 21773
               Peoples Bap Ch, 6648 Carpenter Rd, Frederick 21701
               Pioneer Bap Ch, 13802 Long Rd, Thurmont 21788
               South End Bap Ch, 506 Carrollton Dr, Frederick 21701
               Thurmont Bap Chapel, 7 Sunny Way, Thurmont 21788
               Thurmont Bap Ch, P.O.Box 205, Thurmont 21788
               Victory Bap Ch, 322 W Patrick St, Frederick 21701
Garrett   Deep Creek Bap Ch, Deep Creek Lake, Star Rt 1 Box 119, Oakland
                 21550
               Ferndale Bap Ch, Star Route, Oakland 21550
               Good Shepherd Indep Bap Ch, Rt 219 South, Accident 21520
               Pleasant View Bap Ch, 211 Roanoke Ave, Rt 219 South, Mt Lake
                 Park 21550
               Rush Bap Ch, Rt 1 Old Morgantown Rd, Friendsville 21531
Harford   Antioch Bap Ch, Havre de Grace 21078
               Bel Forest Bap Ch, 603 Vale Rd, Bel Air 21014
               Bethel Bap Ch, 1501 Stockton Rd, Joppa 21085
               Calvary Bap Ch, 206 E Courtland Pl, Bel Air 21014
               Carsins Run Bap Ch, P.O.Box 205, Churchville 21028
               Com Bap Ch, 303 Phila Rd, Joppa 21085
               Dublin Missionary Bap Ch, 1727 Poole Rd, Darlington 21034
               Ebenezer Bap Ch, 508 Foster Branch Rd, Joppa 21085
               Edgewood Bap Ch, 422 Edgewood Rd, Edgewood 21040
               Edgewood Korean Bap Ch, 422 Edgewood Rd, Edgewood 21040
               Emmorton Bap Ch, Emmorton Rd, Bel Air 21014
               Faith Bap Ch, 1305 Joppa Rd, Joppa 21085
               First Bap Ch, 219 E Bel Air Ave, P.O.Box 461, Aberdeen 21001
               First Bap Ch, Congress Ave & Stokes St, Havre de Grace 21078
               Harford Furnace Bap Ch, RD 2, Bel Air 21014
               Jarrettsville Bap Ch, 379 Federal Hill Rd, Jarrettsville
                 21084
               Maple View Bap Ch, 1600 Singer Rd, Joppa 21085
               Mt Calvary Free Will Bap Ch, Cranberry Rd, Perryman 21130
               Mt Zion Bap Ch, 520 Lewis St, Havre de Grace 21078
               New Hope Bap Ch, 116 Alice Anne St, Bel Air 21014
               North Harford Bap Ch, 4008 Old Federal Hill Rd, Jarrettsville
                 21084
               Oak Grove Bap Ch, 2106 Churchville Rd, Bel Air 21014
               Shiloh Bap Ch, 2507 Fallston Rd, Fallston 21047
               Tabernacle Bap Ch, 315 Earlton Rd, Havre de Grace 21078
               Towne Bap Ch, 536 Trimble Rd, Joppa 21085

CHURCH ADDRESSES

| | Trappe Missionary Bap Ch, Rt 136 & Trappe Rd, Darlington 21034 |
| Howard | Bethany Lane Bap Ch, 3030 Bethany Ln, Ellicott City 21043 |

Trappe Missionary Bap Ch, Rt 136 & Trappe Rd, Darlington 21034

Howard
Bethany Lane Bap Ch, 3030 Bethany Ln, Ellicott City 21043
Bethel Bap Ch, 4261 Montgomery Rd, Ellicott City 21043
Chinese Mission, Wilde Lake Interfaith Center, 10431 Twin Rivers Rd, Columbia 21044
Columbia Bap Fellowship, 5885 Robert Oliver Pl, Columbia 21045
Covenant Bap Ch, 5960 Cedar Ln, Columbia 21044
Covenant Bap Ch, 6601 Quiet Hours, Colu$bia 21045
Elkridge Bap Ch, 5929 Setter Dr, Elkridge 21227
First Bap Ch (Washington & Woodward Sts) 8901 Washington St, Savage 20763
First Bap Ch of Elkridge, 5795 Paradise Ave, Elkridge 21227
First Bap Ch of Guilford, 7504 Oakland Mills Rd, Columbia 21046
Gethsemane Bap Ch (Glenelg) 14135 Burntwoods Rd, Glenwood 21738
Glenwood Bap Ch, Rt 97, Glenwood 21738
Harvester Bap Ch, 9605 Old Annapolis Rd, Ellicott City 21043
Howard Bap Assn, 9025 Chevrolet Dr, Ellicott City 21043
Liberty Bap Ch, Lisbon 21765
Rolling Hills Bap Ch, 11510 Johns Hopkins Rd, Clarksville 21029
South Columbia Bap Ch, 8814 Guilford Rd, Columbia 21046
South Columbia Mission, P.O.Box 2248, Columbia 21045

Kent
Chestertown Bap Ch, 401 Morgnec Rd, Chestertown 21620
First Bap Ch, Morgnec Rd, Chestertown 21620

Montgomery
Abba Sung-Shin Bap Ch, 12701 Twinbrook Pkwy, Rockville 20852
Ashton Bap Ch, 17826 New Hampshire Ave, Ashton 20861
Barnesville Bap Ch, 17917 Barnesville Rd, P.O.Box 407, Barnesville 20838
Burtonsville Bap Ch, 3400 Spencerville Rd, P.O.Box 130, Burtonsville 20866
Calverton Bap Ch, 12625 Galway Dr, Silver Spring 20904
Calverton Korean Bap Ch, 12625 Galway Dr, Silver Spring 20904
Clarksburg Bap Ch, 14210 Comus Rd, P.O.Box 4, Clarksburg 20871
Colesville Bap Ch, 13100 Andrew Dr, Silver Spring 20904
Congressional Heights Bap Ch, 11845 Seven Locks Rd, Rockville 20854
Emmanuel Spanish Bap Ch, 832 Wayne Ave, P.O.Box 333, Silver Spring 20907
First Bap Ch, 8850 Main St, P.O.Box 189, Damascus 20872
First Bap Ch, 55 Adclare Rd, Rockville 20850
First Bap Ch, 8415 Fenton St, Silver Spring 20910
First Korean Bap Ch, 13421 Georgia Ave, Silver Spring 20906
First Spanish Bap Ch, c/o Clifton Park Bap Ch, 8818 Piney Branch Rd, Silver Spring 20903
Georgia Avenue Bap Ch, 12525 Georgia Ave, Wheaton 20906
Germantown Bap Ch, 17640 Riffle Ford Rd, P.O.Box 86, Germantown 20874
Glen Echo Bap Ch, Vassar Circle, P.O.Box 595, Glen Echo 20812
Greenridge Bap Ch, 21925 Frederick Rd, P.O.Box 38, Germantown 20874

Baptist

Halpine Bap Ch, 12701 Twinbrook Pkwy, Rockville 20852
Kensington Bap Ch, 10100 Connecticut Ave, Kensington 20895
Korean of Ashton Bap Ch, 17826 New Hampshire Ave, Ashton 20861
Korean of Washington Bap Ch, 310 Randolph Rd, Silver Spring
    20904
Laytonsville Bap Ch, 6855 Olney-Laytonsville Rd, P.O.Box 1027,
    Laytonsville 20879
Montgomery Korean Bap Ch, 55 Adclare Rd, Rockville 20850
Montrose Bap Ch, 5110 Randolph Rd, Rockville 20852
Norbeck Bap Ch, 4601 Muncaster Mill Rd, Rockville 20853
Olney Bap Ch, 17525 Georgia Ave, P.O.Box 325, Olney 20832
Paul Korean Bap Ch, c/o Viers Mill Bap Ch, 12221 Viers Mill
    Rd, Silver Spring 20906
Poolesville Bap Ch, 17600 Willard Rd, P.O.Box 185, Poolesville
    20837
Quince Orchard Bap Ch, Gaithersburg 20877
Redland Bap Ch, 6922 Muncaster Mill Rd, Derwood 20855
Travilah (Travillah) Bap Ch, 12811 Glen Rd, Gaithersburg 20878
Upper Seneca Bap Ch, 23415 Davis Mill Rd, Germantown 20874
Viers Mill Bap Ch, 12221 Viers Mill Rd, Silver Spring 20906
Vietnamese Fellowship, c/o Viers Mill Bap Ch, 12221 Viers Mill
    Rd, Silver Spring 20906
Wheaton Woods Bap Ch, 13200 Arctic Ave, Rockville 20853
Wildwood Bap Ch, 10200 Old Georgetown Rd, Bethesda 20814

Prince
Georges

Belair Bap Ch, 2801 Belair Dr, P.O.Box 796, Bowie 20715
Beltsville Bap Ch, 4700 Odell Rd, Beltsville 20705
Berwyn Bap Ch, 4720 Cherokee St, College Park 20740
Broadview Bap Ch, 5757 Temple Hills Rd SE, Temple Hills 20748
Calvary Bap Ch, 8330 Crain Hwy, Upper Marlboro 20772
Cambodian Mission, West Hyattsville 20783
Carrollan Woods Bap Ch, 7309 Riverdale Rd, Lanham 20706
Central Korean Bap Ch, 5757 Temple Hills Rd SE, Temple Hills
    20748
Chinese Mission (Berwyn) 4720 Cherokee St, College Park 20740
Com Bap Ch of Laurel, 8600 Locust Grove Dr, Laurel 20707
Crusader Bap Ch, 6832 3rd St, Lanham 20706
Emmanuel Bap Ch, 11443 Laurel-Bowie Rd, RFD 2, Laurel 20708
Faith Bap Ch of South Laurel, 12700 Claxton Dr, Laurel 20708
First Bap h, 6 Capitol Heights Blvd, Capitol Heights 20743
First Bap Ch, 5400 Silver Hill Rd, Suitland 20747
First Bap Ch of College Park, 5018 Lakeland Rd, College Park
    20740
First Bap Ch of Laurel, 811 Fifth St, Laurel 20707
Forestville Bap Ch, 7808 Marlboro Pike, Forestville 20747
Greenbelt Bap Ch, Crescent & Greenhill Rds, Greenbelt 20770
Kent Bap Ch, 7006 Flagstaff St, Landover 20785
Kettering Bap Ch, 1 Kettering Dr, Upper Marlboro 20772
Korean Central Bap Ch, c/o Broadview Bap Ch, 5757 Temple Hills
    Rd SE, Temple Hills 20748
Korean of Laurel, c/o First Bap Ch, 811 Fifth St, Laurel 20707
Landover Hills Bap Ch, 4420 73rd Ave, Landover Hills 20784
Laurel Bap Temple, Georgetown Alley, Laurel 20707

CHURCH ADDRESSES

```
              Le Detroit Bap Ch, Oxon Hill 20745
              Maryland City Bap Ch, 326 Brock Bridge Rd, Laurel 20707
              Mitchellville Bap Ch, P.O.Box 1646, Bowie 20716
              Mt Calvary Bap Ch, 6117 Seabrook Rd, Seabrook 20801
              Mt Rainier Bap Ch, 3107 Shepherd St, Mt Rainier 20712
              Mt Sinai Bap Ch, 1811 Mitchellville Rd, Mitchellville 20716
              New Jerusalem Bap Ch, 2218 Columbia Pl, Landover 20785
              Oxon Hill Bap Ch, 6633 St Barnabas Rd SE, Oxon Hill 20745
              Riverside Bap Ch, P.O.Box 55173, Oxon Hill 20745
              Seabrook Bap Ch, 6117 Seabrook Rd, Seabrook 20706
              Village Bap Ch, 1950 Mitchelville Rd, P.O.Box 1634, Bowie
                20716
              West Hyattsville Bap Ch, 3100 Nicholson St, Hyattsville 20782
              Whitehall Bap Ch, 1205 Farmington Rd E, Accokeek 20607
Queen Annes   --
St Marys      Callaway Bap Ch, P.O.Box 105, Callaway 20620
              Calvary Bap Ch, Peggs Rd, Lexington Park 20653
              Grace Bible Bap Ch, 130-A Shangri-La Dr, Lexington Park 20653
              Leonardtown Bap Ch, Rt 1 Box 16-A, Leonardtown 20650
              Lexington Park Bap Ch, 100 S Shangri-La Dr, Lexington Park
                20653
              Victory Bap Ch, Golden Beach Rd, Charlotte Hall 20622
Somerset      Enon Bap Ch of Deliverance, Tyler St, Crisfield 21817
              Fellowship Mission, Deal Isl 21821
              First Bap Ch, Main St & Somerset Ave, Crisfield 21817
              First Bap Ch, Crisfield Ln, Box 396, Princess Anne 21853
              Marion Bap Ch, P.O.Box I, Marion Sta 21838
              Rehobeth Bap Ch, Rehobeth 21857
              St Mary's Bap Ch, W Post Office Rd, Princess Anne 21853
Talbot        Bible Bap Ch, Dover Rd, Easton 21601
              Cordova Bap Ch, Rt 1, Cordova 21625
              First Bap Ch, Idlewild Ave & S Hanson St, Easton 21601
              Union Bap Ch, 335 Glenwood Ave, P.O.Box 1043, Easton 21601
Washington    Bap Temple, Virginia Ave & Davis Dr, Hagerstown 21740
              Emmanuel Bap Ch, nr Huyetts Crossroads, Hagerstown 21740
              Evangel Bap Ch, 1706 Broadfording Rd, Hagerstown 21740
              First Bap Ch, 512 Washington Sq, Hagerstown 21740
              Grace Bap Ch, 2450 Jefferson Blvd, Hagerstown 21740
              Greenbrier Bap Ch, Rt 2 Box 94W, Boonsboro 21713
              Harvest Bap Ch, 951 Woodland Way, Hagerstown 21740
              Mountain View Bap Ch, Walnut Pt Rd, Hagerstown 21740
              Paramount Bap Ch, 2323 Marsh Pike, Hagerstown 21740
              Pinesburg Bap Ch, Rt 2 Box 231, Williamsport 21795
              Virginia Avenue Bap Ch, 2027 Virginia Ave, Hagerstown 21740
              West End Chapel, 101 Buena Vista Ave, Hagerstown 21740
              Zion Bap Ch, 61 Bethel St, Hagerstown 21740
Wicomico      Allen Memorial Bap Ch  (N Division & Chestnut Sts) 231 N
                Division St, Salisbury 21801
              Bible Bap Ch, 729 E Main St, Salisbury 21801
              Calvary Bap Tabernacle, Tilghman Rd, Salisbury 21801
              Eastern Bap Assn, 1514 Ocean City Rd, Salisbury 21801
              Faith Bap Ch, E State St, Delmar 21875
```

First Bap Ch, Delmar 21875
First Bap Ch, 511 W Main St, P.O.Box 27, Fruitland 21826
First Bap Ch, Main St, Mardela Springs 21837
Holy Trinity Bap Ch, Booth St & Delaware Ave, Salisbury 21801
Immanuel Bap Ch, 1514 Ocean City Rd, Salisbury 21801
New Testament Bap Ch, P.O.Box 1509, Salisbury 21801
Oak Ridge Bap Ch, Dixon Rd, P.O.Box 2242, Salisbury 21801
St Mary's Bap Ch, P.O.Box 1590, Salisbury 21801
Salisbury Bap Temple, Hobbs Rd, Salisbury 21801
Weeping Mary Bap Ch, Shavox Rd, Salisbury 21801

Worcester   Bap Chapel of Ocean City, 102 N Division St, Ocean City 21842
First Bap Ch, 613 Williams St, P.O.Box 442, Berlin 21811
First Bap Ch, P.O.Box 37, Girdletree 21829
First Bap Ch (4th & Market Sts) 202 Fourth St, P.O.Box 497, Pocomoke City 21851
Goodwill Bap Ch, Rt 3 Box 43, Pocomoke City 21851
Lynnhaven Bap Ch, 1200 Lynnhaven Dr, P.O.Box 237, Pocomoke City 21851
Macedonia Bap Ch, 6th & Young Sts, Pocomoke City 21851
Mt Carmel Bap Ch, 319 Hampden Ave, Princess Ann 21853
Mt Sinie Bap Ch, Line Rd, Pocomoke City 21851
Mt Zion Bap Ch, Dighton Ave, Snow Hill 21863
Pitts Creek Bap Ch, Cedar Hill Rd Ext, Rt 1 Box 385, Pocomoke City 21851
Spence Bap Ch, Public Landing Rd, Rt 3 Box 164, Snow Hill 21863

Bible

Allegany   Cumberland Bible Ch, 307 Wallace St, Cumberland 21502
Anne Arundel Bible Ch of Lake Shore, 860 Swift Rd, Pasadena 21122
Grace Fellowship, 203 Main Ave SW, Glen Burnie 21061
Grace Fellowship, 419 Madingley Rd, Linthicum Heights 21090
South River Bible Ch, 744 Central Ave, Davidsonville 21035
Trinity Bible Ch, Church Truck House Rd, Severna Park 21146
Baltimore   Berean Bible Ch, 2024 Orleans St, Balto 21231
Bible Speaks, 4210 Belair Rd, Balto 21206
Brooklyn Bible Chapel, 502 Jack St, Balto 21225
Com Bible Fellowship, 1410 Wiseburg Rd, White Hall 21161
Ekklesia Bible Chapel, 2000 N Fulton Ave, Balto 21217
Evan Bible Ch, 2444 Washington Blvd, Balto 21230
Family Bible Ministries, 801 N Brice St, Balto 21217
Hillendale Bible Chapel, 1716 Goodview Rd, Balto 21234
Oakwood Bible Ch, 1602 Linden Ln, Relay 21227
Open Bible Tabernacle, 5814 Harford Rd, Balto 21214
Pilgrim Presb Bible Ch, Kingsville 21087
Towson Bible Ch, 8415 Bellona Ln, Balto 21204
Calvert   Bible Way Ch, Prince Frederick 20678
Calvary Bible Ch, Lusby 20657

115

CHURCH ADDRESSES

	Chris Bible Center, 670 Plum Pt Rd, Huntingtown 20639
Carroll	Clearfield Bible Ch, 1303 Old Westminster Pike, Westminster 21157
	Deer Park Bible Ch, 1950 Deer Park Rd, Finksburg 21048
	Grace Bible Ch, Charmil Dr, Manchester 21102
	Uniontown Bible Ch, Uniontown 21157
	Wakefield Valley Bible Ch, 2214 Old New Windsor Rd, New Windsor 21776
	Westminster Bible Ch, 310 Gorsuch Rd, Westminster 21157
	Winfield Bible Chapel, 5407 Woodbine Rd, Woodbine 21797
Cecil	Bible Fellowship, 325 Cameron Rd, Rising Sun 21911
Dorchester	Open Bible Ch & Academy, 1715 Race St, Cambridge 21613
Frederick	F S K Bible Ch, Scholl's Ln & Burck St, Frederick 21701
Harford	Aberdeen Bible Ch, 529 Edmund St, Aberdeen 21001
	Grace Bible Ch & Chris Academy, 2903 Beechwood Ln, Fallston 21047
Howard	Grace Community Bible Ch, 5744 Yellowrose Ct, Columbia 21045
	Faith Bible Ch, 5810 Timberview Dr, Elkridge 21227
	Lisbon Bible Ch, 16700 Old Frederick Rd, Lisbon 21765
	Open Bible Tabernacle, 2631 Rogers Ave, Ellicott City 21043
St Marys	SAYSF Bible Ch, Rue Purchase Rd, Lexington Park 20653
Talbot	Talbot Bible Ch, 5 Federal St, Easton 21601
Washington	Hagerstown Bible Ch, 203 Summit Ave, Hagerstown 21740
	Sharpsburg Bible Ch, Potomac & Antietam Sts, Sharpsburg 21782
	Trinity Bible Ch, 100 E Antietam St, Hagerstown 21740
Wicomico	Trinity Bible Ch, 700 Roger St, Salisbury 21801

Brethren

Allegany	Cumberland Grace Breth Ch, Williams Rd, Cumberland 21502
	First Breth Ch, 400 Seymour St, Cumberland 21502
	Frostburg Breth Ch, 1 Beall St, Frostburg 21532
	La Vale Com Breth Ch, 25 Doris St, La Vale 21502
	Living Stone Ch of the Breth, W 2d & N Cedar Sts, Cumberland 21502
Anne Arundel	Friendship Breth Ch, 217 Mansion Rd, Linthicum Heights 21090
Baltimore	Breth in Christ Ch, 611 S Marlyn Ave, Balto 21221
	Brooklyn Park Unit Breth in Christ Ch, 201 W Hilltop Rd, Balt 21225
	Dundalk Ch of the Breth, Yorkway & Shipway, Dundalk 21222
	Eastern Gospel Chapel, 103 N Potomac St, Balto 21224
	Glad Tidings Chapel, 4801 Garrison Blvd, Balto 21215
	Grace Breth Fellowship of Balto, 119 Marburth Ave, Towson 21204
	Long Green Valley Breth Ch, Long Green Rd, Glen Arm 21057
	Plymouth Breth Loch Hall Chapel, 6601 Loch Raven Blvd, Balto 21239
	Reisterstown Breth Ch, Berrymans Ln, Reisterstown 21136
	Trinity Ch of the Breth, 4615 Roland Ave, Balto 21210

Brethren

	Unit Breth for Christ, 2112 McCulloh St, Balto 21217
	Woodberry Ch of the Breth, W 36th & Poole Sts, Balto 21211
Caroline	Ch of the Breth, 7th St, Denton 21629
Carroll	Ch of the Breth, Main & Church Sts, Union Bridge 21791
	Ch of the Breth, Park & Bond Sts, Westminster 21157
	Edgewood Breth Ch, Rt 2, New Windsor 21776
	Linwood Breth Ch, Linwood 21764
	Locust Grove Breth Ch, Glissan Mill Rd, Mt Airy 21771
	Meadow Branch Breth Ch, 818 Old Taneytown Rd, Westminster 21157
	Sam's Creek Breth Ch, 2736 Marston Rd, New Windsor 21776
Charles	Grace Breth Ch, Rt 5, Waldorf 20601
Frederick	Breth in Christ, 9407 Glade Ave, Walkersville 21793
	Bush Creek Breth Ch, 4821-A Green Valley Rd, Monrovia 21770
	Ch of the Breth, 201 Fairview Ave, Frederick 21701
	Glade Valley Breth Ch, 2 Chapel Pl, Walkersville 21793
	Grossnickle Ch of the Breth, Myersville 21773
	Harmony Breth Ch, 3924 Brethren Church Rd, Myersville 21773
	Myersville Ch of the Breth, Myersville 21773
	Pleasant View Breth Ch, 101 Main St, Burkittsville 21718
	Pleasant View Breth Ch, Picnic Woods Rd, Burkittsville 21718
Garrett	Oak Park Ch of the Breth, Church St, Oakland 21550
	West Marva District Ch of the Breth, 1009 Dennett Rd, Rt 2 Box 78, Oakland 21550
Howard	Mid Atlantic District Ch of the Breth, 10378 Balto Natl Pike, Ellicott City 21043
	Oakland Mills Uniting Ch, 5885 Robert Oliver Pl, Columbia 21045
Prince Georges	Grace Breth Ch, 8400 Good Luck Rd, Lanham 20706
Somerset	Ch of the Breth, US 13 S, Westover 21871
Talbot	Ch of the Breth, Stewart & Harrison Sts, Easton 21601
Washington	Beaver Creek Breth Ch, Beaver Creek Rd, Hagerstown 21740
	Bible Breth Ch, 533 S Burhans Blvd, Hagerstown 21740
	Broadfording Bible Breth Ch, Broadfording Church Rd, Hagerstown 21740
	Brownsville Breth Ch, Brownsville 21715
	Calvary Breth Ch, W Franklin & Bryan Pl, Hagerstown 21740
	Long Meadow Breth Ch, 31 E Long Meadow Dr, Hagerstown 21740
	Maranatha Breth Ch, 1717 Jefferson Blvd, Hagerstown 21740
	Paramount Breth Ch, 53 W Long Meadow Rd, Hagerstown 21740
	St James Breth Ch, Rt 681, St James 21781
	Valley Grace Breth Ch, 2275 Gay St, Hagerstown 21740
	Van Lear Breth Ch, 4 Van Lear Dr, Williamsport 21795

Catholic

Allegany	St Ambrose Cath Ch, Winchester Rd, Cresaptown 21502
	St Gabriel Cath Ch, Barton 21521

St Joseph Cath Ch, Box 1, Midland 21542
St Mary Cath Ch, 300 Oldtown Rd, Cumberland 21502
St Mary of the Annunciation, 8 St Mary Ter, Lonaconing 21539
St Michael Cath Ch, 28 E Main St, P.O.Box 402, Frostburg 21532
St Patrick Cath Ch, 201 N Centre St, Cumberland 21502
St Patrick Cath Ch, P.O.Box 577, Mt Savage 21545
St Patrick's Cath Ch, Oldtowne Rd & St Patrick Rd, Little
    Orleans 21766
St Peter Cath Ch, 127 Church St, Westernport 21562
SS Peter & Paul Cath Ch, 125 Fayette St, Cumberland 21502

Anne Arundel   Ch of the Crucifixion, 100 Scott Ave, Glen Burnie 21061
Ch of the Good Shepherd, 1451 Furnace Ave, Glen Burnie 21061
Holy Family Cath Ch, 826 W Central Ave, Davidsonville 21035
Holy Trinity Cath Ch (Dorsey Rd & Central Ave) 126 Dorsey Rd,
    Glen Burnie 21061
Holy Trinity Cath Ch, 7436 Balto-Annapolis Blvd, Glen Burnie
    21061
Our Lady of Perpetual Help, 515 Loch Haven Rd, Edgewater 21037
Our Lady of Sorrows, 101 Owensville Rd, West River 20778
Our Lady of the Chesapeake, 1527 Marco Dr, Pasadena 21122
Our Lady of the Fields, 1069 Cecil Ave, Millersville 21108
Pilgrim Com Cath Ch, P.O.Box 60, Severna Park 21146
St Andrew by the Bay, 1257 Hilltop Dr, Cape St Claire 21401
St Bernadette Cath Ch, 801 Stevenson Rd, Severn 21144
St Elizabeth Ann Seton, 1800 Seton Dr, Crofton 21114
St Jane Frances de Chantal, 8499 Virginia Ave, Riviera Beach
    21122
St Joseph Cath Ch, 1250 Baliol St, P.O.Box 172, Odenton 21113
St Lawrence (Jessup Rd & Balto-Wash Pkwy, Rt 175) 2899 Jessup
    Rd, Jessup 20794
St Mary Cath Ch, 109 Duke of Gloucester St, Annapolis 21401
St Philip Neri Cath Ch, 6405 Orchard Rd, Linthicum Hts 21090

Baltimore   All Saints Cath Ch (Liberty Hts & Eldorado Ave) 4408 Liberty
    Hts Ave, Balto 21207
Archdiocese of Balto Cath Center, (Cathedral & Mulberry Sts)
    320 Cathedral St, Balto 21201
Basilica of the Assumption. SEE: Co-Cathedral-Basilica of
    the Assumption of the Blessed Virgin Mary
Cath Com at Relay, 5025 Cedar Ave, Balto 21227
Cath House, 341 S Stricker St, Balto 21223
Christ the King Cath Ch, 335 Sollers Pt Rd, Dundalk 21222
Ch of Nativity of Our Lord Jesus Christ, 1809 Vista Ln,
    Timonium 21093
Ch of the Annunciation, 5212 McCormick Ave, Balto 21206
Ch of the Blessed Sacrament, 4103 Old York Rd, Balto 21218
Ch of the Immaculate Conception (Mosher St & Druid Hill Ave)
    1512 Druid Hill Ave, Balto 21217
Ch of the Immaculate Conception, 200 Ware Ave, Towson 21204
Co-Cathedral-Basilica of the Assumption of the Blessed Virgin
    Mary (Cathedral & Mulberry Sts) 408 N Charles St, Balto
    21201

Catholic

Corpus Christi Cath Ch, (Jenkins Memorial) (Mt Royal &
  Lafayette Aves) 110 W Lafayette Ave, Balto 21217
Holy Cross Cath Ch, 110 E West St, Balto 21230
Holy Cross Cath Ch (Polish) 208 S Broadway, Balto 21231
Holy Family Cath Ch, 9533 Liberty Rd, Randallstown 21133
Holy Redeemer Chapel, 800 S Oldham St, Balto 21224
Holy Rosary Cath Ch, 408 S Chester St, Balto 21231
Immaculate Heart of Mary (Baynesville) 8501 Loch Raven Blvd,
  Balto 21204
Jenkins Memorial. SEE: Corpus Christi Cath Ch
Johns Hopkins Hospital Apostolate, 550 N Broadway, Balto 21205
Katharine of Sienna Cath Ch, 1222 N Luzerne Ave, Balto 21213
Most Precious Blood Cath Ch, 5010 Bowleys Ln, Balto 21206
Most Precious Blood Cath Ch, 4790 Shamrock Ave, Balto 21206
Our Lady of Fatima, 6420 E Pratt St, Balto 21224
Our Lady of Good Counsel, 1532 E Fort Ave, Balto 21230
Our Lady of Hope, 1727 Lynch Rd, Balto 21222
Our Lady of Mt Carmel (Middle River) 1704 Eastern Ave, Balto
  21221
Our Lady of Perpetual Help (Woodlawn) 6950 Dogwood Rd, Balto
  21207
Our Lady of Pompei, 3600 Claremont St, Balto 21224
Our Lady of Victory (Arbutus) 4414 Wilkens Ave, Balto 21229
Our Lady Queen of Peace (Middle River) 10003 Bird River Rd,
  Balto 21220
Patronage of the Mother of God (Ruthenian Cath, Byzantine
  Rite) 1260 Stevens Ave, Arbutus 21227
Sacred Heart Cath Ch, 65 Sacred Heart Ln, Glyndon 21071
Sacred Heart of Jesus, 600 S Conkling St, Balto 21224
Sacred Heart of Mary, 6736 Youngstown Ave, Balto 21222
St Agnes Cath Ch, (Rt 40 at St Agnes Ln) 5422 Old Frederick
  Rd, Catonsville, Balto 21229
St Alphonsus Cath Ch (Lithuanian) (Park Ave & Saratoga St)
  114 W Saratoga St, Balto 21201
St Alphonsus Rodriguez Cath Ch, 10800 Old Court Rd, Woodstock
  21163
St Ambrose Cath Ch, 4502 Park Heights Ave, Balto 21215
St Ann Cath Ch (Greenmount Ave & E 22nd St) 528 E 22nd St,
  Balto 21218
St Anthony of Padua, 4420 Frankford Ave, Balto 21206
St Athanasius Cath Ch (Prudence & Church Sts) 4708 Prudence
  St, Curtis Bay, Balto 21226
St Benedicts Cath Ch, 2612 Wilkens Ave, Balto 21223
St Bernard Cath Ch, 928 Gorsuch Ave, Balto 21218
St Bernardine Cath Ch (Edmondson Ave & Mt Holly St) 3812
  Edmondson Ave, Balto 21229
St Brigid Cath Ch, 911 S Ellwood Ave, Balto 21224
St Casimir Cath Ch (Polish) 2736 O'Donnell St, Balto 21224
St Charles Borromeo Cath Ch, 101 Church Ln, P.O.Box 5783,
  Pikesville, Balto 21208
St Clare Cath Ch, 714 Myrth Ave, Essex, Balto 21221

Catholic

St Clement Cath Ch, 2700 Washington Ave, Lansdowne, Balto
21227
St Clement Mary Hofbauer Cath Ch, 1220 Chesaco Ave, Rosedale,
Balto 21237
St Dominic Cath Ch, (Harford Rd & Gibbons Ave) 2910 Echodale
Ave, Balto 21214
St Edward Cath Ch (Poplar Grove & Prospect Sts) 901 Poplar
Grove St, Balto 21216
St Elizabeth of Hungary Cath Ch, (Balto St & Lakewood Ave)
Belnord Ave & Balto St, Balto 21224
St Francis of Assisi Cath Ch, 3615 Harford Rd, Balto 21218
St Francis Xavier Cath Ch, (Caroline & Oliver Sts) 1501 E
Oliver St, Balto 21213
St Gerard Chapel, Charlotte & Cardiff Aves, Balto 21224
St Gregory the Great Cath Ch, 1542 N Gilmore St, Balto 21217
St Ignatius Cath Ch, (Calvert & Madison Sts) 102 E Madison St,
Balto 21202
St Isaac Jogues Cath Ch, 9215 Old Harford Rd, Balto 21234
St James & St John Cath Ch, (Aisquith & Eager Sts) 1225 E
Eager St, Balto 21202
St Jerome Cath Ch, 775 W Hamburg St, Balto 21230
St John the Baptist Cath Ch, 308 N Paca St, Balto 21201
St John the Evangelist Cath Ch, Long Green Pike, Hydes 21082
St Joseph Cath Ch (Texas) 101 Church Ln, Cockeysville 21030
St Joseph Monastery, 3800 Frederick Ave, Balto 21229
St Katharine of Sienna (Preston St & Luzerne Ave) 1222 N
Luzerne Ave, Balto 21213
St Lawrence Cath Ch, 5801 Security Blvd, Balto 21207
St Leo Cath Ch (Italian) 227 S Exeter St, Balto 21202
St Luke Cath Ch, 7517 North Point Rd, Edgemere, Balto 21219
St Martin Cath Ch (Fulton Ave & Fayette St) 31 N Fulton Ave,
Balto 21223
St Mary of the Assumption, 5502 York Rd, Govans, Balto 21212
St Mary Star of the Sea, 1419 Riverside Ave, Balto 21230
St Matthew Cath Ch, 5401 Loch Raven Blvd, Balto 21239
St Michael (Ukrainian Cath, Byzantine Rite) 524 S Wolfe St,
Balto 21231
St Michael the Archangel, 7 S Wolfe St, Balto 21231
St Michael the Archangel (Overlea) 2 Willow Ave, Balto 21206
St Patrick Cath Ch, 317 S Broadway, Balto 21231
St Peter the Apostle Cath Ch (Poppleton & Hollins Sts) 848
Hollins St, Balto 21201
St Pius V Cath Ch (Schroeder St & Edmondson Ave) 521 N
Schroeder St, Balto 21223
St Pius X Cath Ch (Rodgers Forge) 6428 York Rd, Balto 21212
St Rita Cath Ch, 2903 Dunleer Rd, Dundalk, Balto 21222
St Rose of Lima Cath Ch, 3803 Fourth St, Balto 21225
St Stanislaus Kostka (Polish) 700 S Ann St, Balto 21231
St Stephen Cath Ch, 8030 Bradshaw Rd, Bradshaw 21021
St Thomas Aquinas Cath Ch, 1008 W 37th St, P.O.Box 4821, Balto
21211
St Thomas More Cath Ch, 6806 McClean Blvd, Balto 21234

St Ursula Cath Ch (Parkville) 8801 Harford Rd, Balto 21234
St Veronica Cath Ch, 806 Cherry Hill Rd, Balto 21225
St Vincent de Paul Cath Ch, 120 N Front St, Balto 21202
St Wenceslaus Cath Ch (Bohemian) 2111 Ashland Ave, Balto 21205
St William of York Cath Ch, 4900 Edmondson Ave, Balto 21229
SS Peter & Paul (Ukrainian Cath, Byzantine Rite) 1506 Church
  St, Curtis Bay, Balto 21226
SS Philip & James Cath Ch, 2801 N Charles St, Balto 21218
Shrine of the Little Flower (Belair Rd & Brendan Ave) 2854
  Brendan Ave, Balto 21213
Shrine of the Sacred Heart, 1701 Regent Rd, Balto 21209

Calvert
Our Lady Star of the Sea, P.O.Box 560, Solomons 20688
St Anthony Cath Ch, 8820 Chesapeake Ave, North Beach 20714
St John Mary Bap Vianney Cath Ch, Star Rt 1 Box 264, Prince
  Frederick 20678

Caroline
Immaculate Conception Cath Ch, Marydel 21649

Carroll
St John's Cath Ch, Monroe St, P.O.Box 546, Westminster 21157
St Joseph Cath Ch, P.O.Box 12, Taneytown 21787
St Peter Cath Ch, 9201-A Church St, Rt 2, Union Bridge 21791

Cecil
Immaculate Conception Cath Ch, Bow St, Elkton 21921
St Basil's Ukrainian Cath Ch, Chesapeake City 21915
St Jude Cath Ch, 1/4 mi fr town on Rt 272, North East 21901

Charles
Holy Ghost Cath Ch, Rt 1 Box 97, Newburg 20664
Our Lady Help of Christians, 930 Barrington Dr, Waldorf 20601
Sacred Heart Cath Ch, P.O.Box 2, La Plata 20646
St Catherine of Alexandria, P.O.Box 385, Port Tobacco 20677
St Francis de Sales Cath Ch, P.O.Box 306, Benedict 20612
St Francis de Sales Cath Ch, Rt 1 Box 97, Newburg 20664
St Joseph Cath Ch, P.O.Box 100, Pomfret 20675
St Mary Cath Ch, Bryantown 20617
St Mary Star of the Sea, 30 Mattingly Ave, Indian Head 20640
St Peter Cath Ch, Box 42 St Peter's Church Rd, Waldorf 20601

Dorchester
Our Lady of Good Counsel, Secretary 21664
St Mary's Refuge of Sinners, Glasgow Rd, Cambridge 21613

Frederick
Cath Ch of Walkersville, P.O.Box 184, Walkersville 21793
Cath Com of Middletown, 3240 Old Natl Pike, Middletown 21769
St Anthony Shrine, 16150 St Anthony Rd, Emmitsburg 21727
St Francis of Assisi, 113 First Ave, Brunswick 21716
St Ignatius Loyola, 3523 Urbana Pike, Frederick 21701
St John the Evangelist Cath Ch, 116 E 2nd St, P.O.Box 189,
  Frederick 21701
St Joseph Cath Ch (Carrollton Manor) 5843 Manor Woods Rd,
  Buckeystown 21717
St Joseph Cath Ch, 47 DePaul St, Emmitsburg 21727
St Mary Cath Ch (Petersville) Brunswick P.O. 21716
St Timothy Cath Ch, 40 Main St, Walkersville 21793

Garrett
Immaculate Conception Cath Ch, Rt 38 & Maple St, Kitzmiller
  21538
St Ann's R Cath Ch (New Germany Rd & Rt 40) Rt 2 Box 130,
  Grantsville 21536
St Peter the Apostle Cath Ch, 402 E Oak St, P.O.Box 186,
  Oakland 21550

Harford	Ch of the Holy Spirit, 540 Joppa Farm Rd, Joppa 21085
	Prince of Peace Cath Ch, 2600 Willoughby Beach Rd, Edgewood 21040
	St Francis de Sales Cath Ch, 1450 Abingdon Rd, Abingdon 21009
	St Ignatius Cath Ch (Hickory) 533 E Jarrettsville Rd, Forest Hill 21050
	St Joan of Arc Cath Ch, 257 S Law St, Aberdeen 21001
	St Margaret Cath Ch, 141 Hickory Ave, Bel Air 21014
	St Mark Cath Ch, 812 Reckord Rd, Fallston 21047
	St Mary Cath Ch, 1021 St Mary's Rd, Pylesville 21132
	St Patrick Cath Ch, 615 Congress Ave, Havre de Grace 21078
Howard	Ch of the Resurrection, Paulskirk Dr & Chatham Rd, Ellicott City 21043
	Our Lady of Perpetual Help, 4795 Ilchester Rd, Ellicott City 21043
	St Augustine Cath Ch, 5976 Old Washington Rd, Elkridge 21227
	St John the Evangelist Cath Ch, Wilde Lake, 10431 Twin Rivers Rd, Columbia 21044
	St Louis Cath Ch, 12500 Clarksville Pike, P.O.Box 155, Clarksville 21029
	St Paul Cath Ch, 3755 St Paul St, Ellicott City 21043
Kent	Sacred Heart Cath Ch, 508 W High St, Chestertown 21620
	St Dennis Cath Ch, Galena 21635
Montgomery	Christ the King Cath Ch, 2300 East-West Hwy, Silver Spring 20910
	Holy Cross Cath Ch, 4900 Strathmore Ave, Garrett Park 20896
	Holy Redeemer Cath Ch, 9705 Summit Ave, Kensington 20895
	Little Flower Cath Ch, 5607 Massachusetts Ave, Bethesda 20816
	Mother Seton Cath Ch, P.O.Box 18, Germantown 20874
	Our Lady of Grace, Leisure World, 3134 Adderly Ct, Silver Spring 20906
	Our Lady of Lourdes, 7500 Pearl St, Bethesda 20814
	Our Lady of Mercy, 9200 Kentsdale Dr, Potomac 20854
	Our Lady of Sorrows, 1006 Larch Ave, Takoma Park 20912
	Resurrection Cath Ch, 14505 Perrywood Dr, Burtonsville 20866
	St Andrew the Apostle Cath Ch, 11600 Kempt Mill Rd, Silver Spring 20902
	St Bartholomew Cath Ch, 6900 River Rd, Bethesda 20817
	St Bernadette Cath Ch, 70 University Blvd E, Silver Spring 20901
	St Camillus Cath Ch, 1600 St Camillus Dr, Silver Spring 20903
	St Catherine Laboure Cath Ch, 11801 Claridge Rd, Wheaton 20902
	St Elizabeth Cath Ch, 919 Montrose Rd, Rockville 20852
	St Francis of Assisi, 6704 Mancaster Mill Rd, Rockville 20855
	St Jane Frances de Chantal, 9701 Old Georgetown Rd, Bethesda 20814
	St John Neumann Cath Ch, 19300 Thomas Farm Rd, Gaithersburg 20879
	St John the Bap Cath Ch, 12319 New Hampshire Ave, Silver Spring 20904
	St John the Evangelist Cath Ch, 10103 Georgia Ave, Silver Spring 20902

Catholic

St Martin Cath Ch, 201 S Frederick Ave, Gaithersburg 20877
St Mary Cath Ch, 520 Veirs Mill Rd, Rockville 20852
St Michael the Archangel, 824 Pershing Dr, Silver Spring 20910
St Patrick Cath Ch, 4101 Norbeck Rd, Rockville 20853
St Paul Cath Ch, 9240 Main St, Damascus 20872
St Peter Cath Ch, 3408 King William Dr, Olney 20832
St Raphael Cath Ch, 1590 Kimblewick Rd, Rockville 20854-6198
St Rose of Lima, 11811 Clopper Rd, Gaithersburg 20878
Shrine of St Jude, 12701 Veirs Mill Rd, Rockville 20853

Prince Georges Ascension Cath Ch, 12700 Lanham-Severn Rd, P.O.Box 96, Bowie 20715
Blessed Andrew Kim Korean Pastoral Mission, 8108 54th Ave, College Park 20740
Congregation of Jesus & Mary, 8908 Riggs Rd, Hyattsville 20783
Holy Family Cath Ch, 2210 Callaway St, Hillcrest Hts 20748
Holy Family Cath Ch, P.O.Box 1599, Mitchellville 20716
Holy Redeemer Cath Ch, 4902 Berwyn Rd, College Park 20740
Holy Spirit Cath Ch, 1717 Ritchie Rd, Forestville 20747
Most Holy Rosary Cath Ch, 11704 Duley Sta Rd, Upper Marlboro 20772
Mt Calvary Cath Ch, 6700 Marlboro Pike, Forestville 20747
Resurrection of Our Lord, 8402 Brock Bridge Rd, Laurel 20707
Sacred Heart Cath Ch, 16501 Annapolis Rd, Bowie 20715
St Ambrose Cath Ch, 3107 63rd Ave, Cheverly 20785
St Bernard Cath Ch, 5700 St Bernard's Dr, Riverdale 20737
St Bernardine of Siena, 2400 Brooks Dr, Suitland 20746
St Columba Cath Ch, 7804 Livingston Rd, Oxon Hill 20745
St Edward the Confessor, 16304 Pond Meadow Lane, Bowie 20716
St Gregory Byzantine Cath Ch, 12420 Old Gunpowder Rd, Beltsville 20705
St Hugh Cath Ch, 135 Crescent Rd, Greenbelt 20770
St Ignatius Cath Ch, 2315 Brinkley Rd, Fort Washington 20744
St James Cath Ch, 3628 Rhode Island Ave, Mt Rainier 20712
St Jerome Cath Ch, 5205 43rd Ave, Hyattsville 20781
St John Bap de la Salle, 5706 Sargent Rd, Chillum 20782
St John the Evangelist Cath Ch, 8908 Old Branch Ave, Clinton 20735
St Joseph Cath Ch, 9400 Landover Rd, Landover 20785
St Joseph's Cath Ch, 11011 Montgomery Rd, Beltsville 20705
St Margaret of Scotland, 408 Addison Rd, Seat Pleasant 20743
St Mark Cath Ch, 7501 Adelphi Rd, Hyattsville 20783
St Mary Cath Ch, 13401 Piscataway Rd, Clinton 20735
St Mary Cath Ch, 7401 Buchanan St, Landover Hills 20784
St Mary of the Assumption, 14908 Main St, Upper Marlboro 20772
St Mary of the Mills, 114 8th St, Laurel 20707
St Mathias Cath Ch, 411 Nova Ave, Capital Hts 20743
St Matthias Cath Ch, 9475 Annapolis Rd, Lanham 20706
St Nicholas Cath Ch, 8603 Contee Rd, Laurel 20708
St Philip the Apostle, 5416 Henderson Way, Camp Springs 20746
St Pius X Cath Ch, 3300 Moreland Pl, Bowie 20715

Queen Annes Mother of Sorrows Cath Ch, Corbaley Hall, Centreville 21617
St Christopher's Cath Ch, Chester 21619

CHURCH ADDRESSES

St Marys	St Peter's Cath Ch, Queenstown 21658
	Holy Face Cath Ch, Great Mills 20634
	Immaculate Conception Cath Ch, P.O.Box 166, Mechanicsville 20659
	Immaculate Heart of Mary, Rt 235 Box 6, Lexington Park 20653
	Our Lady of the Wayside, P.O.Box 97, Chaptico 20621
	Our Lady's Ch at Medley's Neck, P.O.Box 111, Leonardtown 20650
	Sacred Heart Cath Ch, Bushwood 20618
	St Aloysius Cath Ch, 120 Washington St, P.O.Box 310, Leonardtown 20650
	St Cecilia Cath Ch, P.O.Box 67, St Mary's City 20686
	St Francis Xavier Cath Ch, Rt 2 Box 50, Leonardtown 20650
	St Francis Xavier Cath Ch, Valley Lee 20692
	St Francis Xavier R Cath Ch, Newtowne 20627
	St George Cath Ch, St George Church Rd, Valley Lee 20692
	St John Cath Ch, Hollywood 20636
	St Joseph Cath Ch, Morganza 20660
	St Mary Cath Ch, Rt 1 Box 213, Charlotte Hall 20622
	St Michael Cath Ch, Ridge 20680
	St Peter Claver Cath Ch, St Peter Claver Church Rd, St Inigoes 20684
Talbot	St Michaels Chapel, Lincoln Ave, St Michaels 21663
Washington	St Ann Cath Ch, 1525 Oak Hill Ave, Hagerstown 21740
	St Ann's R Cath Ch, 1010 Oak Hill Ave, Hagerstown 21740
	St Augustine Cath Ch, 32 E Potomac St, Williamsport 21795
	St James Cath Ch, Ford & Main Sts, Boonsboro 21713
	St Joseph (Half-way) 1837 Virginia Ave, Hagerstown 21740
	St Mary Cath Ch, 224 W Washington St, Hagerstown 21740
	St Michael Cath Ch, Clear Spring 21722
	St Peter Cath Ch, 16 E High St, Hancock 21750
Wicomico	St Francis de Sales Cath Parish, 514 Camden Ave, Salisbury 21801
	St Jude House, 825 E Church St, Salisbury 21801
Worcester	Holy Name of Jesus, By Pass Rd, Pocomoke City 21851
	St Luke's & St Andrews Cath Ch, 403 141st St, Ocean City 21842
	St Mary's Star of the Sea, 208 S Balto Ave, Ocean City 21842

Christian

Allegany	First Chris Ch (Disc of Christ) 312 Bedford St, Cumberland 21502
	Grace Memorial Com Ch, Seton Dr, Cumberland 21502
	Liberty Temple Chris Center, Rt 220, Cresaptown 21502
	Love's Way Chris Fellowship, 103 Mustaphal Dr, La Vale 21502
Anne Arundel	Annapolis Chris Fellowship, 923 Windsor Rd, Annapolis 21403
	Com Gospel Ch of Pasadena, 4374 Mountain Rd, Pasadena 21122
	Faith Com Ch, 1306 Waugh Chapel Rd & Rt 3 North, Gambrills 21054
	First Chris Ch of Glen Burnie, 320 Oak Manor Dr, Glen Burnie 21061

Catholic

First Chris Com Ch, 8111 Hicks Rd, Jessup 20794
Fork Chris Ch of Glen Burnie, Stoney Batter Rd & Sunshine Ave,
  Glen Burnie 21061
New Covenant Ch at Arnold, 804 Windsor Rd, Arnold 21012
Severna Park Chris Ch, 1237 Old Annapolis Blvd, Arnold 21012

Baltimore Agape Chris Fellowship, Randallstown 21133
Balto Chris Fellowship, 9303 Harford Rd, Balto 21234
Boulevard Chris Ch, 920 Essex Ave, Balto 21221
Chinese Chris Ch of Balto, 10012 Harford Rd, Balto 21234
Chris Faith Tabernacle, 914 Middle River Rd, Balto 21220
Chris Gospel Ch, 1501 N Eden St, Balto 21213
Chris House of Prayer, 1639 Browns Rd, Balto 21221
Chris Life Ch, 3306 Garrison Blvd, Balto 21216
Chris Life Ch, 6605 Liberty Rd, Woodlawn, Balto 21207
Chris Memorial Ch, 2001 W North Ave, Balto 21217
Chris Temple (Disc of Christ) (Edmondson Ave & Academy Rd)
  5820 Edmondson Ave, Balto 21228
Chris Unity Temple, 3900 Groveland Ave, Balto 21215
City of God Chris Fellowship, 4141 W Rodgers Ave, Balto 21215
Com Ch in Woodbridge Valley, 7102 Pine Crest Rd, Catonsville
  21228
Cookley's Chris Com Chapel, 710 Poplar Grove St, Balto 21216
Emmanuel Chris Com Ch, 1210 W Lanvale St, Balto 21217
English Consul Chris Ch, 2733 Daisy Ave, Balto 21227
Faith Chris Fellowship, 9306 Winands Rd, Balto 21208
First Chris Ch (Disc of Christ) 5802 Roland Ave, Balto 21210
First Chris Ch of Edgemere, 2618 N Snyder Ave, Edgemere 21222
First Chris Com Ch, 4116 Groveland Ave, Balto 21215
Gateway Ch of Christ Disc, 1563 N Fulton Ave, Balto 21217
Gillis Memorial Com Ch, 4016 Park Heights Ave, Balto 21215
Glen Arm Chris Fellowship, 6300 Loch Raven Blvd, Balto 21239
Good Samaritan Chris Ch (Disc of Christ) 2229 N Fulton Ave,
  Balto 21217
Halethorpe Com Ch, 1312 Francis Ave, Balto 21227
Hiway Chris Ch, 1100 Homewood Ave, Balto 21202
Inter-City Action, 1012 N Carrollton Ave, Balto 21217
Ivory Temple Com Ch, 4802 Liberty Heights Ave, Balto 21207
Jones Creek Chris Ch, 7348 Geise Ave, Balto 21219
Lansdown Chris Ch, Wilmington & Clyde Sts, Balto 21223
Living Word Chris Center, 4536 Harford Rd, Balto 21214
Metropolitan Com Ch of Balto, 2630 St Paul St, Balto 21218
Mt Olivet Chris Ch (Disc of Christ) 1800 Penrose Ave, Balto
  21223
New Chris Memorial Ch, 352 S Caton Ave, Balto 21229
New Creation Chris Ch, 5401 Frankford Ave, Balto 21206
New Creation Chris Ch, 4617 York Rd, Balto 21212
New Fellowship Chris Com Ch, 5202 Park Heights Ave, Balto
  21225
Randall Street Chris Ch, Belt & Randall Sts, Balto 21230
Renew Hope Chris Com Ch, 2601 E Madison St, Balto 21205
Robe of Righteousness Chris Com Ch, 2109 W Pratt St, Balto
  21223

CHURCH ADDRESSES

	Rosedale Com Ch, 7901 Redmore Rd, Balto 21237
	St James Chris Com Ch, 4316 Park Heights Ave, Balto 21215
	St John's Chris Com Ch, 1208 E Lanvale St, Balto 21202
	Second Shiloh Ch of Christ Disc (Disc of Christ) 4 N Broadway, Balto 21231
	Shiloh Chris Com Ch, 2500 W Lombard St, Balto 21223
	Trinity Temple, 914 Essex Ave, Balto 21221
	Unit Council of Com Churches for Maryland & Virginia, 2408 Shirley Ave, Balto 21215
	Victory Villa Com Ch, 9796 Bird River Rd, Victory Villa 21220
	Wilson Park Chris Com Ch, 4629 York Rd, Balto 21212
Calvert	Dunkirk Com Chapel, Dunkirk 20754
Carroll	Evan Chris Ch, 1011 Francis Scott Key Hwy, Keymar 21757
	Mt Airy Chris Com Ch, 703 E Ridgeville Rd, Mt Airy 21771
	Salva Trinity Chris Com Ch, 703 E Ridgeville Rd, Mt Airy 21771
Charles	Shiloh Com Ch, Rt 1 Box 65, Newburg 20664
	Waldorf Com Ch, St Peter's Church Rd, Waldorf 20601
Dorchester	Cambridge Chris Fellowship Ch, 415 Academy St, Cambridge 21613
Frederick	Walkersville Chris Fellowship, 2 W 2nd St, Frederick 21701
Harford	Bible Com Ch, 1609 S Toll Gate Rd, Bel Air 21014
	First Chris Ch, 800 Giles St, Havre de Grace 21078
	Joppatowne Chris Ch, 725 Trimble Rd, Joppatowne 21085
	Mountain Chris Ch, 1824 Mountain Rd, Joppa 21085
Howard	Covenant Com Ch, Joseph Sq Village Center, Columbia 21044
	Elkridge Indep Chris Com Ch, 6327 Meadow Ridge Rd, Elkridge 21227
	Grace Chris Ch, 8850 Balto St, Savage 20763
	Lamplighter Chris Ch, 9160 Red Branch Rd, Columbia 21045
Kent	Evan Chris Ch, Millington 21651
Montgomery	Chris Ch (Disc of Christ) Capital Area, 8901 Connecticut Ave, Chevy Chase 20815
	Downsville Chris Ch, Rt 3 Box 265, Williamsport 21795
	First Chris Ch of Boonsboro, 14 St Paul St, Boonsboro 21713
	Hyattstown Chris Ch, 26012 Frederick Rd, Clarksburg 20871
	Rockville Chris Ch, 301 Adclare Rd, Rockville 20850
Prince Georges	Bread of Life Chris Fellowship, 12411 Sussex Ln, Bowie 20715
	Chris Hope Center, 5301 Edgewood Rd, College Park 20740
	Covenant Faith Com Ch, 8725 Hummingbird Ct, Laurel 20707
	Good Shepherd Chris Ch, 10500 Angora Dr, Cheltenham 20623
	Laurel Chris Fellowship, 701 Montgomery St, Laurel 20707
	Mt Rainier Chris Ch, 33rd & Bunker Hill Rd, Mt Rainier 20712
Somerset	Crisfield Chris Academy, 134 Maryland Ave, Crisfield 21817
	Perryhawkin Chris Ch, Rt 2 Box 134, Princess Anne 21853
Washington	Agape Chris Fellowship, 1725 Pennsylvania Ave, Hagerstown 21740
	Beaver Creek Chris Ch, Rt 9 Box 265, Hagerstown 21740
	First Chris Ch (Disc of Christ) Boonsboro 21713
	First Chris Ch, 1345 Potomac Ave, Hagerstown 21740
	Second Chris Ch, 65 W North Ave, Hagerstown 21741
Wicomico	Chris Covenant Ch, 126 Robins Ave, Salisbury 21801
	Faith Com Ch, 219 N Division St, Salisbury 21801
	Fruitland Chris Ch, Main St, Fruitland 21826
Worcester	Snow Hill Chris Ch, 205 S Church St, Snow Hill 21863

CHURCH ADDRESSES

Christian & Missionary Alliance

Anne Arundel	Severn Alliance Ch, Donaldson Ave, Severn 21144
Baltimore	Chris Missionary Alliance Ch of Dundalk, 1731 Rita Rd, Balto 21222
	Fellowship Ch Chris & Missionary Alliance, 3 Bowleys Quarters Rd, Balto 21220
	Lansdowne Alliance Ch, 2212 Lansdowne Rd, Balto 21227
	Walter Avenue Alliance Ch, 531 Walker Ave, Balto 21212
Frederick	Frederick Alliance Ch, 1631 Opossumtown Pike, Frederick 21701
	Kemptown Alliance Ch, Ijamsville 21754
Harford	Chris & Missionary Alliance Ch of Edgewood, 1980 Trimble Rd, Edgewood 21040
Montgomery	Chris & Missionary Alliance Ch, 7100 Roslyn Ave, Rockville 20855

Christian Science

Allegany	First Ch of Christ Sci, 28 Washington St, Cumberland 21502
Anne Arundel	Chris Sci Reading Rm, 22 West St, Annapolis 21401
	First Ch of Christ Sci, Maryland Ave & Prince Georges St, Annapolis 21401
	First Ch of Christ Sci, 101 1st Ave SE, Glen Burnie 21061
Baltimore	Chris Sci Ch, 702 Cathedral St, Balto 21201
	First Ch of Christ Sci, 1717 Frederick Rd, Balto 21228
	First Ch of Christ Sci, 1314 Eastern Ave, Essex, Balto 21221
	First Ch of Christ Sci, 1 Maryland Ave, Towson 21204
	First Ch of Christ Sci, 102 W University Pkwy, Balto 21210
	Second Ch of Christ Sci, 5720 Old Court Rd, Balto 21207
	Third Ch of Christ Sci, 702 Cathedral St, Balto 21201
Carroll	First Ch of Christ Sci, 346 Old New Windsor Rd, Westminster 21157
Frederick	First Ch of Christ Sci, 5 E Second St, Frederick 21701
Harford	Chris Sci Soc, 2 S Main St, Bel Air 21014
Prince Georges	Chris Sci Reading Rm, 384 Main St, Laurel 20707
St Marys	First Ch of Christ Sci, Rt 235 & Town Creek Rd, Lexington Park 20653
Talbot	First Ch of Christ Sci, 501 S Washington St, Easton 21601
Wicomico	First Ch of Christ Sci, Smith St & South Blvd, Salisbury 21801

Church of Christ

Allegany	Ch of Christ, 221 Memorial Ave, Cumberland 21502
	Winifred Road Ch of Christ, 936 Winifred Rd, Cumberland 21502
Anne Arundel	Annapolis Ch of Christ, 1601 Ritchie Hwy, Arnold 21012
	Ch of Christ of Glen Burnie, 2 Eastern, Glen Burnie 21061
Baltimore	Central Ch of Christ, 4301 Woodridge Rd, Balto 21229
	Ch of Christ, 1810 E Lombard St, Balto 21231
	Ch of Christ, 530 W University Pkwy, Balto 21210
	Ch of Christ, 103 Riverside Dr, Essex 21221
	Ch of Christ, Eastside, 900 Martin Blvd, Balto 21220
	Ch of Christ, Westside, 7009 Johnnycake Rd, Balto 21207
	Ch of Christ Household of Faith, Pillow Ground of Truth, 3503 Fairview Ave, Balto 21216
	Com Ch of Christ, 1002 Somerset St, Balto 21202
	Cornerstone Ch of Christ, 4239 Park Heights Ave, Balto 21215
	Grace Unit Ch of Christ, 1404 S Charles St, Balto 21230
	Highway Ch of Christ, 3413 Hayward Ave, Balto 21215
	Highway Holiness Ch of Christ, 2223 E Madison St, Balto 21205
	Inter Ch of Christ, 2208 Harford Rd, Balto 21218
	Mt Sinai Ch of Christ, 300 S Broadway, Balto 21231
	Slavic Ch of Christ, 516 S East Ave, Balto 21224
Calvert	Bibleway Ch of Christ, Prince Frederick 20678
	Ch of Christ, Huntingtown 20639
	Solid Rock Ch of Christ, Port Republic 20676
Carroll	Westminster Ch of Christ, 114 Liberty St, Westminster 21157
Cecil	Ch of Christ, Colora 21917
Charles	Ch of the Lord Jesus Christ, Ironsides 20643
Dorchester	Cambridge Ch of Christ, 1024 Cosby Ave, Cambridge 21613
Frederick	Frederick Ch of Christ, 1305 N Market St, Frederick 21701
Harford	Ch of Christ, 90 Mt Royal Ave, Aberdeen 21001
	Ch of Christ, 2529 Conowingo Rd, Bel Air 21014
	Creswell Ch of Christ, 2504 Creswell Rd, Bel Air 21014
Prince Georges	Ch of Christ, 7111 Cherry Ln, Laurel 20707
	Ch of Christ Wildercroft, 6330 Auburn Ave, Riverdale 20737
St Marys	Ch of Christ, Great Mills Rd, Lexington Park 20653
Washington	Ch of Christ, Leitersburg Pike, Hagerstown 21740
Wicomico	Ch of Christ, Walnut St, Delmar 21875
	Ch of Christ (Ocean City Rd & Jerome Dr) 2810 Old Ocean City Rd, Salisbury 21801
	Liberty Ch of Christ, 1313 Old Ocean City Rd, Salisbury 21801
	Quantico Road Ch of Christ, Quantico Rd, Salisbury 21801
Worcester	Ch of Christ, 99 Graham Ave, Berlin 21811
	Ch of Christ, Rt 2, Pocomoke City 21851

Church of God

Allegany	Ch of God (Clev Tenn) 401 W Industrial Blvd, Cumberland 21502
	First Ch of God (Anderson Ind) 2 Lagonda St, Cumberland 21502

Church of God

Anne Arundel	Ch of God, 84 Janwall St, Annapolis 21403
	Ch of God of Anderson, Rt 175, Gambrills 21054
	Edgewater Ch of God, 158 Mayo Rd, Edgewater 21037
	Gateway to Heaven Ch of God in Christ, Old Mill & Logan Rd, Pasadena 21122
	Heritage Ch of God, 8146 Quarterfield Rd, Severn 21144
Baltimore	Balto Street Ch of God, 3216 W Balto St, Balto 21229
	Bethel Ch of God 7th Day Inc, 2661 Harlem Ave, Balto 21216
	Bethlehem Chris Com Ch of God, 410 Melvin Ave, Balto 21228
	Bethlehem Ch of God, 3201 Garrison Blvd, Balto 21216
	Carter Memorial Ch of God in Christ, 745 W Fayette St, Balto 21201
	Celestial Pent Ch of God, 1744 W North Ave, Balto 21217
	Chris Com Ch of God, 2701 W Balto St, Balto 21223
	Ch of God, 2149 Division St, Balto 21217
	Ch of God, 4310 Edmondson Ave, Balto 21229
	Ch of God, 1301 Roland Heights Ave, Balto 21211
	Ch of God, 3800 9th St, Brooklyn 21225
	Ch of God, 4710 Curtis Ave, Curtis Bay 21226
	Ch of God, 171 Wiltshire Rd, Essex 21221
	Ch of God by Faith, 301 N Stricker St, Balto 21223
	Ch of God of Anderson, 301 N Monroe St, Balto 21223
	Ch of God of Anderson Ind, 6 Yorkway, Dundalk 21222
	Ch of God of Clev Tenn, 7414 Ellen Ave, Edgemere 21219
	Ch of God of Prophecy, 5th & Arsan Aves, Balto 21225
	Ch of God of Prophecy, 402 Maryland Ave, Essex 21221
	Doswell Cathedral, Ch of God in Christ, 520 Whitmore Ave, Balto 21223
	East Balto Ch of God, 2043 E Balto St, Balto 21231
	Evangel Temple Ch of God, 300 Middle River Rd, Essex 21220
	First Ch of God, Middle River Rd, Balto 21220
	First Ch of God (Anderson Ind) 4801 Sipple Ave, Balto 21206
	Grace Ch of God (Clev Tenn) 7006 Graces Quarters Rd, Balto 21220
	Greater Remnant Ch of God in Christ, 5015 Gwynn Oak Ave, Balto 21207
	Greater Spirit of Trust Ch, 664 Pitcher St, Balto 21217
	Hallelujah Unit Ch of God, 3606 W Rogers Ave, Balto 21215
	Holy Trinity Ch of God in Christ, 2028 Ashland Ave, Balto 21205
	Joppa Ch of God, 513 Philadelphia Rd, Balto 21237
	Lansdowne Ch of God, 2130 Smith Ave, Balto 21227
	Liberty Ch of God in Christ, 6202 Reisterstown Rd, Balto 21215
	Liberty Grace Ch of God, 3400 Copley Rd, Balto 21215
	Maryland Ch of God in Christ, 5100 Denmore Ave, Balto 21215
	Maryland # 26 Ch of God in Christ, 68 S Kossuth St, Balto 21229
	Mason Memorial Ch of God in Christ, 2608 Frederick Ave, Balto 21223
	Memorial Insti Ch of God, 2016 Greenmount Ave, Balto 21218
	Mt Carmel Ch of God in Christ, 4003 Elderon Ave, Balto 21215
	Mt Zion Unit Ch of God, 2217 W North Ave, Balto 21216

	New Friendship Ch of God in Christ, 2400 Denison St, Balto 21216
	New Galilee Ch of God in Christ Jesus, 3016 Oakley Ave, Balto 21215
	New Jerusalem FBH Ch of God, 1905 N Rosedale St, Balto 21216
	Prayer Tower Ch of God in Christ, 4231 York Rd, Balto 21212
	Rehoboth Ch of God, 700 Poplar Grove St, Balto 21216
	St Mark's Ch of God, 1338 W North Ave, Balto 21217
	St Peter's Ch of God True Holiness, 837 W Barre St, Balto 21230
	Star Ch of God, 3716 Windsor Mill Rd, Balto 21216
	True Deliverance Ch of God, 3306 Garrison Blvd, Balto 21216
	West Port Temple Ch of God, 2427 Annapolis Rd, Balto 21230
Caroline	First Ch of God, N Main St, Federalsburg 21632
	Park Lane Ch of God, 209 Park Ln, Federalsburg 21632
Carroll	Carrollton Ch of God, 1901 Carrollton Rd, Finksburg 21048
	Gospel Spreading Ch of God, Priestland Rd, Union Bridge 21791
	Westminster Ch of God, Rt 27 & Lucabaugh Mill Rd, Westminster 21157
	Westminster First Ch of God, 25 N Center St, Westminster 21157
Cecil	Elkton Ch of God, 301 Curtis Ave, Elkton 21921
	North East Ch of God, 302 E Thomas Ave, North East 21901
	Rising Sun Ch of God, 11 Windmill Rd, Rising Sun 21911
Charles	Waldorf Ch of God, Rt 925 & Richards Rd, Waldorf 20601
Dorchester	Center Street Ch of God, 815 Center St, Cambridge 21613
	Natl Ch of God, 807 Washington St, Cambridge 21613
	Natl Ch of God, Lords Crossing Rd, Hurlock 21643
	Souls Harbor Ch of God, 718 Peach Blossom Ave, Cambridge 21613
Frederick	Maranatha Ch of God, 1440 Taney Ave, Frederick 21701
	Maryland Virginia Conference Churches of God, 1730 N Market St, Frederick 21701
	Middletown Valley Ch of God, Main & Church Sts, Middletown 21769
	Parkway Ch of God, 216 Carroll Pkwy, Frederick 21701
Howard	Ch of God of Clev Tenn, Rt 29 Box 98, Simpsonville 21150
	Columbia Ch of God in Christ, 6000 Tamar Dr, Columbia 21045
	First Ch of God of Anderson, 3761 Church Rd, Ellicott City 21043
	Long Reach Ch of God, 6080 Foreland Garth, Columbia 21045
Montgomery	Chesapeake-Delaware-Potomac District Chris Service Board of the Ch of God, 1307 Dilston Pl, Silver Spring 20903
Prince Georges	Laurel Ch of God (Clev Tenn) 613 Montgomery St, Laurel 20707
St Marys	Ch of God, Chancellors Run Rd, Lexington Park 20653
Somerset	Ch of God, 134 Maryland Ave, Crisfield 21817
	Walker Memorial Ch of God, 129 Prince William St, Princess Anne 21853
Talbot	Ch of God, 1009 N Washington St, Easton 21601
	St Michael's Ch of God in Christ, 242 North St, St Michaels 21663
Washington	Antietam Ch of God, Sharpsburg 21782
	Ch of God, 1515 Dual Hwy, Hagerstown 21740

Church of God

Ch of God of Hagerstown, 919 Corbett St, Hagerstown 21740
Germantown Bethel Ch of God, 16924 Raven Rock Rd, Cascade
  21719
Hancock Ch of God, 163 E Main St, Hancock 21750
Mt Calvary Ch of God, Clear Spring 21722
Virginia Avenue Ch of God, 2206 Virginia Ave, Hagerstown 21740
Williamsport Ch of God, 5 Artizan & Sunset Ave, Williamsport
  21795

Wicomico   Ch of God, 661 West Rd, Salisbury 21801
Ch of God of Prophecy, 506 E College Ave, Salisbury 21801
Holy Temple Ch of God in Christ, 326 Delaware Ave, Salisbury
  21801
Parkway Ch of God, Rt 50 & Tilghman St, Salisbury 21801
Trinity Tabernacle Ch of God in Christ, Rt 50 & Dukes Dr,
  Salisbury 21801

Worcester   Berlin-Ocean City Ch of God, Sinepuxent & Lewis Rd, Berlin
  21811
Ch of God, By Pass Rd, Pocomoke City 21851

Episcopal

Allegany   Ch of the Holy Cross, 612 Brookfield Ave, Cumberland 21502
Emmanuel Epis Ch, 16 Washington St, Cumberland 21502
St George's Epis Ch, 6 C St, Mt Savage 21545
St James Epis Ch, 32 Main St, Westernport 21562
St John's Epis Ch, 50 Broadway, Frostburg 21532
St Peter's Epis Ch, 2 St Peter's Pl, Lonaconing 21639

Anne Arundel   All Hallow's Epis Ch (Solomons Isl & Brick Church Rds) Rt 424,
  Davidsonville 21035
Christ Epis Ch, Rt 255, West River 20778
Ch of St Andrew the Fisherman, Carr's Wharf Rd & Central Ave,
  Mayo 21106
Ch of St Christopher, 118 Marydel Rd, Linthicum Heights 21090
Ch of St John the Evangelist, Shady Side 20764
Epiphany Epis Ch, Morgan Rd, Odenton 21113
St Alban's Parish (1st & A Sts SW) 100 A St SW, Glen Burnie
  21061
St Andrew's Epis Ch, 7859 Tick Neck Rd, Pasadena 21122
St Anne's Epis Ch (Church Circle) 199 Duke of Gloucester St,
  Annapolis 21401
St James' Epis Ch, 5757 Solomons Isl Rd, Lothian 20711
St John's Epis Ch, 1429 Snug Harbor Rd, Shady Side 20864
St Luke's Epis Ch (Eastport) 1101 Bay Ridge Ave, Annapolis
  21403
St Margaret's Epis Ch, 1601 Pleasant Plains Rd, Annapolis
  21401
St Mark's Chapel, Deale 20751
St Martin's-in-the-Field, 375 Benfield Rd, Severna Park 21146

St Philips Epis Ch (Bestgate & Severn Grove Rds) 70 Severn
   Grove Rd, Annapolis 21401
St Stephen's Epis Ch, 1110 St Stephen's Church Rd, Crownsville
   21032

Baltimore   All Saints' Epis Ch, 203 Chatsworth Ave, Reisterstown 21136
All Souls' Epis Ch, 3815 Second St, Brooklyn, Balto 21225
Bishop Cummins Memorial Ch, 2001 Frederick Rd, Balto 21228
Cathedral Ch of the Incarnation, E University Pkwy & St Paul
   St, Balto 21218
Ch of the Holy Evangelist, 1001 S Potomac St, Balto 21224
Christ the King Epis Ch, 1930 Brookdale Rd, Balto 21207
Christ's Epis Ch (Chase & St Paul Sts) 1110 St Paul St, Balto
   21202
Ch of St Katherine of Alexandria (Presstman & Division Sts)
   2001 Division St, Balto 21217
Ch of St Mary (Woodlawn) 5610 Dogwood Rd, Balto 21207
Ch of St Mary the Virgin, 3121 Walbrook Ave, Balto 21216
Ch of St Michael & All Angels (St Paul & 20th Sts) 2013 St
   Paul St, Balto 21218
Ch of St Paul the Apostle, 859 Washington Blvd, Balto 21230
Ch of the Advent, 1301 S Charles St, Balto 21230
Ch of the Ascension (Middle River) 1313 Wilson Pt Rd, Balto
   21220
Ch of the Ascension & Prince of Peace, 8334 Liberty Rd, Balto
   21207
Ch of the Good Shepherd (Ruxton) Boyce & Carrollton Aves,
   Balto 21204
Ch of the Guardian Angel, 335 W 27th St, Balto 21211
Ch of the Holy Apostles, 4922 Leeds Ave, Balto 21227
Ch of the Holy Comforter, Seminary & Bellona Aves, Lutherville
   21093
Ch of the Holy Covenant, 560 N Broadway, Balto 21205
Ch of the Holy Cross, Millington Ave & Ashton St, Balto 21223
Ch of the Holy Evangelists (Potomac & Dillon Sts--Canton)
   1001 S Potomac St, Balto 21224
Ch of the Holy Nativity (Forest Park) 3809 Egerton Rd, Balto
   21215
Ch of the Holy Trinity, 2300 W Lafayette St, Balto 21216
Ch of the Messiah, 5801 Harford Rd, Balto 21214
Ch of the Nativity (York & Cedarcroft Rds) 419 Cedarcroft Rd,
   Balto 21212
Ch of the Redeemer, 5603 N Charles St, Balto 21210
Ch of the Redemption, 1401 Towson St, Balto 21230
Ch of the Resurrection, 2900 E Fayette St, Balto 21224
Emmanuel Epis Ch, 811 Cathedral St, Balto 21201
Emmanuel Ref Epis Ch, 3517 Harford Rd, Balto 21218
Epiphany Epis Ch (Dulaney Valley) 2216 Pot Spring Rd, Timonium
   21093
Epis Ch of Christ the King, 1930 Brookdale Rd, Balto 21207
Epis Diocese of Maryland, 105 W Monument St, Balto 21201
Grace & St Peter's Epis Ch, 707 Park Ave, Balto 21201
Grace Epis Ch (Elkridge) 6725 Montgomery Rd, Balto 21227

Episcopal

Holy Epis Ch, 3809 Edgerton Rd, Balto 21204
Holy Trinity Epis Ch, 1131 Mace Ave, Essex, Balto 21221
Immanuel Epis Parish, 1509 Glencoe Rd, Glencoe 21152
Memorial Epis Ch, 1407 Bolton St, Balto 21217
Mt Calvary Epis Ch, 816 N Eutaw St, Balto 21201
Prot Epis Ch Diocese of Md, 105 W Monument St, Balto 21201
St Andrew's Epis Ch, 6515 Loch Raven Blvd, Balto 21239
St Bartholomew's Epis Ch (Edmondson Ave & Uplands Pkwy--Ten
  Hills) 4711 Edmondson Ave, Balto 21229
St David's Epis Ch (Oakdale & Roland Ave--Roland Park) 4700
  Roland Ave, Balto 21210
St George's & St Matthew's Epis Parish, 2900 Dunleer Rd, Balto
  21222
St James' Epis Ch, 801 N Arlington Ave, Balto 21217
St James Epis Ch (Irvington) 205 S Augusta Ave, Balto 21229
St James Epis Ch (Rt 45) 19200 York Rd, Parkton 21120
St James Epis Ch, 1005 W Lafayette St, Balto 21217
St James Parish (My Lady's Manor) 3100 Monkton Rd, Monkton
  21111
St John's Epis Ch (Huntingdon) Greenmount Ave & Old York Rd,
  Balto 21218
St John's Epis Ch (Mt Washington) 1700 South Rd, Balto 21209
St John's Epis Ch (Western Run Parish) 3738 Butler Rd, Glyndon
  21071
St John's Epis Ch, 11901 Belair Rd, Kingsville 21087
St Luke's Epis Ch, 217 N Carey St, Balto 21223
St Margaret's Epis Ch (Coventry) 1819 Cromwood Rd,Balto 21234
St Mark's-on-the-Hill (Pikesville) 1620 Reisterstown Rd, Balto
  21208
St Mary's Epis Ch (Hampden) 3900 Roland Ave, Balto 21211
St Matthias' Epis Ch, 6400 Belair Rd, Balto 21206
St Paul's Parish, Charles & Saratoga Sts, Balto 21201
St Stephen's Chapel, 2401 St Stephen's Ct, 2A, Balto 21216
St Thomas' Epis Ch (Garrison Forest) 232 St Thomas' Ln, Owings
  Mills 21117
St Thomas' Epis Ch (Homestead) 1108 Providence Rd, Balto 21204
St Timothy's Epis Ch (Catonsville) 200 Ingleside Ave, Balto
  21228
Sherwood Epis Ch, Sherwood & York Rds, Cockeysville 21030
Trinity Epis Ch, 120 Allegheny Ave, Towson 21204
Trinity Epis Ch (Long Green) 12400 Manor Rd, Long Green 21092

Calvert   All Saints Epis Ch, Junction Rts 2 & 4, Sunderland 20689
Christ Epis Ch, Brooms Isl Rd, Port Republic 20676
Middleham Epis Ch, Lusby 20657
Parish of Middleham & St Peter's, Box 277, Lusby 20657
St Paul's Parish, Prince Frederick 20678
St Peter's Epis Ch, Solomons 20688

Caroline   Christ Epis Ch, 105 Gay St, Denton 21629
St Mary's Whitechapel, Denton 21629

Carroll   Ch of the Ascension, 23 N Court St, Westminster 21157
St Barnabas' Epis Ch (Forsythe Rd) 14 Main St, Sykesville
  21784

CHURCH ADDRESSES

Cecil	St George's Epis Ch, Cape Horn Rd, Manchester 21102

St George's Epis Ch, Cape Horn Rd, Manchester 21102
St James' Epis Ch, 302 N Main St, Mt Airy 21771

Cecil
Good Shepherd Epis Ch, Chesapeake City 21919
St Augustine's Epis Ch, Chesapeake City 21919
St Mark's Epis Ch, Aiken, Perryville 21903
St Mary Anne's Epis Ch, 317 S Main St, North East 21901
St Stephen's Epis Ch, Cecilton 21913
St Stephen's Epis Ch, 14 Glebe Rd, Earleville 21919
Trinity Epis Ch, 105 Bridge St, Elkton 21921

Charles
Christ Epis Ch, Charles St, P.O.Box 760, La Plata 20646
Christ Epis Ch (Ironsides) Nanjemoy 20662
Christ Epis Ch (Wayside) P.O.Box 177, Newburg 20664
St James' Epis Ch, 7 Potomac Ave, Indian Head 20640
St Paul's Epis Ch, Piney Church Rd, P.O.Box 272 Waldorf 20601
Trinity Epis Ch (Newport) Rt 1 Box 253-A, Hughesville 20637

District of Columbia
Epis Diocese of Washington, Mt St Albans, Washington, DC 20016

Dorchester
Christ Epis Ch, 601 Church St, Cambridge 21613
Grace Epis Ch, Taylor's Isl 21669
Old Trinity Epis Ch, Parish Hall, Church Creek 21622
St Andrew's Epis Ch, Hurlock 21643
St John's Epis Ch (Cornersville) Cambridge 21613
St Paul's Epis Ch, Vienna 21869
St Stephen's Epis Ch, East New Market 21631

Frederick
All Saints' Parish, 108 W Church St, Frederick 21701
Catoctin Parish, 12625 Catoctin Furnace Rd, Thurmont 21788
Ch of the Transfiguration, Maryland & Urner Aves, Braddock
  Heights 21714
Grace Epis Ch, 114 A St, Brunswick 21716
Grace Epis Ch, E Main St, New Market 21774
Harriet Chapel, 12625 Catoctin Furnace Rd, Thurmont 21788
St Barnabas' Chapel, Winchester St, Frederick 21701
St Paul's Parish, 1917 Ballenger Creek Rd, Point of Rocks
  21777
Timothy's Epis Ch, Franklin St, Frederick 21701

Garrett
Our Father's House, Rt 135, Altamont 21527
St John's Epis Ch, Rt 135, Deer Park 21527
St Matthew's Parish (2nd & Liberty Sts) 126 E Liberty St,
  Oakland 21550

Harford
Christ Epis Ch, Intersection Rts 23 & 24, Forest Hill 21050
Ch of the Ascension, (1 mi s of Rt 136) Rt 440, Street 21154
Ch of the Holy Trinity, (Rt 155) 2929 Level Rd, Churchville
  21028
Ch of the Prince of Peace, Old Fallston Rd, Fallston 21047
Ch of the Resurrection (Gunpowder Hundred) Bridge Rd & Anchor
  Dr, Joppa 21085
Emmanuel Epis Ch, Main St & Broadway, Bel Air 21014
Grace Memorial Ch, (1 mi s of Rt 1) Rt 161, Darlington 21034
Grace Ref Epis Ch, 560 Fountain St, Havre de Grace 21078
Holy Cross Epis Ch (The Rocks) Rt 24, Street 21154
St George's Parish, Perryman Rd, P.O.Box 22, Perryman 21130
St John's Epis Ch, Union & Congress Aves, Havre de Grace 21078

Episcopal

	St Mary's Epis Ch, 1 St Mary's Church Rd, Abingdon 21009
Howard	Christ Epis Ch, 6800 Oakland Mills Rd, Columbia 21045
	St Andrew's Epis Ch, Rt 97 & Union Chapel Rd, Glenwood 21738
	St John's Epis Ch, 9120 Frederick Rd, Ellicott City 21043
	St Mark's Epis Ch (Rt 216 & Hall Shop Rd) 12700 Hall Shop Rd, Highland 20777
	St Paul's Epis Ch (Poplar Springs) 16457 Old Frederick Rd, Lisbon 21765
	St Peter's Epis Ch (Rogers Ave & Frederick Rd) 3695 Rogers Ave, Ellicott City 21043
	Trinity Epis Ch (Waterloo) 7474 Washington Blvd, Elkridge 21227
Kent	Christ Epis Ch, Worton 21678
	Emmanuel Epis Ch, Chestertown 21620
	Holy Cross Epis Ch, Millington 21651
	St Clement's Epis Ch, Massey 21650
	St Paul's Epis Ch, Fairlee Rd, Chestertown 21620
	Shrewsbury Epis Ch, Kennedyville 21645
Montgomery	All Saints' Epis Ch, 3 Chevy Chase Circle, Chevy Chase 20815
	Chapel of the Holy Spirit, P.O.Box 319, Germantown 20874
	Christ Epis Ch, 4001 Franklin St, Kensington 20895
	Christ Epis Ch, 109 S Washington St, Rockville 20850
	Ch of Our Saviour, 1700 Powder Mill Rd, Silver Spring 20903
	Ch of St Mary Magdalene, 3820 Aspen Hill Rd, Wheaton 20906
	Ch of the Ascension, 201 S Summit Ave, Gaithersburg 20877
	Ch of the Ascension, 630 Silver Spring Ave, Silver Spring 20910
	Ch of the Good Shepherd, 818 University Blvd W, Silver Spring 20906
	Ch of the Redeemer (Glen Echo) 6201 Dunrobbin Dr, Bethesda 20816
	Ch of the Transfiguration, 13925 New Hampshire Ave, Silver Spring 20904
	Grace Epis Ch, 1607 Grace Church Rd, Silver Spring 20910
	St Anne's Epis Ch, 25100 Ridge Rd, Damascus 20872
	St Bartholomew's Epis Ch, 21615 Laytonsville Rd, Laytonsville 20879
	St Dunstan's Epis Ch (Sumner) 5450 Massachusetts Ave, Bethesda 20816
	St Francis' Epis Ch, 10033 River Rd, Potomac 20854
	St James Epis Ch, 11815 Seven Locks Rd, Potomac 20854
	St John's Epis Ch, 6701 Wisconsin Ave, Chevy Chase 20815
	St John's Epis Ch, 3247 Olney-Laytonsville Rd, Olney 20832
	St Luke's Epis Ch, 6100 Grosvenor Ln, Bethesda 20814
	St Luke's Epis Ch, 1001 Brighton Dam Rd, Brookeville 20833
	St Mark's Epis Ch (Fairland) 12621 Old Columbia Pike, Silver Spring 20904
	St Peter's Epis Ch, P.O.Box 387, Poolesville 20837
Prince Georges	All Saints Epis Ch (Annapolis Junction) 8207 Washington St, Laurel 20810
	Chapel of the Incarnation, Brandywine 20613
	Christ Epis Ch, 600 Farmington Rd W, Accokeek 20607

Christ Epis Ch, 8710 Old Branch Ave, Clinton 20735
Ch of St Michael & All Angels, 8501 New Hampshire Ave, Adelphi 20783
Ch of the Nativity, 5203 Manchester Dr, Camp Springs 20748
Epiphany Epis Ch, 3111 Ritchie Rd, Forestville 20747
Holy Trinity Epis Ch (Collington) P.O.Box 560, Bowie 20715
Memorial Chapel, University of Maryland, College Park 20740
St Andrew's Epis Ch, 4512 College Ave, College Park 20740
St Barnabas' Epis Ch (Oxon Hill) 5203 St Barnabas' Rd, Temple Hills 20748
St Barnabas' Epis Ch (Leeland) 14111 Oak Grove Rd, Upper Marlboro 20772
St Christopher's Epis Ch, 8001 Annapolis Rd, New Carrollton 20784
St George's Epis Ch, P.O.Box 188, Glenn Dale 20769
St James' Chapel, 8th & Chapel Sts, P.O.Box 187, Bowie 20715
St John's Epis Ch, 11040 Balto ave, P.O.Box 14, Beltsville 20705
St John's Epis Ch (Broad Creek) 9801 Livingston Rd, Fort Washington 20744
St John's Epis Ch, 34th St & Rainier Ave, Mt Rainier 20712
St Luke's Epis Ch, 4006 53rd St, Bladensburg 20710
St Luke's Epis Ch, Annapolis Rd & 53rd St, Bladensburg 20710
St Mary's Chapel, Aquasco 20608
St Matthew's Epis Ch, 5901 36th Ave, Hyattsville 20782
St Paul's Epis Ch (Baden) 13301 Baden-Westwood Rd, Brandywine 20613
St Philip's Chapel (Baden) 13801 Baden-Westwood Rd, Brandywine 20613
St Philip's Epis Ch (6th & Main Sts) 522 Main St, Laurel 20810
St Thomas' Epis Ch, 10303 Croom Rd, Upper Marlboro 20772
Trinity Epis Ch, 14515 Church St, Upper Marlboro 20772

Queen Annes   Christ Epis Ch, Stevensville 21666
St Andreew's Epis Ch, Sudlersville 21668
St Luke's Epis Ch, Church Hill 21623
St Paul's Epis Ch, Centreville 21617

St Marys   All Faith Epis Ch (Huntersville) Charlotte Hall 20622
All Saints' Epis Ch (Oakley) Avenue 20609
Christ Epis Ch, P.O.Box 8, Chaptico 20621
Ch of the Ascension, Great Mills Rd & Essex Dr, Lexington Park 20653
St Andrews Epis Ch, St Andrews Church Rd, California 20619
St George's Epis Ch, P.O.Box 30, Valley Lee 20692
St Mary's Chapel, Ridge 20680
St Peter's Chapel, P.O.Box 115, Leonardtown 20650
Trinity Epis Ch, P.O.Box 3, St Mary's City 20686

Somerset   Grace Epis Ch, Mt Vernon RFD, Princess Anne 21853
St Andrew's Epis Ch, 1 Washington St, Princess Anne 21853
St Mark's Epis Ch, Kingston 21834
St Paul's Epis Ch, Marion Sta 21836

Talbot   All Faiths Epis Ch, Tunis Mills 21601
Christ Epis Ch, Easton 21601

Episcopal

Christ Epis Ch, Willow St, St Michaels 21663
Epis Diocese of Easton, P.O.Box 1027, Easton 21601
Holy Trinity Epis Ch, Morris St, Oxford 21654
Old Wye Parish, Wye Mills 21679
St Luke's Epis Ch, Queenstown 21658
St Luke's Epis Ch (Old Wye) Wye Mills 21679
St Paul's Epis Ch, Main St, Trappe 21673
Trinity Cathedral, Cathedral Green, Easton 21601

ashington St Andrew's Epis Ch, (Rt 40) 22 Cumberland St, Clear Springs 21722
St Ann's Epis Ch, Maple Ave, Smithburg 21783
St James Chapel, St James 21781
St John's Parish, 101 S Prospect St, Hagerstown 21740
St Luke's Epis Ch, Old Rt 67, Brownsville 21715
St Mark's Epis Ch (Lappans) RFD 1, Boonsboro 21713
St Paul's Epis Ch, Sharpsburg 21782
St Thomas Epis Ch, 2 E High St, Hancock 21750

icomico St Alban's Epis Ch, Mt Hermon Rd & St Alban Dr, P.O.Box 1272, Salisbury 21801
St Bartholomew's Epis Ch, Green Hill, Tyaskin 21865
St Paul's Epis Ch, Hebron 21830
St Philip's Epis Ch, Quantico 21856

orcester All Hallows Epis Ch, 101 N Church St, Snow Hill 21863
Holy Cross Epis Ch, Stockton 21864
Holy Spirit Epis Ch, N Ocean City 21842
St Martin's Epis Ch, Showell 21862
St Mary the Virgin Epis Ch, Third St, Pocomoke City 21851
St Paul's Epis Ch, Church St, P.O.Box 429, Berlin 21811
St Paul's-by-the-Sea, 302 N Baltimore Ave, Ocean City 21842

Friends

ltimore Balto Monthly Meet (Homewood) 3107 N Charles St, Balto 21218
Balto Monthly Meet (Stony Run) 5116 N Charles St, Balto 21210

strict of Society of Friends, 1250 Irving St NE, Washington, DC 20017
Columbia

ntgomery Society of Friends, 1700 Quaker Ln, Sandy Spring 20860

lbot Third Haven Friends Meet, 405 S Washington St, Easton 21601

Holiness

legany Mountain Top Holiness Ch, Rts 40 & 2, Flintstone 21530

ne Arundel Grace of God Holiness Ch, 113 W Earleight Hts Rd, Severna Park 21146

ltimore Archbishop Charles Malloy Sunrise Spirtual Temple, 1302 N Gay St, Balto 21213

137

CHURCH ADDRESSES

Balto Tabernacle, 1922 Edmondson Ave, Balto 21228
Balto Tabernacle of Prayer, 1500 Harford Ave, Balto 21202
Blood Wash Holiness Ch, 2558 Druid Hill Ave, Balto 21217
Christ Temple Holiness Ch, 2117 Pennsylvania Ave, Balto 21217
Holy Trinity Ch, 2100 Vine St, Balto 21223
James Tabernacle Apos Holiness Ch, 3400 Mondawmin ave, Balto
    21216
Macdeonia Holiness Ch, 1400 N Mount St, Balto 21217
Mt Sinai Holiness Ch, 3069 Spaulding Ave, Balto 21215
New St Paul Holy Ch, 1340 N Calhoun St, Balto 21217
Resurrection Prot Holiness Ch, 3510 Clifton Ave, Balto 21216
Revelation Gospel Holiness Ch of Deliverance, 3008 W North
    Ave, Balto 21216
St Matthews Holiness Ch, 1110 W Balto St, Balto 21223
St Michael's Ref House of God, 1506 E Hoffman St, Balto 21213
St Paul Apos Holiness Ch, 1725 E Balto St, Balto 21231
Unit Temple of God, 1035 W Balto St, Balto 21223
Whole Truth of God in Christ Jesus Ch, 2247 Eutaw Pl, Balto
    21217

Calvert   Bethel Way of the Cross Ch, Cherry Hill Rd, Huntingtown 20639
Caroline   King's Apostle Holiness Ch, N 4th St, Denton 21629
Harford   Highway Holiness Ch, 511 Edmund St, Aberdeem 21001
Wicomico   Mt Enoch Holiness Ch, 703 Delaware Ave, Salisbury 21801
Worcester   St James Holiness Ch, Dighton Ave, Snow Hill 21863
   Unit Faith Body of Deliverance, 4th & Willow St, Pocomoke City
    21851

Jehovah's Witnesses

Allegany   Jeh Wit, Country Club Rd, Cumberland 21502
Anne Arundel   Jeh Wit Kingdom Hall, 1301 Williams St, Glen Burnie 21061
   Jeh Wit of Crownsville, 1200 Sunrise Beach Rd,, Crownsville
    21032
   Jeh Wit Pasadena, June Dr, Pasadena 21122
Baltimore   Essex Congregation of Jeh Wit, 364 Upperlanding Rd, Balto
    21221
   Jeh Wit Catonsville Congregation, 1928 Powers Ln, Balto 21228
   Jeh Wit Freeland Congregation, 21135 Ridge Rd, Parkton 21120
   Jeh Wit Information Center for Balto, P.O.Box 571, Balto 21203
   Jeh Wit Kingdom Hall, 7824 Eddlynch Rd, Balto 21222
   Jeh Wit Kingdom Hall, 1007 Veronica Ave, Balto 21225
   Jeh Wit Kingdom Hall, 930 Wilmington Ave, Balto 21223
   Kingdom Hall of Jeh Wit, 1107 N Broadway, Balto 21213
   Kingdom Hall of Jeh Wit, 1925 N Dukeland St, Balto 21216
   Kingdom Hall of Jeh Wit, 1323 Edmondson Ave, Balto 21228
   Kingdom Hall of Jeh Wit, 3627 Greenmount Ave, Balto 21218
   Kingdom Hall of Jeh Wit, 211 N Highland Ave, Balto 21224
   Kingdom Hall of Jeh Wit, 1701 W Mulberry St, Balto 21223
   Kingdom Hall of Jeh Wit, 2432 E North Ave, Balto 21213

Jehovah's Witnesses

Kingdom Hall of Jeh Wit, 5010 Park Heights Ave, Balto 21215
Kingdom Hall of Jeh Wit, 4423 Pimlico Rd, Balto 21215
Kingdom Hall of Jeh Wit, 1400 Weyburn Rd, Balto 21237
Kingdom Hall of Jeh Wit, Pulaski Hwy, White Marsh 21162
Kingdom Hall of Jeh Wit, South Congregation, 1110 Church St,
    Balto 21225
Rosemont Congregation of Jeh Wit, 3204 Presstman St, Balto
    21216

Carroll	Eldersburg Kingdom Hall, 6328 Sykesville Rd, Sykesville 21784
	Jeh Wit, 207 Greenwood Ave, Westminster 21157
Cecil	Jeh Wit Kingdom Hall, 1120 Telegraph Rd, Rising Sun 21911
Charles	Kingdom Hall of Jeh Wit, Washington Ave, La Plata 20646
Dorchester	Jeh Wit, 609 Governors Ave, Cambridge 21613
Frederick	Kingdom Hall of Jeh Wit, 1 W 9th St, Frederick 21701
Garrett	Kingdom Hall of Jeh Wit, Oakland 21550
Harford	Bel Air Congregation of Jeh Wit, Wilgis Rd, Fallston 21047
	Kingdom Hall of Jeh Wit, Mitchell Ln, Perryman 21130
Howard	Jeh Wit Kingdom Hall, 3589 Centennial Ln, Ellicott City 21043
Prince	Jeh Wit Kingdom Hall, 3609 Metzerott Rd, College Park 20740
Georges	Jeh Wit Kingdon Hall, Lyons Ave & All Saints Rd, Laurel 20707
St Marys	Jeh Wit, Chancellors Run Rd, Lexington Park 20653
Somerset	Jeh Wit, US 13, Westover 21871
Washington	Jeh Wit, 30 Nottingham Rd, Hagerstown 21740
Wicomico	Jeh Wit, 108 Louise Ave, Salisbury 21801
Worcester	Jeh Wit, West St, Berlin 21811

Judaism

Baltimore	Anshe Emunah-Altz Chaim Orth Syn, 8615 Church Ln, Balto 21207
	Arugas Habosern Orth Syn, 6615 Park Hts Ave, Balto 21215
	Balto Hebrew Ref Congregation, 7401 Park Hts Ave, Balto 21208
	Beth-Am-in-Town Syn, Eutaw Pl nr Chauncey, Balto 21217
	Beth Arn Orth Syn, 2501 Eutaw Pl, Balto 21217
	Beth El Conserv Congregation, 8101 Park Hts Ave, Balto 21208
	Beth Isaac Adath Israel Orth Congregation, 4398 Crest Hts Rd, Balto 21215
	Beth Israel Syn, 9411 Liberty Rd, Balto 21207
	Beth Jacob Anshe Riga Syn, 5713 Park Hts Ave, Balto 21215
	Beth Jacob Orth Congregation, 5713 Park Hts Ave, Balto 21215
	Beth Tfiloh Syn, 3300 Old Court Rd, Balto 21208
	B'nai Jacob Orth Congregation, 3615 Seven Mill Ln, Balto 21208
	B'nai Jacob Syn, 6605 Liberty Rd, Balto 21207
	Chizuk Amuno Conserv Congregation, 8100 Stevenson Rd, Balto 21208
	Har Sinai Ref Congregation, 6300 Park Hts Ave, Balto 21215
	Moses Montefiore Congregation, 3605 Coronado Rd, Balto 21207
	Oheb Shalom Ref Congregation, 7310 Park Hts Ave, Balto 21208
	Ohel Yakov Orth Congregation, 3200 Glen Ave, Balto 21215

CHURCH ADDRESSES

Ohr-Knesseth Israel Anshe Sphard Congregation, 3910 W Rogers
Ave, Balto 21215
Pickwick Jewish Center, 6221 Greenspring Ave, Balto 21209
Randallstown Syn, 8729 Church Ln, Randallstown 21133
Rosh Pina Congregation, Pikesville 21208
Shaarei Zion Orth Congregation, 6602 Park Hts Ave, 21215
Shomrei Emanah Orth Syn, 6213 Greenspring Ave, Balto 21209
Suburban Orth Syn, 7504 Seven Mile Ln, Balto 21208
Synagogue Center, 7124 Park Hts Ave, Balto 21215
Temple Emanuel, 3301 Milford Mill Rd, Balto 21207
Winands Road Synagogue Center, Winands & Carthage Rds,
Randallstown 21133

Howard   Beth Shalom Conserv Congregation, 5639 Thunder Hill Rd,
Columbia 21045
Columbia Jewish Congregation, 5885 Robert Oliver Pl, Columbia
21045
Temple Isaiah Ref Congregation, 5885 Robert Oliver Pl,
Columbia 21045

Latter Day Saints

Allegany   Ch of Jesus Christ of LDS, Gramlich Rd, Rt 1 Box 1-F, La Vale
21502
Anne Arundel Annapolis Ward, 1875 Ritchie Hwy, Annapolis 21401
Ft Meade Ward, 524 Higgins Dr, Odenton 21113
Glen Burnie Ward, 206 A St SW, Glen Burnie 21061
Baltimore   Balto Ward, 3501 The Alameda, Balto 21218
Ch of Jesus Christ of LDS, Balto Stake, 1400 Dulaney Valley
Rd, Lutherville 21204
Essex Ward, 1400 Dulaney Valley Rd, Lutherville 21204
Perry Hall Ward, 1400 Dulaney Valley Rd, Lutherville 21204
Towson Ward, 1400 Dulaney Valley Rd, Lutherville 21204
Calvert   Ch of Jesus Christ of LDS, Clyde Jones Rd, Sunderland 20689
Caroline Ch of Jesus Christ of LDS, 110 Maryland Ave, Ridgely 21660
Carroll   Ch of Jesus Christ of LDS, 4117 Lower Beckleysville Rd,
Hampstead 21074
Ch of Jesus Christ of LDS, Rt 27, Mt Airy 21771
Cecil   Ch of Jesus Christ of LDS, 601 Elkton Blvd, Elkton 21921
Charles   Ch of Jesus Christ of LDS, Rt 227 & Padgett Rd, White Plains
20695
Frederick Ch of Jesus Christ of LDS, Middletown Ward, 199 North Pl,
Frederick 21701
Harford   Bel Air Ward, 3836 Level Rd, Havre de Grace 21078
Chesapeake Ward, 3836 Level Rd, Havre de Grace 21078
Howard   Catonsville Ward, 4100 St Johns Ln, Ellicott City 21043
Columbia Stake, 4100 St Johns Ln, Ellicott City 21043
Patapsco Ward, 4100 St Johns Ln, Ellicott City 21043
Prince   Reorganized Ch of Jesus Christ of LDS, 7310 Sandy Spring Rd,
Georges   Laurel 20707

Latter Day Saints

St Marys	Ch of Jesus Christ of LDS, Old Rolling Rd, Lexington Park 20653
Washington	Ch of Jesus Christ of LDS, Mt Aetna Rd, Hagerstown 21740
	Ch of Jesus Christ of LDS, Douglas St, Hancock 21750
Wicomico	Ch of Jesus Christ of LDS, Greenlawn Ln, Salisbury 21801

Lutheran

Allegany	Christ Luth Ch, Vocke Rd & Martz Ln, La Vale 21502
	Mt Calvary Luth Ch, Front & Fusner Sts, Westernport 21562
	St John's Luth Ch, 8619 Black's Mill Rd, Creagerstown 21701
	St John's Luth Ch, 406 Arch St, Cumberland 21502
	St Luke's Luth Ch, 1601 Frederick St, Cumberland 21502
	St Paul Luth Ch, Lonaconing 21539
	St Paul's Luth Ch (Washington & Smallwood Sts) 15 N Smallwood St, Cumberland 21502
	St Paul's Luth Ch, 34 W Main St, P.O.Box 227, Frostburg 21532
	Trinity Luth Ch, 326 N Centre St, Cumberland 21502
Anne Arundel	Christ Luth Ch, 8245 Jumpers Hole Rd, Millersville 21108
	Emmanuel Luth Ch, P.O.Box 336, Rivera Beach 21122
	Emmanuel Luth Ch, 8615 Fort Smallwood Rd, Stoney Creek 21226
	First Luth Ch, Telegraph & Odenton Rd, Odenton 21113
	Galilee Luth Ch (Lake Shore) 4652 Mountain Rd, Pasadena 21122
	Glen Luth Ch, 106 Carroll Rd, Glen Burnie 21061
	Gloria Dei Luth Ch, 539 Bay Green Dr, Arnold 21012
	Magothy-Chelsea Luth Ch, 268 Magothy Beach Rd, Pasadena 21122
	Our Redeemer Luth Ch, 7606 Quarterfield Rd, Glen Burnie 21061
	Our Shepherd Luth Ch, 400 Benfield Rd, Severna Park 21146
	Peace Luth Ch (Ferndale Hts) 800 Wellham Ave, Glen Burnie 21061
	Resurrection Luth Ch, Hammonds Ln & Robinwood Rd, Brooklyn Park 21225
	St Johns Luth Ch, 300 W Maple Rd, Linthicum 21090
	St Martin's Evan Luth Ch (Spa Rd & Hilltop Ln) 1120 Spa Rd, Annapolis 21403
	St Paul Luth Ch, Roscoe Rowe Blvd, Annapolis 21401
	St Paul's Evan Luth Ch, 1370 Defense Hwy, Gambrills 21054
	St Paul's Evan Luth Ch, 308 Oak Manor Dr, Glen Burnie 21061
Baltimore	Ascension Evan Luth Ch, 7601 York Rd, Towson 21204
	Atonement Luth Ch, 9121 Old Harford Rd, Balto 21204
	Augsburg Luth Ch, 2610 Garrison Blvd, Balto 21216
	Augsburg Luth Home, 6811 Campfield Rd, Balto 21207
	Augustana Luth Ch, 3401 Mannasota Ave, Balto 21213
	Balto Conference Amer Luth Ch, Luth University Ministry, 7909 York Rd, Balto 21204
	Berea Luth Ch, 2200 E Oliver St, Balto 21213
	Bethany Luth Ch, Madison St & N Lakewood Ave, Balto 21205
	Bethany Luth Ch (Violetville) 1022 Haverhill Rd, Balto 21229
	Bethlehem Evan Luth Ch, 4815 Hamilton Ave, Balto 21206

CHURCH ADDRESSES

Calvary Luth Ch, Old Harford Rd & Northern Pkwy, Balto 21214
Calvary Luth Ch, 1950 W North Ave, Balto 21217
Christ Luth Ch (Charles & Hill Sts) 9 E Hill St, Balto 21230
Christ Luth Ch, 5700 Edmondson Ave, Balto 21228
Christ Luth Ch, 7041 Sollers Pt Rd, Dundalk 21222
Christ Luth Ch, Trenton Church Rd, Upperco 21155
Christ the King Luth Ch, 515 Academy Ave, Owings Mills 21117
Christus Victor Luth Ch, 9833 Harford Rd, Parkville 21234
Divinity Luth Ch, 1220 Providence Rd, Towson 21204
Emmanuel Luth Ch, 3121-31 E Balto St, Balto 21224
Emmanuel Luth Ch (Ingleside & Craigmont) 929 Ingleside Ave)
  Catonsville 21228
Epiphany Luth Ch, 4301 Raspe Ave, Balto 21206
Faith Evan Luth Ch, 1900 E North Ave, Balto 21213
Faith Luth Ch, 8 Sherwood Rd, Cockeysville 21030
Faith Luth Ch, 2200 Old Eastern Ave, Middle River 21220
First Eng Luth Ch (Charles & 39th Sts) 3807 N Charles St,
  Balto 21218
First Luth Ch, 40 E Burke Ave, Towson 21204
First Luth Ch of Gray Manor, 212 Oakwood Rd, Balto 21222
Glen Luth Ch, 106 Carroll Rd, Balto 21228
Good Shepherd Luth Ch, 3103 Sollers Pt Rd, Dundalk 21222
Grace Eng Luth Ch, 8601 Valleyfield Rd, Lutherville 21093
Grace Luth Ch of Hamilton, 5205 Harford Rd, Balto 21214
Holy Comforter Luth Ch, 5513 York Rd, Balto 21212
Holy Cross Luth Ch, 8516 Loch Raven Blvd, Towson 21204
Holy Nativity Luth Ch (Linden & Shelbourne Aves) 1200 Linden
  Ave, Balto 21227
Holy Trinity Luth Ch, 4000 Sinclair Ln, Balto 21213
Hope Evan Luth Ch, 1901 Middleborough Rd, Balto 21221
Immanuel Luth Ch, Loch Raven Blvd & Belvedere Ave, Balto 21239
Jerusalem Luth Ch, 4605 Belair Rd, Balto 21206
Lamb of God Luth Ch, 8912 Philadelphia Rd, Rossville 21237
Luther Memorial Luth Ch, 5401 Eastern Ave, Balto 21224
Luth Ch in Amer, Maryland Synod, 7604 York Rd, Balto 21204
Luth Ch, Missouri Synod, 4501 Harcourt Rd, Balto 21214
Martin Luth Ch, 401-409 N Patterson Park Ave, Balto 21231
Martini Luth Ch, Hanover & Henrietta Sts, Balto 21230
Messiah Luth Ch (Potomac & O'Donnell Sts) 1025 S Potomac St,
  Balto 21224
Mt Olive Luth Ch, Belair Rd & Cliftmont Ave, Balto 21213
Nativity Luth Ch, 14 Ratna Ct, Balto 21236
Nazareth Luth Ch (Bank St & Highland Ave) 3401 Bank St, Balto
  21224
Norwegian Seamens Ch, 300 S Patterson Park Ave, Balto 21231
Our Savior Luth Ch, 141 Laverne Ave, Lansdowne 21227
Our Saviour Luth Ch, 3301 The Alameda, Balto 21218
Pilgrim Luth Ch, Liberty & Latham Rds, Milford 21207
Prince of Peace Luth Ch, 8212 Philadelphia Rd, Balto 21237
Redeemer Luth Ch, 4211 Vermont Ave, Balto 21229
Reformation Luth Ch, 6200 Loch Raven Blvd, Balto 21239
St Andrew's Luth Ch, 1201 Taylor Ave, Parkville 21234

Lutheran

St James Evan Luth Ch, 8301 Liberty Rd, Balto 21207
St James Luth Ch (Overlea) 8 W Overlea Ave, Balto 21206
St John Luth Ch, 7801 North Point Rd, Balto 21219
St John Luth Ch, 224 Washburn Ave, Brooklyn 21225
St John Luth Ch, Dulaney Valley & Manor Rds, Long Green 21092
St John Luth Ch, 3911 Sweet Air Rd, Phoenix 21131
St John's Evan Luth Ch, 4403 Pimlico Rd, Pimlico, Balto 21215
St John's Evan Luth Ch, 518 Franklin Ave, Essex 21221
St John's Luth Ch, 8808 Harford Rd, Parkville 21234
St Luke Luth Ch, 1803 Dundalk Ave, Balto 21222
St Luke Luth Ch (Harford Rd & Woodhome Ave) 7001 Harford Rd,
  Balto 21234
St Luke Luth Ch, W 36th St & Chestnut Ave, Balto 21211
St Marc Estonian Luth Ch, 2905 Fleetwood Ave, Balto 21214
St Mark Estonian Luth Ch, 1900 St Paul St, Balto 21218
St Mark Luth Ch, 101 N Broadway, Balto 21231
St Mark Luth Ch, 2206 Lake Ave, Balto 21213
St Mark Luth Ch of the Deaf, 40 E Burke Ave, Towson 21204
St Matthew Luth Ch, 1901 Druid Hill Ave, Balto 21217
St Matthew Luth Ch, 3620 Red Rose Farm Rd, Balto 21220
St Michael Luth Ch (Perry Hall) 9534 Belair Rd, Balto 21236
St Paul Evan Luth Ch, 2111 Hollins Ferry Rd, Balto 21230
St Paul Evan Luth Ch, 2001 Old Frederick Rd, Catonsville 21228
St Paul Evan Luth Ch, 12022 Jerusalem Rd, Kingsville 21087
St Paul Evan Luth Ch, 1609 Kurtz Ave, Lutherville 21093
St Paul Luth Ch, 141 S Clinton St, Balto 21224
St Paul Luth Ch (Curtis Bay) 3909 Pennington Ave, Balto 21226
St Paul Luth Ch, Dover Rd, Upperco 21155
St Paul's Evan Luth Ch, 7902 Liberty Rd, Balto 21207
St Peter Evan Luth Ch (Fullerton) 7910 Belair Rd, Balto 21236
St Peter Evan Luth Ch of Northwood, 4215 Loch Raven Blvd,
  Balto 21218
St Peter's Evan Luth Ch (Colgate) 7834 Eastern Ave, Balto
  21224
St Philip's Evan Luth Ch, 501 N Caroline St, Balto 21205
St Stephen Luth Ch (Wilkins Ave & Courtney Rd) 901 Courtney
  Rd, Balto 21227
St Thomas Luth Ch, 339 S Pulaski St, Balto 21223
St Timothy Luth Ch, 100 E Timonium Rd, Timonium 21093
St Timothy's Evan Luth Ch, Dundalk Ave & Willow Spring Rd,
  Balto 21222
SS Stephen & James Luth Ch, Hanover & Hamburg Sts, Balto 21230
Salem Evan Luth Ch (Battery Ave & Randall St) 214 E Randall
  St, Balto 21230
Salem Luth Ch, 905 Frederick Rd, Catonsville 21228
Second Eng Luth Ch, 5010 Briarclift Rd, Balto 21229
Third Eng Luth Ch, 3000 Hillen Rd, Balto 21218
Trinity Luth Ch, 2424 McElderry St, Balto 21205
Trinity Luth Ch, 109 Main St, Reisterstown 21136
Zion Evan Luth Ch (Grindon & Mainfield Aves) 2715 Grindon Ave,
  Balto 21214
Zion Luth Ch (City Hall Plaza) 400 E Lexington St, Balto 21202

CHURCH ADDRESSES

Calvert	First Luth Ch (Rt 2 & 4) Pushaw Rd, Sunderland 20689
Caroline	Immanuel Luth Ch, Main St & Back Landing Rd, P.O.Box 39, Preston 21655
Carroll	Calvary Luth Ch, 7721 Woodbine Rd, Woodbine 21797
	Christ Luth Fellowship, 6 E Ridgeville Blvd, Mt Airy 21771
	Emmanuel Luth Ch, P.O.Box 83, Uniontown 21157
	Faith Luth Ch, 6400 Ridge Rd, Eldersburg 21784
	Grace Luth Ch, 21 Carroll St, Westminster 21157
	Holy Spirit Luth Ch, 2205 Old Liberty Rd, Eldersburg 21784
	Immanuel Luth Ch, 3184 Church St, Manchester 21102
	Jerusalem Luth Ch, P.O.Box 53, Lineboro 21088
	Keysville Evan Luth Ch, 2 mi n, Detour 21725
	Lazarus Luth Ch, P.O.Box 53, Lineboro 21088
	Messiah Luth Ch (Rt 97) 5600 Old Washington Rd, Sykesville 21784
	Mt Union Luth Ch, P.O.Box 83, Uniontown 21157
	St Abraham Luth Ch, 1305 Taylor St, ·Hampstead 21074
	St Benjamin's Luth Ch (Krider's) Kriders Church Rd, Rt 140, Westminster 21157
	St James Luth Ch, 14 S Benedum St, Union Bridge 21791
	St John Luth Ch, 162 Pennsylvania Ave, Westminster 21157
	St Luke Luth Ch, 701 Green Valley Rd, New Windsor 21776
	St Mark Luth Ch, 3 mi w, Hampstead 21074
	St Mark Luth Ch, 1373 N Main St, Hampstead 21074
	St Mary Evan Luth Ch (Rt 140 & Mayberry Rd) 1436 E Mayberry Rd, Westminster 21157
	St Matthew Luth Ch, Silver Run 21157
	St Matthew Luth Ch, Pleasant Valley, 6 mi nw, Westminster 21157
	St Paul Luth Ch, P.O.Box 83, Uniontown 21157
	St Peters Evan Luth Ch, 4300 Church Rd, Hampstead 21074
	Trinity Luth Ch, 38 W Balto St, Taneytown 21787
	Trinity Luth Ch, 821 Deer Park Rd, Smallwood, Westminster 21157
Cecil	Bethel Luth Ch, (Rts 40 & 272) 24 Cameron Rd, North East 21901
Charles	Grace Luth Ch, Rts 6 & 488, La Plata 20646
	Messiah Luth Ch, Mattawoman-Beantown Rd, Waldorf 20601
	Our Savior Luth Ch, Rt 210, Bryans Road 20616
District of Columbia	Missouri Synod, Southeastern District of the Luth Ch, 5121 Colorado Ave NW, Washington, DC 20011
Dorchester	Our Shepherd Luth Ch, 1312 Race St, Cambridge 21613
Frederick	Bethany Luth Ch, A St & First Ave, Brunswick 21716
	Bethel Luth Ch, 9664 O'Possumtown Pike, Frederick 21701
	Braddock Luth Ch, Braddock 21714
	Chapel Luth Ch, Daysville Rd, Woodsboro 21798
	Elias Luth Ch, 100 W Main St, Emmitsburg 21727
	Evan Luth Ch, 35 E Church St, Frederick 21701
	Evan Luth Ch, Main St, Woodsboro 21798
	Good Shepherd Luth Ch, 1415 W 7th St, Frederick 21701
	Grace Luth Ch, 12223 Woodsboro Pike, Keymar 21757
	Grace Luth Ch, 10825 Coppermine Rd, Woodsboro 21798
	Luther Chapel Luth Ch (3 mi e Brunswick) Petersville 21716

Manor Luth Ch, 5136 Doubs Rd, Adamstown 21710
Mt Moriah Luth Ch, Foxville Rt 1, Lantz 21760
Mt Tabor Luth Ch, 10043 Long's Mill Rd, Rocky Ridge 21778
Mt Zion Luth Ch, 5709 Mt Phillip Rd, Feagaville 21701
Mt Zion Luth Ch, 12223 Woodsboro Pike, Keymar 21757
Mt Zion Luth Ch, Haugh's Church Rd, Ladiesburg 21759
Peace in Christ Luth Ch, 8325 Yellow Springs Rd, Frederick
    21701
St John Luth Ch, Church Hill Rd, Myersville 21773
St John's Luth Ch, 15 Church St, Thurmont 21788
St Luke Luth Ch, 5464 Jefferson Pike, Feagaville 21701
St Luke Luth Ch, Ballenger Creek Rd, Point of Rocks 21777
St Mark Luth Ch, 5132 Doubs Rd, Adamstown 21710
St Mark Luth Ch, P.O.Box 13, Myersville 21773
St Mark Luth Ch, 17015 Sabillasville Rd, Sabillasville 21780
St Matthew Luth Ch, Rt 1 Box 329, Adamstown 21710
St Paul Luth Ch, 4 Main St, Burkittsville 21718
St Paul Luth Ch, Main St, Jefferson 21755
St Paul Luth Ch, Lewistown 21701
St Paul Luth Ch, 400 Main St, Myersville 21773
St Paul Luth Ch, 11148 Old Frederick Rd, Thurmont 21788
St Paul Luth Ch, 14 W Pennsylvania Ave, Walkersville 21793
St Paul's Luth Ch, Rt 5 & 6, New Market 21774
Trinity Luth Ch, Knoxville 21758
Zion Luth Ch, 100 W Main St, Middletown 21769

Garrett
Accident Evan Luth Ch, Main St, Accident 21520
Emmanuel Luth Ch, Star Rt Box 90, Grantsville 21536
Grace Luth Ch, P.O.Box 74, Accident 21520
St John Luth Ch, Cove Rd, Accident 21520
St John Luth Ch, Star Rt Box 90, Grantsville 21536
St John Luth Ch, Rt 2 Box 159, Oakland 21550
St Mark's Luth Ch, 6 S 2nd St, Oakland 21550
St Paul Luth Ch, P.O.Box 74, Accident 21520
Zion Luth Ch, Rt 219 Box 171, Accident 21520
Zion Luth Ch, Star Rt Box 90, Grantsville 21536

Harford
Good Shepherd Luth Ch, 1515 Emmorton Rd, Bel Air 21014
Holy Communion Luth Ch, Fallston 21047
Jerusalem Evan Luth Ch, 708 Highland Rd, Street 21154
Jerusalem Luth Ch, Old Pylesville Rd, P.O.Box 90, Whiteford
    21160
Lord of Life Luth Ch (Willoughby Beach Rd & Sequoia Dr) 501
    Sequoia Dr, Edgewood 21040
St Matthew Luth Ch, 1200 Churchville Rd, Bel Air 21014
St Paul Luth Ch, 201 Mt Royal Ave, Aberdeen 21001
Salem Luth Ch, 3825 Morrisville Rd, Jarrettsville 21084
Trinity Luth Ch, 1100 Philadelphia Rd, Joppa 21085

Howard
Abiding Savior Luth Ch, 10689 Owen Brown Rd, Columbia 21044
Amer Luth Ch, 608 Amer City Bldg, Columbia 21044
First Luth Ch, 3604 Chatham Rd, Ellicott City 21043
Living Word Luth Ch, 5885 Robert Oliver Pl, Columbia 21045
St John Evan Luth Ch, 6004 Waterloo Rd, Columbia 21045
St John Luth Ch, Wilde Lake Village Green, Columbia 21044

CHURCH ADDRESSES

	St Paul's Luth Ch, Rt 216 Lime Kiln Rd, Fulton 20759
Kent	Trinity Luth Ch, Rt 213 College Hts, Chestertown 21620
Montgomery	Bethany Luth Ch, A St & First Ave, Potomac 21716
	Calvary Luth Ch, 9545 Georgia Ave, Silver Spring 20910
	Christ Luth Ch, 8011 Old Georgetown Rd, Bethesda 20814
	Christ Luth Ch, 9600 E Main St, Damascus 20872
	Christ the Servant Luth Ch, 10016 Battle Ridge Pl, Gaithersburg 20879
	Cross Luth Ch, 1350 Falls Rd, Rockville 20854
	Crusader Luth Ch, 1605 Veirs Mill Rd, Rockville 20851
	Emmanuel Luth Ch, 7730 Bradley Blvd, Bethesda 20817
	Epiphany Luth Ch, 14411 Old Columbia Pike, Burtonsville 20866
	Good Shepherd Luth Ch, 16420 S Westland Dr, Gaithersburg 20877
	Messiah Luth Ch, 20701 Frederick Rd, Germantown 20874
	Prince of Peace Luth Ch, 11900 Darnestown Rd, Gaithersburg 20878
	Redeemer Luth Ch, 27015 Ridge Rd, Damascus 20872
	Resurrection Luth Ch, 3101 University Blvd W, Kensington 20895
	St Andrew Luth Ch, 12247 Georgia Ave, Silver Spring 20902
	St John Luth Ch, 4629 Aspen Hill Rd, Rockville 20853
	St Luke Luth Ch, 17740 Muncaster Rd, Derwood 20855
	St Luke Luth Ch, 9100 Colesville Rd, Silver Spring 20910
	St Stephen Luth Ch, 11612 New Hampshire Ave, Silver Spring 20904
	Shepherd of the Valley Luth Ch, 4414 Muncaster Mill Rd, Rockville 20853
	Trinity Luth Ch, 11200 Old Georgetown Rd, Rockville 20852
	Washington Estonian Luth Ch, 10236 New Hampshire Ave, Silver Spring 20903
	Zion Luth Ch, 7410 New Hampshire Ave, Takoma Park 20912
Prince Georges	Abiding Presence Luth Ch, 11310 Montgomery Rd, Beltsville 20705
	All Saints Luth Ch, 16404 Pointer Ridge Dr, Bowie 20716
	Ascension Luth Ch, 7420 Ardmore Rd, Landover Hills 20784
	Concordia Luth Ch, 10201 Old Indian Head Rd, Cheltenham 20623
	Concordia Luth Ch, Upper Marlboro 20772
	Divine Peace Luth Ch, 1500 Brown Sta Rd, Largo 20870
	Faith Luth Ch, 5701 Livingston Rd, Oxon Hill 20745
	First Luth Ch, 12710 Duckettown Rd, Bowie 20715
	Good Samaritan Luth Ch, 10110 Greenbelt Rd, Lanham 20706
	Grace Luth Ch, 2503 Belair Dr, Bowie 20715
	Grace Luth Ch, 10928 Indian Head Hwy, Fort Washington 20744
	Holy Cross Luth Ch, 6905 Greenbelt Rd, Greenbelt 20770
	Holy Trinity Luth Ch, 7607 Sandy Spring Rd, Laurel 20707
	Hope Luth Ch, 7801 Coventry Way, Clinton 20735
	Hope Luth Ch, 4201 Guilford Dr, College Park 20740
	Our Savior Luth Ch, 13611 Laurel-Bowie Rd, Laurel 20708
	Our Savior Luth Ch, 4915 St Barnabas Rd, Temple Hills 20748
	Oxon Hill Luth Ch, 3415 Brinkley Rd, Oxon Hill 20745
	Redeemer Luth Ch, 3799 East West Hwy, Hyattsville 20782
	St John Luth Ch, 5820 Riverdale Rd, Riverdale 20737

Lutheran

	St Michael Luth Ch, Central Ave nr Capital Beltway, Largo 20027
	St Michael Luth Ch, 10703 Phillips Dr, Upper Marlboro 20772
	Trinity Luth Ch, 6600 Laurel-Bowie Rd, Bowie 20715
	Trinity Luth Ch, 30th & Bunker Hill, Mt Rainier 20712
Queen Annes	Galilee Luth Ch, Harbor View, Chester 21619
	St Matthew Luth Ch, Church Hill 21623
St Marys	St Paul Luth Ch, Box 65, Charlotte Hall 20622-0065
	Trinity Luth Ch, Shangri-La Dr, P.O.Box 157, Lexington Park 20653
Somerset	--
Talbot	Grace Luth Ch (Brookletts Ave & Hanson St) 111 Brookletts Ave, Easton 21601
	Immanuel Luth Ch, Rt 50, Easton 21601
	St Paul Luth Ch, RD 1, Cordova 21625
Washington	Christ Luth Ch, 216 N Cleveland Ave, Hagerstown 21740
	Concordia Luth Ch, 1799 Garden Ln, Hagerstown 21740
	Foxville-Greensburg Luth Ch, Edgemont Rd, Smithsburg 21783
	Haven Luth Ch, 1035 Haven Rd, Hagerstown 21740
	Holy Trinity Luth Ch, 201 E Main St, Sharpsburg 21782
	Maryland Synod Luth Ch of Amer, 601 Washington Ave, Hagerstown 21740
	Mt Moriah Luth Ch, Edgemont Rd, Rt 3 Box 3288, Smithsburg 21783
	Mt Tabor Luth Ch, Rt 1 Box 148 Clear Spring 21722
	Mt Tabor Luth Ch, Fairview 21722
	Mt Zion Luth Ch, 1 mi n Locust Grove Rd, Rohrersville 21779
	St John Luth Ch, 141 S Potomac St, Hagerstown 21740
	St Mark's Luth Ch, 601 Washington Ave, Hagerstown 21740
	St Matthew Luth Ch, P.O.Box 192, Keedysville 21756
	St Matthew's Luth Ch, Beaver Creek Church Rd, Beaver Creek 21740
	St Paul Luth Ch, 24 E Balto St, Funkstown 21734
	St Paul Luth Ch, Edgemont & Greensbury Rds, Greensburg 21783
	St Paul Luth Ch, Resley Rd, Hancock 21750
	St Paul Luth Ch, Leitersburg 21740
	St Paul Luth Ch, 3 mi e Rt 40, Western Pike 21722
	St Peter Luth Ch, 30 S Martin St, Clear Spring 21722
	St Peter Luth Ch, Rt 5 Box 109, Hagerstown 21740
	St Peter Luth Ch, 53 N Main St, Keedysville 21756
	St Peter's (Beard's) Luth Ch, Old Forge Rd, Rt 1, Leitersburg 21740
	Salem Luth Ch, 6 mi n Sharpsburg, Bakersville 21782
	Trinity Luth Ch, 64 S Main St, Boonsboro 21713
	Trinity Luth Ch, 15 Randolph Ave, Hagerstown 21740
	Trinity Luth Ch, 16 N Main St, Smithsburg 21783
	Zion Luth Ch, 35 W Potomac St, P.O.Box 156, Williamsport 21795
Wicomico	Bethany Luth Ch, Camden Ave & South Blvd, Salisbury 21801
	Faith Luth Ch, 1416 Ocean City Rd, Salisbury 21801
Worcester	St Peter's Luth Ch, 10301 Coastal Hwy, P.O.Box 1983, Ocean City 21842

Mennonite

Allegany	Friendship Haven Chapel, 930 Gay St, Cumberland 21502
	Pinto Menn Ch, Pinto 21556
Anne Arundel	Guilford Road Menn Ch, 10140 Guilford, Jessup 20794
Baltimore	Balto Menn Mission, 1616 Wilkens Ave, Balto 21223
Carroll	Mt Airy Menn Ch, 7101 Watersville Rd, Mt Airy 21771
Garrett	Maple Glen Menn Ch, Dorsey Hotel Rd, Grantsville 21536
	Oak Grove Menn Ch, Grantsville 21536
Howard	First Menn Ch of Columbia, 5022 Avoca Ave, Ellicott City 21043
Kent	Lake View Menn Ch, Urieville Lake, Chestertown 21620
Washington	Mt Zion Menn Ch, Benevola Church Rd, Boonsboro 21713
	North Side Memm Ch, 716 N Locust St, Hagerstown 21740
Worcester	Holly Grove Menn Ch, Mennonite Rd, Pocomoke City 21851
	Ocean City Menn Ch, Rt 50, Ocean City 21842

Methodist

Allegany	Allegany Unit Meth Ch (Rt 36) P.O.Box 444, Frostburg 21532
	Barton Unit Meth Ch, Box 247, Barton 21521
	Bethel Unit Meth Ch, 3rd & Seymour Sts, Cumberland 21502
	Calvary Unit Meth Ch, 28 E Mary St, Cumberland 21502
	Carlos Unit Meth Ch (Front & Main Sts) P.O.Box 444, Frostburg 21532
	Catalpa (Orchard Rd) 722 Valley View Dr, La Vale 21502
	Centenary Unit Meth Ch, Rt 3 Box 333, Cumberland 21502
	Central Unit Meth Ch, 15 S George St, Cumberland 21502
	Centre Street Unit Meth Ch, 217 N Centre St, Cumberland 21502
	Christ Unit Meth Ch, 4th & Race Sts, Cumberland 21502
	Cresaptown Unit Meth Ch, 14805 McMullen Hwy, P.O.Box 5206, Cresaptown 21502
	Davis Memorial Unit Meth Ch (Rt 4) Oldtown Rd, Cumberland 21502
	Dawson Unit Meth Ch, Rt 3 Box 93A, Rawlings 21557
	Eckhart Unit Meth Ch (Main & Porter) P.O.Box 444, Frostburg 21532
	Ellerslie Unit Meth Ch, Box 358, Ellerslie 21529
	Elliott Memorial Unit Meth Ch (Hazen Rd) 128 Virginia Ave, Cumberland 21502
	Emmanuel Unit Meth Ch, 18 Humbird St, Cumberland 21502
	Emmanuel Unit Meth Ch, Rt 40 West & Rt 2, Frostburg 21532
	Fairview Avenue Unit Meth Ch, 640 Fairview Ave, Cumberland 21502
	First Unit Meth Ch, 1707 Frederick St, Cumberland 21502
	First Unit Meth Ch, 14 Church St, Lonaconing 21539
	Flintstone Unit Meth Ch, Box 2, Flintstone 21530
	Frostburg Unit Meth Ch, 48 W Main St, Frostburg 21532
	Grace Unit Meth Ch, 130 Virginia Ave, Cumberland 21502
	Mt Fairview Unit Meth Ch (Rt 4) 13A Yoder Ct, Cumberland 21502

Methodist

Mt Hermon Unit Meth Ch, Box 2, Flintstone 21530
Mt Pleasant Unit Meth Ch (Mt Pleasant Rd) 128 Virginia Ave,
    Cumberland 21502
Mt Savage Unit Meth Ch, Church Hill & Old Row Sts, Mt Savage
    21545
Mt Tabor Unit Meth Ch (Spring Gap) Rt 1 Box 19, Oldtown 21555
Mt Zion Unit Meth Ch (Orleans Crossroad) Rt 4 Box 302,
    Cumberland 21502
Mt Zion Unit Meth Ch, Rt 40, Frostburg 21532
Murley's Branch Unit Meth Ch, Box 2, Flintstone 21530
Oldtown Unit Meth Ch, Rt 1 Box 19, Oldtown 21555
Oliver's Grove Unit Meth Ch (Walnut Ridge Rd) Rt 1 Box 19,
    Oldtown 21555
Park Place Unit Meth Ch, 80 Natl Hwy, La Vale 21502
Piney Plains Unit Meth Ch (Mann Rd) 722 Valley View Dr, La
    Vale 21502
Pleasant Grove Unit Meth Ch (Rt 40) 128 Virginia Ave,
    Cumberland 21502
Potomac Park Unit Meth Ch (McMullen Hwy & Marigold Ave) 12011
    Marigold Ave SW, Cumberland 21502
Prosperity Unit Meth Ch (Rt 2) 23 Mary St, Cumberland 21502
Rawlings Unit Meth Ch, Box 228, Rawlings 21557
Shaft Unit Meth Ch, Box 56, Midland 21542
Trinity Unit Meth Ch, 122 Grand Ave, Cumberland 21502
Vale Summit Unit Meth Ch (Rt 55) P.O.Box 444, Frostburg 21532
Westernport Unit Meth Ch, 434 Vine St, Westernport 21562
Woodland Unit Meth Ch, Box 56, Midland 21542
Zion Unit Meth Ch, Rt 3 Box 333, Cumberland 21502

Anne Arundel   Adams Unit Meth Ch, Browns Woods Rd, Box 161, Annapolis 21401
Alberta Gary Memorial Unit Meth Ch (Rt 32) 106 E Maple Rd,
    Linthicum 21090
Andover Unit Meth Ch, Andover & Nursery Rds, Linthicum 21090
Asbury Unit Meth Ch, 87 West St, Annapolis 21401
Asbury Unit Meth Ch, 78 Church Rd, Arnold 21012
Asbury Unit Meth Ch, Rt 32, Jessup 20794
Asbury-Broadneck Unit Meth Ch, 657 Broadneck Rd, Annapolis
    21401
Asbury-Town Neck Unit Meth Ch, 429 Balto-Annapolis Blvd,
    Severna Park 21146
Baldwin Memorial Unit Meth Ch (General's Hwy & Indian Landing
    Rd) 921 General's Hwy, Millersville 21108
Broadneck Unit Meth Ch, Broadneck Rd, Annapolis 21401
Calvary Unit Meth Ch, 301 Rowe Blvd, Annapolis 21401
Cape St Claire Unit Meth Ch (Summit & Chestnut Tree Drs) 855
    Chestnut Tree Dr, Annapolis 21401
Carters Unit Meth Ch, Friendship 20758
Cecil Memorial Unit Meth Ch, 15 Parole St, Annapolis 21401
Cedar Grove Unit Meth Ch, 710 Mason's Beach Rd, Deale 20751
Centenary Unit Meth Ch, P.O.Box 276, Shady Side 20764
Chews Memorial Unit Meth Ch, 418 Mill Swamp Rd, Edgewater
    21037
Chews Unit Meth Ch, 492 Owensville Rd, West River 20778

149

Com Unit Meth Ch (Reidel Rd & Rt 424) 1690 Reidel Rd, Crofton 21114

Com Unit Meth Ch (8680 Fort Smallwood Rd) 238 Harlem Rd, Pasadena 21122

Davidsonville Unit Meth Ch, Hwy 214, Davidsonville 21035

Delmont Unit Meth Ch, 1217 Delmont Rd, Severn 21144

Eastport Unit Meth Ch, 926 Bay Ridge Ave, Annapolis 21403

Edgewater Unit Meth Ch, 41 Mayo Rd, P.O.Box 325, Edgewater 21037

Faith Unit Meth Ch (Edgewood Rd & Duvall Hwy) 905 Duvall Hwy Pasadena 21122

Ferndale Unit Meth Ch (117 Ferndale Rd) 7 S Hollins Ferry Rd Glen Burnie 21061

First Korean Unit Meth Ch, 251 Pershing St, Glen Burnie 2106

Fowler's Unit Meth Ch,133 Bestgate Rd, Annapolis 21401

Franklin Unit Meth Ch, 5375 Deale-Churchton Rd, Churchton 20733

Friendship Unit Meth Ch, Friendship 20758

Galesville Unit Meth Ch, 4825 Church Ln, Box 131, Galesville 20765

Glen Burnie Unit Meth Ch, 5 Second Ave SE, Glen Burnie 21061

Harwood Park Unit Meth Ch, Harwood Park 20776

Hope Memorial Unit Meth Ch, 4738 Idlewild Rd, Churchton 2073

Hope Unit Meth Ch, 3672 Muddy Creek Rd, Edgewater 21037

John Wesley Unit Meth Ch (Crain Hwy & Furnace Branch Rd) 692 Ritchie Hwy, Glen Burnie 21061

John Wesley Unit Meth Ch, 1350 Ritchie Hwy N, Glen Burnie 21061

John Wesley Unit Meth Ch (Eastport) 327 Jennings Rd, Severna Park 21146

John Wesley Unit Meth Ch (Waterbury) 3036 Rock Dr, Riva 2114

Linthicum Heights Unit Meth Ch, 200 School Ln, Linthicum Hts 21090

Macedonia Unit Meth Ch, Discus Mill Rd, Odenton 21113

Magothy Unit Meth Ch (Rt 177 w of Hog Neck Rd) 3703 Mountain Rd, Pasadena 21122

Magothy Unit Meth Ch of the Deaf (Rt 177 w of Hog Neck Rd) 3703 Mountain Rd, Pasadena 21122

Marley Unit Meth Ch, Marley Neck Rd & Second Ave, Glen Burni 21061

Mayo Memorial Unit Meth Ch, 1012 Turkey Pt Rd, Edgewater 21C

Messiah Unit Meth Ch (Furnace Branch Rd & Country Club Dr) 2 Thomas Rd, Glen Burnie 21061

Metropolitan Unit Meth Ch, 548 Queenstown Rd, Severn 21144

Mt Calvary Unit Meth Ch, 1236 Jones Sta Rd, Arnold 21012

Mt Carmel Unit Meth Ch, Lake Shore, Pasadena 21122

Mt Olive Meth Ch, 2 Hicks Ave, Annapolis 21401

Mt Tabor Meth Ch (St Stephen Rd) 569 Queenstown Rd, Severn 21144

Mt Tabor Unit Meth Ch, 1421 St Stephens Church Rd, Crownsvil 21032

Mt Zion Unit Meth Ch, 612 Second St, Annapolis 21403

Mt Zion Unit Meth Ch, 122 Bayard Rd, P.O.Box 159, Lothian
  20711
Nichols-Bethel Unit Meth Ch, 1239 Murray Rd, Odenton 21113
Oakland Unit Meth Ch, Churchton 20733
Parkwood Unit Meth Ch, 41 Mayo Rd, P.O.Box 325, Edgewater
  21037
Pasadena Unit Meth Ch, 213 Governor Ritchie Hwy, Pasadena
  21122
St Andrews Unit Meth Ch, 926 Bay Ridge Ave, Annapolis 21403
St Mark's Unit Meth Ch, 4738 Idlewild Rd, Churchton 20733
St Mark's Unit Meth Ch, 1440 Dorsey Rd, Hanover 21076
St Mark's Unit Meth Ch, 705 Beverly Ave, Mayo 21106
St Matthew's Unit Meth Ch, 5375 Deale-Churchton Rd, Churchton
  20733
St Matthews Unit Meth Ch, Shady Side Rd, Shady Side 20764
Severn Unit Meth Ch, 1215 Old Camp Meade Rd, Severn 21144
Severna Park Unit Meth Ch, 731 Benfield Rd, Severna Park 21146
Sollers Unit Meth Ch, 1219 Wrighton Rd, Lothian 20711
Solley Unit Meth Ch (7600 Solley Rd) 7895 Cheverly Ln, Glen
  Burnie 21061
Trinity Unit Meth Ch (Locust Ave & West St) 1300 West St,
  Annapolis 21401
Trinity Unit Meth Ch (968 Patuxent Rd) 586 Sixth St, Pasadena
  2122
Union Unit Meth Ch, Browns Woods Rd, Box 161, Annapolis 21401
Union Unit Meth Ch, 274 W Bay Front Rd, Lothian 20711
Union Unit Meth Ch (3328 Davidsonville Rd) 107 Magothy Bridge
  Rd, Severna Park 21146
Ward's Memorial Unit Meth Ch (Ward Chapel Rd) 445 Collins Rd,
  Edgewater 21037
Wesley Chapel Unit Meth Ch (Rt 175) 7761 Jessup Rd, Jessup
  20794
Wesley Chapel Unit Meth Ch (Bristol-Deale Rd) P.O.Box 276,
  Shady Side 20764
Wesley Grove Unit Meth Ch, 1320 Dorsey Rd, Hanover 21076
White Rock Unit Meth Ch, 3274 Arundel Rd, Annapolis 21401
Wilson Unit Meth Ch, 1113 Rt 3, N Gambrills 21054

altimore A W Wilson Memorial Unit Meth Ch (Charles St & University
  Pkwy) 304 Southway, Balto 21218
Aldersgate Unit Meth Ch, Falls Rd & 42nd St, Balto 21211
Ames Memorial Unit Meth Ch (Carey & Baker Sts) 615 Baker St,
  Balto 21217
Ames Unit Meth Ch, 9 Walker Ave, Pikesville 21208
Andrew Chapel Unit Meth Ch, 4102 Frankford Ave, Balto 21206
Arbutus Unit Meth Ch (Shelbourne Rd & Maple Ave) 1201 Maple
  Ave, Balto 21227
Arlington Unit Meth Ch, 5268 Reisterstown Rd, Balto 21215
Arnolia Unit Meth Ch, 1776 E Joppa Rd, Balto 21234
Asbury Unit Meth Ch, 12234 Eastern Ave, Chase 21027
Asbury Unit Meth Ch, Rt 32, Jessup 20794
Ayres Chapel Unit Meth Ch (Norrisville & Ayres Chapel Rds)
  5415 Norrisville Rd, White Hall 21161

CHURCH ADDRESSES

Back River Unit Meth Ch, 544 Back River Neck Rd, Balto 21221
Beechfield Unit Meth Ch, 541 S Beechfield, Balto 21229
Bentley Springs Unit Meth Ch (5 Forks & Bentley) 423 Bentley
   Rd, Parkton 21120
Bethesda Unit Meth Ch, 6300 Harford Rd, Balto 21214
Boring Unit Meth Ch, 15200 Old Hanover Rd, Upperco 21155
Bosley Unit Meth Ch, Thornton Mill Rd, Sparks 21152
Brooklyn Heights Unit Meth Ch, 110 Townsend Ave, Balto 21225
Brooklyn Unit Meth Ch (4th St & Pontiac Ave) 401 Pontiac Ave,
   Balto 21225
Brown's Chapel Unit Meth Ch, Howard Rd, Balto 21208
Camp Chapel Unit Meth Ch, 5000 E Joppa Rd, Perry Hall 21128
Canton Unit Meth Ch, 1000 S Ellwood Ave, Balto 21224
Carroll's Unit Meth Ch, 11525 Greenspring Ave, Lutherville
   21093
Catonsville Unit Meth Ch, 6 Melvin Ave, Balto 21228
Cedar Grove Unit Meth Ch, 2015 Mt Carmel Rd, Parkton 21120
Centennial-Caroline Street Unit Meth Ch, 1029 E Monument St,
   Balto 21202
Cherry Hill Unit Meth Ch, 3225 Round Rd, Balto 21225
Chesaco Avenue Unit Meth Ch (Rosedale) 901 Chesaco Ave, Balto
   21237
Christ Ch of the Deaf, 4499 Loch Raven Blvd, Balto 21218
Christ Edmondson Unit Meth Ch, 3600 Edmondson Ave, Balto 21229
Christ Unit Meth Ch (Chase & Washington Sts) 2201 Chase St,
   Balto 21213
Christ Unit Meth Ch (Florida & Brian) 2833 Florida Ave, Balto
   21227
Clynmalira Unit Meth Ch, Old York & Stockton Rds, Phoenix
   21131
Cowenton Unit Meth Ch, 10838 Red Lion Rd, White Marsh 21162
Curtis Bay Unit Meth Ch (Church St & Fairhaven Ave) 1429
   Church St, Balto 21226
Deer Park Unit Meth Ch, 6107 Deer Park Rd, Reisterstown 21136
Dorguth Memorial Unit Meth Ch (Scott & Carroll Sts) 525 Scott
   St, Balto 21230
Dorsey Emmanuel Unit Meth Ch, 6951 Dorsey Rd, Balto 21227
Dundalk Free Meth Ch, 1517 Vesper Ave, Dundalk 21222
Dundalk Unit Meth Ch, 6903 Mornington Rd, Balto 21222
Eastern Unit Meth Ch (North Ave & Caroline St) 1429 E North
   Ave, Balto 21213
Ebenezer Unit Meth Ch (Ebenezer & Earl's Rds) 6601 Ebenezer
   Rd, Balto 21220
Ecumenical Campus Ministry, 10 E Mt Vernon Pl, Balto 21202
Elderslie-St Andrew's Unit Meth Ch, 5601 Pimlico Rd, Balto
   21209
Emanuel Unit Meth Ch, 6517 Frederick Rd, Catonsville 21228
Emmanuel Unit Meth Ch, 6951 Dorsey Rd, Balto 21227
Emmarts Unit Meth Ch (Dogwood & Rolling Rds) 7110 Dogwood Rd,
   Woodlawn, Balto 21207
Emory Unit Meth Ch, 1600 Emory Rd, Upperco 21155

Methodist

Epworth Chapel Unit Meth Ch, Liberty Rd & St Luke's Ln, Balto
  21207
Epworth Unit Meth Ch (600 Warren Rd) 13 Hillary Way,
  Cockeysville 21030
Essex Unit Meth Ch (Maryland Ave & Woodward Dr) 600 Maryland
  Ave, Balto 21221
Eutaw Unit Meth Ch, 2204 Mayfield Ave, Balto 21213
Fairview Unit Meth Ch, 13916 Jarrettsville Pike, Phoenix 21131
First Free Meth Ch, 3441 Keswick Rd, Balto 21211
Fork Unit Meth Ch, 12800 Fork Rd, Fork 21051
Frames Memorial Unit Meth Ch (Phoenix) 303 Warren Rd,
  Cockeysville 21030
Free Meth Ch, 2510 Brannon Ave, Edgemere 21219
Fulton Siemers Memorial Unit Meth Ch, Beechfield & Leeds Ave,
  Balto 21227
Garrison Boulevard Unit Meth Ch, 2506 Garrison Blvd, Balto
  21216
Gatch Memorial Unit Meth Ch, 5738 Belair Rd, Balto 21206
Gill's Unit Meth Ch, Walnut Ave, Owings Mills 21117
Glyndon Unit Meth Ch, 4713 Butler Rd, Glyndon 21071
Good Shepherd Unit Meth Ch, 301 E Fort Ave, Balto 21230
Good Shepherd Unit Meth Ch, 1500 Patapsco St, Balto 21230
Gough Unit Meth Ch, Cuba Rd, Cockeysville 21030
Govans-Boundary Parish Unit Meth Ch, 5210 York Rd, Balto 21212
Grace Unit Meth Ch (N Charles & Belvedere Ave) 5405 N Charles
  St, Balto 21210
Grace Unit Meth Ch (Falls & Ridge Rds) 1814 Ridge Rd,
  Reisterstown 21136
Graceland Park Unit Meth Ch, 6714 Youngstown Ave, Balto 21222
Greenspring Unit Meth Ch (Valley Rd & RR Ave) 5907 Gwynn Oak
  Ave, Apt C, Balto 21207
Halethorpe Unit Meth Ch, 4513 Ridge Ave, Balto 21227
Hall Unit Meth Ch, Julius F Ford, 221 Cedar Hill Ln, Balto
  21225
Hampden Unit Meth Ch, 3449 Falls Rd, Balto 21211
Harwood Park Unit Meth Ch, Highland & Euclid Aves, Balto 21227
Hereford Unit Meth Ch, 16931 York Rd, P.O.Box 99, Monkton
  21111
Hillsdale-Chatsworth Unit Meth Ch (Windsor Mill Rd & Forest
  Park Ave) 5112 Windsor Mill Rd, Balto 21207
Hiss Unit Meth Ch, 8700 Harford Rd, Balto 21234
Homestead Unit Meth Ch, Kirk & Gorsuch Aves, Balto 21218
Howard Park Unit Meth Ch, 5020 Gwynn Oak Ave, Balto 21207
Hunt's Memorial Unit Meth Ch, 1901 W Joppa Rd, Balto 21204
Idlewylde Unit Meth Ch, 1000 Regester Ave, Balto 21239
Immanuel of Brooklyn Unit Meth Ch (Annabel Ave & 5th St) 504
  Annabel Ave, Balto 21225
John Wesley Unit Meth Ch, 3202 W North Ave, Balto 21216
John Wesley Unit Meth Ch, 12234 Eastern Ave, Chase 21027
Keen Memorial Unit Meth Ch, 3002 Huntington Ave, Balto 21211
Korean of Balto Unit Meth Ch, N Charles St & University Pkwy,
  Balto 21218

CHURCH ADDRESSES

Lansdowne Unit Meth Ch, 114 Laverne ave, Balto 21227
Lauraville Unit Meth Ch, 4800 Harford Rd, Balto 21214
Lewin Unit Meth Ch, 4820 Reisterstown Rd, Balto 21215
Linden Heights Unit Meth Ch, 9941 Harford Rd, Balto 21234
Loch Raven Unit Meth Ch, 6622 Loch Raven Blvd, Balto 21239
Lodge Forest Unit Meth Ch (Lodge Forest Dr & North Point Rd) 2715 Lodge Forest Dr, Balto 21219
Lovely Lane Unit Meth Ch (St Paul & 22nd Sts) 2200 St Paul St, Balto 21218
Maryland Line Unit Meth Ch, 21500 York Rd, Maryland Line 21105
Melville Chapel Unit Meth Ch, 5660 Furnace Ave, Balto 21227
Memorial Unit Meth Ch, 3340 Frederick Ave, Balto 21229
Metropolitan Unit Meth Ch, 1121 W Lanvale St, Balto 21217
Milford Mill Unit Meth Ch, 901 Milford Mill Rd, Balto 21208
Milton Avenue Unit Meth Ch, Milton Ave & Oliver St, Balto 21213
Monkton Unit Meth Ch, 1930 Monkton Rd, Monkton 21111
Monroe Street Unit Meth Ch, 400 S Monroe St, Balto 21223
Mt Carmel Unit Meth Ch (Mt Carmel & Prettyboy Dam Rds) 2533 Mt Carmel Rd, Parkton 21120
Mt Gilead Unit Meth Ch, 13900 Hanover Rd, Reisterstown 21136
Mt Gregory Unit Meth Ch, 2325 Washington Rd, Balto 21222
Mt Olive Unit Meth Ch, 5115 Old Court Rd, Randallstown 21133
Mt Olivet Unit Meth Ch, 823 Edmondson Ave, Balto 21228
Mt Pisgah C M E Ch (Riggs & N Fulton Aves) 1034 N Fulton Ave, Balto 21217
Mt Vernon Place Unit Meth Ch (N Charles St & Mt Vernon Pl) 10 E Mt Vernon Pl, Balto 21202
Mt Vernon Unit Meth Ch (W 33rd St & Chestnut Ave) 3261 Chestnut Ave, Balto 21211
Mt Washington Unit Meth Ch, 5800 Cottonwood Ave, P.O.Box 65070, Balto 21209
Mt Winans Unit Meth Ch, 2501 Hollins Ferry Rd, Balto 21230
Mt Zion Unit Meth Ch (Liberty Hts & Wabash Aves) 3050 Liberty Hts Ave, Balto 21215
Mt Zion Unit Meth Ch, Mt Zion Rd, Freeland 21053
Mt Zion Unit Meth Ch, Black Rock Rd, Upperco 21155
Multiple Charge Parish, 16 York Ct, Balto 21218
Norrisville Unit Meth Ch (Norrisville Rd & Church Ln) 5415 Norrisville Rd, White Hall 21161
Northwood Appold Unit Meth Ch (Loch Raven Blvd & Cold Spring Ln) 4499 Loch Raven Blvd, Balto 21218
Oakland Unit Meth Ch, Oakland Rd, Freeland 21053
Old Otterbein Unit Meth Ch (Conway & Sharp Sts) 112 W Conway St, Balto 21201
Olive Branch Unit Meth Ch, 5 W Fort Ave, Balto 21230
Orangeville Unit Meth Ch, 924 N Janney St, Balto 21205
Orems Unit Meth Ch, 1020 Orems Rd, Balto 21220
Otterbein Memorial Unit Meth Ch (38th St & Roland Ave) 1000 W 38th St, Balto 21211
Overlea Unit Meth Ch (Overlea & Cedonia Aves) 3900 Overlea Ave, Balto 21206

154

Methodist

Parke Memorial Unit Meth Ch, 18908 York Rd, Parkton 21120
Parkside Unit Meth Ch, 4400 Parkside Dr, Balto 21206
Patapsco Unit Meth Ch, 7800 Wise Ave, Balto 21222
Patapsco Unit Meth Ch, 5302 Glen Falls Rd, Reisterstown 21136
Perry Hall Unit Meth Ch, 9515 Belair Rd, Perry Hall 21136
Pine Grove Unit Meth Ch (Rayville) 19246 Middletown Rd,
  Parkton 21120
Pine Grove Unit Meth Ch, 20105 Kirkwood Shop Rd, White Hall
  21161
Piney Grove Unit Meth Ch, 201 Bowleys Quarters Rd, Balto 21220
Piney Grove Unit Meth Ch, Old Hanover & Piney Grove Rds,
  Boring 21020
Pleasant Grove Unit Meth Ch (Dover & Pleasant Grove Rds) 15311
  Dover Rd, Reisterstown 21136
Pleasant Hill Unit Meth Ch, 10911 Reisterstown Rd,
  Reisterstown 21136
Poplar Grove Unit Meth Ch,, Poplar Hill Rd, Phoenix 21131
Providence Unit Meth Ch, 1318 Providence Rd, Balto 21204
Providence Unit Meth Ch, 10 E Seminary Ave, Lutherville 21093
Reisterstown Unit Meth Ch, 246 Main St, Reisterstown 21136
Relay Unit Meth Ch, 1716 Arlington Ave, Balto 21227
Rodgers Forge Unit Meth Ch, 56 Stevenson Ln, Balto 21212
Roland Avenue-Evergreen Unit Meth Ch, Roland Ave & W 40th St,
  Balto 21211
St James Meth Ch, 415 Jefferson Ave, Balto 21204
St James Unit Meth Ch, 1901 W Lexington St, Balto 21223
St John Unit Meth Ch, 6019 Belle Grove Rd, Balto 21225
St John's of Hamilton Unit Meth Ch, (Harford Rd & Gibbons Ave)
  5315 Harford Rd, Balto 21214
St John's Unit Meth Ch, 3300 Glen Ave, Balto 21215
St John's Unit Meth Ch (St Paul & 27th Sts) 2705 St Paul St,
  Balto 21218
St John's Unit Meth Ch, 216 W Seminary Ave, Lutherville 21093
St Luke Unit Meth Ch (16810 Hereford Rd) 2506 Edgecombe Cir,
  Apt H, Balto 21215
St Luke's Unit Meth Ch, 2119 Gwynn Oak Ave, Balto 21207
St Luke's Unit Meth Ch, 1100 N Gilmor St, Balto 21217
St Luke's Unit Meth Ch, 60 Bond Ave, Reisterstown 21136
St Mark's Unit Meth Ch, 1440 Dorsey Rd, Balto 21227
St Mark's Unit Meth Ch (Garrison Blvd & Liberty Hts Ave) 3900
  Liberty Hts Ave, Balto 21207
St Matthew's Unit Meth Ch, 416 E 23rd St, Balto 21218
St Matthew's Unit Meth Ch (129 Main St) 1100 Walnut Ave, Balto
  21222
St Matthew's Unit Meth Ch (Monument & Bouldin Sts) 614 N
  Bouldin St, Balto 21205
St Paul Unit Meth Ch, 630 N Linwood Ave, Balto 21205
St Paul Unit Meth Ch, 1000 W Saratoga St, Balto 21223
St Paul Unit Meth Ch (St Paul Rd) 19246 Middletown Rd, Parkton
  21120
Salem Unit Meth Ch, 3405 Gough St, Balto 21224
Salem Unit Meth Ch, 7509 Windsor Mill Rd, Balto 21207

155

Salem Unit Meth Ch, 7901 Bradshaw Rd, Upper Falls 21156

Sexton Unit Meth Ch, 1721 Sexton St, Balto 21230

Sharp Street Memorial Unit Meth Ch, 1206 Etting St, Balto 21217

Sharp Street Unit Meth Ch, 12234 Eastern Ave, Chase 21027

Stabler's Unit Meth Ch (Stablerville & Stabler's Church Rds) 16929 York Rd, Monkton 21111

Stevenson Unit Meth Ch, Greenspring Valley & Stevenson Rds, Balto 21208

Stone Chapel Unit Meth Ch, 18 Stone Chapel Rd, Pikesville 21208

Strawbridge Unit Meth Ch, Park Ave & Wilson St, Balto 21217

Sudbrook Unit Meth Ch, 501 Reisterstown Rd, Pikesville 21208

Texas Unit Meth Ch (Galloway Ave) 303 Warren Rd, Cockeysville 21030

Timonium Unit Meth Ch, Pot Spring & Chantry Rds, Timonium 21093

Towson Unit Meth Ch (Hampton Ln & Dulaney Valley Rd) 501 Hampton Ln, Towson 21204

Trinity Unit Meth Ch (Westchester & Rockwell Aves) 2100 Westchester Ave, Balto 21228

Union Memorial Unit Meth Ch (Harlem & Warwick Aves) 2500 Harlem Ave, Balto 21216

Union Square Unit Meth Ch, 1401 W Lombard St, Balto 21223

Union Unit Meth Ch (Sweet Air & Patterson Rds; 5225 Sweet Air Rd) 12635 Manor Rd, Long Green 21092

Union Unit Meth Ch (Trover Rd) 2506 Edgecombe Cir, Apt H, Balto 21215

Unit Meth Ch Balto Conference, 516 N Charles St, Balto 21201

Unit Meth Ch Balto Conference Center, 5124 Greenwich Ave, Balto 21229

Unity Unit Meth Ch, 1433 Edmondson Ave, Balto 21223

Vernon Unit Meth Ch, Vernon Rd, White Hall 21161

Violetville Unit Meth Ch (Coolidge & Joh Aves) 3646 Coolidge Ave, Balto 21229

Ward's Chapel Unit Meth Ch (Liberty & Ward's Chapel Rds) 11023 Liberty Rd, Randallstown 21133

Waugh Unit Meth Ch, Long Green Pike & Hannibal Rd, Glen Arm 21057

Waverly Unit Meth Ch, 644 E 33rd St, Balto 21218

Wesley Memorial Unit Meth Ch (Johnnycake Rd & Balto Natl Pike) 5606 Johnnycake Rd, Balto 21207

Wesley Unit Meth Ch (Highland & Pratt Sts) 200 S Highland Ave, Balto 21224

West Balto Unit Meth Ch (Charing Cross Rd & Greenwich Ave) 5130 Greenwich Ave, Balto 21229

West Liberty Unit Meth Ch (W Liberty & Meredith Rds) 20400 W Liberty Rd, White Hall 21161

Wildwood Parkway Unit Meth Ch, 700 Wildwood Pkwy, Balto 21229

Wilson Unit Meth Ch (Manor & Long Green Rds) 4507 Long Green Rd, Long Green 21092

Wiseburg Unit Meth Ch, Wiseburg Rd, White Hall 21161

Methodist

Woodberry Unit Meth Ch, (Clipper Rd & Druid Park Dr) 2000
   Druid Park Dr, Balto 21211

Calvert Brooks Unit Meth Ch, Box 22, Port Republic 20676

Carroll—Western Unit Meth Ch (Adelina Rd) P.O.Box 821, Prince
   Frederick 20678

Cooper's Unit Meth Ch, Rt 4, Dunkirk 20754

Eastern Unit Meth Ch, Olivet Rd, Lusby 20657

Emmanuel Unit Meth Ch (Emmanuel Church Rd) P.O.Box 216,
   Huntingtown 20639

Huntingtown Unit Meth Ch, Rt 521, P.O.Box 216, Huntingtown
   20639

Lower Marlboro Unit Meth Ch, RR Box 260, Owings 20736

Mt Harmony Unit Meth Ch (Mt Harmony Hwy) P.O.Box 260, Owings
   20736

Mt Hope Unit Meth Ch (Dalrymple Rd) Box 117, Sunderland
   20689-0117

Mt Olive Unit Meth Ch (Dares Beach Rd) P.O.Box 821, Prince
   Frederick 20678

Olivet Unit Meth Ch, Solomons 20688

Patuxent Unit Meth Ch (Rt 4) 4230 Hunting Creek Rd,
   Huntingtown 20639

Peter's Unit Meth Ch, Chaney Rd, Dunkirk 20754

Plum Point Unit Meth Ch (Stinnett Rd) 4230 Hunting Creek Rd,
   Huntingtown 20639

St Edmond's Unit Meth Ch, Chesapeake Beach 20732

St John Unit Meth Ch, Solomons Rd, Lusby 20657

St Paul Unit Meth Ch, Box 203 Lusby 20657

Smithville Unit Meth Ch, P.O.Box 175, Dunkirk 20754

Solomons Unit Meth Ch, Solomons 20688

Trinity Unit Meth Ch, Box 171, Prince Frederick 20678

Wards Memorial Meth Ch, Ward Chapel Rd, Owings 20736

Waters Memorial Meth Ch, MacKall Rd, Box 3AA, St Leonard 20685

Young's Unit Meth Ch, 4230 Hunting Creek Rd, Huntingtown 20639

Caroline Ames Unit Meth Ch (Hobbs) P.O.Box 66, Denton 21629

Bethel Unit Meth Ch, Harper Rd, Federalsburg 21632

Bethesda Unit Meth Ch (N Main St) Box 147, Preston 21655

Bloomery Unit Meth Ch (nr Smithville) 109 Park Ln,
   Federalsburg 21632

Bridgetown Unit Meth Ch (Bridgetown) Box 424, Ridgely 21660

Calvary Unit Meth Ch, Marydel 21649

Chestnut Grove Unit Meth Ch (Chipman Ln) 109 Park Ln,
   Federalsburg 21632

Christ Unit Meth Ch,, 5 S Main St & Maple Ave, Federalsburg
   21632

Concord Unit Meth Ch, Dion Rd, Denton 21629

Grove Unit Meth Ch, Preston—Harmony Rd, Box 147 Preston 21655

Henderson Unit Meth Ch, Henderson 21640

Hillsboro—Queen Anne Unit Meth Ch, Hillsboro 21641

John Wesley Unit Meth Ch (Chipman Ln) 206 Denton Rd,
   Federalsburg 21632

Lockerman Unit Meth Ch (Lockerman) P.O.Box 216, Greensboro
   21639

CHURCH ADDRESSES

Metropolitan Unit Meth Ch, 206 Denton Rd, Federalsburg 21632
Mt Calvary Unit Meth Ch, P.O.box 418, Preston 21655
Mt Pleasant Unit Meth Ch, P.O.Box 216, Greensboro 21639
Mt Zion Unit Meth Ch (Mt Zion Rd) P.O.Box 216, Greensboro
  21639
Preston-Harmony Unit Meth Ch, Rt 1 Box 236, Preston 21655
Replanted Zion Unit Meth Ch (Ridgely) P.O.Box 216, Greensboro
  21639
Ridgely Unit Meth Ch, 109 Central Ave, Box 424, Ridgely 21660
St Luke's Unit Meth Ch, 5th Ave & Franklin Sts, P.O.Box 66,
  Denton 21629
St Paul's Unit Meth Ch, Sunset & Academy Sts, P.O.Box 57,
  Greensboro 21639
Thawley's Unit Meth Ch (nr Denton) Box 424, Ridgely 21660
Trinity Unit Meth Ch, P.O.Box 153, Goldsboro 21636
Union Grove Unit Meth Ch, Osborne Rd, P.O.Box 418 Preston
  21655
Union Unit Meth Ch, N Main & Greenridge Rd, Federalsburg 2163?
Union Unit Meth Ch, P.O.Box 216, Greensboro 21639
Union Unit Meth Ch (Burrsville) P.O.Box 57, Greensboro 21639
Washington Unit Meth Ch (n of Hurlock) P.O.Box 418, Preston
  21655
Wheatley Hall Meth Ch, Academy St & Sunset Ave, Greensboro
  21639
Zion Unit Meth Ch, 206 Denton Rd, Federalsburg 21632
Zorah Unit Meth Ch (Hurlock off Rt 331) P.O.Box 418, Preston
  21655

Carroll   Bethel Unit Meth Ch (Sam's Creek & Buffalo Rds) 3280 Charmil
  Dr, Manchester 21102
Bethesda Unit Meth Ch, 328 N Klee Mill Rd, Sykesville 21784
Bixler's Unit Meth Ch, Bixler's Church Rd, Westminster 21157
Brandenburg Unit Meth Ch (Berrett) 4356 Ridge Rd, Mt Airy
  21771
Brick Unit Meth Ch, Brick Church Rd, Box 30, Uniontown 21157
Calvary Unit Meth Ch, 3939 Gamber Rd, Finksburg 21048
Calvary Unit Meth Ch, 401 S Main St, Mt Airy 21771
Deer Park Unit Meth Ch, 684 Brandy Ln, Westminster 21157
Dorsey Unit Meth Ch, Rt 1, Mt Airy 21771
Dover Unit Meth Ch, 14505 Dover Rd, Hampstead 21074
Ebenezer Unit Meth Ch, 4901 Woodbine Rd, Sykesville 21784
Fairview Unit Meth Ch (Rt 2) 1128 Western Chapel Rd, New
  Windsor 21776
Falls Road Unit Meth Ch (Falls & String Rds) 18221 Falls Rd,
  Hampstead 21074
Flohrville Unit Meth Ch (Church & Central) 1718 Yorkland Rd,
  Finksburg 21048
Gaither Unit Meth Ch, 105 Estelle Ct, Sykesville 21784
Grace Unit Meth Ch (Black Rock & Grace Rds) 4700 Black Rock
  Rd, Hampstead 21074
Greenmount Unit Meth Ch, 2001 Hanover Pike, Hampstead 21074
Howard Chapel Unit Meth Ch, Longcorner Rd, Mt Airy 21771

Methodist

Jennings Chapel Unit Meth Ch, 2551 Jennings Chapel Rd,
   Woodbine 21797
Johnsville Unit Meth Ch, Johnsville Rd, Eldersburg 21784
Johnsville Unit Meth Ch (Rt 75) P.O.Box 460, Union Bridge
   21791
Marriottsville Unit Meth Ch, 1718 Yorkland Rd, Finksburg 21048
Messiah Unit Meth Ch, 25 Middle St, Taneytown 21787
Middleburg Unit Meth Ch (Simpson Mill & Middleburg Rds) 25
   Washington Ln Apt B, Willowwood Gardens, Westminster 21157
Miller's Unit Meth Ch, Warehime & Miller's Sta Rd, Millers
   21107
Morgan Chapel Unit Meth Ch (Rt 94) 2917 Gillis Falls Rd, Mt
   Airy 21771
Mt Gregory Unit Meth Ch, 7359 Spout Hill Rd, Sykesville 21784
Mt Olive Unit Meth Ch, 2917 Gillis Falls Rd, Mt Airy 21771
Mt Zion Unit Meth Ch, 3006 Old Westminster Pike, Finksburg
   21048
Oakland Unit Meth Ch, 5969 Mineral Hill Rd, Sykesville 21784
Poplar Springs Unit Meth Ch, Watersville Rd, Mt Airy 21771
Ridgeville Unit Meth Ch, Ridgeville Blvd, Mt Airy 21771
St James Unit Meth Ch, Marston Rd, New Windsor 21776
St John's Unit Meth Ch, 1205 N Main St, Hampstead 21074
St Luke Unit Meth Ch, 7359 Spout Hill Rd, Sykesville 21784
St Paul Unit Meth Ch, 200 Main St, P.O.Box 4, New Windsor
   21776
St Paul Unit Meth Ch (Church & Main Sts) 105 Estelle Ct,
   Sykesville 21784
Salem Unit Meth Ch, 18217 Falls Rd, Hampstead 21074
Salem Unit Meth Ch (Salem Bottom & Bear Branch Rds) 2815 Ridge
   Rd, Westminster 21157
Sandy Mount Unit Meth Ch, 2101 Old Westminster Pike, Finksburg
   21048
Shiloh Unit Meth Ch, 3106 Shiloh Rd, Hampstead 21074
Simpson Unit Meth Ch, Hardy Rd, Mt Airy 21771
Stone Chapel Unit Meth Ch (Stone Chapel & Bowersox Rds) 2815
   Ridge Rd, Westminster 21157
Strawbridge Meth Epis Ch, 969 Wampler Ln, Westminster 21157
Strawbridge Unit Meth Ch, Rt 3, New Windsor 21776
Taylorsville Unit Meth Ch, 4360 Ridge Rd, Mt Airy 21771
Union Bridge Unit Meth Ch, 7 S Main St, P.O.Box 460, Union
   Bridge 21791
Union Street Unit Meth Ch, 22 Union St, Westminster 21157
Uniontown Unit Meth Ch, Uniontown Rd, Box 30, Uniontown 21157
Watersville Unit Meth Ch (Watersville Rd) 2917 Gillis Falls
   Rd, Mt Airy 21771
Wesley-Freedom Unit Meth Ch, 1043 Liberty Rd, Sykesville 21784
Wesley Unit Meth Ch (Carrollton, Houcksville & Wesley Rds)
   3239 Carrollton Rd, Hampstead 21074
Westminster Unit Meth Ch (Main & Center Sts) 165 E Main St,
   Westminster 21157
White Rock Meth Ch, 6300 White Rock Rd, Sykesville 21784
Zion Unit Meth Ch, 2716 Old Washington Rd, Westminster 21157

CHURCH ADDRESSES

Cecil

Asbury Unit Meth Ch (Craigtown Rd) 100 N Main St, Port Deposit
   21904
Baldwin Unit Meth Ch, 13 Elk Mills Rd, Elkton 21921
Bethel Unit Meth Ch (Bethel Church Rd) 370 Old Bayview Rd,
   North East 21901
Cecilton Unit Meth Parish, 164 W Main St, Cecilton 21913
Cherry Hill Unit Meth Ch, 13 Elk Mills Rd, Elkton 21921
Cokesbury Unit Meth Ch (Rt 222) 100 N Main St, Port Deposit
   21904
Ebenezer Unit Meth Ch (Ebenezer Church Rd) 94 Old Zion Rd,
   North East 21901
Elkton Unit Meth Ch, 219 E Main St, Elkton 21921
Hart's Chapel Unit Meth Ch, North East 21901
Hopewell Unit Meth Ch (1713 Liberty Rd) 1708 Liberty Grove Rd,
   Colora 21917
Hopewell Unit Meth Ch, Hopewell Rd, Rising Sun 21911
Janes Unit Meth Ch, Box 242 Rising Sun 21911
Johnson's Chapel Unit Meth Ch, Warwick 21912
Leeds Unit Meth Ch (Rt 545) 1579 Blue Ball Rd, Elkton 21921
Moore's Chapel Unit Meth Ch, 396 Blake Rd, Elkton 21921
Mt Olivet Unit Meth Ch, Warwick 21912
Mt Pleasant Unit Meth Ch, 1708 Liberty Grove Rd, Colora 21917
North East Unit Meth Ch, 308 S Main St, P.O.Box 522, North
   East 21901
Perryville Unit Meth Ch, Broad & Susquehanna Ave, Box 312,325,
   Perryville 21903
Principio Unit Meth Ch (Principio Furnace) Box 312,325
   Susquehanna Ave, Perryville 21903
Providence Unit Meth Ch (E High St) 229 E Main St, Elkton
   21921
Rosebank Unit Meth Ch (Rt 272) 94 Old Zion Rd, North East
   21901
St John's Unit Meth Ch, Box 82, Charlestown 21914
St John's Unit Meth Ch, 396 Blake Rd, Elkton 21921
St Paul's Unit Meth Ch (Earleville) P.O.Box 326, Cecilton
   21913
Shelemiah Unit Meth Ch, 370 Old Bayview Rd, North East 21901
Town Point Meth Ch, P.O.Box 196, Chesapeake City 21915
Trinity Ch AUMP, Trinity Church Rd, Rising Sun 21911
Trinity Unit Meth Ch, 3rd & Bohemia Ave, P.O.Box 196,
   Chesapeake City 21915
Union Unit Meth Ch (Union Church Rd) 1579 Blue Ball Rd, E$kto
   21921
Unit Providence Meth Ch, 150 E High St, Elkton 21921
Wesley Unit Meth Ch, 41 Justice Way, Elkton 21921
Wesley Unit Meth Ch (Elk Neck) 304 Hance Pt Rd, North East
   21901
Zion Unit Meth Ch, P.O.Box 326, Cecilton 21913

Charles

Alexandria Chapel Unit Meth Ch, Pisgah 20640
Alexander Unit Meth Ch, Rt 244, Rison 20658
Calvary Unit Meth Ch, Ironsides 20643
Calvary Unit Meth Ch, Hwy 5 Box 359, Waldorf 20601

Methodist

Chicamuxen Unit Meth Ch (Rt 224) 17 Mattingly Ave, Indian Head 20640
Emory Chapel Unit Meth Ch, Box 121, Pisgah 20640
Good Shepherd Unit Meth Ch, 305 E Smallwood Dr, Waldorf 20601
Indian Head Unit Meth Ch, 19 Mattingly Ave, Indian Head 20640
La Plata Unit Meth Ch, 3 Port Tobacco Rd, La Plata 20646
Metropolitan Unit Meth Ch (Pomonkey) Rt 1 Box 119, Indian Head 20640
Pisgah Unit Meth Ch (Rts 484 & 424) 17 Mattingly Ave, Indian Head 20640
St Matthew's Unit Meth Ch, Rt 6, La Plata 20646
Shiloh Unit Meth Ch, Bryans Road 20616
Smith's Chapel Unit Meth Ch, Box 121, Pisgah 20640
Zion Wesley Unit Meth Ch, Berry Rd, Rt 7 Box 359, Waldorf 20601

Dorchester   Antioch Unit Meth Ch (Town Point), Rt 3 Box 164A, Cambridge 21613
Beckwith (Cornersville) Rt 343, Cambridge 21613
Bethany Unit Meth Ch (Crocheron) Box 93, Wingate 21675
Bounds Unit Meth Ch (Andrews) Crapo 21626
Brookview Unit Meth Ch, Rt 14 box 95, East New Market 21631
Bucktown Unit Meth Ch, Box 98, Secretary 21664
Christ Rock Unit Meth Ch, Taylor's Isl 21669
Christ Unit Meth Ch (Aireys) P.O.Box 275, Cambridge 21613
Ebenezer Unit Meth Ch, Crapo 21626
Eldorado Unit Meth Ch, Rt 313 Box 95, East New Market 21631
Elliotts Unit Meth Ch (Elliotts Isl) Box 278 Vienna 21869
First Unit Meth Ch, Main & Academy Sts, Box 98 Secretary 21664
Friendship Unit Meth Ch (Aireys) Box 98, Secretary 21664
Grace Unit Meth Ch, Race & Muir Sts, Cambridge 21613
Hoopers Memorial Unit Meth Ch (Hoopersville) Fishing Creek 21634
Hosier Memorial Unit Meth Ch, Fishing Creek 21634
Jefferson Unit Meth Ch (Smithville) Taylor's Isl 21669
John Wesley Unit Meth Ch, Liners Rd, Church Creek 21622
Lane Unit Meth Ch, Church Rd, Taylor's Isl 21669
Madison Unit Meth Ch, Rt 16, Madison 21648
Malone Unit Meth Ch, White Marsh Rd, Madison 21648
Milton Unit Meth Ch, Rt 16, Woolford 21677
Mt Pleasant Unit Meth Ch (Salem) Rt 50, East New Market 21631
Mt Zion Unit Meth Ch, East New Market 21631
Reid's Grove Unit Meth Ch, Box 278, Vienna 21869
St James Unit Meth Ch, Hicksburg Rd, East New Market 21631
St John's Unit Meth Ch (Golden Hill) Crapo 21626
St Luke Unit Meth Ch, 908 Pine St, Cambridge 21613
St Paul Unit Meth Ch (Hawkeye Rd) East New Market 21631
St Paul's Unit Meth Ch, 205 Maryland Ave, Cambridge 21613
St Paul's Unit Meth Ch (Harrisville) Taylor's Isl 21669
St Thomas Unit Meth Ch, Bishops Head 21611
Salem Unit Meth Ch, Box 98, Secretary 21664
Secretary Unit Meth Ch, Main St, Secretary 21664
Spedden Unit Meth Ch (Hudson) Rt 3 Box 164A, Cambridge 21613

Taylor's Isl Unit Meth Ch, Rt 16 Box 46, Church Creek 21622
Thompson Chapel Unit Meth Ch (Thompsontown) East New Market 21631
Trinity Unit Meth Ch, Main St, Box 95, East New Market 21631
Unity-Washington Unit Meth Ch, Main & Oak Sts, Box 298, Hurlock 21643
Vienna Unit Meth Ch, Church St, Box 278, Vienna 21869
Waters Unit Meth Ch (Fork Neck) P.O.Box 275, Cambridge 21613
Waugh Unit Meth Ch, 429 High St, P.O.Box 275, Cambridge 21613
Wesley Unit Meth Ch (Andrews) Crapo 21626
Wesley Unit Meth Ch (Rt 313, Finchville) Box 298, Hurlock 21643
Wesley Unit Meth Ch, Vienna 21869
White Haven Unit Meth Ch, Rt 16 Box 46, Church Creek 21622
Wingate Unit Meth Ch, Box 93, Wingate 21675
Zion Unit Meth Ch, 612 Locust St, Cambridge 21613
Zion Unit Meth Ch, Toddville 21672
Zoar Unit Meth Ch (Reid's Grove) 715 Bradley Ave, Cambridge 21613

Frederick   Araby Unit Meth Ch (Rt 2) 4619 Araby Church Rd, Frederick 21701
Asbury Unit Meth Ch (W All Saints & Court Sts) 200 W All Saints St, Frederick 21701
Brook Hill Unit Meth Ch, 8946 Indian Springs Rd, Frederick 21701
Buckeystown Unit Meth Ch, Rt 80 Box 86, Buckeystown 21717
Calvary Unit Meth Ch (W 2nd & Bentz Sts) 131 W 2nd St, Frederick 21701
Catoctin Unit Meth Ch (Rt 3) 7912 Rocky Ridge Rd, Thurmont 21788
Centennial Memorial Unit Meth Ch, 8 W 2nd St, Frederick 21701
Central Unit Meth Ch, Rt 75 Box 6, Libertytown 21762
Deerfield Unit Meth Ch (Foxville-Deerfield Rd, Lantz) 101 Dogwood Ave, Thurmont 21788
Doubs Unit Meth Ch, 5131 Doubs Rd, Adamstown 21710
Ebenezer Unit Meth Ch, Rt 1, Ijamsville 21754
Epworth Unit Meth Ch, 5131 Doubs Rd, Adamstown 21710
Firlt Unit Meth Ch, 7 S Maryland Ave, Brunswick 21716
Flint Hill Unit Meth Ch (Rt 2) 4619 Araby Church Rd, Frederick 21701
Garfield Unit Meth Ch (Stottlemyer Rd) 12477 Wolfsville Rd, Myersville 21773
Hope Hill Unit Meth Ch, Box 86, Buckeystown 21717
Ijamsville Unit Meth Ch, 3519 Urbana Pike, Frederick 21701
Jackson Chapel Unit Meth Ch, Rt 6, Frederick 21701
Jefferson Unit Meth Ch, 5131 Doubs Rd, Adamstown 21710
Jefferson Unit Meth Ch, 3882 Jefferson Pike, Jefferson 21755
Key's Chapel Unit Meth Ch (Coppermine Rd) 1412 Rolling House Dr, Frederick 21701-6036
Lewistown Unit Meth Ch, Rt 1, Frederick 21701
Libertytown Unit Meth Ch, Rt 26 Box 6, Libertytown 21762

Linganore Unit Meth Ch, 8919 Clemsonville Rd, Union Bridge
21791
Middletown Unit Meth Ch (Fountaindale) 7102 Fern Circle,
Middletown 21769
Mt Carmel Unit Meth Ch (Rt 144) 6102 Dover St, Frederick 21701
Mt Pleasant Unit Meth Ch (Liberty & Crum Rds) 7933 McKaig Rd,
Frederick 21701
Mt Zion Unit Meth Ch (McKaig Rd & Gashouse Pike) 7933 McKaig
Rd, Frederick 21701
Mt Zion Unit Meth Ch, Box 106, Myersville 21773
New Market Unit Meth Ch, Rt 874 & North Alley, New Market
21774
New York Hill Unit Meth Ch, 9th & Park, Brunswick 21716
Pleasant Grove Unit Meth Ch, Rt 75, Monrovia 21770
Pleasant View Unit Meth Ch, Rt 1, Adamstown 21710
Pleasant Walk Unit Meth Ch, Box 106, Myersville 21773
Providence Unit Meth Ch (Kemptown) 3735 Kemptown Church Rd,
Monrovia 21770
Salem Unit Meth Ch (Rt 17) 12477 Wolfsville Rd, Myersville
21773
Sandy Hook Unit Meth Ch (Sandy Hook Rd) 4500 Mass Ave NW, Box
16, Washington DC 20016
Silver Hill Unit Meth Ch (Old Rt 26 nr Water St) 7933 McKaig
Rd, Frederick 21701
Sunnyside Unit Meth Ch, Rt 4, Frederick 21701
Thurmont Unit Meth Ch (Church St) 13738 Hillside Ave, Thurmont
21788
Tom's Creek Unit Meth Ch (Tom's Creek & Simmons Rds) 16252
Tom's Creek Church Rd, Emmitsburg 21727
Trinity Unit Meth Ch, 313 W Main St, Emmitsburg 21727
Trinity Unit Meth Ch, 705 W Patrick St, Frederick 21701
Walkersville Unit Meth Ch, 40 Main St, Walkersville 21793
Warren Unit Meth Ch, 1412 Rolling House Dr, Frederick
21701-6036
Weller Unit Meth Ch, 101 Altamont Rd, Thurmont 21788
Wesley Chapel Unit Meth Ch, 3519 Urbana Pike, Frederick 21701

Garrett   Bethel Unit Meth Ch, Balto & H St, Mountain Lake Park 21550
Bloomington Unit Meth Ch, Box 175, Bloomington 21523
Chestnut Grove Unit Meth Ch, Box 175, Bloomington 21523
Crellin Unit Meth Ch, 205 Seneca Ave, Mountain Lake Park 21550
Deer Park Unit Meth Ch, Paradise Rt 4, Deer Park 21550
Friendsville Unit Meth Ch, Riverdrive Rd, Friendsville 21531
Grantsville Unit Meth Ch, Box 442, Grantsville 21536
Hoyes Unit Meth Ch, Box 176, McHenry 21541
Jennings Unit Meth Ch, Box 442 Grantsville 21536
Kurtz Chapel Unit Meth Ch, 205 Seneca Ave, Mountain Lake Park
21550
McHenry Unit Meth Ch, Deep Creek Lake, McHenry 21541
Mt Bethel Unit Meth Ch, Kitzmiller 21538
Mt Zion Unit Meth Ch, Box 442, Grantsville 21536
Mt Zion Unit Meth Ch, Rt 1, Swanton 21561

Mountain Lake Park Bethel Unit Meth Ch, Box 276, Mountain Lake Park 21550
North Glade Unit Meth Ch, Rt 2, Swanton 21561
Pleasant Dale Unit Meth Ch, 205 Seneca Ave, Mountain Lake Park 21550
St Andrews Unit Meth Ch, Kitzmiller 21538
St Paul's Unit Meth Ch, 316 E Oak St, Oakland 21550
Selby's Port Unit Meth Ch, Old Morgantown Rd, Friendsville 21531

Methodist

State Line Unit Meth Ch, Box 442, Grantsville 21536
Swanton Otterbien Unit Meth Ch, Box 175, Bloomington 21523
White Unit Meth Ch, 205 Seneca Ave, Mountain Lake Park 21550

Harford   Ames Unit Meth Ch, 116 Balto Ave, Bel Air 21014
Asbury Unit Meth Ch, Asbury Rd, Bel Air 21014
Bel Air Unit Meth Ch, 21 Linwood Ave, Bel Air 21014
Calvary Unit Meth Ch, 1321 Calvary Rd, Churchville 21028
Cambria Unit Meth Ch, Main St, Box 152, Whiteford 21160
Centre Unit Meth Ch, 2409 Rocks Rd, Forest Hill 21050
Clarks Chapel Unit Meth Ch, Churchville 21028
Clarks Unit Meth Ch, 2001 Kalmia Rd, Bel Air 21014
Cokesbury Unit Meth Ch, 2968 Dumbarton Dr, Abingdon 21009
Cranberry Unit Meth Ch (Perryman Rd) 3031 Bellechasse Rd, Fallston 21047
Darlington Unit Meth Ch, 2117 Shuresville Rd, Darlington 21034
Deer Creek Unit Meth Ch (Chestnut Hill & Deer Creek Church Rds) 729 Chestnut Hill Rd, Forest Hill 21050
Dublin Unit Meth Ch, 1524 Whiteford Rd, Street 21154
Ebenezer Unit Meth Ch (Rt 152 & Charles St) 3345 Charles St, Fallston 21047
Edgewood Unit Meth Ch, 1430 Bellona Ave, Edgewood 21040
Emory Unit Meth Ch, Emory Church Rd, Street 21154
Evan Meth Ch (1 mi n of Dublin, Hwy 136) 1736 Whiteford Rd, Street 21154
Fallston Unit Meth Ch, 1501 Fallston Rd, Fallston 21047
Grace Unit Meth Ch (110 W Bel Air Ave) 445 Ruby Dr, Aberdeen 21001
Havre de Grace Unit Meth Ch (Union Ave & Congress St) 101 N Union Ave, Havre de Grace 21078
Hopewell Unit Meth Ch, 3600 Level Village Rd, Havre de Grace 21078
Jarrettsville Unit Meth Ch, 1733 Jarrettsville Rd, Jarrettsville 21084
John Wesley Unit Meth Ch, Rt 7, Abingdon 21009
Mt Tabor Unit Meth Ch, 2350 Conowingo Rd, Forest Hill 21050
Mt Vernon Unit Meth Ch, Rt 136 Box 152, Whiteford 21160
Mt Zion Unit Meth Ch, 1643 Churchville Rd, Bel Air 21014
Mt Zion Unit Meth Ch, 1915 N Singer Rd, Joppa 21085
Presbury Unit Meth Ch, 806 Edgewood Rd, Edgewood 21040
Rock Run Unit Meth Ch, Rock Run Rd, Havre de Grace 21078
St James Unit Meth Ch, 617 Green St, Havre de Grace 21078

CHURCH ADDRESSES

St James Unit Meth Ch, 4080 Federal Hill Rd, Jarrettsville 21084

St Pauls Unit Meth Ch, St Pauls & Telegraph Rds, Pylesville 21132

Smith's Chapel Unit Meth Ch, 3111 Churchville Rd, Churchville 21028

Union Chapel Unit Meth Ch, 1012 Old Joppa Rd, Joppa 21085

Union Unit Meth Ch (Rt 3) 700 Old Post Rd, Aberdeen 21001

Wesleyan Chapel Unit Meth Ch (Paradise & Wesleyan Rds) 3602 Level Village Rd, Havre de Grace 21078

William Watters Unit Meth Ch, 1452 W Jarrettsville Rd, Jarrettsville 21084

Howard

Alberta Gary Memorial Meth Ch, 9405 Guilford Rd, Columbia 21046

Bethany Unit Meth Ch, 2875 Bethany Ln, Ellicott City 21043

Christ Unit Meth Ch, 7246 Cradlerock Way, Columbia 21045

Daniels-Gary Memorial Unit Meth Ch, Daniels Rd, Ellicott City 21043

Emory Unit Meth Ch (Church & Emory Rds) 8794 Autumn Hill Dr, Ellicott City 21043

Glen Mar Unit Meth Ch, 8430 Glen Mar Rd, Ellicott City 21043

Glenelg Unit Meth Ch, 13900 Burnt Woods Rd, Glenelg 21737

Harwood Park Meth Ch, Highland & Euclid Aves, Elkridge 21227

Hopkins Unit Meth Ch, Rt 216 & Hopkins Rd, Highland 20777

Linden-Linthicum Unit Meth Ch, 12175 Rt 108, Clarksville 21029

Lisbon Unit Meth Ch, 16515 Frederick Rd, Mt Airy 21771

Locust Unit Meth Ch, Martin & Freetown Rds, Columbia 21044

Locust Unit Meth Ch, Rt 32, Simpsonville 21150

Mt Zion Unit Meth Ch, 8565 Main St, Ellicott City 21043

Mt Zion Unit Meth Ch, Rt 216, Highland 20777

Rockland Unit Meth Ch (8949 Old Frederick Rd) 8971 Chapel Ave, Ellicott City 21043

St James Unit Meth Ch (12470 Rt 99) P.O.Box 9, West Friendship 21794

St John Unit Meth Ch (Wilde Lake Village Green) 10431 Twin Rivers Rd, Columbia 21044

Savage Unit Meth Ch, Balto & Foundry Sts, Savage 20763

West Liberty Unit Meth Ch, 2000 Sand Hill Rd, Woodstock 21163

Kent

Aaron Chapel Unit Meth Ch (Piney Neck Rd) Rt 1 Box 230, Rock Hall 21661

Asbury Unit Meth Ch (Chesterville) Rt 2 Box 513, Chestertown 21620

Asbury Unit Meth Ch, Cypress St, P.O.Box 187, Millington 21651

Asbury Unit Meth Ch (Georgetown) Rt 1 Box 230, Rock Hall 21661

Betterton Unit Meth Ch, Betterton 21610

Christ Unit Meth Ch, 405 W High St, Chestertown 21620

Crumpton Unit Meth Ch (Third St) Cypress St, P.O.Box 187, Millington 21651

Double Creek Unit Meth Ch (nr McGinns Corner) Cypress St, P.O.Box 187, Millington 21651

Emmanuel Unit Meth Ch (Quaker Neck Rd, Pomono) Washington Park, RD 4 Box 450, Chestertown 21620

CHURCH ADDRESSES

First Unit Meth Ch, High & Mill Sts, P.O.Box 227, Chestertown 21620

Fountain Unit Meth Ch (Big Wood) 12 Montpelier Ct, New Castle DE 19720

Janes Unit Meth Ch (Cross & Cannon Sts) Washington Park, RD 4 Box 450, Chestertown 21620

John Wesley Unit Meth Ch (Millington) Rt 2 Box 513, Chestertown 21620

John Wesley Unit Meth Ch (Sassafras) Rt 4 Box 462, Chestertown 21620

Joshua Chapel Unit Meth Ch (Morgnec) Rt 2 Box 513, Chestertown 21620

Kennedyvile Unit Meth Ch, Kennedyville 21645

Lynch Unit Meth Ch, Lynch 21646

Mt Pisgah Unit Meth Ch (Melitota) Rt 1 Box 230, Rock Hall 21661

Mt Pleasant Unit Meth Ch (Fairlee) Rt 1 Box 230, Rock Hall 21661

Mt Pleasant Unit Meth Ch (Pondtown) Rt 2 Box 513, Chestertown 21620

Olivet Unit Meth Ch, Box 107, Galena 21635

Raum Chapel Unit Meth Ch, Rt 2 Box 127, Rock Hall 21661

Rock Hall Unit Meth Ch, Rt 2 Box 127, Rock Hall 21661

St Georges Unit Meth Ch (Worton Pt) 12 Montpelier Ct, New Castle DE 19720

St James Unit Meth Ch, Worton 21678

Salem Unit Meth Ch (Fairlee) Rt 2 Box 245, Chestertown 21620

Still Pond Unit Meth Ch, Box 36, Still Pond 21667

Union Unit Meth Ch (Coleman, Rt 433) 12 Montpelier Ct, New Castle DE 19720

Wesley Chapel Unit Meth Ch, Rt 2 Box 127, Rock Hall 21661

Worton Unit Meth Ch, Worton 21678

Montgomery   Asbury Unit Meth Ch, 17540 Black Rock Rd, ermantown 20874

Ashton Unit Meth Ch (17314 New Hampshire Ave) 801 Tucker Ln, Ashton 20861

Bethesda Unit Meth Ch, 8300 Old Georgetown Rd, Bethesda 20814

Bethesda Unit Meth Ch (11900 Bethesda Church Rd) 27909 Kemptown Church Rd, Damascus 20872

Brooke Grove Unit Meth Ch, 7700 Brink Rd, Laytonsville 20879

Cabin John Unit Meth Ch (77th St & MacArthur Blvd) 7703 MacArthur Blvd, Cabin John 20818

Chevy Chase Unit Meth Ch, 7001 Connecticut Ave, Chevy Chase 20815

Chinese Unit Meth Ch (7001 Connecticut Ave) 11802 Seven Locks Rd, Potomac 20854-3395

Clarksburg Unit Meth Ch (Spire St at 121 & 355) 22925 Frederick Rd, Clarksburg 20871

Colesville Unit Meth Ch, 52 Randolph Rd, Silver Spring 20904

Concord-St Andrews Meth Ch, River & Goldsboro Rds, 6308 Blackwood Rd, W Bethesda 20817

Covenant Unit Meth Ch, 20301 Pleasant Ridge Dr, Gaithersburg 20879

Damascus Unit Meth Ch, 9700 New Church St, Damascus 20872
Dickerson Unit Meth Ch, 20341 Dickerson Church Rd, Dickerson
20842
Elijah Unit Meth Ch (Elgin & Jerusalem) 15451 Hoyles Mill Rd,
Boyds 20841
Emory Grove Unit Meth Ch, 8200 Emory Grove Rd & Rt 124)
P.O.Box 123, Dickerson 20842
Epworth Unit Meth Ch, 9008 Rosemont Dr, Gaithersburg 20877
Fairhaven Parish Unit Meth Ch (12801 Darnestown Rd) 19006
Perrone Dr, Germantown 20874
Faith Unit Meth Ch, 6810 Montrose Rd, Rockville 20852
Forest Grove Unit Meth Ch, Dickerson 20842
Francis Asbury Unit Meth Ch, 2181 Balto Rd, Rockville 20851
Friendship Unit Meth Ch (27747 Ridge Rd) 9700 New Church St,
Damascus 20872
Glenmont Unit Meth Ch, 12901 Georgia Ave, Wheaton 20906
Good Hope-Union Unit Meth Ch, 14655 Good Hope Rd, Silver
Spring 20904
Good Shepherd Unit Meth Ch, 9701 New Hampshire Ave, Silver
Spring 20903
Grace Meth Ch, 7001 New Hampshire Ave, Takoma Park 20912
Grace Unit Meth Ch, 119 N Frederick Ave, Gaithersburg 20877
Hispanic Mission, 7001 New Hampshire Ave, Takoma Park 20912
Hughes Unit Meth Ch, 10700 Georgia Ave, Wheaton 20902
Hyattstown Unit Meth Ch (26121 Frederick Rd) 14463 Lewisdale
Rd, Clarksburg 20871
Jerusalem Unit Meth Ch (21 Wood Ln) 16920 Cherry Valley Dr,
Olney 20832
John Wesley Unit Meth Ch, 22420 Frederick Rd, Clarksburg 20871
Korean Unit Meth Ch UM Mission of Washington (River &
Goldsboro Rds) 8304 Jeb Stuart Rd, Potomac 20854
Liberty Grove Unit Meth Ch, 15124 Liberty Grove Dr,
Burtonsville 20866
Marvin Chapel Unit Meth Ch (Woodville Rd) Box 302, Damascus
20872
Marvin Memorial Unit Meth Ch, 33 University Blvd E, Silver
Spring 20901
McKendree Unit Meth Ch (205 Paca St) 2011 Featherwood St,
Silver Spring 20904
Memorial Unit Meth Ch, 1782 Elgin Rd, Poolesville 20837
Memorial Unit Meth Ch, 9226 Colesville Rd, Silver Spring 20910
Mill Creek Parish Unit Meth Ch, 7101 Horizon Ter, Rockville
20855
Millian Memorial Unit Meth Ch (Parkland & Grenoble Drs) 13016
Parkland Dr, Rockville 20853
Montgomery Unit Meth Ch, 28325 Kemptown Rd, Damascus 20872
Mt Carmel Unit Meth Ch, 22222 Georgia Ave, Box 177, Rockville
20833
Mt Pleasant Unit Meth Ch (4012 Muncaster Mill Rd) 16920 Cherry
Valley Dr, Olney 20832
Mt Tabor Unit Meth Ch, 24101 Laytonsville Rd, Gaithersburg
20879

CHURCH ADDRESSES

Mt Zion Unit Meth Ch, 5000 Brookeville Rd, Brookeville 20833
Mt Zion Unit Meth Ch, 21020 Beallsville Rd, Dickerson 20842
Mountain View Unit Meth Ch, 11501 Mountain View Rd, Damascus
 20872
North Bethesda Unit Meth Ch, 10100 Old Georgetown Rd, Bethesda
 20814
Oak Chapel Unit Meth Ch (Layhill & Argyle Club Rds) 14503
 Argyle Club Rd, Silver Spring 20906
Oakdale-Emory Unit Meth Ch (Georgia Ave & Emory Church Rd)
 3415 Emory Church Rd, Olney 20832
Potomac Korean Unit Meth Ch, 10100 Old Georgetown Rd, Bethesda
 20814
Potomac Unit Meth Ch (S Glen & Falls Rd) 9908 S Glen Rd,
 Potomac 20854
Prospect Unit Meth Ch, Woodville Rd, Box 302, Damascus 20872
Rockville Unit Meth Ch, 112 W Montgomery Ave, Rockville 20850
St Andrews Unit Meth Ch, River & Goldsboro Rds, W Bethesda
 20817
St Marks Unit Meth Ch, 19620 White Ground Rd, Boyds 20841
St Paul Meth Ch, 2601 Colston Dr, Chevy Chase Md 20815-3092
St Paul Unit Meth Ch, 21720 Laytonsville Rd, Laytonsville
 20879
St Paul Unit Meth Ch, Sugarland Rd, Poolesville 20837
St Paul's Unit Meth Ch, Armory Ave & Mitchell St, Kensington
 20895
Salem Unit Meth Ch, 8 High St, Brookeville 20833
Salem Unit Meth Ch, Cedar Grove 20767
Salem Unit Meth Ch (23725 Ridge Rd) 10601 Radstock Ct,
 Damascus 20872
Sharp Street Unit Meth Ch, 1310 Sandy Spring Rd, Sandy Spring
 20860
Stewarttown Unit Meth Ch, 19615 Goshen Rd, Laytonsville 20879
Trinity Unit Meth Ch, 19225 Germantown Rd, P.O.Box 477,
 Germantown 20874
Warren Unit Meth Ch (22625 Whites Ferry Rd) 21020 Beallsville
 Rd, Dickerson 20842
Washington Ch of the Deaf, 7001 New Hampshire Ave, Takoma Park
 20912
Washington Grove Unit Meth Ch, 305 Chestnut Ave, Washington
 Grove 20880
Wesley Grove Unit Meth Ch, 23640 Woodfield Rd, Gaithersburg
 20879
Wesley Korean Unit Meth Ch, 10700 Georgia Ave, Silver Spring
 20902
Woodside Unit Meth Ch, 8900 Georgia Ave, Silver Spring 20910

Prince
Georges

Ager Road Unit Meth Ch, 6301 Ager Rd, Hyattsville 20782
Asbury Unit Meth Ch, 4004 Accokeek Rd, Brandywine 20613
Asbury Unit Meth Ch, 8513 Madison St, New Carrollton 20784
Bells Unit Meth Ch, 6016 Allentown Rd, Suitland 20746
Bethel Unit Meth Ch, 16101 Swanson Rd, Upper Marlboro 20772
Bowie Unit Meth Ch, 13009 Sixth St, Bowie 20715

Brentwood Unit Meth Ch (37th & Tilden Sts) 4214 37th St,
  Brentwood 20722
Brookfield Unit Meth Ch (Naylor) 17400 Aquasco Rd, Brandywine
  20613
Cheltenham Unit Meth Ch, Rt 301 Box 18, Cheltenham 20623
Cheverly Unit Meth Ch, 2801 Cheverly Ave, Cheverly 20785
Chinese Unit Meth Ch, 2601 Colston Dr, Chevy Chase 20815-3092
Christ Unit Meth Ch, Church Rd, Aquasco 20608
Christ Unit Meth Ch (69th Ave & Annapolis Rd) 4805 Glen Oak
  Dr, Landover Hills 20784
Ch of the Redeemer, 1901 Iverson St, Temple Hills 20748
Clinton Unit Meth Ch, 10700 Brandywine Rd, Clinton 20735
College Park Unit Meth Ch, 9601 Rhode Island Ave, College Park
  20740
Com Unit Meth Ch, 300 Brock Bridge Rd, Laurel 20707
Corkran Memorial Unit Meth Ch, 5200 Temple Hills Rd, Temple
  Hills 20748
Ebenezer Unit Meth Ch (4912 Whitefield Chapel Rd) 6949
  Nashville Rd, Lanham 20706
Emmanuel Unit Meth Ch, 11416 Cedar Ln, Beltsville 20705
Emmanuel Unit Meth Ch, 10755 Scaggsville Rd, Laurel 20707
Faith Unit Meth Ch, 15769 Livingston Rd, Accokeek 20607
First Unit Meth Ch, Queensbury & Queens Chapel Rds,
  Hyattsville 20782
First Unit Meth Ch, 424 Main St, Laurel 20707
First Unit Meth Ch (5512 Whitefield Chapel Rd) 9207 Sheridan
  St, Seabrook 20706
Forest Memorial Unit Meth Ch, 3111 Forestville Rd, Forestville
  20747
Fort Washington Unit Meth Ch, 12919 Indian Head Hwy, Fort
  Washington 20744
Gethsemane Unit Meth Ch, 910 Addison Rd S, Capitol Hts 20743
Gibbons Unit Meth Ch, 14107 Gibbons Church Rd, Brandywine
  20613
Glenn Dale Unit Meth Ch, Springfield & Goodluck Rds, Glenn
  Dale 20769
Grace Unit Meth Ch, 716 59th Ave, Fairmount Hts 20743
Grace Unit Meth Ch, 11700 ld Fort Rd, Fort Washington 20744
Grace Unit Meth Ch, 7001 New Hampshire Ave, Takoma Park 20912
Greenbelt Unit Meth Ch, 40 Ridge Rd, Greenbelt 20770
Hopkins Unit Meth Ch, 8513 Madison St, New Carrollton 20784
Immanuel Unit Meth Ch, 17400 Aquasco Rd, Brandywine 20613
Korean First Unit Meth Ch, 11416 Cedar Ln, Beltsville 20705
Locust Unit Meth Ch, 4523 Kinmount Rd, Lanham 20706
Maryland City Free Meth Ch, 314 Brock Bridge Rd, Laurel 20707
Mt Oak Unit Meth Ch, 14110 Mt Oak Rd, Mitchellville 20716
Mt Rainier Unit Meth Ch, 3501 Bunker Hill Rd, Mt Rainier 20712
Mt Zion Unit Meth Ch, 1937 Tanow Pl, District Hts 20747
Mt Zion Unit Meth Ch, 3592 Whiskey Bottom Rd, Laurel 20707
Mt Zion Unit Meth Ch, Rt 1 Box 178 1/2, Laurel 20707
Mowatt Memorial Unit Meth Ch, 2-A Northway Rd, Greenbelt 20770

CHURCH ADDRESSES

Nottingham-Myers Unit Meth Ch, 15601 Brooks Church Rd, P.O.Box 267, Upper Marlboro 20772
Oxon Hill Unit Meth Ch, 6400 Livingston Rd, Oxon Hill 20745
Providence Unit Meth Ch, 10610 Old Fort Rd, Fort Washington 20744
Queen's Chapel Unit Meth Ch, 7410 Muirkirk Rd, Beltsville 20705
St Mark's Unit Meth Ch, 8th & West St, Laurel 20707
St Matthew's Unit Meth Ch, 14900 Annapolis Rd, Bowie 20715
St Paul Unit Meth Ch, 2601 Colston Dr, Chevy Chase 20815-3092
St Paul Unit Meth Ch, 6634 St Barnabas Rd, Suitland 20745
Union Unit Meth Ch, 14418 Old Marlboro Pike, Upper Marlboro 20772
University Unit Meth Ch, 3621 Campus Dr, College Park 20740
Washington Ch of the Deaf, 7001 New Hampshire Ave, Takoma Park 20912
Westphalia Unit Meth Ch, 8511 Westphalia Rd, Upper Marlboro 20772
Zion Wesley Unit Meth Ch (Rt 228) 14205 Waters Way, Brandywine 20613

Queen Annes
Bethany Unit Meth Ch (Price) Box 6, Church Hill 21623
Bryan Unit Meth Ch, Grasonville 21638
Calvary Unit Meth Ch, Box 7, Queenstown 21658
Calvary-Asbury Unit Meth Ch, P.O.Box 202, Sudlersville 21668
Centreville Unit Meth Ch, Rt 213 & Hope Rd, Centreville 21617
Charles Wesley Unit Meth Ch, 423 S Liberty, Centreville 21617
Church Hill Unit Meth Ch, Box 6, Church Hill 21623
Ezion Unit Meth Ch (Batt's Neck) Rt 1 Box 16, Chester 21619
Immanuel Unit Meth Ch, Grasonville 21638
John Wesley Unit Meth Ch (Carmichael) P.O.Box 516, Queenstown 21658
Kent Isl Unit Meth Ch (Rt 301 & Cox Neck Rd) Harbor View, Chester 21619
Marvin Memorial Unit Meth Ch, Barclay 21607
Mt Olive Unit Meth Ch (Hope) Rt 1 Box 63, Church Hill 21623
Mt Vernon Unit Meth Ch (Salem) Rt 1 Box 63, Church Hill 21623
Mt Zion Unit Meth Ch (Burrisville) Rt 1 Box 63, Church Hill 21623
St Daniels Unit Meth Ch, Barclay 21607
St Paul's Unit Meth Ch, Ingleside 21644
Sudlersville Unit Meth Ch, Sudlersville 21668
Union Wesley Unit Meth Ch, Rt 1 Box 16, Chester 21619
Wye of Carmichael Meth Ch, Box 7, Queenstown 21658

St Marys
Bethesda Unit Meth Ch (Valley Lee) 1 Windsor Dr, Lexington Park 20653
First Friendship Unit Meth Ch (Ridge) 150 Great Mills Rd, Lexington Park 20653
Hollywood Unit Meth Ch, Rt 1 Box 100, Hollywood 20636
Lexington Park Unit Meth Ch, 150 Great Mills Rd, Lexington Park 20653
Mt Calvary Unit Meth Ch, Rt 6, Charlotte Hall 20622

Mt Zion Unit Meth Ch (235 Laurel Grove) Rt 1 Box 84A, Mechanicsville 20659

Mt Zion Unit Meth Ch, P.O.Box 38, St Inigoes 20684

St George Isl Unit Meth Ch, Star Rt Box 264A, Piney Pt 20674

St Luke Unit Meth Ch, Scotland 20687

St Paul Unit Meth Ch, Washington St on Town Sq, Leonardtown 20650

Zion Unit Meth Ch, 1 Windsor Dr, Lexington Park 20653

Somerset   Antioch Unit Meth Ch, 200 S Somerset Ave, Princess Anne 21853

Asbury Unit Meth Ch (Main St & Asbury Ave) Rt 1 Box 231A, Crisfield 21817

Calvary Unit Meth Ch, Rhodes Pt 21858

Christ Unit Meth Ch, Box 165, Upper Fairmount 21867

Cokesbury Unit Meth Ch, P.O.Box 297, Princess Anne 21853

Ebenezer Unit Meth Ch, 33 E Broad St, Princess Anne 21853

Ewell Unit Meth Ch, P.O.Box 52, Ewell 21824

Flower Hill Unit Meth Ch, Eden 21822

Friendship Unit Meth Ch, P.O.Box 297, Princess Anne 21853

Grace Unit Meth Ch (Venton) Rt 1 Box 144, Princess Anne 21853

Handys Memorial Unit Meth Ch, Rt 357 Box 95, Marion Sta 21838

Immanuel Unit Meth Ch, P.O.Box 109, Crisfield 21817

John Wesley Meth Ch, Cottage Grove, Westover 21871

John Wesley Unit Meth Ch (Rt 353) Rt 3 Box 316, Princess Anne 21853

Liberia Unit Meth Ch, P.O.Box 95, Marion Sta 21838

Macedonia Unit Meth Ch, Rt 353, Dames Quarter 21820

Mariners Unit Meth Ch, Mariners & Old St Rds, Crisfield 21817

Metropolitan Unit Meth Ch, 3 E Broad St, Princess Anne 21853

Mt Olive Unit Meth Ch, Revel Neck Rd, Box 165, Upper Fairmount 21867

Mt Peer Unit Meth Ch (Rt 357) P.O.Box 95, Marion Sta 21838

Mt Pleasant Unit Meth Ch (1st & Main Sts) 37 W Main St, Crisfield 21817

Mt Zion Unit Meth Ch, Polks Rd, Rt 1 Box 144, Princess Anne 21853

Quindocqua Unit Meth Ch (2 mi w of Marion Sta) 37 W Main St, Crisfield 21817

Rehoboth Unit Meth Ch (Rehoboth) Box 165, Upper Fairmount 21867

Rock Creek Unit Meth Ch (Chance) P.O.Box 28, Deal Isl 21821

St Charles Unit Meth Ch (Rt 353, Chance) Rt 3 Box 316, Princess Anne 21853

St James Unit Meth Ch, Rt 413, Westover 21871

St Johns Unit Meth Ch, P.O.Box 28, Deal Isl 21821

St Mark Unit Meth Ch, Rt 2 Perry Hawkin Rd, Princess Anne 21853

St Paul Unit Meth Ch (Mt Vernon) Rt 1 Box 144, Princess Anne 21853

St Paul's Unit Meth Ch (Wenona) P.O.Box 28, Deal Isl 21821

St Peter's Unit Meth Ch, Box 62, Oriole 21848

St Stephen's Unit Meth Ch (Monie) Box 62, Oriole 21853

Shiloh Unit Meth Ch, N 4th St, Crisfield 21817

Somerset Unit Meth Ch, Dames Quarter 21820
Union Asbury Unit Meth Ch, Rt 1 Box 231A, Crisfield 21817
Union Unit Meth Ch, Tylerton 21866
Waters Chapel Unit Meth Ch (Kingston) Rt 1 Box 336, Eden 21822

Talbot   Asbury Unit Meth Ch (18 S Higgins) 420 Dover St, Easton 21601
Asbury Unit Meth Ch, Wittman 21676
Bozman Unit Meth Ch, Bozman 21612
Claiborne Unit Meth Ch, Claiborne 21624
Deshields Unit Meth Ch (Copperville) 420 Dover St, Easton
   21601
Faith Chapel Unit Meth Ch (Bruceville) P.O.Box 46, Trappe
   21673
John Wesley Unit Meth Ch (Chapel Rd) 420 Dover St, Easton
   21601
John Wesley Unit Meth Ch, McDaniel 21647
McGee Unit Meth Ch (Longwoods) 420 Dover St, Easton 21601
Neavitt Unit Meth Ch, Neavitt 21652
Oxford Unit Meth Ch, Morris St, P.O.Box 117, Oxford 21654
Royal Oak Com Unit Meth Ch, P.O.Box 126, Royal Oak 21662
St James Unit Meth Ch, Sherwood 21665
St John's Unit Meth Ch, Rt 33 Box 192, Tilghman 21671
St John's Unit Meth Ch, P.O.Box 162, Wittman 21676
St Luke's Unit Meth Ch, Talbot St, P.O.Box 27, St Michaels
   21663
St Mark's Unit Meth Ch (Oxford Rd) 522 Trippe Ave, Easton
   21601
St Paul Unit Meth Ch, Royal Oak 21662
Scott's Unit Meth Ch, 150 Main St, Trappe 21673
Sherwood Unit Meth Ch, Sherwood 21665
Staten Chapel Unit Meth Ch, Denton Rd, Easton 21601
Tilghman Unit Meth Ch, Main St, P.O.Box 192, Tilghman 21671
Trappe Unit Meth Ch, E Maple St, P.O.Box 46, Trappe 21673
Union Unit Meth Ch (Fremont & Railway Ave) 210 Talbot St, St
   Michaels 21663
Water Unit Meth Ch, Banks & Market Sts, P.O.Box 125, Oxford
   21654
Williamsburg Unit Meth Ch, Williamsburg 21643
Wye Mills Unit Meth Ch, Wye Mills 21679

Washington   Asbury Unit Meth Ch, 155 N Jonathan St, Hagerstown 21740
Benevola Unit Meth Ch, Benevola Church Rd, Rt 1 Box 1,
   Boonsboro 21713
Bethel Unit Meth Ch, Rt 62 Box 37, Chewsville 21721
Bethel Unit Meth Ch, Box B, Rohrersville 21779
Emmanuel Unit Meth Ch (Summit Ave & Howard St) 812 Summit Ave
   Hagerstown 21740
Grace Unit Meth Ch (Church & Winter Sts) 712 W Church St,
   Hagerstown 21740
Hancock Unit Meth Ch (Main St & Methodist Ave) 168 W Main St,
   Hancock 21750
John Wesley Unit Meth Ch, 129 N Potomac St, Hagerstown 21740
Mt Bethel Unit Meth Ch (Foxville Rd) 14532 Stottlemyer Rd,
   Smithsburg 21783

Methodist

Mt Carmel Unit Meth Ch, Rt 1 Box 4, Big Pool 21711
Mt Carmel Unit Meth Ch, Rt 67, Boonsboro 21713
Mt Lena Unit Meth Ch, Rt 1 Box 1, Boonsboro 21713
Mt Nebo Unit Meth Ch, 134 S Main St, Boonsboro 21713
Mt Zion Unit Meth Ch (Rt 63 Cearfoss) 1142 Luther Dr,
 H gerstown 21740
Mt Zion Unit Meth Ch, Mt Zion Rd, Smithsburg 21783
Otterbein Unit Meth Ch, 108 E Franklin St, Hagerstown 21740
Parkhead Unit Meth Ch, Rt 1 Box 4, Big Pool 21711
Rehoboth Unit Meth Ch, 30 E Salisbury St, Williamsport 21795
St Andrew's Unit Meth Ch, 1020 Maryland Ave, Hagerstown 21740
St Matthew's Unit Meth Ch (Franklin & High Sts) 505 W Franklin
 St, Hagerstown 21740
St Paul Unit Meth Ch, Rt 1 Box 4, Big Pool 21711
St Paul Unit Meth Ch, 51 S Main St, P.O.Box 205, Smithsburg
 21783
Salem Unit Meth Ch, 16 S Main St, Keedysville 21756
Shiloh Unit Meth Ch, 111 Jackson Dr, Williamsport 21795
Tolson Chapel Unit Meth Ch, Sharpsburg 21782
Washington Square Unit Meth Ch, 538 Washington Ave, Hagerstown
 21740
Williamsport Unit Meth Ch, 25 E Church St, Williamsport 21795

Wicomico   Aaron Chapel Unit Meth Ch, Sharptown 21861
Asbury Unit Meth Ch (Mt Vernon) Box 123, Allen 21810
Asbury Unit Meth Ch, 1401 Camden Ave, Box 463, Salisbury 21801
Asbury Unit Meth Ch, 601 Main St, Sharptown 21861
Ayres Unit Meth Ch (Delaware Rd) Main St, Pittsville 21850
Bethel Unit Meth Ch, Walston's Switch, Box 88, Parsonsburg
 21849
Bethesda Unit Meth Ch, 406 N Division St, Salisbury 21801
Bishop's Memorial Unit Meth Ch, Parsonsburg 21849
Bivalve Unit Meth Ch, Main St, P.O.Box 111, Nanticoke 21840
Centennial Unit Meth Ch, P.O.Box D, Nanticoke 21840
Charity Unit Meth Ch, Jersey & Nlr M Rds, Box 331, Hebron
 21830
Christ Unit Meth Ch, Phillip Morris Dr, Rt 3, Salisbury 21801
Ebenezer Unit Meth Ch, Rt 1 Box 78, Hebron 21830
Eden Unit Meth Ch, Main St, Pittsville 21850
Elzey Unit Meth Ch (Jesterville) Box 463, Salisbury 21801
Emmanuel Unit Meth Ch, Main St, Box 126, Mardela Springs 21837
First Unit Meth Ch, Rt 1 Box 78, Hebron 21830
Freedman's Meth Ch, Tyaskin Wetipquin Rd, Tyaskin 21865
Friendship Unit Meth Ch, 372 Tourmaline Dr, Hebron 21830
Friendship Unit Meth Ch, Friendship Rd, P.O.Box 8, Powellville
 21852
Galestown Unit Meth Ch (Galestown) Box 203, Sharptown 21861
Grace Unit Meth Ch, Main St, Pittsville 21850
Grace Unit Meth Ch, Anne & Church Sts, Salisbury 21801
Jerusalem Unit Meth Ch, Box 88, Parsonsburg 21849
John Wesley Unit Meth Ch (Mt Vernon) Box 123, Allen 21810
John Wesley Unit Meth Ch (Athol Rd) Rt 2 Box 136, Mardela
 Springs 21837

CHURCH ADDRESSES

John Wesley Unit Meth Ch, P.O.Box D, Nanticoke 21840
Mt Calvary Unit Meth Ch, S Division St Ext, P.O.Box 417,
  Fruitland 21826
Mt Hermon Unit Meth Ch, Rt 7 Box 66, Salisbury 21801
Mt Hermon Unit Meth Ch, Box 203, Sharptown 21861
Mt Nebo Unit Meth Ch, Rt 2 Box 136, Mardela Springs 21837
Mt Pleasant Unit Meth Ch (Athol Rd) Box 126, Mardela Springs
  21837
Mt Pleasant Unit Meth Ch, Willards 21874
Mt Vernon Unit Meth Ch, Box 203, Sharptown 21861
Mt Zion Unit Meth Ch, Quantico 21856
Nanticoke Unit Meth Ch, Main St, P.O.Box 111, Nanticoke 21840
Nelson Memorial Unit Meth Ch, Main & Church Sts, Box 331,
  Hebron 21830
Powellville Unit Meth Ch, P.O.Box 8, Powellville 21852
Riverside Meth Ch, 608 Riverside Dr, Salisbury 21801
Riverton Unit Meth Ch (Riverton) 601 Main St, Sharptown 21861
St Andrews Unit Meth Ch, P.O.Box D, Nanticoke 21840
St Andrews Unit Meth Ch, 400 E Vine St, Salisbury 21801
St John's Unit Meth Ch, Main St, Box 236, Fruitland 21826
St Luke Unit Meth Ch, 372 Tourmaline Dr, Hebron 21830
St Mark Unit Meth Ch (nr Princess Anne) Rt 2 Box 332A, Berlin
  21811
St Paul's Unit Meth Ch, Walnut & Howard Sts, Box 331, Hebron
  21830
Samuel Wesley Unit Meth Ch, P.O.Box D, Nanticoke 21840
Showell Unit Meth Ch, Bethel Rd, Box 218A, Willards 21874
Siloam Unit Meth Ch, Box 123, Allen 21810
Snethen Unit Meth Ch, Box 126, Mardela Springs 21837
Trinity Unit Meth Ch, N Division & Broad Sts, Salisbury 21801
Tyaskin Unit Meth Ch, Tyaskin 21865
Union Unit Meth Ch, Pine & Maryland, Box 236, Fruitland 21826
Washington Unit Meth Ch (Shad Pt) Box 123, Allen 21810
Wesley Temple Unit Meth Ch (West Rd) Rt 2 Box 182, Salisbury
  21801
Wheatley's Unit Meth Ch (nr Galestown) Box 203, Sharptown
  21861
Zion Unit Meth Ch, Zion & Zion Church Rds, Box 88, Parsonsburg
  21849
Zion Unit Meth Ch, Zion Rd, Salisbury 21801
Zion Unit Meth Ch, Cooper Mill Rd, Sharptown 21861
Zion Unit Meth Ch (Sandomingo) Rt 2 Box 136, Mardela Springs
  21837

Worcester   Atlantic Unit Meth Ch, Balto Ave & 4th St, P.O.box 88, Ocean
  City 21842
Bates Memorial Unit Meth Ch (Market & Washington Sts) 116 N
  Washington St, Snow Hill 21863
Bethany Unit Meth Ch, Snug Harbor Rd & Rt 611, Berlin 21811
Bethany Unit Meth Ch (Sinepunxent) P.O.Box 36, Newark 21841
Bethany Unit Meth Ch (2nd & Market Sts) 200 Walnut St,
  Pocomoke City 21851
Bishopville Meth Ch, Main St, Bishopville 21813

Bowen Unit Meth Ch, Main St, P.O.Box 36, Newark 21841
Collins Temple Ch, Castle Hill Rd, Snow Hill 21863
Cool Springs Unit Meth Ch, P.O.Box 2, Girdletree 21829
Curtis Unit Meth Ch, Bishopville 21813
Ebenezer Unit Meth Ch, 105 S Collins St, Snow Hill 21863
Friendship Unit Meth Ch, 18 S Main St, Berlin 21811
Friendship Unit Meth Ch, 107 S Collins St, Snow Hill 21863
Girdletree Unit Meth Ch, Rt 1 Box 22, Girdletree 21829
Hutt's Memorial Unit Meth Ch, 107 S Collins St, Snow Hill
    21863
John Wesley Unit Meth Ch (Cottage Grove) Rt 2 Box 332A, Berlin
    21811
Mt Olive Unit Meth Ch (nr Snow Hill) 116 N Washington St, Snow
    Hill 21863
Mt Wesley Unit Meth Ch, P.O.Box 2, Girdletree 21829
Mt Zion Unit Meth Ch, 407 Oxford St, Pocomoke City 21851
New Bethel Unit Meth Ch, 111 Branch St, Berlin 21811
New Hope Unit Meth Ch, New Hope Rd, Box 6, Whaleysville 21872
Ocean City Unit Meth Ch, P.O.Box 88, Ocean City 21842
Ocean Pines Unit Meth Ch (nr Berlin) P.O.Box 306, Berlin 21811
Porterville Unit Meth Ch (2 mi e Stockton) Rt 1 Box 22,
    Girdletree 21829
Pullet's Unit Meth Ch, Rt 1 Box 138A, Whaleysville 21872
Remson Unit Meth Ch (5 mi s Stockton) Rt 1 Box 22, Girdletree
    21829
St James Unit Meth Ch (7 mi s) 407 Oxford St, Pocomoke City
    21851
St John's Unit Meth Ch (Sinepunxent Rd) 111 Branch St, Berlin
    21811
St Matthew Unit Meth Ch (Box Iron) P.O.Box 2, Girdletree 21829
St Paul's Unit Meth Ch (Flower St) 111 Branch St, Berlin 21811
St Paul's Unit Meth Ch (Shiloh nr Pocomoke) 115 N Delano Ave,
    Salisbury 21801
Salem Unit Meth Ch (2nd & Walnut Sts) 200 Walnut St, Pocomoke
    City 21851
Shiloh Meth Ch, Johnsons Neck Rd, Pocomoke City 21851
Stevenson Unit Meth Ch, 123 N Main St, Berlin 21811
Taylorville Unit Meth Ch, P.O.Box 88, Ocean City 21842
Trinity Unit Meth Ch, Main St, P.O.Box 36, Newark 21841
Trinity Unit Meth Ch (Clocke St Rd) 407 Oxford St, Pocomoke
    City 21851
Wesley Unit Meth Ch, Stockton 21864
Whaleysville Unit Meth Ch, Box 6, Whaleysville 21872
Whatcoat Unit Meth Ch (Federal & Washington Sts) 102 W Federal
    St, Snow Hill 21863
Wilson Unit Meth Ch, Bethel Rd, Box 218A, Willards 21874
Zion Unit Meth Ch, Bethel Rd, Box 218A, Willards 21874

CHURCH ADDRESSES

Nazarene

Allegany	Frostburg Ch of the Naz, 150 Center St, Frostburg 21532
Anne Arundel	Ch of the Naz, 1309 Bay Ridge Ave, Annapolis 21403
	Glen Burnie Ch of the Naz, Westfield & Midland Rds, Margate 21061
Baltimore	Balto Faith Ch of the Naz, 2033 Frederick Ave, Balto 21228
	Brooklyn Ch of the Naz, 120 Audrey Ave, Balto 21225
	Ch of the Naz Hallmark, 8505 David Ave, Parkville 21234
	Dundalk Ch of the Naz, 1626 Lynch Rd, Dundalk 21222
	Marley Park Ch of the Naz, 7741 Balto Annapolis Blvd, Balto 21225
Caroline	Ch of the Naz, Denton-Greensboro, Denton 21629
Carroll	S Carroll Ch of the Naz, 351 Liberty Rd, Eldersburg 21784
Cecil	Elkton Ch of the Naz, 377 Nottingham Rd, Elkton 21921
	North East Ch of the Naz, 107 Mechanics Valley Rd, North East 21901
	Rising Run ch of the Naz, 2626 Tome Hwy, Rising Sun 21911
Charles	Ch of the Naz, 3409-B White Fir Ct, Waldorf 20601
	Indian Head Ch of the Naz, 35 Raymond Ave, Indian Head 20640
	La Plata Ch of the Naz, La Plata 20646
Dorchester	Ch of the Naz, Hambrooks Blvd, Cambridge 21613
Harford	Ch of the Naz, 1705 conowingo Rd, Bel Air 21014
Howard	Ch of the Naz, 2509 Jonathon Rd, Ellicott City 21043
	First Ch of the Naz, 8801 Rogers Ave, Ellicott City 21043
Kent	Chestertown Ch of the Naz, Chestertown 21620
Prince Georges	College Park Ch of the Naz, 9704 Rhode Island Ave, College Park 20740
St Marys	Hollywood Ch of the Naz, Sotterley Rd, Rt 3 Box 827, Hollywood 20636
Talbot	Ch of the Naz, Hollyday St & Glebe Rd, Easton 21601
Washington	Ch of the Naz, 141 N Edgewood Dr, Hagerstown 21740
Wicomico	Ch of the Naz, 800 Johnson St, Salisbury 21801
Worcester	Pocomoke Ch of the Naz, 1300 Market St, Pocomoke City 21851

Orthodox

Anne Arundel	Hellenic Center, 2647 Riva Rd, Annapolis 21401
	St Constantine & St Helen Greek Orth Ch, 4 Constitution Ave, Annapolis 21401
Baltimore	Cathedral of the Annunciation Greek Orth Ch (Preston St & Maryland Ave) 24 W Preston St, Balto 21201
	Holy Trinity Russian Orth Ch, 1723 E Fairmount Ave, Balto 21231
	Nativity of the Theotokos Antiochian Orth Ch, Lutherville 21093
	St Andrew's Russian Orth Ch, 2028 E Lombard St, Balto 21231
	St Demetrios Greek Orth Ch, 2504 Cub Hill Rd, Balto 21234
	St Nicholas Greek Orth Com Ch, 520 S Ponca St, Balto 21224

Orthodox

	St Mary Antiochian Orth Ch, 18 N Hampton Rd, Timonium 21093
Montgomery	St George Greek Orth Ch, 7701 Bradley Blvd, Bethesda 20817
Prince Georges	St Theodore Greek Orth Ch, 12404 Brandywine Rd, Brandywine 20613
Washington	St Catherine's Eastern Orth Ch, 433 Liberty St, Hagerstown 21740
Wicomico	Greek Orth Com of the Eastern Shore, Mt Hermon Rd & St Alban's Dr, Salisbury 21801
Worcester	St George Greek Orth Ch, 8805 Coastal Hwy, Ocean City 21842

Pentecostal

Allegany	Bethel Pent Holiness Ch, Rt 36 N, Lonaconing 21539
Anne Arundel	Unit Pent Ch of Glen Burnie, 996 Pt Pleasant Rd, Glen Burnie 21061
Balto	Alpha & Omega Pent Ch, 3023 Clifton Ave, Balto 21216
	Alpha & Omega Pent Ch of Amer, 2021 Barclay St, Balto 21218
	Balto Tabernacle Deliverence Center, 1231 E Biddle St, Balto 21202
	Bethel Holy Tabernacle, 1606 Ashland Ave, Balto 21205
	Bethel Pent Ch, 2703 Hilldale Ave, Balto 21215
	Catonsville Pent Holiness Ch, 1928 Frederick Rd, Balto 21228
	Ch of the Living God, 2402 W Fayette St, Balto 21223
	East Balto Deliverance Evening Center, 1001 N Caroline St, Balto 21205
	Ezekiel Pent Ch, 1204 Druid Hill Ave, Balto 21217
	Faith Mission Gospel Tabernacle, 1712 E Madison St, Balto 21205
	Faith Outreach Chapel, 1713 Rittenhouse Ave, Balto 21227
	Faith Temple, 2301 Edmondson Ave, Balto 21223
	First Pent Ch, 301 N Gilmor St, Balto 21223
	First Unit Pent Ch, 200 N Marlyn Ave, Balto 21221
	Gospel Tabernacle of Dundalk, 6601 Cleveland Ave, Balto 21222
	Grace Holy Tabernacle First Born Ch of the Living God, 1329 W Saratoga St, Balto 21223
	Greater Balto Temple Unit Pent Ch, 1014 W 36th St, Balto 21211
	Greater Harvest Pent Ch of Deliverance, 923 W Balto St, Balto 21223
	Holy Faith Ch, 501 N Gilmor St, Balto 21223
	Holy Mt Zion Temple, 1201 N Monroe St, Balto 21217
	Holy Tabernacle of God, 3457 Park Hts Ave, Balto 21215
	Holy Temple Ch of Truth, 900 N Chester St, Balto 21205
	Holy Trinity Ch, 2601 Pennsylvania Ave, Balto 21217
	House of God Ch, 2660 Polk St, Balto 21218
	Israelite Pent Holiness Ch, 1611 W Saratoga St, Balto 21223
	Macedonia Deliverance Ch, 3538 Old York Rd, Balto 21218
	Mt Airy Pent Ch, 1318 N Broadway, Balto 21213
	Mt Calvary Pent Faith, 1204 Eutaw Pl, Balto 21217
	Mt Nebo Holy Ch, 1700 W Balto St, Balto 21223

CHURCH ADDRESSES

Pent Faith Ch, 718 N Fremont Ave, Balto 21217
Pent Holiness Ch, 1116 N Gilmor St, Balto 21217
Pent Holiness Ch, 6000 Loch Raven Blvd, Balto 21239
Pent Unit Holy Ch, 204 N Mount St, Balto 21223
Peoples Pent Ch of Maryland, 2117 E Fayette St, Balto 21231
Prayer Chapel, 1752 N Gay St, Balto 21213
Prayer Mission, 1209 W Fayette St, Balto 21223
St James Alpha Omega Pent Ch, 1432 Hollins St, Balto 21223
St Johns Alpha Omega Pent Ch, 1950 W North Ave, Balto 21217
St Matthews Pent Ch, 3112 W Morth Ave, Balto 21216
Solid Rock Pent Ch, 1354 W North Ave, Balto 21217
Temple of God Ch, 3301 Edgewood St, Balto 21216
True Fellowship Pent Ch of Amer, 4238 Pimlico Rd, Balto 21215
Unit Pent Miracle Center, 2620 Quantico Ave, Balto 21215
Zion Miracle temple, 1940 W Pratt St, Balto 21223
Zion Tabernacle, 4015 Liberty Hts Ave, Balto 21207

Calvert	Bethel Way of the Cross Ch, Cherry Hill Rd, Huntingtown 20639
	Calvert Lighthouse Tabernacle, 40 Clay Hammond Rd, Prince Frederick 20678
Caroline	Greensboro Pent Ch of God, Greensboro 21639
Cecil	New Life Faith Center Ch, 1820 Jacob Tome Hwy, Colora 21917
	Unit Pent Ch, Rt 40, North East 21901
Frederick	Gospel Temple Ch, 46 W J St, Brunswick 21716
Garrett	Unit Pent Ch, Friendsville 21531
Harford	Evangelistic Ch of Deliverance, 463 Franklin St, Havre de Grace 21078
	Upper Room Gospel Tabernacle, Heim Ln, Joppa 21085
Howard	Full Gospel Pent Ch, Westchester Ave, Ellicott City 21043
Kent	Unit Pent Ch, Creamery St, Kennedyville 21645
Queen Annes	Queen Annes First Unit Pent Ch, Church Hill, Centreville 21617
St Marys	First Pent Ch, 313 Midway Dr, Lexington Park 20653
Somerset	Liberty Rock Ch, Crisfield 21817
Washington	Calvary Temple, 350 N Jonathan St, Hagerstown 21740
	Faith Chapel, 38 S Locust St, Hagerstown 21740
	People's Gospel Tabernacle, 543 Security Rd, Hagerstown 21740
Wicomico	Deliverance House of Prayer, Allen Cut-off Rd, Fruitland 21826
Worcester	Refuge Temple, Rt 12, Stockton 21864

Presbyterian

Allegany	Barrelville Presb Ch, Mt Savage 21545
	Faith Presb Ch of Amer, 418 N Centre St, Cumberland 21502
	First Presb Ch of Barton, Box 312, Barton 21521
	First Presb Ch of Cumberland, 11-47 Washington St, Cumberland 21502
	First Presb Ch of Frostburg, 33 Broadway, Frostburg 21532
	First Presb Ch of Lonaconing, E Main St, Lonaconing 21539
	Koinonia Presb Ch, 605 N 3rd St, La Vale 21502
	Southminster Presb Ch, 310 Race St, Cumberland 21502

Presbyterian

Anne Arundel	Christ Our Anchor Unit Presb Ch, 1006 Bayberry Dr, Arnold 21012
	Evan Presb Ch, Ridgely Ave & Wilson Rd, Annapolis 21401
	First Presb Ch of Annapolis, 144 Conduit St, Annapolis 21401
	Glen Burnie Evan Presb Ch, 7855 Cindy Dr, Glen Burnie 21061
	Harundale Presb Ch (Eastway & Guilford Rd) 1020 Eastway, Glen Burnie 21061
	Prince of Peace Presb Ch, 1657 Crofton Pkwy, Crofton 21114
	Severna Park Evan Presb Ch, 138 Ritchie Hwy, Pasadena 21122
	Union of Herald Harbor Presb Ch, Box 272, Crownsville 21032
	Woods Memorial Presb Ch, 611 Balto-Annapolis Blvd, Severna Park 21146
Baltimore	Abbott Memorial Presb Ch, 3426 Bank St, Balto 21224
	Aisquith Presb Ch, 7515 Harford Rd, Balto 21234
	Arlington Presb Ch, 3215 W Belvedere Ave, Balto 21215
	Ashland Presb Ch, 118 Ashland Rd, Cockeysville 21030
	Babcock Memorial Presb Ch, 8240 Loch Raven Blvd, Balto 21204
	Bethel Korean Presb Ch, 11301 Liberty Rd, Randallstown 21133
	Bethel Presb Ch, 4135 Norrisville Rd, White Hall 21161
	Brown Memorial Presb Ch (Charles St & Woodbrook Ln) 6200 N Charles St, Balto 21212
	Brown Memorial Presb Ch (Park & Lafayette Aves) 1316 Park Ave, Balto 21217
	Catonsville Presb Ch (Frederick Rd & Beechwood Aves) 1400 Frederick Rd, Balto 21228
	Central Presb Ch, 7308 York Rd, Balto 21204
	Chapel Hill Presb Ch, 1501 N Rolling Rd, Balto 21228
	Cherry Hill Presb Ch, 819 Cherry Hill Rd, Balto 21225
	Chestnut Grove Presb Ch, Sweet Air Rd, Phoenix 21131
	Crisp Memorial Presb Ch, 301 E Patapsco Ave, Balto 21225
	Cub Hill Bible Presb Ch, 2927 Cub Hill Rd, Balto 21234
	Dickey Memorial Presb Ch, 5112 Wetheredsville Rd, Balto 21207
	Dundalk Presb Ch, Merritt Blvd & Stansbury Rd, Balto 21222
	Emmanuel Presb Ch, 7017 Queen Anne Rd, Balto 21207
	Evan Presb Ch, 3599 E Northern Pkwy, Balto 21206
	Faith Presb Ch, 5400 Loch Raven Blvd, Balto 21239
	First & Franklin Street Presb Ch (Park Ave & Madison St) 808 Park Ave, Balto 21201
	First Presb Ch of Randallstown, 9019 Liberty Rd, Randallstown 21133
	Forest Park Presb Ch, 3805 Fairview Ave, Balto 21216
	Franklinville Presb Ch (Franklinville & Reynolds Rds) 11846 Franklinville Rd, Bradshaw 21021
	Govans Presb Ch, 5828 York Rd, Balto 21212
	Grace Presb Ch, 2604 Banister Rd, Balto 21215
	Grace Ref Presb Ch, 29 Holmehurst Ave, Catonsville 21228
	Hamilton Presb Ch, 5532 Harford Rd, Balto 21214
	Hampden Presb Ch, 37th St & Falls Rd, Balto 21211
	Havenwood Presb Ch, Ridgely & Charmuth Rds, Lutherville 21093
	Hope Presb Ch (Shelbourne & Ten Oaks Rd) 4748 Shelbourne Rd, Balto 21227
	Hughes Memorial Presb Ch, 3008-10 Sparrows Pt Rd, Balto 21219

CHURCH ADDRESSES

Hunting Ridge Presb Ch, Edmondson Ave & Winans Way, Balto
    21229
Inverness Presb Ch, 49 Inverness Ave, Balto 21222
Kenwood Presb Ch, 4601 Fullerton Ave, BalOo 21236
Knox Presb Ch, 1300 N Eden St, Balto 21213
Korean Presb Ch of Balto, Highland Ave & Bank St, Balto 21224
Lakeland Presb Ch, 2926 Hollins Ferry Rd, Balto 21230
Liberty Ref Presb Ch, Liberty Rd, Randallstown 21133
Light Street Presb Ch, 809 Light St, Balto 21230
Loch Raven Village Presb Ch, 1600 White Oak Ave, Balto 21234
Lochearn Presb Ch, 3800 Patterson Ave, Balto 21207
Madison Avenue Presb Ch, 2110 Madison Ave, Balto 21217
Maryland Presb Ch, 1105 Providence Rd, Balto 21204
Merritt Boulevard Presb Ch of Dundalk, 1973 Merritt Blvd,
    Balto 21222
Mission to N Amer, 231-A W Timonium Rd, Timonium 21093
Montebello Presb Ch, 1910 E 30th St, Balto 21218
Mt Paran Presb Ch, 10308 Liberty Rd, Randallstown 21133
Northminster Presb Ch, 705 Main St, P.O.Box 306, Reisterstown
    21136
Perry Hall Presb Ch, 8848 Belair Rd, Balto 21236
Presb Synod of the Piedmont, 6600 York Rd, Suite 205A, Balto
    21212
Presbytery of Balto, 5400 Loch Raven Blvd, Balto 21239
Ref Presb Ch, Ashland & Wright Aves, Armistead Gardens, Balto
    21205
Relay Presb Ch, 5025 Cedar Ave, Balto 21227
Ridgley Street Presb Ch, 941 Ridgley St, Balto 21230
Roland Park Presb Ch, 4801 Roland Ave, Balto 21210
Second Presb Ch, St Paul St & Stratford Rd, Balto 21218
Timonium PCA Presb Ch, 303 W Timonium Rd, Balto 21093
Tollgate Ref Presb Ch, 12 S Tollgate Rd, Owings Mills 21117
Towson Presb Ch, Chesapeake & Highland Aves, Balto 21204
Trinity Presb Ch, 3200 Walbrook Ave, Balto 21216
Valley Presb Ch, W Joppa Rd & The Beltway, Lutherville 21093
Waverly Presb Ch, Old York Rd & 34th St, Balto 21218
Westminster Presb Ch, 515 W Fayette St, Balto 21201

Carroll   First Presb Ch, 65 Washington Rd, Westminster 21157
           Kirkridge Assoc Ref Presb Ch, 2740 Old Fort Schoolhouse Rd,
               Manchester 21102
           New Windsor Assoc Ref Presb Ch, Church & High Sts, New Windso:
               21776
           Piney Creek Assoc Ref Presb Ch, Harney Rd, Taneytown 21787
           Springfield Presb Ch, 7300 Spout Hill Rd, Sykesville 21784
           Taneytown Presb Ch, 36 York St, Box 101, Taneytown 21787
Cecil   Evan Presb Ch, Singerly Rd, Elkton 21921
           West Nottingham Unit Presb Ch, Colora 21917
Charles   Good Samaritan Presb Ch, Rt 5 Box 925, Waldorf 20601
District of Natl Capital Union Presbytery, 4125 Nebraska Ave NW,
  Columbia   Washington DC 20016
Frederick Emmitsburg Presb Ch, Emmitsburg 21727
           Faith Ref Presb Ch, 8158 Yellow Springs Rd, Frederick 21701

Presbyterian

Frederick Presb Ch, 115 W Second St, Frederick 21701

Harford   Christ Our King Presb Ch (Emmorton & Lexington Rds) 10 Lexington Rd, Bel Air 21014

Churchville Presb Ch, P.O.Box 8, Churchville 21028

Deer Creek Harmony Presb Ch, Rt 161, Darlington 21034

Fallston Presb Ch, 600 Fallston Rd, Box 54, Fallston 21047

First Presb Ch (Main St & Broadway) 226 N Main St, Bel Air 21014

Good Shepherd Unit Presb Ch, Joppa Farm Rd & Towne Center Dr, P.O.Box 57, Joppa 21085

Grove Presb Ch, 50 E Bel Air Ave, Aberdeen 21001

Havre de Grace Presb Ch, 551 Franklin St, Havre de Grace 21078

Highland Presb Ch, 701 Highland Rd, Street 21154

New Covenant Presb Ch, 6 N Main St, Bel Air 21014

New Hope Presb Ch, Box 934, Edgewood 21040

Slate Ridge Presb Ch, Cardiff 21024

Howard   Bethel Korean Presb Ch, 9802 Pushcart Way, Columbia 21045

Chapelgate Presb Ch, 3291 N St Johns Ln, Ellicott City 21043

Christ Memorial Presb Ch, 6410 Amherst Ave, Columbia 21046

First Presb Ch of Howard Co (Rt 108 nr Rt 29) 9325 Old Annapolis Rd, Columbia 21045

Granite Presb Ch, 10637 Old Court Rd, Woodstock 21163

Mt Hebron Presb Ch (Mt Hebron Dr & Calvin Circle) 2330 Mt Hebron Dr, Ellicott City 21043

St John Unit Presb Ch, 10431 Twin Rivers Rd, Columbia 21044

Montgomery   Bethesda Presb Ch, 7611 Clarendon Rd, Bethesda 20814

Boyds Presb Ch, 19901 White Ground Rd, Boyds 20841

Bradley Hills Presb Ch, 6601 Bradley Blvd, Bethesda 20817

Chevy Chase Presb Ch, 1 Chevy Chase Circle, Washington DC 20015

Colesville Unit Presb Ch, 12800 New Hampshire Ave, Silver Spring 20904

Covenant Orth Presb Ch, 4515 Sandy Spring Rd, Burtonsville 20866

Darnestown Presb Ch, 15120 Turkey Foot Rd, Gaithersburg 20878

Fourth Presb Ch, 5500 River Rd, Bethesda 20816

Gaithersburg Presb Ch, 16700 S Frederick Ave, Gaithersburg 20877

Geneva Unit Presb Ch, 11931 Seven Locks Rd, Rockvile 20854

Gunton-Temple Memorial Presb Ch, 7009 Wilson Ln, Bethesda 20817

Harmon Presb Ch, 7801 Persimmon Tree Ln, Bethesda 20817

Korean Presb Ch, 1905 Ventura Ave, Wheaton 20902

Neelsville Presb Ch, 20701 Frederick Rd, Germantown 20874

Northwood Presb Ch, 1200 University Blvd W, Silver Spring 20902

Poolesville Presb Ch, Box 68, Pooleville 20837

Potomac Unit Presb Ch, 10301 River Rd, Potomac 20854

St Mark Unit Presb Ch, 10701 Old Georgetown Rd, Rockville 20852

St Matthew Unit Presb Ch, Georgia Ave & Bel Pre Rd, Wheaton 20906

CHURCH ADDRESSES

Silver Spring Presb Ch, 580 University Blvd E, Silver Spring 20901
Takoma Park Presb Ch, Maple & Tulip Aves, Takoma Park 20912
Unit Korean Presb Ch, 7009 Wilson Ln, Bethesda 20817
Warner Memorial Presb Ch, 10123 Connecticut Ave, Kensington 20895
Wheaton Presb Ch, Newport Mill Rd & Church Ln, Wheaton 20902

Prince Georges
Adelphi Unit Presb Ch, 9401 Riggs Rd, Adelphi 20783
Beltsville Unit Presb Ch, 4216 Powder Mill Rd, Beltsville 20705
Berwyn Unit Presb Ch, 6301 Greenbelt Rd, Berwyn Hts 20740
Camp Springs Presb Ch, 4401 Brinkley Rd, Temple Hills 20748
Chris Com Presb Ch, 3120 Belair Dr, Bowie 20715
Clinton Unit Presb Ch, 9901 Brandywine Rd, Clinton 20735
Cornerstone Com Bap-Presb Ch, 3636 Dixon St, Temple Hills 20748
District Heights Presb Ch, 6330 Gateway Blvd, District Hts 20747
Eastminster Presb Ch, 5601 Randolph St, Hyattsville 20784
First Korean Presb Ch of Maryland, 6513 Queens Chapel Rd, Hyattsville 20782
Grace Unit Presb Ch, 5924 Princess Garden Pkwy, Lanham 20801
Hope Presb Ch, 1100 Enterprise Rd, Mitchellville 20716
Hyattsville Presb Ch, 3120 Nicholson St, Hyattsville 20782
Laurel Presb Ch, 7610 Sandy Spring Rd, Laurel 20707
Maryland Korean Presb Ch, 6605 Mallery Dr, Lanham 20801
Oaklands Unit Presb Ch, 14301 Laurel-Bowie Rd, Laurel 20708
Riverdale Unit Presb Ch, 6513 Queens Chapel Rd, Hyattsville 20782
St Paul's Unit Presb Ch, 41st Ave & Parkwood St, Brentwood 20722
Southminster Presb Ch, 7801 Livingston Rd, Oxon Hill 20745
Unit Parish of Bowie, 16011 Pennant Ln, Bowie, 20716
Wallace Memorial Unit Presb Ch, 7201 16th Pl, Hyattsville 20783

St Marys
First Presb Ch, 235 Town Creek Dr, Lexington Park 20653
First Presb Ch of St Mary's Co, P.O.Box 75, California 20619

Somerset
Rehobeth Presb Ch, Rt 1 Box 184, Rehobeth 21857

Talbot
Presb Ch, 617 N Washington St, Easton 21601

Washington
Covenant Presb Ch, 250 Green Hill Dr, Hagerstown 21740
Grace Presb Ch, Locker Mansion, Hancock 21750
Hagerstown Presb Ch, 20 S Prospect St, Hagerstown 21740
Mt Olivet Presb Ch, Exline Rd, Hancock 21750

Wicomico
Wicomico Presb Ch, 129 Broad St, Salisbury 21801

Worcester
First Presb Ch, 13th St & Phila Ave, Ocean City 21842
Buckingham Presb Ch, 20 S Main St, Berlin 21811
Makemie Memorial Presb Ch, 115 Franklin St, Snow Hill 21863

Reformed

Baltimore	Christ Ref Ch, 1718 N Fulton Ave, Balto
	Faith Ref Ch, 130 S Patterson Park Ave, Balto
	First Ref Ch, 822 N Calvert St, Balto
	Grace Ref Ch, 1218 Hanover St, Balto
	St Luke's Ref Ch, 1811 Penrose Ave, Balto
	St Mark's Ref Ch, 2811 E Preston St, Balto
	St Paul's Eng Ref Ch, 410 N Calhoun St, Balto
	St Stephen's Ref Ch, 306 E 23rd St, Balto
	Third Ref Ch, 822 N Eutaw St, Balto
	Trinity Ref Ch, 342 W 36th St, Balto
Caroline	St Paul's Ref Ch, Ridgely
Carroll	Emmanuel Ref Ch, Union Bridge
	Jerusalem Ref Ch, Westminster
	Keysville Ref Ch, Taneytown
	St Mary's Ref Ch, RFD 1, Westminster
	St Matthew's Ref Ch, Westminster
	St Paul's Ref Ch, Union Bridge
	St Paul's Ref Ch, Westminster
Frederick	Braddock Ref Ch, Frederick
	Evan Ref Ch, Burkittsville
	First Ref Ch, Brunswick
	Grace Ref Ch, Knoxville
	Grace Trinity Ref Ch, RD 1, Frederick
	St John Ref Ch, Adamstown
	St Paul's Ref Ch, RFD 7, Frederick
	St Paul's Ref Ch, Ladiesburg
	St Stephen's Ref Ch, Sabillasville
	Trinity Ref Ch, Thurmont
	Union Chapel Ref Ch, RD 1, Frederick
	Zion Ref Ch, RFD 7, Frederick
Washington	Christ Ref Ch, Funkstown
	Christ Ref Ch, 133 W Washington St, Hagerstown
	Christ Ref Ch, Sharpsburg
	Mt Moriah Ref Ch, Keedysville
	Ref Ch, 441 Simmit Ave, Hagerstown

Salvation Army

Allegany	Salva Army, 701 E First St, Cumberland 21502
	Salva Army, P.O.Box 2436, Cumberland 21502-0282
Anne Arundel	Salva Army, 351 Hilltop Ln, Annapolis 21403
Baltimore	Salva Army (Hampden) Box 4742, Balto 21211
	Salva Army (Maryland & Northern West Virginia) 2641 Maryland Ave, Balto 21218
	Salva Army (Patterson Park) 519 S Ellwood Ave, Balto 21224
	Salva Army (South) Box 6338, Balto 21230
	Salva Army (Temple) P.O.Box 4323, Balto 21223-2331
Dorchester	Salva Army, 200 Washington St, Cambridge 21613
Frederick	Salva Army, 223 W 5th St, Frederick 21701

CHURCH ADDRESSES

	Salva Army, Box 1003, Frederick 21701
Harford	Salva Army, Box 309, Havre de Grace 21078-0309
	Salva Army, Weber St Ext, Havre de Grace 21078
Washington	Salva Army, P.O.Box 747, Hagerstown 21741
	Salva Army, 534 W Franklin St, Hagerstown 21740
Wicomico	Salva Army, 407 Oak St, Salisbury 21801
New York	Salva Army & Research Center (Archives) 145 W 15th St, New York NY 10011

Seventh Day Adventist

Allegany	7th Day Adv Ch, 800 Hill Top Dr, Cumberland 21502
	Frostburg 7th Day Adv Ch, 82 W College Ave, Frostburg 21532
Anne Arundel	Annapolis 7th day Adv Ch, Bell Branch Rd, Gambrills 21054
	Beacon Light 7th Day Adv Ch, 1903 Drew St, P.O.Box 307, Annapolis 21401
	Bell Branch Road 7th Day Adv Ch, 2365 Bell Branch Rd, Gambrills 21054
	Glen Burnie 7th Day Adv Ch, 508 Aquahart Rd, Glen Burnie 21061
	Korean 7th Day Adv Ch, 510 Aquahart Rd, Glen Burnie 21061
	Korean 7th Day Adv Ch, Rt 4 Box 200, Pasadena 21122
	Linthicum 7th Day Adv Ch, 951 Andover Rd, Linthicum 21090
	Pasadena 7th Day Adv Ch, Rt 4 Box 200, Pasadena 21122
Baltimore	Berea Temple 7th Day Adv Ch, 1901 W Madison Ave, Balto 21217
	Brooklyn 7th Day Adv Ch, 4th & Annabel Sts, Balto 21225
	Cherry Hill 7th Day Adv Ch, 2802 Joplea Ave, Balto 21225
	Dundalk 7th Day Adv Ch, 210 Balto Ave, Balto 21222
	Edmondson Heights 7th Day Adv Ch, 810 Walnut Ave, Balto 21229
	Essex 7th Day Adv Ch, 624 Eastern Ave, Balto 21221
	First 7th Day Adv Ch, 5110 Frederick Ave, Balto 21229
	First 7th Day Adv Ch, 305 Ingleside Ave, Balto 21228
	Liberty Heights 7th Day Adv Ch, 5020 Gwynn Oak Ave, Balto 21207
	Lutherville 7th Day Adv Ch, 2123 W Joppa Rd, Lutherville 21093
	Maranatha 7th Day Adv Ch, 2224 Harford Rd, Balto 21218
	Northwest 7th Day Adv Ch, 5113 Old Court Rd, Randallstown 21133
	Parkville-Essex 7th Day Adv Ch, 3033 Oak Forest Dr, Balto 21234
	Reisterstown 7th Day Adv Ch, Beverly Rd & Berryman's Ln, Reisterstown 21136
	Sharon 7th Day Adv Ch, 1100 N Calvert St, Balto 21201
	Towson 7th Day Adv Ch, 2123 W Joppa Rd, Lutherville 21204
Calvert	Emmanuel 7th Day Adv Ch, Dares Beach Rd, Prince Frederick 20678
	Prince Frederick 7th Day Adv Ch, Broome Isl Rd, Prince Frederick 20678
	Regional 7th Day Adv Ch, Dares Beach Rd, Prince Frederick 20678

Seventh Day Adventist

Caroline	Federalsburg 7th Day Adv Ch, Mowberry Creek Rd, Federalsburg 21632
Carroll	7th Day Adv Ch, 320 Crest Ln, Westminster 21157
	Sykesville 7th Day Adv Ch, Spout Hill Rd, Sykesville 21784
	Westminster 7th Day Adv Ch, 320 Crest Ln, Westminster 21157
Cecil	Blythedale 7th Day Adv Ch, 40 Homehurst Ln, Elkton 21921
	Perryville 7th Day Adv Ch, Rt 1 Box 50, Blythedale 21903
	Providence 7th Day Adv Ch, 3085 Singerly Rd, Elkton 21921
	Rising Sun 7th Day Adv Ch, Rt 2 Walnut St, Rising Sun 21911
Charles	Pisgah 7th Day Adv Ch, Bumpy Oak Rd, Indian Head 20640
	Waldorf 7th Day Adv Ch, Rt 2 Berry Rd, Waldorf 20601
Dorchester	Cambridge 7th Day Adv Ch, Rt 50 Bonnie Brook, Cambridge 21613
	Faith 7th Day Adv Ch, 1011 Phillips St, Cambridge 21613
	Regional 7th day Adv Ch, Center & Robbins Sts, Bonnie Brook, Cambridge 21613
	7th Day Adv Ch, Rt 50, Cambridge 21613
Frederick	Frederick 7th Day Adv Ch, 80 Adventist Dr, Frederick 21701
	Thurmont 7th day Adv Ch, Hwy 15, Thurmont 21788
Garrett	Mountain Top 7th Day Adv Ch, Rt 219 N, Oakland 21550
Harford	Norrisville 7th Day Adv Ch, 2015 Channel Rd, Pylesville 21132
	Wilna 7th day Adv Ch, 1010 Old Joppa Rd, Joppa 21085
Howard	Atholton 7th day Adv Ch, 6520 Martin Rd, ColOmbia 21044
	Chesapeake Conference 7th Day Adv Churches of N Amer, 6600 Martin Rd, Columbia 21044
	Columbia Union Conference 7th Day Adv Churches of N Amer, 5427 Twin Knolls Rd, Columbia 21045
	Tridelphia 7th Day Adv Ch, 12950 Brighton Dam Rd, Clarksville 21029
Kent	Chestertown 7th Day Adv Ch, Kent Circle, Chestertown 21620
	Rock Hall 7th Day Adv Ch, Sharp & Judefind Aves, Rock Hall 21661
Montgomery	Burnt Mills 7th Day Adv Ch, 10915 Lockwood Dr, Silver Spring 20901
	Damascus 7th Day Adv Ch, 9600 Main St, Damascus 20872
	Korean 7th Day Adv Ch, 419 E Indian Spring Dr, Silver Spring 20901
	Korean 7th Day Adv Ch, Good Hope & Spencerville Rds, Spencerville 20868
	Laurel 7th Day Adv Ch, 15121 McKnew Rd, Burtonsville 20866
	Olney 7th day Adv Ch, 4100 Olney-Laytonsville Rd, Olney 20832
	Regional 7th Day Adv Ch, 18800 New Hampshire Ave, Brinklow 20862
	Rockville 7th Day Adv Ch, 727 W Montgomery Ave, Rockville 20850
	Silgo 7th Day Adv Ch, Carroll & Flower Aves, Takoma Park 20912
	Silver Spring 7th Day Adv Ch, 8900 Colesville Rd, Silver Spring 20910
	Spanish 7th day Adv Ch, Takoma Park 20912
	Spencerville 7th Day Adv Ch, 16325 New Hampshire Ave, Spencerville 20868
	Takoma Park 7th Day Adv Ch, 6951 Carroll Ave, Takoma Park 20912

CHURCH ADDRESSES

Washington Adv Hospital Chapel, 7600 Carroll Ave, Takoma Park 20912

Wheaton 7th Day Adv Ch, 3132 Bel Pre Rd, Wheaton 20906

Prince Georges	Beltsville 7th Day Adv Ch, 4200 Ammendale Rd, Beltsville 20705
	Brazilian 7th Day Adv Ch, 2601 Powder Mill Rd, Adelphi 20783
	Clinton 7th Day Adv Ch, Brandywine Rd, Clinton 20735
	Hyattsville 7th Day Adv Ch, 4905 42nd Pl, Hyattsville 20781
	Regional 7th Day Adv Ch, Accokeek 20607
	Regional 7th Day Adv Ch, 4105 54th St, Bladensburg 20710
	Regional 7th Day Adv Ch, 5909 Riggs Rd, Hyattsville 20783
	Seabrook 7th Day Adv Ch, 8900 Good Luck Rd, Seabrook 20706
Queen Annes	Grasonville 7th Day Adv Ch, Rt 1, Grasonville 21638
St Marys	Patuxent 7th Day Adv Ch, Whirlwind Rd & Rt 5, Leonardtown 20650
Washington	Hagerstown 7th Day Adv Ch, Dual Hwy 40 E, Hagerstown 21740
	Highland View Academy 7th Day Adv Ch, Rt 1 Box 286, Hagerstown 21740
	Mountain Top 7th day Adv Ch, Rt 219 N, Mountain Lake Park, Mountain Top 21550
	7th Day Adv Ch of Hagerstown, 709 Dual Hwy, Hagerstown 21740
	Willow Brook 7th Day Adv Ch, Rt 66, Boonsboro 21713
Wicomico	Park 7th Day Adv Ch, Hobbs Rd, Salisbury 21801
	Regional 7th day Adv Ch, Jersey Rd, Salisbury 21801
	Salisbury 7th Day Adv Ch, Hwy 50 & Hobbs Rd, Salisbury 21801
Worcester	Pocomoke 7th Day Adv Ch, Hwy 113 & 13, Pocomoke City 21851

Unitarian Universalist

Anne Arundel	Unitar Ch of Anne Arundel Co, 333 Dubois Rd, Annapolis 21401
Baltimore	Balto Unit Fellowship, c/o Rev Fred Rutledge, 1208 Argonne Dr, Balto 21218
	First Unitar Ch, 1 W Hamilton St, Balto 21201
	Towson Unitar Univ Ch, 1710 Dulaney Valley Rd, Lutherville 21093
	Unitar Univ Ch of Balto, Charles & Franklin Sts, Balto 21201
Frederick	Unitar Fellowship, P.O.Box 1032, Frederick 21701
Harford	Unitar Univ Fellowship of Harford Co, 210 Lee Way, Bel Air 21014
Howard	Unitar Univ Soc of Howard Co, P.O.box 849, Columbia 21044
Montgomery	Cedar Lane Unitar Ch, 9601 Cedar Ln, Bethesda 20814
	River Road Unitar Ch, 6301 River Rd, Bethesda 20817
	Seneca Valley Unitar Univ Fellowship (Seneca Valley High Sch) Box 2311, Gaithersburg 20879
	Unitar Ch, 501 Mannakee St, Rockville 20850
	Unitar Univ Ch, 10309 New Hampshire Ave, Silver Spring 20903
Prince Georges	Davies Memorial Unitar Ch, 7400 Temple Hill Rd, Camp Springs 20748
	Paint Branch Unitar Ch, 3215 Powder Mill Rd, Adelphi 20783
Talbot	Unitar Fellowship, P.O.Box 1162, Easton 21601

Unitarian Universalist

Washington   Unitar Univ Ch, 465 N Potomac St, Hagerstown 21740
                Unitar Univ Ch of Hagerstown, P.O.Box 1268, Hagerstown 21740
Wicomico   Unitar Fellowship, 325 Snow Hill Rd, Salisbury 21801

United Church of Christ

Allegany   Redeemer UCC, Ellerslie 21529
                St Marks UCC, 221 E Harrison St, Cumberland 21502
                St Matthews UCC, 12400 Bowling St SW, Cumberland 21502
                Salem UCC, 78 Broadway, Frostburg 21532
                Zion UCC, 405 N Mechanic St, Cumberland 21502
                Zion UCC, 160 E Main St, Frostburg 21532
Anne Arundel Annapolis UCC, 8 Carvel Circle, Edgewater 21037
Baltimore   Bethany UCC (Woodlawn) 1928 Gwynn Oak Ave, Balto 21207
                Bethel UCC, 3033 E Balto St, Balto 21224
                Catonsville Immanuel UCC, 1905 Edmondson Ave, Balto 21228
                Central Atlantic Conference UCC, 1905 Edmondson Ave, Balto
                  21228
                Christ UCC (Beason & Decatur Sts) 1308 Beason St, Balto 21230
                Faith & St Mark's UCC, 4839 Hazelwood Ave, Balto 21206
                First & St Stephen's UCC, 6915 York Rd, Balto 21212
                First Unit Evan Ch, 1728 Eastern Ave, Balto 21231
                Grace UCC, 1404 S Charles St, Balto 21230
                Heritage UCC, 3106 Liberty Heights Ave, Balto 21215
                Huber Memorial UCC, The Alameda & 29th St, Balto 21218
                Immanuel UCC, 1905 Edmondson Ave, Balto 21228
                Messiah UCC, 5615 The Alameda, Balto 21218
                Park Com UCC, 3608 Mohawk Ave, Balto 21207
                Prot Com UCC, 155 Orville Rd, Balto 21221
                St John's UCC (S Rolling Rd & Wilkens Ave) 1000 S Rolling Rd,
                  Balto 21228
                St Luke's UCC (W Fayette & Carey Sts) 1301 W Fayette St, Balto
                  21223
                St Mark's UCC, 1805 Wickes Ave, Balto 21230
                St Matthew's UCC, 3400 Norman Ave, Balto 21213
                St Paul's UCC, 620 S Beechfield Ave, Balto 21227
                Trinity UCC, 1224 W 36th St, Balto 21211
                Trinity UCC, 29 Belclare Circle, Sparks 21152
                Unit Evan UCC, East Ave & Dillon St, Balto 21224
                Zion Evan Luth UCC, 7146 Golden Ring Rd, Balto 21221
                Zion UCC, Harford Rd at 3000 Iona Terrace, P.O.box 3615, Balto
                  21214
Carroll   Benjamin's UCC (1/10 mi n on Rt 32) 619 Augusta Ave,
                  Westminster 21157
                Emmanuel (Baust) UCC (7 mi w on Rt 32) 2950 Old Taneytown Rd,
                  Westminster 21157
                Grace UCC, 2049 Keysville-Bruceville Rd, Keysville 21757
                Grace UCC, 49 W Balto St, Taneytown 21787
                Kriders UCC, Kriders Church Rd, Westminster 21157

CHURCH ADDRESSES

	Lazarus Ref UCC (Lineboro) 3244 Main St, Box 64, Manchester 21102
	St Mark's Ref UCC (Snydersburg) 3244 Main St, Box 64, Manchester 21102
	St Mary's UCC, 1441 E Mayberry Rd, Silver Run, Westminster 21157
	St Matthews UCC (Pleasant Valley) 619 Augusta Ave, Westminster 21157
	St Paul's UCC (Bond & Green Sts) 17 Bond St, Westminster 21157
	Trinity Ref UCC, 3244 Main St, Box 64, Manchester 21102
Dorchester	Immanuel UCC, 900 Peach Blossom Ave, Cambridge 21613
Frederick	Apples UCC, Apples Church Rd, Thurmont 21788
	Catoctin UCC Resource Center, 29-A W Patrick St, Frederick 21701
	Christ Ref UCC, 12 S Church St, Box 333, Middletown 21769
	Ch of the Incarnation, 124 W Main St, Box 255, Emmitsburg 21727
	Coffman Chapel, Hood College, Frederick 21701
	Evan Ref UCC, 15 W Church St, Frederick 21701
	Faith-Mt Pleasant UCC, Rt 2, Frederick 21701
	Faith UCC (Charlesville) 9337 Opossumtown Pike, Frederick 21701
	Glade UCC, 2818 Wildwood Ct, Walkersville 21793
	Grace Ref UCC, 25 E Second St, Frederick 21701
	Grace Trinity UCC, 9501 Balto Rd, Frederick 21701
	Jefferson UCC, 3831 Jefferson Pike, Box 179, Jefferson 21755
	Mt Pleasant UCC, 9337 Opossumtown Pike, Frederick 21701
	Mt Tabor UCC, 10019 Longs Mill Rd, Rocky Ridge 21778
	Resurrection Ref UCC, P.O.Box 333, Burkittsville 21718
	St John's UCC, 17001 Sabillasville Rd, Sabillasville 21780
	St John's UCC (Woodsboro) 2818 Wildwood Ct, Walkersville 21793
	Trinity Evan & Ref Ch, 5605 Mountville Rd, Adamstown 21710
	Trinity UCC, 101 E Main St, Thurmont 21788
Garrett	St Johns UCC, Main St, Box 25, Grantsville 21536
	Trinity UCC (Grantsville) RD 2, New Germany 21536
Harford	Webster Cong Chris Ch of the UCC, 4102 Webster Rd, Havre de Grace 21078
Howard	Oakland Mills Uniting Ch, 5885 Robert Oliver Pl, Columbia 21045
Montgomery	Central Atlantic Conference, 620 Pershing Dr, Silver Spring 20910
	Christ Cong UCC, 9525 Colesville Rd, Silver Spring 20901
	Pilgrim UCC, 2206 Briggs Rd, Wheaton 20906
	Rockville UCC, 355 Linthicum St, Rockville 20851
	Seneca Valley UCC, 11 Melmark Ct, Gaithersburg 20878
	Trinity UCC, 7300 New Hampshire Ave, Takoma Park 20912
	UCC, 10010 Fernwood Rd, Bethesda 20817
	Westmoreland UCC, 1 Westmoreland Circle, Bethesda 20816
Prince Georges	Greenbelt Com UCC (Hillside & Crescent Rds) 1 Hillside Rd, Greenbelt 20770
	St Paul UCC (Lanham) 9721 Good Luck Rd, Seabrook 20706
	Unit Chris Parish, 810 Rollins Ave, Capitol Heights 20743

United Church of Christ

Washington

Unit Parish of Bowie, 16029 Pennant, Bowie 20715
Christ UCC, 35 Potomac St, Boonsboro 21713
Christ UCC, Center Ln, P.O.Box 100, Cavetown 21720
Christ's Ref UCC, 130 W Franklin St, Hagerstown 21740
Ch of the Holy Trinity, 733 W Oak Ridge Dr, Hagerstown 21740
Mt Moriah UCC, Main St, Sharpsburg 21782
Mt Vernon Evan & Ref Ch, Rt 1 Box 52, Keedysville 21756
St Johns UCC, 215 Main St, Clear Spring 21722
St Paul's UCC, Rt 1 Box 407-A, Clear Spring 21722
St Stephen's UCC (Highfield) 17001 Sabillasville Rd,
  Sabillasville 21780
Salem Ref UCC (Hagerstown, 2 mi w Cearfoss Pike) P.O.Box 296,
  Maugansville 21767
Trinity Evan & Ref Ch, 35 Potomac St, Boonsboro 21713
Zion Evan & Ref Ch, 201 N Potomac St, Hagerstown 21740

Wesleyan

Allegany	First Wes Ch, 15003 Wyoming Ave SW, Cresaptown 21502
Anne Arundel	Wes Oakwood Ch, 505 Oakwood Sta Rd, Glen Burnie 21061
Caroline	Bethel Wes Ch, Goldsboro 21636
Charles	Wes Ch, Rt 925, Waldorf 20601
Dorchester	Wes Ch, 803 Race St, Cambridge 21613
Montgomery	Damascus Wes Ch, 25520 Woodfield Rd, Damascus 20872
Prince Georges	College Park Wes Ch, 4915 Edgewood Rd, College Park 20740
Talbot	First Wes Ch, 620 Goldsboro St, Easton 21601
Wicomico	Faith Wes Ch, 500 Lincoln Ave, Salisbury 21801
	Wango Wes Ch, Wango Rd, Salisbury 21801
	Wes Ch Emmanuel, 142 Shamrock Dr, Salisbury 21801

Other

Allegany	Ch of the Living Christ, 913 Natl Way, La Vale 21502
	First Cong Ch, Bowery St, Frostburg 21532
	God's Ark of Safety, Frostburg Plaza Shopping Center, Frostburg 21532
	Interfaith Consortium, 209 N Centre St, Cumberland 21502
	Potomac Valley Revival Center, McMullen Hwy, Rawlings 21557
	Souls Harbor Ch, 1308 River Ave, Cumberland 21502
Anne Arundel	Annapolis Gospel Center, 829 Hazel Trail, Crownsville 21032
	Calvary Chapel, Ridge Rd, Hanover 21076
	Calvary Temple, Old Mill Rd, Millersville 21108
	Ch of the Sacred Mother, 2282 Patuxent Rd, Gambrills 21054
	Full Gospel Temple, Maryland Ave & Telegraph Rd, Severn 21144
	Glen Burnie Universal Life Ch, Empire Towers, Glen Burnie 21061

CHURCH ADDRESSES

Grace of God Fellowship, 8430 New Cut Rd, Severn 21144
Living Waters, 211 Arunah Ave, Mayo 21106
Manna Fellowship Ch, 139 Truck House Rd, Severna Park 21146
New Covenant Ch, 1071 Bay Ridge Rd, Annapolis 21403
New Covenant Ch at Arnold, 804 Windsor Rd, Arnold 21012
St Charles the Martyr Anglican Ch, 166 Defense Hwy, Annapolis
   21401
South Co New Covenant Ch, Edgewater 21037
Triumph Faith Center, 8222 Telegraph Rd, Odenton 21113
Unity Ch of Severna Park, Gambrills 21054
Word of Faith Center, 7930 Ritchie Hwy, Glen Burnie 21061
Word of Faith Center, 206 Magothy Beach Rd, Pasadena 21122

Baltimore
Ahmadiyya Movement in Islam, 4406 Garrison Blvd, Balto 21215
Ariel Ministries, 7900 Liberty Rd, Balto 21207
Baha'i Faith, 5301 Gwynn Oak Ave, Balto 21207
Baha'i Faith, Balto Co Com, Randallstown 21133
Balto Ethical Soc, 601 E 38th St, Balto 21218
Balto Masjid, 514 Wilson St, Balto 21217
Believer's Chapel, 12 W 22nd St, Balto 21218
Believers Haven Fellowship, 1606 Harlem Ave, Balto 21217
Beth Sar Shalom Hebrew Chris Fellowship, 900 Reisterstown Rd,
   Pikesville 21208
Better Way Minstery, 3604 Belair Rd, Balto 21213
Christ & Country Ch, 6020 Old Harbord Rd, Balto 21214
Christ Deliverance Ch, 711 Walnut Ave, Balto 21229
Christadelphian Ch, 600 Frederick Rd, Balto 21228
Christadelphian Ch Central, 2606 Gwynndale Ave, Balto 21207
Ch of the New Jerusalem, 901 Dartmouth Rd, Balto 21212
Divine Life Ch, 5928 Falls Rd, Balto 21209
Elisha's Spiritual Temple, 900 N Stricker St, Balto 21217
Emmanuel Temple F B H Ch, 2500 Frederick Ave, Balto 21228
Free Gospel Tabernacle Ch, 3201 Lynch Rd, Balto 21219
Full Gospel Tabernacle, 100 Winters Ln, Balto 21228
Gospel Tabernacle of Balto, 8855 Belair Rd, Perry Hall 21236
Grace Fellowship Ch, 6071 Falls Rd, Balto 21209
Hillside Chapel--Swed, 901 Dartmouth Rd, Balto 21212
Jesuits of Jamshedpur India, 7027 Bellona Ave, Balto 21212
Korean Unit Ch of Balto, 1501 N Rolling Rd, Balto 21228
Little Tabernacle Ch of the Saviour, 1503 E Balto St, Balto
   21231
Miracle Tabernacle of God, 931 N Broadway, Balto 21205
Mission to Seamen, 2700 Broening Hwy, Balto 21222
Mission to Seamen, North Point Blvd & Snyder Ave, Balto 21222
New Birth Holy Ch on the Rock, 929 W Fayette St, Balto 21223
New Covenant Ch, 1705 E Joppa Rd, Balto 21234
New Life Inspirational Ch, 2621 Oswego Ave, Balto 21215
Outreach for God, 306 S Broadway, Balto 21231
Pleasant Hill Chapel, 1800 Worthington Hts Pkwy, Cockeysville
   21030
Revival Mission Ch & Holy Ghost Sta, 24 S Fulton Ave, Balto
   21223
Rock Ch, 1607 Cromwell Bridge Rd, Balto 21234

	Second Cong Ch, 5 Highland Ave & Elliott St, Balto 21224
	Solid Rock Ch, 1517 N Gay St, Balto 21213
	Spirit and the Bride Fellowship, 1815 Woodside Ave, Arbutus 21227
	Spirit of Liberty Ch, 1126 W Saratoga St, Balto 21223
	Star of Bethlehem Spiritual Temple, 1111 W Lanvale St, Balto 21217
	Unification Ch, 3101 N Calvert St, Balto 21218
	Unity Center of Christianity, 2901 N Charles St, Balto 21218
	Universal Conference Tabernacle, 1800 N Payson St, Balto 21217
	Upper Room Prayer Garden of Balto, 7 Roberts Ave, Catonsville 21228
	Wilson Chapel, 2120 E Fairmount Ave, Balto 21231
	Word & Faith Fellowship, 1800 N Gay St, Balto 21213
	Word Faith Delivernace Chris Center, 5168 S Marlyn Ave, Balto 21221
	Word of Faith Cathedral, 212 E 25th St, Balto 21218
Calvert	Rock Ch, Broomes Isl Rd, Port Republic 20676
Caroline	His Lighthouse Fellowship Ch, Railroad Ave, Federalsburg 21632
Carroll	Ch of the Open Door, 550 Balto Blvd, Westminster 21157
	Faith Evan Free Ch, 649 Lake View Dr, Mt Airy 21771
	Foursquare Gospel Ch, 495 S Center St, Westminster 21157
	Liberty Ch of Maryland, 613 Uniontown Rd, Westminster 21157
	Miracle Valley Ch, Rt 91 & Lawndale Rd, Finksburg 21048
	Mt Airy Full Gospel Ch, 13949 Penn Shop Rd, Mt Airy 21771
	South Carroll Full Gospel Ch, 2015 Old Liberty Rd, Sykesville 21784
Cecil	Little Wedding Chapel, 142 E Main St, Elkton 21921
Charles	Calvary Gospel Ch, Hwy 925 N Box 179, Waldorf 20601
	New Covenant Ch, Hwy 5 box 387, Waldorf 20601
Dorchester	Faith Chapel, Oak St, Hurlock 21643
	Muhammad Temple, 313 Pine St, Hurlock 21643
Frederick	Frederick Worship Center, 1722 N Market St, Frederick 21701
Harford	Aberdeen Korean Missionary Ch, 203 Plaza Ct, Aberdeen 21001
	Chesapeake Covenant Ch, 900 Trimble Rd, Joppa 21085
	Child Evangelism Fellowship of Harford-Cecil Co, 1916 Harford Rd, Benson 21018
	Chris Kids Call, 3934 Paddrick Rd, Darlington 21034
	Fellowship Chapel, 4043-A Federal Hill Rd, Jarrettsville 21084
	Temple of Faith Non-Denominational Ch, 616 Green St, Havre de Grace 21078
	Victorious Faith Fellowship, 2700 Phila Rd, Edgewood 21040
Howard	Full Gospel Tabernacle Ch, 14340 Frederick Rd, Cooksville 21723
	Interfaith Center, 10431 Twin Rivers Rd, Columbia 21044
Prince	Solid Rock Ch, 4917 Niagara Rd, College Park 20740
Georges	Sri Siva Vishnu Temple, 6905 Cipriano Rd, Lanham 20706
	Tabernacle, 11601 S Laurel Dr, Laurel 20708
	Trinity Moravian Ch, 7011 Good Luck Rd, New Carrollton 20784
Queen Annes	New Covenant Ch, Main St & Bowlingly Ln, Queenstown 21658
St Marys	Gospel Tabernacle of Prayer, Morganza 20660
	St Mark's Uame Ch, Happlyland Rd, Valley Lee 20692

CHURCH ADDRESSES

St Mary's Abbey Ch of Absolute Monism, Cape St Mary's Rd,
   Mechanicsville 20659

Washington   Co Council of Churches, 15 Randolph Ave, Hagerstown 21740

Hagerstown Indep Ch, 146 S Potomac St, Hagerstown 21740

Tri State Fellowship, 1185 Mt Aetna Rd, Hagerstown 21740

Wicomico   Baha'i Faith, 405 Park Ave, Salisbury 21801

Delmarvia Evangelistic Ch, Gordy Rd & Hudson Dr, P.O.Box 986,
   Salisbury 21801

Evangelistic Ch of Deliverance, West Rd, Salisbury 21801

Full Gospel Fellowship Center, 630 Robin Hood Dr, Parsonsburg
   21849

Salisbury Revival Center, Rose St & Westover Circle, Salisbury
   21801

Tabernacle of Prayer Ch, Rt 50 & Lake St, Salisbury 21801

Unit Ch of the First Born, Robinson St, Salisbury 21801

1 -   List of addresses of Protestant Episcopal churches from the 1983
        Journal of Proceedings, 199th Convention, List of Parishes,
        Separate Congregations and Missions, furnished by F Garner Ranney,
        Historiographer of the Diocese of Maryland, Maryland Diocesean
        Archives, 201 W Monument St, Balto 21201
2 -   List of addresses of Roman Catholic churches furnished by Sr M
        Felicitas Powers, RSM, Archivist, Archdiocese of Balto, 320
        Cathedral St, Balto 21201
3 -   The Official Catholic Directory. 1983 ed. published by P J Kenedy &
        Sons, P.O.Box 265, Skokie, IL 60077. pp 52-56, 1009-1011
4 -   Directory. Unitarian Universalist Assn, 25 Beacon St, Boston MA
        02108
5 -   Letter dated May 8, 1984 from Richard M Kelly, Exec Dir, Maryland
        Churches United, An Inter-church Agency for Christian Cooperation,
        4 E University Pkwy, Balto 21218
6 -   An Index of the Source Records of Maryland, by Eleanor Phillips
        Passano. 1940. pp 401-430
7 -   Annual of the Baptist Convention of Maryland....1982 Session Held
        with Middle River Baptist Church, Balto Nov 15-17, 1982. pp 174-
        200, 221-228
8 -   The Convention Journal of the Episcopal Diocese of Washington. 1983.
        pp 56-88
9 -   Letter dated Mar 11, 1984 from Florence M Bricker, Archivist, The
        Evangelical & Reformed Historical Society, Lancaster Central
        Archives & Library, 555 W James St, Lancaster PA 17603 with a list
        of churches from the 1983 United Church of Christ Yearbook
0 -   ....with a list of churches from the Act & Proceedings, General
        Synod Reformed Church in the United States, Summary of Synods and
        the Classes for the Year 1911
1 -   Letter dated Mar 23, 1984 from the Salvation Army Archives &
        Research Center, 145 W 15th St, New York NY 10011 with a list of
        Salvation Army Corps (churches) that existed in Maryland prior to
        1910 with the current location of their records
2 -   List of Seventh-Day Adventist churches from Stephen Cooper, Project
        Coordinator, Hall of Records, P.O.Box 828, Annapolis 21404
3 -   List of Lutheran churches from Stephen Cooper
4 -   List of Presbyterian churches from Stephen Cooper
5 -   List of black churches in the Baltimore area from Eva Slezak,
        Librarian in Charge Afro-American Collection, Enoch Pratt Free
        Library, 400 Cathedral St, Balto 21201
6 -   The Garden of Methodism, by E C Hallman. Published at the request
        of the Peninsula Annual Conference of the Methodist Church
7 -   A Survey of American Church Records, by E Kay Kirkham. 4th ed.
        1978. Everton Publishers, Inc. P.O.Box 368, Logan UT 84321 pp
        140-148
8 -   Synagogue Directory and The Historical and Geographical Distribution
        Pattern of Jewish Synagogues in Balto. Prepared by the Jewish
        Historical Society of Maryland, Embassy Apartments Lower Level,
        3809 Clarks Ln, Balto 21215
9 -   Letter dated May 1, 1984 from Stephen Cooper with a list of United
        Methodist churches and charges in Maryland from the Balto & Penin-
        sula Conference directories

SOURCES

20 - The Old Otterbein Church Story--The Old Otterbein Evangelical United
      Brethren Church, Conway and Sharp Sts, Balto, Established 1771, by
      Paul E. Holdcraft. Translations by August C. Wagner
21 - Letter dated June 14, 1984 from the Methodist Historical Society,
      West Virginia Wesleyan College Library, Buckhannon,WV 26201 with a
      list of Garrett County churches--Methodist, Methodist Episcopal
      South, United Methodist
22 - Letter dated July 30, 1984 from Concordia Historical Institute,
      Department of Archives and History, The Lutheran Church--Missouri
      Synod, 801 DeMun Ave, St Louis MO 63105 with a list of churches
      and list of records available at CHI
23 - Letter dated July 11, 1984 from Neil L Irons, Dist Supt, Romney
      District, The United Methodist Church, 380 Woodland Way, Romney,
      WV 26757 with a list of churches in Garrett Co
24 - List of United Church of Christ churches from Rev. Bernie Zerkel,
      Catoctin Assn, 29A W Patrick St, Frederick 21701
25 - Letter dated Aug 2, 1984 from Rev Constantine M Monios, Dean, Greek
      Orthodox Cathedral of the Annunciation with list of churches in
      Maryland
26 - List of African Methodist Episcopal churches received from Bishop
      John Hurst Adams, 615 G St SW, Washington DC 20024 in reply to my
      letter of July 25, 1984
27 - Letter dated July 31, 1984 from Christian Science Committee on
      Publication for Maryland, 156 South St, P.O.Box 1585, Annapolis
      21404 with a list of Christian Science churches
28 - Reply to my letter of July 28, 1984 to the Balto Conference American
      Lutheran Church, Lutheran University Ministry, 7909 York Rd, Balto
      21204 with a list of churches
29 - Letter dated Aug 7, 1984 from Central Atlantic Conference, 620
      Pershing Dr, Silver Spring 20910 with a list of United Church of
      Christ churches
30 - Letter dated Aug 7, 1984 from Central Atlantic Conference, 1905
      Edmondson Ave, Balto 21228 with a list of United Church of Christ
      churches
31 - Letter dated Aug 16, 1984 from Elisabeth Wittman, Asst Archivist,
      Lutheran Church in America, 1100 E 55th St, Chicago IL 60615 with
      a list of Maryland Synod LCA churches from Minutes of the 22nd
      Annual Convention June 17-19, 1983
32 - Letter dated Aug 13, 1984 from The American Lutheran Church, 333
      Wartburg Pl, Dubuque, IA 52001 with a list of the ALC churches in
      Maryland and information on two Norwegian Lutheran churches
33 - Letter dated Aug 23, 1984 from the Christian Church, Capital Area
      (Disciples of Christ) The Church House, 8901 Connecticut Ave,
      Chevy Chase 20815 with a list of Christian churches (Disciples of
      Christ) in Maryland
34 - Letter dated Aug 23, 1984 from Chesapeake Conference of Seventh-
      Day Adventists, 6600 Martin Rd, Columbia 21044 with a list of SDA
      churches
35 - Letter dated Aug 21, 1984 from the Christian Methodist Episcopal
      Church, 7th Episcopal District, 557 Randolph St NW, Washington
      20011

SOURCES

36 -   Letter dated Aug 24, 1984 from Robert C Wiederaenders, Archivist,
        The American Lutheran Church, 333 Wartburg Pl, Dubuque IA 52001
        with a Congregation Master List dated Aug 22, 1984 for Maryland
        (computer printout), an explanation sheet, a chart of the American
        Lutheran Church Family, and a listing of congregations on micro-
        film
37 -   Minutes of the 199th Annual Session Baltimore Annual Conference,
        Official Journal 1983 of United Methodist Church, Frostburg State
        College, Frostburg, June 7-10, 1983. Printed by TM/UME Produc-
        tions, Dallas TX -- "Appointments and Directrory, 1983-84"
        pp 182-234
38 -   United Church of Christ, Mergers of Congregations with a Map from
        Rev Ralph Cook, St Matthews UCC, Mayfield, Norman and Lake Aves,
        Balto 21213
39 -   Letter dated Sept 5, 1984 from Church of the Nazarene, 2509 Jonathan
        Rd, Ellicott City 21043 with list of churches
40 -   Letter dated Sept 4, 1984 from William J Netting, The Presbytery of
        Balto, Presbyterian Church (USA), 5400 Loch Raven Blvd, Balto
        21239 with lists of churches
41 -   Photocopies of pages 80-84 from Yearbook 1983 United Church of
        Christ "That They May All Be One" from the Archives of the United
        Church of Christ
42 -   Letter dated Sept 11, 1984 from Rev Ronald D Marcy with information
        on the Unitarian Universalist Church in Maryland
43 -   Letter dated Sept 26, 1984 from Judith A Koucky, Archivist, South-
        eastern District, The Lutheran Church--Missouri Synod, 2712 Hicko-
        ry St, Alexandria VA 22305 with list of churches
44 -   The Catholic Directory of the Archdiocese of Baltimore 1984-1985.
        Published by the Catholic Review, P.O.Box 777, 320 Cathedral St,
        Balto 21201
45 -   Official Catholic Directory, Archdiocese of Washington, P.O.Box
        29260, Washington DC 20017. 1985
46 -   The Manuscript Collections of the Maryland Historical Society, com-
        piled by Avril J M Pedley. 1968
47 -   Guide to the Research Collections of the Maryland Historical Socie-
        ty, edited by Richard J Cox and Larry E Sullivan. 1981
48 -   Quaker Records in Maryland by Phebe R Jacobsen. Pub # 14. The Hall
        of Records Commission, State of Maryland, Annapolis. 1966
49 -   Church and Pastoral Records in the Archives of the United Church of
        Christ and the Evangelical and Reformed Historical Society, Lan-
        caster, PA, compiled and edited by Florence M Bricker. Published
        by the Evangelical and Reformed Historical Society. 1982
50 -   The Records of Baltimore's Private Organizations--A Guide to
        Archival Resources, by John T Guertler. Adele M Newburger,
        Project Dir, Garland Publishing Co, New York. 1981
51 -   Frederick County Maryland Genealogical Research Guide, by Donna V.
        Russell. 1987 Catoctin Press, 709 E Main St, Middletown 21769
52 -   Minutes of the 202nd Annual Session of the Baltimore Annual Confer-
        ence of the United Methodist Church, University of Maryland,
        Baltimore County, Catonsville, June 17-20, 1986. pp 176-228
53 -   C&P Telephone Books. 1986-1987 (20 books covering the state of
        Maryland)